Palgrave Studies in Populisms

Series Editor
Ihsan Yilmaz, Alfred Deakin Institute, Deakin University, Burwood, VIC, Australia

This Palgrave Macmillan book series addresses the phenomenon of populism which has become part of mainstream politics. Its contested meanings and various shapes inform many aspects of political and social life across the world. In some cases, it emerges in the form of an individual leader; in others, in the form of a social movement or a political party. It is thus important that we understand not merely its defining features and causes, but also its relationship with other social phenomena. While populism's relationships with globalisation, nationalism, and race are regularly discussed in scholarly literature, there is still need and also great interest in studies that look at different manifestations of populism in different parts of the world and in relation to a rich variety of contexts, polities, religions, and movements. This series includes works on political science, political psychology, sociology, anthropology, political economy and theology. It makes a significant contribution to populism studies and literature from different angles. There is an enormous interest among the scholars from different backgrounds in studying populism and this books series is an important avenue of publication for their studies.

Ihsan Yilmaz · Nicholas Morieson

Religions and the Global Rise of Civilizational Populism

palgrave
macmillan

Ihsan Yilmaz
Alfred Deakin Institute for
Citizenship and Globalisation
Deakin University
Burwood, VIC, Australia

Nicholas Morieson
Alfred Deakin Institute for
Citizenship and Globalisation
Deakin University
Burwood, VIC, Australia

ISSN 2731-3069 ISSN 2731-3077 (electronic)
Palgrave Studies in Populisms
ISBN 978-981-19-9054-0 ISBN 978-981-19-9052-6 (eBook)
https://doi.org/10.1007/978-981-19-9052-6

© The Editor(s) (if applicable) and The Author(s), under exclusive license to Springer Nature Singapore Pte Ltd. 2023
This work is subject to copyright. All rights are solely and exclusively licensed by the Publisher, whether the whole or part of the material is concerned, specifically the rights of translation, reprinting, reuse of illustrations, recitation, broadcasting, reproduction on microfilms or in any other physical way, and transmission or information storage and retrieval, electronic adaptation, computer software, or by similar or dissimilar methodology now known or hereafter developed.
The use of general descriptive names, registered names, trademarks, service marks, etc. in this publication does not imply, even in the absence of a specific statement, that such names are exempt from the relevant protective laws and regulations and therefore free for general use.
The publisher, the authors, and the editors are safe to assume that the advice and information in this book are believed to be true and accurate at the date of publication. Neither the publisher nor the authors or the editors give a warranty, expressed or implied, with respect to the material contained herein or for any errors or omissions that may have been made. The publisher remains neutral with regard to jurisdictional claims in published maps and institutional affiliations.

Cover illustration: Özgür Kesedar/EyeEm

This Palgrave Macmillan imprint is published by the registered company Springer Nature Singapore Pte Ltd.
The registered company address is: 152 Beach Road, #21-01/04 Gateway East, Singapore 189721, Singapore

Contents

1 **Religions and the Global Rise of Civilizational Populism**   1
   1.1 Introduction   1
   1.2 Significance and Research Questions of the Book   12
   1.3 Structure of the Book   12
   References   21

2 **Civilizationalism, Religions, and Populism**   25
   2.1 Introduction   25
   2.2 What is Populism?   30
   2.3 Civilizational Populism   36
   References   40

3 **Islam and Civilizational Populism**   45
   3.1 Introduction   45
   3.2 Relationship Between Islam and Populism   47
   3.3 Case Studies   59
      3.3.1 Turkey: Justice and Development Party (AKP)   59
      3.3.2 Indonesia: The Islamic Defenders Front (FPI)   71
   3.4 Discussion of Case Studies   87
   References   96

4 **Christianity and Civilizational Populism**   111
   4.1 Introduction   111
   4.2 Civilizational Populism in Christian Majority Nations   114

	4.3	Case Studies		121
		4.3.1 Hungary: Victor Orbán and Fidesz		121
		4.3.2 Netherlands: Party for Freedom		132
		4.3.3 USA: The Trump Administration		146
	4.4	Discussion of Case Studies		156
	References			168
5	**Hinduism and Civilizational Populism**			181
	5.1	Introduction		181
	5.2	Relationship Between Hinduism and Populism		183
		5.2.1 Understanding Hinduism		183
		5.2.2 Variants of Populism in India		184
		5.2.3 Hindu Nationalism: The Birth of Hindutva		185
	5.3	Case Study: Hindutva Nationalism to Populism		188
		5.3.1 Rashtriya Swayamsevak Sangh (RSS) and its Affiliates		188
		5.3.2 BJP: From Right-Wing Nationalism to Populism		191
		5.3.3 Legislative Changes		194
		5.3.4 Reshaping History		195
		5.3.5 BJP Leadership: Beyond Modi		196
		5.3.6 Political Affiliates: Shiv Sena (SS)		199
		5.3.7 Grass Roots Organizations: RSS and the SP		200
		5.3.8 Online Populism		202
	5.4	Discussion of the Case Study		204
	References			209
6	**Buddhism and Civilizational Populism**			225
	6.1	Introduction		225
	6.2	Case Studies		227
		6.2.1 Myanmar: Religion in the Political Landscape		227
		6.2.2 Sri Lanka: Religion in the Political Landscape		238
	6.3	Discussion of Case Studies		249
	References			254
7	**Judaism and Civilizational Populism**			263
	7.1	Introduction		263
	7.2	Civilizationalism in Israel		265
	7.3	Case Study: Civilizational Populism of the National Liberal Movement (Likud)		268

	7.3.1 Civilizationalism in Netanyahu's Populist Discourse	273
7.4	Discussion of Case Study	282
References		286
8	**Predicament of Civilizational Populism**	291
8.1	Conclusions	291
References		302
Index		305

List of Tables

Table 3.1	Comparison of Islamist populist case studies	89
Table 3.2	Narratives of AKP and FPI	94
Table 4.1	Narratives of Christian populist parties	164
Table 4.2	Comparison of Christian populist case studies	167
Table 5.1	Hindutva populist case study	205
Table 5.2	Populism at Present in India	206
Table 6.1	Narratives of Buddhist populist parties	251
Table 6.2	Comparison of Buddhist case studies	252
Table 7.1	Likud/Netanyahu Judaist populist case study	284
Table 7.2	Populism in Likud/Netanyahu Politics	285

CHAPTER 1

Religions and the Global Rise of Civilizational Populism

1.1 Introduction

In the second half of the twentieth century, and as a response to the horrors of fascism and war, governments around the world sought to implement human rights and increase democratic participation. As a result, the late twentieth century witnessed the decline of autocratic governance and the creation of many new democracies across the world. After the collapse of the Soviet Union, so triumphant did liberal democracy appear, that many began to describe the period as the 'end of history'. The phrase, borrowed from Francis Fukuyama (who used it in a complex and rather ambivalent way to describe the victory of capitalism and liberal democracy over its once powerful rival ideologies), described the growing sense that humankind had reached its optimal state, and that liberal democratic values were now almost axiomatic and without rival (Fukuyama 2006).

By the mid-2000s, and following a series of political events of world historical importance, the euphoria surrounding the collapse of the Soviet Union began to disappear. The attacks on the United States on September 11, 2001, and the subsequent and disastrous wars in Afghanistan and Iraq, along with the rise of authoritarian China and the growth of extremist movements such as Islamic State in the Middle East, suggested that history had not ended, and that liberal democracy would continue to face many challenges. Russia's transformation into a brutal dictatorship under Vladimir Putin, culminating in his expansionist war against Ukraine, signals perhaps a fundamental shift in international relations and a powerful challenge to liberal democracy.

Yet the most potent challenge to democracy may be coming from within, and from the corruption of many supposed liberal democracies, rather than from rival ideologies. On the one hand, while Russia and China may appear to represent an ideological challenge to the liberal democratic world, the two regimes require extreme information control and the punishment of dissidents in order to maintain authoritarian non-liberal governance. However, since the mid-2000s there has been a sharp decline in basic freedoms, and a deterioration of democratic institutions, in a significant number of democratic countries around the world (Repucci and Slipowitz 2021; The Economist Intelligence Unit 2021; IDEA 2019). A survey revealed that the global North, widely considered the most democratic region of the world, has since 2005 suffered from a gradual deterioration of democratic values. The report stated that,

> The impact of the long-term democratic decline has become increasingly global in nature, broad enough to be felt by those living under the cruelest dictatorships, as well as by citizens of long-standing democracies. Nearly 75 percent of the world's population lived in a country that faced deterioration last year. (Repucci and Slipowitz 2021)

According to Thomas Hobbes, there exists a social contract regulating the affairs between the state and its people (or the monarch and their subjects). This contract effectively ensures that a government will guarantee the safety of the people it represents (Gauthier 1988). Hobbes believed that human actions are driven by rational self-interest, and therefore argued that people would willingly enter into this social contract with the other people, on the basis that it was rational for individuals to "submit to the authority of a Sovereign in order to be able to live in a civil society" (Friend 2021).

However, in the twenty-first century, the contract between citizens and their democratic governments appears to be breaking down. For example, Loke (2020) argues that the United States and other democratic nations have become 'flawed' democracies, in which the intangible yet meaningful bind between the state and its citizens has degraded. This disillusionment with the 'elite', 'establishment', or 'managerial class', has led to a loss of trust in elected officials, and perhaps a loss of belief in the democratic process itself. The degrading of democratic politics, and the rise of an elite which is increasingly remote from the majority of citizens, has created an environment conducive to populism. The rise of populism makes sense if we understand populism as the "redemptive face" of democracy, which at once promises to redeem an oppressed and downtrodden people, and yet by its own nature threatens to destroy the key liberal elements—pluralism, rule of law—which prevent democracy from falling into dictatorship (Canovan 1999).

The growth of populism is one of the most significant political developments of the twenty-first century. Populist leaders, movements, and parties, across the world offer an alternative form of politics, one which promises to liberate 'the people' from elite rule, and to 'save' them from the existential crisis elites have brought upon them through their corrupt misrule. What, then, is populism, and why have populists in particular achieved political success in the democratic world while embracing civilizationalist rhetoric? Populism is described in a number of ways by scholars, as a set of ideas, a thin-centered populist ideology, a type of political strategy, a discourse, or a style (Gidron and Bonikowski 2013). The most widely used approach defines populism as a group of ideas that together "considers society to be ultimately separated into two homogenous and antagonistic groups, 'the pure people' versus 'the corrupt elite', and which argues that politics should be an expression of the volonté générale (general will) of the people" (Mudde 2004, 543). However, Mudde argues that 'lacking the sophistication of other ideologies like socialism or liberalism', populism—according to this approach—'is a thin-centred ideology and could be combined with other beliefs and ideas of politics' (De la Torre 2019, 7). This definition is satisfactory insofar as it identifies the core of populism: the division of society into two categories: 'us' and 'them', and acknowledges that populism must always be blended with a 'thick' ideology in order to give it content. Aside from this vertical dimension, populism may contain a second horizontal cultural dimension, in which 'the pure people' (who are morally good) are distinguished from morally 'bad' and dangerous 'others' within society who are accused of threatening 'the people' and their way of life (Mudde 2017; Taguieff 1995, 32–35). Sengul (2022, 3) writes, "both left and right populisms are characterized by the antagonistic pitting of "the people" vs "the elite", but the populist radical right is distinguished by the presence of the 'Other'. The choice of Other is dependent on the particular historical traditions in particular national, regional and local contexts". Populism, then, is a 'thin' ideology or loose set of ideas which pits a virtuous and homogeneous people against a set of elites and dangerous 'others' who are together depicted as depriving (or attempting to deprive) the sovereign people of their rights, values, prosperity, identity, and voice. Populist leaders portray themselves as true representatives and saviors of 'the people' and defenders of their sovereignty, and protectors of the 'good' and 'common' people from their 'corrupt' and inauthentic enemies: elites and 'others' (Muddle 2017). In this way they attempt to turn politics into a Manichean and existential struggle between the forces of good and evil, represented by 'the people' on one hand, and 'elites' and 'others' on the other.

Populism is ultimately a product of democratic societies (Canovan 1999), yet populists frequently violate liberal democratic norms. First, insofar as populism creates a political environment in which the rule of law or the rights of minorities may be discarded if they appear to obstruct the 'will of the people', which populists claim is sacrosanct. Second, because populism encourages an antagonistic politics in which two groups, 'the people' and 'corrupt elites', are pitted against one another in an existential struggle for the nation (Panizza 2005). Populism thus flourishes on the divisive politics of 'the people' versus 'the elite' and 'others', which deepens socio-political-economic rifts and exploits societies' emotional pressure points and vulnerabilities (Yilmaz and Morieson 2021; Rico et al. 2017). One particular form of populism, which categorizes people according to their civilizational identities, and asserts the incompatibility of different cultures and religions, has proven especially influential in the twenty-first century. We call this form of populism 'civilizational populism', which we define as "a group of ideas that together considers that politics should be an expression of the volonté générale (general will) of the people, and society to be ultimately separated into two homogenous and antagonistic groups, 'the pure people' versus 'the corrupt elite' who collaborate with the dangerous others belonging to other civilizations that are hostile and present a clear and present danger to the civilization and way of life of the pure people" (Yilmaz and Morieson 2022a; 2022b).

We understand civilizationalism to be playing a similar role to other ideas and ideologies that may be adhered to populism and which give its signifiers (i.e. 'the pure people', 'corrupt elites', 'dangerous others') meaning. In other words, in the different forms of populism, thicker ideologies or ideas shape define key signifiers 'the people', 'elites', and 'others', and provide content which describes why 'the people' are pure, authentic, and good and why 'elites' and 'others' are bad and inauthentic. In populism, 'the people' are held to be morally good and pure (Mudde 2017). 'Elites', however, are perceived to be morally 'bad', because while they are of 'the people' (however defined) they have betrayed 'the people' by either introducing an economic scheme contrary to the interests of 'the people', or permitting mass immigration which threatens the racial purity or cultural hegemony of 'the people', or for some other reason (Mudde 2017). Civilizationalism is an idea which posits that the world and its peoples can be divided into several 'civilizations', most of them defined by religion. Adhered to populism, civilizationalism defines self and other not primarily in national terms, but civilizational terms (Brubaker 2017). It gives content to populism's signifiers by, first, categorizing people via civilizational identity (whether self-imposed or imposed by populists). Thus we define civilizational populism "as a group of ideas that together considers that politics should be an expression of the volonté générale (general will) of the people, and society to be ultimately separated into two homogenous and antagonistic groups, 'the pure people' versus 'the corrupt elite' who collaborate with the dangerous others belonging to other civilizations that are hostile and present a clear and present danger to the civilization and way of life of the pure people" (Yilmaz and Morieson 2022a). Second, by framing 'the people' as morally good because the civilization to which they belong is morally good, and derived from good religious values. Conversely, civilizationalism adhered to populism allows populists to frame 'elites' as morally bad insofar as they have betrayed and abandoned the values and culture of the people's civilization. Equally, 'others' within the same society are framed as morally 'bad' because they belong to a foreign civilization with inferior values derived from an inferior religion.

The growth of this political phenomenon not only demonstrates disillusionment with liberal democracy, but suggests that key lessons of the twentieth century have been largely forgotten. Ironically, having reached the 'end of history', we witness a worldwide democratic regression symbolized by the growth of civilizationalism, whether in the form of expansionist civilizational powers such as Russia and China, or in the form of civilizational populism. The decay of the liberal order, which just twenty-five years ago seemed all but invincible, haunts the present, and the rise of civilizational populism threatens further harm to our democratic institutions and, furthermore, imperils religious and ethnic minorities the world over.

In an essay written in 2020, Aris Roussinos, for example, argues that the liberal West is today haunted by the rise of civilizationalism and civilization-states. "In 1996", he writes, "the political theorist Samuel P. Huntington observed that 'in the emerging world of ethnic conflict and civilizational clash, the Western belief in the universality of Western culture suffers three problems: It is false, it is immoral and it is dangerous. Imperialism is the necessary logical consequence of universalism'. Yet Huntington, like his critics, was writing at a time of unchallenged American pre-eminence. Critics of Huntington's civilizational thesis, like modern academic critics of the concept of civilization-states, are challenging a construct that no longer exists, of an all-powerful West arrogantly dismissing the rest from a standpoint of political superiority" (Roussinos 2020). "Now", he writes "it is we in the West who are in decline and it is in the universalising myths of liberalism that our powerful civilisational rivals trace the root causes of our failure" (Roussinos 2020). Roussinos (2020) argues that "the rising civilisation-states of Eurasia define themselves against the liberal West" while "the West, and Europe, struggle to define their own very natures, and place greater intellectual emphasis on deconstructing it than on defending it: an urge that is, like the impetus to deny the existence of civilisations as bounded entities, itself ironically a unique marker of our own civilization". The collapse of liberal universalism and the rise of civilizationalism suggests to Roussinos (2020) that the future of global politics will be "stranger and more complex than our current political discourse allows". He sees signs of this new world emerging when he finds French President Emmanuel "Macron struggling to rally European civilisation for the coming age of empires", and "European strongmen like Viktor Orbán, hailed by many Anglo-Saxon conservatives as the saviour of Western civilisation, railing against the West with all the passion and fury of an anti-colonial revolutionary" (Roussinos 2020). Observing that Huntington's clash thesis has proven inaccurate insofar as we do not see a worldwide clash of civilizations, Roussinos (2020) ends his essay by suggesting that "in the new age of the civilisation-state, perhaps the greatest challenge to our social harmony will come not from the challengers beyond our cultural borders, but from the battle within them to define who and what they defend".

We, too, observe the rise of civilizationalism in global politics, and not only in the civilization-states of China and Russia, but in populist-dominated democracies such as India, Turkey, and Hungary. Equally, we agree that rather than worldwide civilizational conflict, the future is more likely to bring about conflict within states over their civilizational identity. The purpose of this book, then, is to explore the rise of civilizational populism throughout the world and its consequences. Civilizational populism posits that democracy ought to be based upon enacting the 'people's will', yet it adds a new and troubling dimension to populism's thin ideology: a civilization-based classification of peoples and division of society. From Western Europe to Turkey, and from India and Pakistan to Indonesia, populist leaders, parties, and movements are increasingly employing a civilization-based classification of peoples, in order to define the identities of 'the people' and their enemies. Religion plays a defining role in delineating the boundaries between these civilizations, and civilizational populism is most often intrinsically bound up with religious identity and practice (Yilmaz and Morieson 2022a; Yilmaz et al. 2021). As a result, Hinduism, Buddhism, Islam, and Christianity have all been commandeered by populist parties and movements, each adept at using the power of religion to define the boundaries of people, nation, and civilization. Religion is thus an important—at times central—aspect of civilizational populist movements across the world.

There is something, then, particularly dangerous about civilizational populism. As Mudde observes, in populism 'the people' are held to be morally good and authentic (Mudde 2017). 'Elites', however, are perceived to be morally 'bad', because while they are of 'the people' (however defined) they have betrayed 'the people' by either introducing an economic scheme contrary to the interests of 'the people', or permitting mass immigration which threatens the racial purity or cultural hegemony of 'the people', or for some other reason (Mudde 2017). Civilizationalism is an idea which posits that the world and its peoples can be divided into several 'civilizations', most of them defined by religion (Huntington 1993). Adhered to populism, then, civilizationalism defines self and other not primarily in national terms, but civilizational terms (Brubaker 2017). It gives content to populism's signifiers by, first, categorizing people via civilizational identity (whether self-imposed or imposed by populists). Second, by framing 'the people' as morally good because the civilization to which they belong is morally good, and derived from good religious values. Conversely, civilizationalism adhered to populism allows populists to frame 'elites' as morally bad insofar as they have betrayed and abandoned the values and culture of the people's civilization. Equally, 'others' within the same society are framed as morally 'bad' because they belong to a foreign civilization with inferior values derived from an inferior religion. Equally, populism thrives on a sense of crisis. Moffitt (2015) claims populists must essentially perform a crisis in order to win power and to perpetuate their rule. Whether or not this is true, populists' distinction between the 'pure people' and 'corrupt elites' and dangerous 'others' can be made more concrete if populists can convince the public that elite corruption and immorality has driven their society into total crisis. Therefore, as the following chapters show, civilizational populists will often argue that proof of elite corrupt and immorality lies in the 'crisis' into which they have driven society. Thus, as the case study chapters show, civilizational populists they often claim that the nation and 'the people' are threatened by people belonging to a foreign civilization (e.g. Islam, 'the West') who with the help of traitorous elites are invading their society and destroying its core values and identity.

The global rise of civilizational populism is significant for several reasons. First, populism itself is a threat to liberal democracy. While populists portray themselves as democrats and call for politicians to obey the 'will of the people', populism's inherent rejection of checks and balances on power and cultivation of a direct connection with 'the people' in their place, often places the societies they govern on the path to authoritarianism and ultimately dictatorship. Civilizational populism poses, in certain respects, a greater threat to democratic society than other forms of the phenomenon. The addition of religion to populist divisions of society between, on the one hand, 'the people' and on the other 'the corrupt elite', quickly undermines social cohesion and threatens the rights of religious minorities. Furthermore, when civilizational populism empowers religious fundamentalists, the result is often an attack on scientific institutions if not the scientific method itself.

The dangers inherent in civilizational populism are becoming visible across the world insofar as they sometimes have an international and transnational dimension (Löfflmann 2022; Wajner 2022). For example, under the rule of the populist Justice and Development Party (AKP), which has embraced a civilizational politics based on identification with Islam, Turkish ethnicity, and the Ottoman Empire, Turkey's government has become increasingly hostile toward religious and secular minorities. At the same time, Turkey has also adopted a foreign policy based upon a rhetorical rejection of the 'Judeo-Christian' West and sought leadership of the Sunni Muslim world. India, under the populist rule of the Bharatiya Janata Party (BJP) and its charismatic leader Narendra Modi, has turned toward Hindu ethnoreligious nationalism, alienating non-Hindus within India and casting them as villains or threats within a political drama. Despite its name, Hindu Nationalism—especially as it is conceived by the BJP—posits that India is a Hindu civilization which was deeply wounded in the past by Muslims and British invaders, and which must now recover its authentic Hindu self in order to be successful. Under BJP rule, India has become progressively more hostile toward Muslims, who have been marginalized and suffered violence at the hands of Hindu mobs.

In the case of the AKP and BJP, religious belief and practice play important roles in defining the culture, values, and heritage of 'nation' and 'people', but also the characteristics of the enemies of the people. In this way, religion is co-opted by political forces, who instrumentalize it in order to create a sense of crisis which helps perpetuate populist rule. This does not mean, however, that a religious population is required for civilizational populism—based on religious identity—to thrive. If the rise of civilizational populism were confined to regions in which religious belief and practice remained a part of everyday life, or was axiomatic, we might comprehend it as the natural and unsurprising merger of two powerful forces: religion and populism. But religion has a role to play in the populist politics of some of the most secular and secularized nations. France, the Netherlands, the United Kingdom, and Hungary all have seen the rise of successful populist movements and parties which draw on the power of religion to define national and civilizational culture and identity. In France, for example, the leader of the right-wing populist National Rally, Marine Le Pen, has described France as a primarily Christian, yet highly secularized, civilization, and Islam as incompatible with French secularism. According to Le Pen, secularism is a product of Christianity, and reflects the core values of Christian civilization. A similar argument is made by Geert Wilders, leader of the Dutch populist Party for Freedom. Wilders describes the culture of the Netherlands as "Judeo-Christian and Humanist", suggesting that he similarly believes that secularism (or as he puts it, humanism) is a product of the West's Christian heritage. Wilders, like Le Pen, argues that Islam is incompatible with the secular values of the West, which are born of Europe's Christian civilizational heritage.

Civilizationalism, then, is playing an important discursive role in populist politics throughout the world, both in religious and secular environments. While this civilizationalism is not necessarily connected with religious belief and practice, it is always connected with religious identity. Indeed, the boundaries of each identified civilization are essentially delineated by religion. Understanding the role played by religion is vital if we are to ever comprehend the reasons behind the global rise of populism. This book argues that not only is civilizational populism a rising political force, but that populists are increasingly turning toward religion because it can be used to help produce public demand for civilizational populism. Through a series of case studies of civilizational populist movements across the world, the book investigates how populists construct civilizational identities, and how they create demand for civilizational populism by claiming there is a clash of civilizations occurring that threatens 'the people', and requires a change of national government in order to 'save' the nation.

While a pervasive political force, populism can be difficult to define. In this book, we understand populism as a set of ideas based upon the notion that society can be "separated into two homogenous and antagonistic groups, 'the pure people' versus 'the corrupt elite,' and which argues that politics should be an expression of the volonté générale (general will) of the people" (Mudde 2004, 543). Populism, therefore, is a 'thin' ideology or set of ideas which pits a virtuous and homogeneous people against a set of elites and dangerous 'others' who are together depicted as depriving the sovereign people of their rights, values, prosperity, identity, and voice. Populist leaders portray themselves as saviors of 'the people' and defenders of their sovereignty, and protectors of the 'good' and 'common' people from their 'corrupt' and inauthentic enemies: elites and 'others' (Muddle 2017). In this way, populism is an attempt to turn politics into a Manichean and existential struggle between the forces of good and evil, represented by 'the people' on one hand, and 'elites' and 'others' on the other.

Our intention in this book is to define civilizational populism and determine where it is present in the world. Our book is thus intended as a starting point for future examinations of the phenomena of civilizational populism. It investigates a hypothesis that may be presented in the form of third contentions. First, that civilizational populism—defined by Yilmaz and Morieson (2022a) as "a group of ideas that together considers that politics should be an expression of the volonté générale (general will) of the people, and society to be ultimately separated into two homogenous and antagonistic groups, 'the pure people' versus 'the corrupt elite' who collaborate with the dangerous others belonging to other civilizations that are hostile and present a clear and present danger to the civilization and way of life of the pure people"—is a growing phenomenon which is challenging democracy and pluralism the world over, and across a wide variety of societies.

Second, that civilizationalism—which emphasizes the civilizational aspect of social and especially national identity—when adhered to populism gives content to populism's signifiers: 'the people', 'elites', and 'others', defining them in civilizational terms. Third, the book contends that civilizational populism incorporates religion, though different civilizational populisms incorporate religion in different ways. The book shows how religion is one aspect of civilization in populist civilizationalism, but most often the key element which defines the boundaries of each civilization. Therefore, we devote entire chapters to 'Christian based civilizational populism', 'Islamic based civilizational populism', 'Hindu based civilizational populism', 'Judaism based civilizational populism', and 'Buddhist based civilizational populism'. It is not possible, of course, to study every manifestation of civilizational populism. Thus, the book examines only the most significant and powerful civilizational populist movements and parties, especially those parties and movements which have achieved either sustained electoral success, or which have considerably affected or altered the course of mainstream politics without winning elections. The book places the study of civilizational populist discourse at the center of its focus. Populism is a thin ideology, or a set of ideas, but it attempts to re-shape societies primarily through discourse. Therefore, this book examines the discourse used by civilizational populists required to create public demand for populist solutions. The book does this by mapping, through a series of case studies, populist narratives and their relationship with religion across a wide range of societies. The book thus identifies in civilizational populist movements pro-violence rhetoric, links or overlaps with far-right movements, efforts to develop transnational movements, identity narratives, crisis narratives, civilization narratives, and victimhood narratives. The book therefore examines the speech and texts produced by populist parties, movements, and especially populist leaders. The book's focus on leader discourse is important: successful populist movements and parties often portray their leader as a messianic figure who will 'save' the people from a crisis brought on by elites and others, and which threatens to engulf the nation. At the same time, we augment our analysis of leader discourse with studies of the wider movement to which the leader is attached, including examinations of party or movement manifestos, and of the wider appeal of the leader.

The book's examination and analysis of civilizational populism and its causes will help future scholars understand the rise of civilizational populism, and also assist policymakers in finding ways to combat this frequently anti-democratic and anti-pluralist phenomenon.

1.2 Significance and Research Questions of the Book

This book is the first to discuss civilizational populism in a global context, and to try to understand, on a global level, how civilizational populism operates, whether it has a transnational dimension, and how it effects societies.

The following four questions are the focus of our investigation:

1. What is civilizational populism and how widespread has it become?
2. How do populists across the world, and in a variety of different religious, geographic, and political contexts, incorporate ideas of 'civilization' into their discourses?
3. What are the consequences of civilizational populism entering the political mainstream?
4. Is there a transnational dimension to civilizational populism?

1.3 Structure of the Book

This book has eight chapters. The first chapter of this book introduces civilizational populism to the reader and describes the theoretical basis for the book and the book's significance. The chapter begins with a historical overview of how divisional politics previously led to grave consequences in a variety of polities, and discusses the decline of democratic freedoms in the contemporary world due to the decay of liberal democracy and the subsequent rise of populism globally. To do this, we discuss the relationships between populist leaders, movements, and parties and the world's major religions.

The second chapter discusses the literature, concepts, and methods we use to examine civilizational populism. The chapter begins by discussing the concept of civilizationalism, and the salience and impact of Samuel P. Huntington's argument that international politics in the post-Cold War period would be dominated by clashing civilizations. The chapter then argues that the civilizational rhetoric we observe in democratic societies does not represent a clash of civilizations precisely as Huntington conceived of it, but is instead a discourse primarily aimed at a domestic audience, closely associated with nationalism and populism, and is an attempt to define national identity through a civilization-based classification of peoples.

The chapter then examines the relationship between populism and civilizationalism, and shows how civilizationalism has become a significant part of right-wing populist discourse not merely in Europe, where it has been observed by several scholars (Brubaker 2017; Kaya 2021; Kaya and Tecmen 2019) but across a wide variety of political and religious contexts the world over. Surveying a wide variety of societies across the world, from the Americas to Europe, and from West and South Asia to Africa, the chapter defines civilizational populism as a group of ideas that together considers that politics should be an expression of the volonté générale (general will) of the people, and society to be ultimately separated into two homogenous and antagonistic groups, 'the pure people' versus 'the corrupt elite' who collaborate with the dangerous others belonging to other civilizations that are hostile and present a clear and present danger to the civilization and way of life of the pure people.

Chapter 3 marks the beginning of the case study section of the book, in which we test our key arguments in a series of case studies of populist parties, movements, and leaders that incorporate civilizational populism into their political discourse. It explores the relationship between Islam and populism by looking at case studies of Muslim majority countries including Pakistan, Tunisia, Egypt, Indonesia, and Turkey. The chapter contends that the Islam and populism nexus is closely related to the political form of Islam: Islamism. This concept is deeply wedded to Islamic ideas of justice, and for that reason can easily be attached to populism, which is itself based on notions of elites acting unjustly toward 'the people'". Second, populism in the Islamic world is often ethnoreligious nationalist, but due to the combination of the emphasis placed on the concept of the *ummah*, and the anti-West agenda of many of Islamist populist movements, there is an inherently transnational and civilizational element in Islamist populism. Civilizationism is, therefore, the chapter shows, a common feature of Islamic populism in the Muslim majority world.

The chapter tests these propositions with case studies of two Islamist populist movements: Turkey's ruling Islamist and Neo-Ottomanist AKP, and the now banned Indonesian Islamist Islamic Defenders Front (FPI). The case studies involve discourse analysis of the statements of the leaders of these two respective movements in the 2010–2020 period, combined with wider socio-political analysis of their impact on Indonesian and Turkish politics and society, respectively.

The chapter argues that the civilizationism of the Turkish ruling party the AKP consists of an *ummah* centric discourse combined with Turkish ethnonationalism and nostalgia for the Ottoman period. Inside this discourse, the party—and in particular its leader Recep Tayyip Erdoğan— use civilizationalism to define ingroups and outgroups in Turkish society. The AKP's ingroup consists of Turkish Sunni Muslims, while the outgroups include secularists, dissident Kurds, non-Sunni Muslims, Christians, and followers of the Gülen Movement. While the ingroups are portrayed as the 'pure people' who belong to the land of Turkey, the outgroups are accused of working with the Judeo-Christian West to destroy Turkey and its people, and of attacking the Islamic faith. We describe how the AKP has successfully integrated Islamist civilizationalism into its populist discourse. Furthermore, the chapter demonstrates how the AKP uses the organs of the state and friendly religious authorities to inculcate the young people of Turkey with civilizationalist ideas in order to create a 'pious generation' which will help perpetuate their rule. The chapter also shows how Turkish foreign policy is influenced by the AKP's civilizationalism, and the manner in which it uses civilizationalism to influence and instrumentalize the Turkish diaspora.

The chapter finds that the FPI uses a discourse which incorporates civilizationalism. The FPI have found only limited success in Indonesia, due to its banning in 2020, and the powerful moderating role played by Indonesia's largest civil Islamic groups. However, the chapter finds the FPI have had a significant impact on Indonesian politics and society. The group's populist discourse, we find, is based around distinguishing 'the people'—essentially Indonesian Sunni Muslims or the *ummah*—from an outgroup consisting of secular 'elites' and non-Orthodox Muslims. Inside this discourse, the outgroup is framed as a persistent and existential threat to the *ummah* which must be overcome. While the FPI is essentially a nationalist group, their categorization of 'the people' as *ummah* and anti-West, anti-Chinese agenda lends the movement a civilizationalist element. Equally, we find, the FPI has a significant transnational aspect, made possible by the civilizational element within their populist ideology, which emphasizes Muslims' solidarity with one another over national belonging.

While the FPI is now banned, the group's civilizational discourse has had a demonstrable influence over Indonesian politics and society. The chapter shows how the FPI played an important role in shifting political discourse in Indonesia to the right. For example, the FPI helped stage large-scale rallies calling for the jailing of former Jakarta governor Ahok, a Chinese Christian who was accused of insulting Islam. Indonesia's government and civil Islamic groups were taken aback by the level of support the FPI's calls to jail Ahok, and fearful of upsetting their movement and its supporters, allowed Ahok to be imprisoned on obviously false charges of blasphemy.

Chapter 4 explores the relationship between Christianity, civilizationalism, and populism. It provides a historical overview of the relationships between Christianity and populism. This relationship is comparatively old, and can be traced back to the United States People's Party (nicknamed 'the Populists'), which blended Protestant Christian teachings with a typically populist anti-elite, anti-government agenda. Yet as the chapter shows, today Christianity has been incorporated into the populist agendas of a wide variety of populist movements the world over. The chapter surveys Christian-based civilizational populism in the United States, Australia, Western Europe, Central and Eastern Europe, Latin America, and Africa.

The chapter argues that the relationship between Christianity and civilizational populism is complex and multifaceted, and often more connected to identity than faith. However, it is possible to contrast genuinely religious Christian populisms from secular 'Christian identitarian' populism. What the Christian populisms have in common, however, is that they often place Christianity within a sacred matrix of ethnos, nation, and civilization, in which Christianity acts as a signifier of all three.

To test these propositions, the chapter presents case studies of three populist movements and their respective leaders: the Dutch Party for Freedom and its leader Geert Wilders, the Hungarian Fidesz Party and its leader Viktor Orbán, and the Trump Administration in the United States and President Trump. The case studies consist of discourse analysis of the statements of the leaders of these two respective parties in the 2010–2020 period, combined with wider socio-political analysis of their impact on Dutch, American, and Hungarian politics and society. The chapter finds that civilizationalism is important in both Wilders and Orbán's respective discourses, and to an extent Trump's, yet in strikingly different ways. Wilders and Orbán are adept at using creating a fearful sense of national crisis, in which elites and Muslims threaten their respective national cultures and identities. Equally, both call upon Europeans to love their own indigenous cultures and identities, and to reject multiculturalism and cultural relativism. For Wilders and Orbán alike Christianity or Judeo-Christianity is not primarily a religion, but a term used to describe the character of Western civilization, and to divide it from rival civilizations. Trump, however, used civilizational rhetoric almost exclusively when running for president and in his first year as president, but it was never a primary element of his discourse. Another key difference between the three groups lies in their relationships with secularism. Wilders and his Party for Freedom are broadly secularist, liberal, and demand Muslims be excluded from the Netherlands due to their alleged authoritarian and illiberal religious worldview. Trump also largely, and perhaps surprisingly, conforms to this pattern. However, the chapter argues, Orbán's civilizationalism is aimed at reifying traditional values, and protecting them from European and American efforts to introduce a progressive agenda to Hungary in which multiculturalism is normalized, and LGBT rights and women's reproductive rights affirmed by the state.

Chapter 5 examines the relationship between Hinduism, civilizationalism, and populism. India is the only majority Hindu nation, therefore, the chapter focuses on Hindu civilizationalist populism in India, and in particular on the power of the Hindu nationalist (and civilizationalist) ideology Hindutva. The chapter begins with a history of Hindu nationalist politics, and describes the way nationalism, religion, and civilizationalism are blended together in *Hindutva*. The chapter then identifies the Narendra Modi-led BJP as the most significant Hindu populist and civilizationalist political party in India, while also examining the influence of Rashtriya Swayamsevak Sangh (RSS) and Shiv Sena.

The chapter examines the political discourse of the BJP and its leader Narendra Modi to determine how their populist narratives incorporate civilizationalism and religion. We also investigate whether the BJP's use of emotional rhetoric has played a key role in eliciting the negative and positive emotions required to create demand for civilizationalist populism. Our investigation finds that the BJP use the *Hindutva* ideology to elicit emotions which produce demand for their nationalist and civilizationalist populism. The BJP is the ruling party of India, and has adapted Hindutva to a populist framework in which Hindus are identified as 'the people', and secular nationalists (such as the former governing party Indian National Congress) are demonized as corrupt and traitorous elites. Muslims, and to perhaps a lesser extent Christians and certain other religious minorities, are 'othered' by the BJP, and categorized as enemies of 'the people' insofar as they are outside of Hindu culture. While the BJP has strong links to religious organizations and individuals, the chapter observes that Hindutva is an ethnoreligious and nationalist ideology which was devised as a response to the rise of Pan-Islamic political movements among Indian Muslims, which Hindutva's founders believed ought to be countered by a similar movement among Hindus.

The chapter then examines the political discourse of the BJP and its leader Narendra Modi. The case study involves discourse analysis of the statements made by Prime Minister Modi and the BJP during the 2010–2020 period, combined with wider socio-political analysis of their impact on Indian politics and society. In particular, we use the data generated by our analysis to comprehend the role emotions play in creating demand for populist solutions in India, and more broadly to help answer the five key questions at the heart of this book. The BJP's Hindutva is used to help frame 'the people' in an ethnoreligious manner, yet also frame them as an eternal victim of Muslim violence and elite misrule. Together these 'others' are blamed by the BJP for all of India's society problems. At the same time, Modi identifies "Congress leader Rahul Gandhi" as "a shahzada (princeling) of the Delhi Sultanate", and in doing so, associates him with the period of Islamic rule (Peker 2019, 32). Conversely, Modi on the one hand "stresses his own underdog background as a *chaiwala*", yet also presents himself at times as a "humble yet anointed Hindu leader" who is in certain posters "sacralised with a halo indicating Hindu symbolism of gods who glow like surya (the sun god)" (Peker 2019, 32). Equally, the BJP, and other supporters of Hindu Nationalism, attack the Indian constitution over its supposed "pseudo-secularism", which they claim favors non-Hindus, and Modi has himself called for Congress to "stop hiding behind the burqa of secularism" (Peker 2019, 32). Finally, the chapter finds that while the BJP much resembles the identitarian populists of Europe, insofar as both use religion as a civilization-based identity marker in order to construct "the people", the BJP are more closely connected with Hinduism than the "Christianist" parties of Europe with Christianity.

The chapter thus describes how the BJP's Hindutva populist-nationalist framework is used to identify Hindus as 'the people' and the secular nationalists (such as the former governing party Indian National Congress) are demonized as 'elites' beholden to foreign ideologies (especially secularism) along with non-Hindus such as Muslims and Christians. We also focus on cyber space, and the manifestation of this civilizational populism in that domain. In this case cow-lynching and the spread of Hindutva narratives are central points of our discussions, and we show how populists use social media to spread narratives about non-Hindus that lead to violence and hatred.

Chapter 6 investigates the relationship between Buddhism, civilizationism, and populism. Buddhist-based populism is rarely discussed by scholars. Therefore in this chapter we examine Buddhist nationalism and nationalist Buddhist creeds, which are politically important in Myanmar and Sri Lanka, in order to understand the larger religious and civilizational populist trend in Asia and across the world.

Myanmar's ethnic diversity has made it impossible for a purely ethnic-based conception of nation and people to succeed. Instead, the country has adopted a religion-based classification of peoples and nationalist understanding of Buddhism. This religion-based classification has allowed space for extremist religious nationalism to, at times, thrive in Myanmar. In Buddhist nationalism, the Buddhist majority of Myanmar become 'the people', and the Muslim minority population become the 'other', the undesired people who threaten the Buddhist identity of the people and the nation. In this chapter we trace the roots of this antagonistic relationship between 'the people' and 'others' to the colonial period. We then discuss contemporary politics in Myanmar, and find that Buddhist nationalist-populist actors have increasingly demonized Muslims during the last three decades, and have spent much energy on scapegoating and othering them in order to create the antagonistic environment in which populist thrives. We also discuss how the actions of groups such as the Taliban, who demolished the Bamiyan Buddhas has contributed to the growing antagonism between Muslims and Buddhists in Myanmar.

The chapter examines two influential and related ethnoreligious nationalist groups in Myanmar: MaBaTha (or Ma Ba Tha) and the 969 movement. Populism is deeply embedded in the discursive practices of these groups, which seek to 'safeguard' the county's Buddhist majority and national identity. Muslims—Myanmar's 'other'—are constructed in the discourse of these two groups as an existentialist threat to the Buddhist society. The chapter also explores how Buddhist nationalist-populist groups influence other parties and political movements. We show how secularist and democratic forces and figures have consistently bowed before the pressure put on them by the nationalist-populist groups, and attempted to avoid upsetting their supporters. For example, fearful of Buddhist nationalists, during her term in office Aung San Suu Kyi turned a blind eye to the growing hatred and violence perpetrated by nationalist Buddhist groups against the Muslim minority. We argue that mainstream parties' tolerant attitude toward Buddhist nationalist violence has exacerbated the problem. The chapters show how mainstream parties have inadvertently encouraged Buddhist nationalism and populism in Myanmar, by allowing the nationalist-populists to extract concessions from them, particularly in the form of laws banning interfaith marriage and religious conversion. Equally, we demonstrate the close relationship between Myanmar's military elites and Buddhist nationalist-populist groups.

The chapter also focuses on Sri Lanka, where Sinhalese Buddhists make up 70% of the population. This majority status has led the Sinhalese Buddhists to largely determine Sri Lanka's political agenda and identity. The chapter discusses populism in colonial and post-colonial Sri Lanka, and describes how Buddhist nationalists have long perceived Tamils and Muslims as threats to the nation's Buddhist and Sinhalese identity. The chapter focuses on the period of civil war in Sir Lanka and its aftermath, and describes how Sinhalese-Buddhist Nationalism (SBN) has been the driving force behind populism in Sri Lanka throughout this period. Our key case study is that of former Sri Lanka Prime Minister Mahinda Rajapaksa, and his use of discursive materials to pursue populist politics. We note how Rajapaksa and his political allies have promoted and espoused a civilizationalist discourse in which a crises situation divides society between the patriot (dēshapremi) and the traitor (dēshadrōhi). We show that this discourse has allowed Rajapaksa to assume an increasingly authoritarian role, and legitimized his unlawful activities, including violence against Tamils, Muslims, and other minorities. The chapter observes that ethnic tensions which existed during the civil war in Sri Lanka are increasingly replaced by religious tensions. For example, the chapter describes the growth of nationalist and anti-Muslim groups in Sri Lanka, and the manner in which their violence against Muslims and other minorities is either ignored or tacitly legitimized by the SBN-dominated state.

Chapter 7 examines Judaism and civilizational populism. It examines civilizational populism in Israel, and focuses on the largest and most powerful party in Israel since the 1980s, Likud, and its most significant leader of the past twenty years, Benjamin Netanyahu. Netanyahu is widely regarded as a populist, and to have moved Likud toward right-wing populism since becoming party chairman in 1993. This move toward right-wing populism has proven electorally successful for Likud, although it has had serious consequences for Israeli society and for the Palestinians. The civilizational narratives within Netanyahu's populist discourses have not been explicitly examined previously. However, this chapter shows how Netanyahu incorporates civilizationalism into his populist discourses by, first, using the notion that Jewish civilization predates all others in the region to establish the legitimacy of the state of Israel, the hegemony of Jewish culture within Israel, and at times his own political decisions. Second, through his portrayal of the Arab-Muslim world as an anti-semitic and barbaric bloc that, far from being a civilization, threatens Western civilization through its barbarism. Equally, this chapter shows how Netanyahu argues that Israel is akin to a protective wall that protects Western civilization from the Islamist barbarians who wish to destroy it, and therefore on this basis calls for Europeans and North Americans to support Israel in its battle for civilization and against the forces of barbarism. Combined, these narratives serve to assist Netanyahu in his populist division of Israeli society into three antagonistic groups: 'the people', the 'elite', and 'others'. In Netanyahu's discourse, the chapter shows, 'others' are non-civilized Arab-Muslims who desire the destruction of both the Jewish people and Western civilization; 'elites' are left-wing parties and liberal Jews who Netanyahu portrays as abandoning Jewish culture and helping Arabs destroy civilization; 'the People' are all the Jewish people, who are authentic and morally good: authentic because their ancestors were the first people of the land, and morally good because they are civilized Jews. This chapter begins with an overview of Israel's history, which is followed by a discussion on civilizational in Israel, and following this an examination of the use of civilizationalism within the populist rhetoric of Likud Party leader Benjamin Netanyahu.

The final chapter compares our major case studies and answers the key questions posed in the introduction. The chapter argues, first, that civilizational populism is a growing phenomenon and a threat to democracy and pluralism throughout the world. This is due to, the chapter shows, the anti-plural ideology of civilizational populism, which perceives religious difference as a threat to the identity and culture of the majority group, and maintains that democracy ought to represent only the will of the majority. Second, the chapter argues that civilizational populism is a group of ideas that together considers that politics should be an expression of the volonté générale (general will) of the people, and society to be ultimately separated into two homogenous and antagonistic groups, 'the pure people' versus 'the corrupt elite' who collaborate with the dangerous others belonging to other civilizations that are hostile and present a clear and present danger to the civilization and way of life of the pure people. Third, the chapter discusses the consequences of civilizational populism, which include a diminishing of pluralism and tolerance within a society, and attacks on the separation of powers.

Finally, the chapter addresses the possibility of transnational civilizational populism. The chapter notes that while civilizational populism remains almost entirely within the bounds of individual nation-states, and nationalist in orientation, religion provides an ideal bridge across nations upon which may be built a common populist agenda, if not a new transnational 'Christian' or 'Islamic' identity. We conclude that although transnational populism is rare, it may become more common due to the power of networked media to draw populists together across the world in common projects.

References

Ádám, Zoltan and Bozóki, András. 2016. "State and Faith: Right-Wing Populism and nationalized Religion in Hungary". *Intersections: East European Journal of Society and Politics* 2, no. 1, 98–122.

Alamgir, Jalal and D'cota, Bina. 2011. "The 1971 Genocide: War Crimes and Political Crimes." *Economic and Political Weekly* 46, no. 13, 2011, 38–41. www.jstor.org/stable/41152283.

Brass, R. Paul. 2003. The Partition of India and Retributive Genocide in the Punjab, 1946–47: Means, Methods, and Purposes. *Journal of Genocide Research* 5 (1): 71–101. https://doi.org/10.1080/14623520305657.

Brubaker, Rogers. 2017. Between nationalism and civilizationism: the European populist moment in comparative perspective. *Ethnic and Racial Studies* 40 (8): 1191–1226. https://doi.org/10.1080/01419870.2017.1294700.

Canovan, Margaret. 1999. Trust the People! Populism and the Two Faces of Democracy. *Political Studies* 47 (1): 2–16. https://doi.org/10.1111/1467-9248.00184.

Chatterji, P.., B. Thomas. Hansen, and Christophe Jaffrelot. 2020. Majoritarian State: How Hindu Nationalism is Changing India. *Oxford Scholarship Online*. https://doi.org/10.1093/oso/9780190078171.001.0001.

Cleminson, Richard. 2019. *Anarchism and Eugenics: An Unlikely Convergence, 1890–1940*. 1st ed., Manchester University Press. www.jstor.org/stable/j.ctv n96hnk.

Friend, Celeste. Last updated 2021. "Social Contract Theory". *Internet Encyclopaedia of Philosophy*. https://iep.utm.edu/soc-cont/.

Fukuyama, Francis. 2006. *The End of History and the Last Man*. New York: Free Press.

Gauthier, David. 1988. "Hobbes's Social Contract." *Noûs* 22: 71–82.

Gidron, Noam, and Bart Bonikowski. 2013. Varieties of Populism: Literature Review and Research Agenda. *SSRN Electronic Journal*. https://doi.org/10.2139/ssrn.2459387.

Huntington, Samuel P. 1993. The Clash of Civilizations? *Foreign Affairs* 72 (3): 22–49. https://doi.org/10.2307/20045621.

IDEA. 2019. "Summary: The Global State Of Democracy 2019". https://www.idea.int/publications/catalogue/summary-global-state-of-democracy-2019.

Kaya, Ayhan. 2021. The use of the past by the Alternative for Germany and the Front National: heritage populism, Ostalgia and Jeanne D'Arc. *Journal of Contemporary European Studies* 1–141. https://doi.org/10.1080/14782804.2021.1981835.

Kaya, Ayhan, and Tecmen, Ayşe. 2019. Europe versus Islam?: Right-Wing Populist Discourse and the Construction of a Civilizational Identity. *The Review of Faith & International Affairs* 17 (1): 49–645. https://doi.org/10.1080/15570274.2019.1570759.

Löfflmann, Georg. 2022. 'Enemies of the people': Donald Trump and the security imaginary of America First. *The British Journal of Politics and International Relations*. 24 (3): 543–560. https://doi.org/10.1177/13691481211048499.

Loke, Andras. 29 October 2020. "Democracy's Decline and Erosion of the Social Contract". *GMF*. https://www.gmfus.org/news/democracys-decline-and-erosion-social-contract. Last accessed September 21, 2022.

McDonnell, Duncan and Cabrera, Luis. 2019. "The right-wing populism of India's BharatiyaJanata Party (and why comparativists should care)". *Democratization* 26, no. 3. https://doi.org/10.1080/13510347.2018.1551885.

Moffitt, Benjamin. 2015. How to Perform Crisis: A Model for Understanding the Key Role of Crisis in Contemporary Populism. *Government and Opposition* 50: 189–217.

Morieson, Nicholas. 2021. *Religion and the Populist Radical Right: Secular Christianism and Populism in Western Europe*. Vernon Press.

Mudde, Cas. 2004. The Populist Zeitgeist. *Government and Opposition* 39 (4): 541–563.

Mudde, Cas. 2017. "Populism: An Ideational Approach". In Kaltwasser et al (editors) *The Oxford Handbook of Populism*. Oxford Handbooks Online Edition. https://doi.org/10.1093/oxfordhb/9780198803560.013.1.

Peker, Efe. 2019. Religious Populism, Memory, and Violence in India. *New Diversities* 17: 23.

Repucci, Sarah and Slipowitz, Amy. 2021. "Freedom in the World 2021 Democracy under Siege". *Freedom House*. https://freedomhouse.org/report/freedom-world/2021/democracy-under-siege Last accessed September 21, 2022.

Rico, Guillem, Marc Guinjoan, and Eva Anduiza. 2017. The Emotional Underpinnings of Populism: How Anger and Fear Affect Populist Attitudes. *Swiss Political Science Review* 23 (4): 444–461. https://doi.org/10.1111/spsr.12261.

Roussinos, Aris. 2020. "The irresistible rise of the Civilization-state". *Unherd*. https://unherd.com/2020/08/the-irresistible-rise-of-the-civilisation-state/. Last accessed September 21, 2022.

Sengul, Kurt Adam. 2022. Performing islamophobia in the Australian parliament: The role of populism and performance in Pauline Hanson's "burqa stunt". *Media International Australia* 184 (1): 49–62. https://doi.org/10.1177/1329878X221087733.

Taguieff, P.A. 1995. Political Science Confronts Populism: From a Conceptual Mirage to a Real Problem. *Telos* 103: 9–43, https://doi.org/10.3817/0395103009.

The Economist: Intelligence Unit. 2021. "Democracy Index 2020: In sickness and in health?." https://www.eiu.com/n/campaigns/democracy-index-2020/. Last accessed September 21, 2022.

Wajner, Daniel F. 2022. The populist way out: Why contemporary populist leaders seek transnational legitimation. *The British Journal of Politics and International Relations*. 24 (3): 416–436. https://doi.org/10.1177/13691481211069345.

Yilmaz, Ihsan. 2021a. *Creating the Desired Citizen: Ideology, State and Islam in Turkey*. Cambridge and New York: Cambridge University Press.

Yilmaz, Ihsan. 2021b. 5 February 2021b. "The AKP's Authoritarian, Islamist Populism: Carving out a New Turkey". *European Center for Populism Studies*. https://www.populismstudies.org/the-akps-authoritarian-islamist-populism-carving-out-a-new-turkey/. Last accessed September 21, 2022.

Yilmaz, Ihsan. 2021c. 14 February 2021c. "Erdoğan's Political Journey: From Victimised Muslim Democrat to Authoritarian, Islamist Populist". *European Center for Populism Studies.* https://www.populismstudies.org/Erdoğans-political-journey-from-victimised-muslim-democrat-to-authoritarian-islamist-populist/. Last accessed September 21, 2022.

Yilmaz, Ihsan and Morieson, Nicholas. 2021. "A Systematic Literature Review of Populism Religion and Emotions". *Religions*12, no. 4, 272. https://doi.org/10.3390/rel12040272

Yilmaz, Ihsan, Nichols Morieson, and Mustafa Demir. 2021. "Exploring Religions in Relation to Populism: A Tour around the World". *Religions* 12: 301. https://doi.org/10.3390/rel12050301.

Yilmaz, Ihsan, and Morieson, Nicholas. 2022a. "Civilizational Populism: Definition, Literature, Theory, and Practice" *Religions.*

Yilmaz, Ihsan, and Morieson, Nicholas. 2022b. "Religious Populisms in the Asia Pacific" *Religions* 13, no. 9: 802. https://doi.org/10.3390/rel13090802.

Zúquete, Jose Pedro. 2017. "Populism and Religion". In *The Oxford Handbook of Populism,* edited by Cristóbal Rovira Kaltwasser, Paul Taggart, Paulina Ochoa Espejo, and Pierre Ostiguy. Oxford: Oxford University Press.

CHAPTER 2

Civilizationalism, Religions, and Populism

2.1 Introduction

Civilizationalism exerts a significant influence on contemporary international politics and state relations, and also on domestic politics across a wide variety of societies. Since it was first powerfully articulated in 1993 by Samuel P. Huntington, the notion that the world can be divided into clashing civilizational blocs, largely defined by religious identity, has gained currency and has arguably influenced some of the most important international political events of the twenty-first century. It is possible to conceive, then, that the belief in a perceived 'clash of civilizations' has played a key role in precipitating, for example, the United States-led 'War on Terror', the rise of al-Qaeda and other radical Islamist organizations, China's increasingly aggressive posturing in Asia, the European Union's refusal to admit Muslim majority Turkey as a member state, and in Russia's violent attempts to expand its territory and sphere of influence beyond its borders. For example, Russia's invasion of Ukraine, while predicated on the dubious notion that Ukraine's neo-Nazi and ultra-nationalist groups pose a direct threat to Russia and an existential menace to Russian speakers in Ukraine, cannot be entirely separated from the Putin regime's ambition to expand Russian civilization beyond Russia's national borders. Indeed, Russian President Vladimir Putin has long attempted to legitimize his domestic and foreign policies by claiming

© The Author(s), under exclusive license to Springer Nature Singapore Pte Ltd. 2023
I. Yilmaz and N. Morieson, *Religions and the Global Rise of Civilizational Populism*, Palgrave Studies in Populisms, https://doi.org/10.1007/978-981-19-9052-6_2

that he is defending Russia's Christian-based civilization from the decadent and expansionist liberal West (Silvius 2015). Blackburn (2021, 11), for example, observes that "a new direction in [Russian] state discourse became visible in 2012, one that focused more on the need for internal unity and patriotism, emphasizing Russia's distinctiveness from the West as a civilization and underlining the need to struggle against Western-backed anti-Russian schemes". In 2013, for example, Putin claimed that many European and North American nations were "rejecting their roots, including the Christian values that constitute the basis of western civilisation" (Costello 2022). Furthermore, Putin said, these Western nations "are denying the moral principles and all traditional identities: national, cultural, religious and even sexual" (Costello 2022).

American and Western European liberalism, which Putin appears to regard as decadent, immoral, and dangerous, is thus perceived to be a direct threat to Russian civilization and to the values of Orthodox Christianity. Putin has vowed to defend Russia from these civilizational threats, and to expand the boundaries of Russian civilization in part as a way of combating the liberal West (Adamsky 2022). Russian Orthodox Patriarch Archbishop Kirill, a powerful Putin ally, has given religious support for Putin's expansionism, remarking once that when he said 'Russian', he was using "the ancient expression from 'A Tale of Bygone Years – Where from has the Russian land come,' the land which now includes Russia and Ukraine and Belarus and other tribes and peoples" (Interfax Religion 2022).

Putin's antipathy toward liberalism and the social and sexual mores it either permits or encourages—at least prior to his invasion of Ukraine[1]—drew varying degrees of support from conservatives and, particularly, right-wing populists throughout the democratic West, many of whom admired Putin's defense of Christian values and traditional sexual mores. For example, *Lega* leader Matteo Salvini, derided as "Putin's man in Europe", drew his party close to Putin throughout the 2010s (Jack 2022). Hungary's right-wing populist Prime Minister Viktor Orbán once praised Putin for making "his country great again", sought to create closer ties with Russia (Janjevic, 2018) and appears to share Putin's belief that the liberal West is decadent, and that liberalism is ultimately the enemy of Western civilization and its Christian values. Equally, like

---

[1] As Viktor Jack (2022) has shown, the invasion of Ukraine has persuaded right-wing populists to revoke their support for Putin and Russia.

Putin, many European right-wing populist parties claim to be protecting the Judeo-Christian values of Western civilization from a combination of enemies ranging from Islam and Muslim immigrants, to elites who support globalization and cultural relativism (Brubaker 2017; Kaya and Tecmen 2019; Morieson 2021; Roy 2016a, b; Roy 2016a; Roy 2013). Civilizationalism, then, is not merely a type of rhetoric employed by leaders of authoritarian 'civilizational states', but also very present in democratic politics, particularly among populist parties, movements, and individual politicians.

What, then, is civilizationalism, and why has it become such a powerful tool in the hands of populists the world over? Civilizationalism, and in particular the notion that the world's great civilizations are doomed to clash in the post-Cold War international environment, has been a widely debated concept in the social sciences—and in particular in International Relations—since the publication of Huntington's essay "The Clash of Civilizations?" in 1993. In his essay and subsequent book *The Clash of Civilizations*, Huntington argued that civilizations, or the "highest cultural grouping of people and the broadest level of social identity" (Huntington 1993) would define international politics in the post-Cold War world. This new world, he argued, would be multipolar, as nations organized themselves around civilizational "core" states (Huntington 1996). Where Francis Fukuyama (2006) argued that, following the collapse of the Soviet Union, liberal democracy no longer faced any strong ideological opposition, Huntington argued that the end of ideological conflict might initiate a new period of civilizational conflict. He argued that the relative decline of the West and the rise of Asian nations, and the growing instability of the Middle East and broader Muslim majority world, would precipitate an era of clashing civilizations (Huntington 1996). In this era nations, Huntington claimed, would naturally draw themselves close to similar nations and "group themselves around the lead or core states of their civilization". Some nations would, he claimed, be 'torn' between civilizations (Huntington 1993, 42–43) and face the deleterious prospect of civil conflict. The rise of the non-West would, Huntington (1993, 40–41) argued, demonstrate to Western peoples that their own culture and worldview was anything but universal, but rather a product of their own histories. In order to keep their unique cultures and to prevent global conflict, he suggested, Western peoples should desist from forcing their culture on other civilizations, and instead embrace and preserve their cultural identity (1996, 20–21).

Huntington described nine world civilizations: Western, Latin American, African,[2] Islamic, Sinic, Hindu, Orthodox, Buddhist, and Japanese. Four of these supposed civilizations are defined by religion, and in his original 'clash' essay Huntington defined 'Sinic' civilization as Confucian (1993, 40). Moreover, Huntington claims that "to a very large degree the major civilizations in human history have been closely identified with the world's great religions" (1996, 42). The importance Huntington placed on religious identity in defining civilizations was novel in the 1990s, and the explosion of interest in religion's relationship with politics and international relations only occurred as a response to the 9/11 attacks on New York and Washington D.C. (Snyder 2011). Huntington was perhaps prescient, then, when discussing the significance of religion on global politics and international relations, and in particular on civilizational identity. Indeed, we have found that religion plays a vital role in defining civilizational identity throughout the world, including in secularized regions such as much of Western Europe (Yilmaz and Morieson 2021; Yilmaz et al. 2021a, b).

Huntington's clash thesis has, of course, been much criticized by scholars. Bottici and Challand (2010, 3) describe the clash of civilizations as a "political myth" which is increasingly used to attack globalization and the "global village" it has created. Amartya Sen has attacked Huntington for placing all humanity within a handful of simple religion and/or ethnic-based monolithic civilizations (Sen 2006). For Sen, Huntington's classification of peoples is not merely simplistic and ignorant, but it perpetuates divisions within societies and between nations, and may even encourage acts of violence (Sen 2006). Ahmad (1995) has likewise critiqued Huntington's lack of nuance when describing the histories of entire nations of people, and argues that it is not possible to place nations and indeed individuals within one simple civilizational tradition. Qureshi and Sells, moreover, claim that Huntington is actively encouraging civilizational conflict (Qureshi and Sells 2003; see also Shahi 2017; Said 2001). Said (2001) argued that Huntington relied too much on Orientalist scholar Bernard Lewis, who believed that a clash between Islam and the West was inevitable (Said 2001; Qureshi and Sells 2003). According to Said, Huntington's thesis—like Lewis' scholarship—constructed Islam

---

[2] Huntington claims to be unsure whether African civilization exists due to the lack of a coherent and common African identity, and the significant presence of Islam and Christianity throughout sub-Saharan Africa (1996, 47).

as a monolithic civilization and opposite of Western (Christian) civilization, and moreover as a threat to Western and particularly American hegemony. It is not difficult, indeed, to draw a line between Huntington's clash thesis and the U.S. government's response to the 9/11 attack, which was at times conceptualized as the first shots in a religious war between radical Islam and the West.

It may be that Huntington's clash thesis was something of a self-fulling prophesy, and thus itself a form of civilizationalism. A distinction may be made between civilization and civilizationalism: if a civilization is the "highest cultural grouping of people and the broadest level of social identity" (Huntington 1993), civilizationalism is a discourse that emphasizes the importance of civilizational difference in global and/or domestic politics above other factors. Civilizationalism, as discourse, explains the world in terms of clashing civilizations, and posits that 'our' civilization is threatened by a foreign civilization, or peoples from that civilization, and that 'we' must defend ourselves. Huntington's clash thesis, viewed in this manner, appears to have encouraged the deleterious foreign policy of the George W. Bush Administration by legitimizing the idea that radical Islam was at war with the West, and that Middle Eastern societies were 'torn' places with bloody borders and required re-orienting toward the West. It would of course be foolish to blame Huntington for the excesses of the Bush Administration or indeed the wave of civilizationalism that has followed the publication of his clash thesis. Equally, elements of the original clash thesis were indeed prescient, particularly Huntington's observation of the importance of religion in creating civilizational identity. Perhaps the greatest flaw in Huntington's thesis is his insistence that there is something entirely natural about civilizational identity, and his acceptance that it should come to dominate international politics and—in the case of torn nations—domestic politics. Indeed, we find all over the world cases in which political parties and movements are deliberately constructing civilizational identities and/or justifying foreign and domestic policies through civilizational discourses. Moreover, as we have already shown, populist parties and movements, in particular, are particularly adept at constructing civilizational narratives and identities, and using them to achieve political and electoral success. European populists' use of civilizational discourse has been identified by a number of scholars; non-Western populists' use of civilization rhetoric, however, has rarely been discussed in scholarly literature. What, then, is the relationship between populism and civilizationalism, and how do populists construct civilizational identities?

2.2 What is Populism?

Populism was once widely considered a political phenomenon found only in weak democracies, or a strategy used by authoritarian and personalistic regimes in Latin America (Glaser 2017; Moffitt 2016; Bjerre-Poulsen 1986). Today, however, populism has become a global phenomenon, and its flexibility has allowed it to adapt to a wide variety of political environments. For example, Kyle and Gultchin, (2018, 4) surveying the global rise of populism, found that:

"Between 1990 and 2018, the number of populists in power around the world has increased a remarkable fivefold, from four to 20. This includes countries not only in Latin America and in Eastern and Central Europe—where populism has traditionally been most prevalent—but also in Asia and in Western Europe". Populism is a contested concept and infamously difficult to define. The sociologist Edward Shills set out an early and minimal definition of populism, which he argued consisted of "popular resentment against the order imposed on society by a …ruling class which is believed to have a monopoly on power, property, breeding, and culture" (Shils 1956, 100–1). He further argued that three other ideas may be inherent to populism: first, that 'the people' are sovereign and above their rulers; second, that there ought to be a direct connection between 'the people' and their government; third, that the 'will of the people' is an "associate with justice and morality" (Shils 1956, 98). To a large degree, these notions continue to influence scholarship on populism. Yet there has been a great deal of scholarly contestation over whether these concepts could be said to form a coherent populist set of ideas, a populist ideology—albeit a 'thin-centred' one—or elements of populist practice (Gidron and Bonikowski 2013).

The ideational approach to populism has, according to Mudde (2017), become the "most broadly used in the field today". While there are variants of this approach, the most significant is perhaps Mudde's own ideological approach, which emerged as dominant among scholars of European populism, many of whom study the large and growing number of right-wing populist parties in the region (Gidron and Bonikowski 2013). The ideological approach conceives of populism as a group of ideas that together "considers society to be ultimately separated into two homogenous and antagonistic groups, 'the pure people' versus 'the corrupt elite', and which argues that politics should be an expression of the volonté générale (general will) of the people" (Mudde 2004, 543). However, 'lacking the sophistication of other ideologies like socialism or liberalism', populism—according to this approach—'is a thin-centred ideology and could be combined with other beliefs and ideas of politics' (de la Torre 2019, 7).

There are three key elements in the ideology of populism, or in populist ideation, according to this approach. The first key element of populism ideology/ideation, according to this approach is, of course, 'the people' and their opposition to 'elites'. In the discursive approach references to 'the people' are often held to be—to use Laclau's term—'empty signifiers' (Laclau 2012). In the ideological/ideational approach 'the people' is a flexible but not empty signifier. According to Mudde (2017), the people in populist ideation are 'pure', and elites impure. This 'moral' difference requires populists to define the boundaries of 'the people' and 'elites' in terms that make sense within their respective political and social environments, or as Mudde (2017) puts it, "no American populist will describe the people as atheist and no West European populist will define the people as Muslim". In their quest to create a 'heartland' (Taggart 2004), populists—according to this approach—define the people in ways "related to the self-perception (or self-idealization) of the targeted people" (Mudde 2017).

'Elites' are viewed by populists—according to the ideological/ideational approach—as immoral and inauthentic insofar as they do not conform to the standards of behavior common to 'the people', but this does not mean that each different populist movement or leader would describe elites' immorality in the same manner. For example, in the United States, according to Nicholson and Segura (2012), right-wing populists describe 'elites' as 'latte-drinking, sushi-eating, Volvo-driving, *New York Times*-reading, Hollywood-loving liberal elite' (Nicholson and Segura 2012, 369), a description which might be a little out of date now, but which serves as a useful example of how populists view 'elites' in one political context.

Populists may also introduce an ethnic or racial or religious dimension to populism. While Mudde (2017, 2004) describes populism as in its core a vertical phenomenon insofar as it distinguishes people 'the people' and 'elites', it is obvious that populists at times introduce a horizontal element, and distinguish between 'the people' and 'others'—another immoral and inauthentic group or groups who may not govern the nation, but harm 'the people' in other ways (see Taguieff 1995). Populists who thus combine populism with religion, or with a form of nationalism or racism, or indeed any form of nativism, exclude people from the heartland or 'the people' based on criteria other than 'morality'. This criteria might be ethnic, religious, or a combination of the two. While most common in right-wing forms of populism, certain left-wing populisms have also incorporated racialism, including in Latin America, where an ethnopopulism "fully merges nativism and populism (e.g. Madrid 2008). For example, Bolivian President Evo Morales has regularly pitted the indigenous pure people against the mestizo corrupt elite (e.g. Mudde and Rovira Kaltwasser 2017; Ramirez 2009)" (Mudde 2017). Equally, the left-wing populist Economic Freedom Fighters (EFF) party in South Africa combines Marxism–Leninism with anti-white, anti-Boer racism and pro-violence rhetoric (Mbete 2015). On the other hand, Satgar disagrees with this categorization and instead (2019) describes the EFF as a "black neofascist" party, and thus a right-wing party.

The 'will of the people' is the third key concept in the ideational/ideological approach. Mudde (2017), following Canovan (1981, 1999) and Taggart (2004), claims that populists believe that politics "should follow the general will of the people". The inherent goodness and purity of 'the people' is the basis, Mudde suggests, of this claim, which populists frame as being merely 'common sense'. In other words, populists believe that 'the people' are pure and good, and that it therefore naturally follows that politics ought to be based on satisfying the wants and desires of 'the people'. Equally, populists believe that those who refuse to obey the 'will of the people' either lack common sense, or are putting their own "special interests" above those of 'the people (Mudde 2017).

Some scholars working within the broad ideational approach do not believe populism is an ideology, and prefer to describe populism as a loose set of ideas that are expressed discursively, or as part of an overall political style. All accept, however, the notion that there are a set of ideas, i.e. 'the people' vs. 'the elite', and the notion that the people's will must be obeyed, that can be grouped together and called populism. This ideational approach may be contrasted against the organizational or 'strategy' approach favored by scholars who predominantly study Latin American populism. These scholars define populism as "a political strategy through which a personalistic leader seeks or exercises government power based on direct, unmediated, uninstitutionalized support from large numbers of mostly unorganized followers" (Weyland 2001, 14). Therefore, when they attempt to measure populism in a political leader and/or movement, they make no attempt to analyze the values or beliefs expressed. Rather, the strategy approach posits that populists attempt to cultivate—through a political strategy—a direct relationship between 'the people' and a populist leader. This strategy is understood to be an attempt to convince 'the people' (however constituted) to support a particular populist leader/movement/party on the basis that (1) the leader of this movement/party understands their 'will', or in some way perhaps even embodies the people themselves, and (2) that no other political leader understand the people's will, and therefore ought not to be supported but, rather, be opposed. Political leaders/parties/movements that can be understood as using such a strategy are described by proponents of this approach as populist. Indeed, scholars in this group often perceive populism to be a 'strategy' in the hands of strongmen, which they use to revise the democratic structure and capture power (Barr 2009; Weyland 2001).

A third group of scholars define populism as a discourse. Some of these scholars, such as Hawkins (2010) work within the ideational framework, but study the manner in which populism is expressed through discourse. However, the earlier proponents of the discourse approach, in particular Laclau, defined populism as a discursive practice and political logic that brings into existence 'the people' (Laclau 2005, 154). According to this approach, in populism "the identity of both 'the people' and 'the other' are political constructs, symbolically constituted through the relation of antagonism, rather than sociological categories" (Panizza 2005, 3). Moreover, "antagonism is thus a mode of identification in which the relation between its form (the people as signifier) and its content (the people as signified) is given by the very process of naming – that is, of establishing who the enemies of the people (and therefore the people itself) are" (Panizza 2005, 3). Laclau's complex approach is summed up by Moffitt (2016, 23), who writes that Laclau argues that "when a demand is un-satisfied within any system, and then comes into contact with other unsatisfied demands, they can form an equivalential chain with one another, as they share the common antagonism/enemy of the system". For populists, then, this would be achieved through the rhetorical division of society into two groups: 'the people' and 'others'.

Further developing these notions, De Cleen and Stavrakakis argue that the discourse of populism is vertical as it is able to engage with multiple factors and thematic areas for instance it distinguishes 'the people' as the 'underdog' and the other as the 'elite' it also engages with the various socio-economic divides within these two basic dichotomies as well (De Cleen and Stavrakakis 2017, 312).

The final and most recently developed manner of defining populism is the performative or 'political style' approach associated with Moffitt and Ostiguy. Moffitt defines populism as "a political style that features an appeal to 'the people' versus 'the elite'; 'bad manners' and the performance of crisis, breakdown or threat" (Moffitt 2016, 45). He describes populism as a political style consisting of "repertoires of embodied, symbolically mediated performance made to audiences that are used to create and navigate the fields of power that comprise the political, stretching from the domain of government through to everyday life" (Moffitt 2016, 38).

In this book we define populism according to the most widely used minimal definition: as a set of ideas which together "considers society to be ultimately separated into two homogenous and antagonistic groups, 'the pure people' versus 'the corrupt elite', and which argues that politics should be an expression of the volonté générale (general will) of the people" (Mudde 2004, 543). At the same time, we draw on ideas from other approaches to populism, many of which can be worked into the ideational approach. Mudde himself does this when acknowledging that populists may create 'heartlands', or that Laclau's notion of populism having key signifiers is helpful, ideas which came from non-ideational approaches (Mudde 2017). We acknowledge the helpfulness of the distinction made by Taguieff (1995) between the vertical and horizontal dimensions of certain populisms, or the 'people vs elite' and 'people vs others' element of certain forms of populism. Equally, we draw on Canovan and Moffitt, who ascribe a "mood" (Canovan 1981, 1999) and "style" (Moffitt 2016), respectively, to populism, often categorized as involving heightened emotions. However, we do not argue that this mood or style is the core of populism. Rather, we argue that populist rhetoric, like all forms of democratic politics, is emotional, and that like other politicians or political activists populists use emotional rhetoric to draw the public's attention to their cause, and to convince the public of its rightness. However, we also wish to draw attention to the specific ways in which politics use emotional rhetoric, and try to show how populists often win power by creating a sense of 'crisis' and fear among their supporters, as well as feelings of anger, nostalgia for a past 'golden age', and hope for a better future. This emotional rhetoric, we argue, is an expression of the civilizational populist ideas, and important to understand if we are to make intelligible civilizational populism.

Populism appears to be a type of democratic politics based on the sacralization of the 'will of the people', and thus emerges almost uniformly in societies in which there is a perception that the people's wishes are being ignored by governments (Canovan 1999, 2–16). Populism thus often emerges when, as Taggart (2021a, b) puts it, "something is not working well with democracy" or at the very least when populists are able to generate a belief that democratic government has failed 'the people'. Populists, however, do not automatically win government merely because the public has lost faith in the democratic process within a nation. Rather, the power of populism lies in its ability to co-opt or graft itself onto 'thicker' ideologies and other ideas. Populism therefore can be combined with socialism, or a left-wing agenda, or with right-wing ideologies, or indeed with a more eclectic or centrist set of ideas and discourses. As a result, populist parties can be very different from one another. Indeed, left-wing populists often divide society into two categories: 'the corrupt elite' and 'the people'; that is, between the 'bad' people at the top who dominate economic relations within a society and the 'good' working-class people at the bottom (Kyle and Gultchin 2018, 21–22).Taguieff (1995) has described this as the 'vertical' dimension of populism, or the top vs bottom or 'people' vs 'elite' dimension, which all forms of populism possess. Of course, there are exceptions, especially in Latin America, where left-wing populists have added an enthnonationist element to populism which categorizes indigenous and black citizens within the ingroup 'the people', and excludes most others (Mudde 2017). Right-wing populism also contains what Taguieff calls the vertical dimension. However, right-wing populists may not distinguish the virtuous community from the corrupt elite based solely on wealth. Instead, right-wing populists most often introduce what Taguieff calls a horizontal dimension to populism, in which 'the people' are distinguished from the 'non-people' or 'others' based on some other characteristic (e.g. ethnicity, race, ideology, religion, or a combination of several characteristics).

According to Kyle and Gultchin (2018, 21), right-wing "cultural populism tends to emphasize religious traditionalism, law and order, sovereignty". Furthermore, right-wing cultural populism, they contend, possesses three key elements: nativism, majoritarianism, and penalism/authoritarianism (Kyle and Gultchin 2018). Right-wing populist majoritarianism affirms the right of the majority population of a nation to have its collective will obeyed, even if this means rule of law and minority rights are discarded. Nativism in right-wing populism in Europe, for example, is presently expressed in anti-immigration policies and rhetoric, and through attempts to 'protect' European Christian or Judeo-Christian culture (Brubaker 2017; Morieson 2021; Roy 2016a, b) Right-wing populist penalism/authoritarianism is evident when populist governments, parties, movement, or individual politicians call for deviants within the nation to be punished and/or excluded on the grounds that their presence threatens the virtuous majority group (i.e. 'the people'). Thus Kyle and Gultchin (2018, 34) observe that right-wing "populism tends to promote punitive short-term solutions to multifaceted problems, often at the expense of human rights". For Europe's right-wing populist parties, these deviants are frequently people within the nation who do not share the ethnicity, religion, and/or political and social views of 'the people'. Populism itself, of course, does not provide a thick ideology around which political parties can determine who these deviants might be. Thus, populists must always combine populism with a thicker ideology or set of ideas.

2.3 Civilizational Populism

Civilizationalism is an idea which provides content through which populists can determine who belongs to 'the people', and who to the outgroups 'elites', and 'others'. Scholars have largely studied populist civilizationalism in the European context (Brubaker 2017; Kaya and Tecmen 2019). Across Europe, populists have achieved varying degrees of political and electoral success while portraying themselves as defenders not merely of the nation, but of Western 'Judeo-Christian' civilization (Kaya 2021; Kaya and Tecman 2019; Marzouki et al. 2016; Yilmaz and Morieson 2021; Yilmaz and Morieson 2022). There is now a well-established body of literature examining and describing Christianity based civilizational populism in Europe, much of which describes how right-wing populists across the continent frame Muslim immigrants as threats to Christian or Judeo-Christian identity, culture, and civilization in Europe (Brubaker 2017; Vollard 2013; Roy 2013, 2016a, b; Apahideanu 2014; van Kessel 2016; Brubaker 2017; Ozzano and Bolzonar 2020).

The civilization turn among populists in Europe was first reported by the sociologist Rogers Brubaker. Brubaker noticed that (2017, 1193) a number of right-wing populist parties in North-Western Europe could be grouped together insofar as they perceived "opposition between self and other not in narrowly national but in broader civilizational terms". The cause of the 'civilizational turn' in North-West European populism appears to be the large number of Muslims immigrating to the region, and the visible presence of Islam, which is held to be deleterious by some right-wing parties in Europe. Islam's growth and the concomitant decrease in European fertility, has perhaps led to fears that Muslims will 'take over' Europe and, in time become the majority socio-religious group on the continent, or at least in certain European nations. Brubaker observes how this new presence of Muslims has changed some European in the North-West of the continent, or to put it another way, in the most secularized region of Western Europe. He observes that as Muslims have increased in number in the region, there has been a curious merging of secularism and Christianity in right-wing populist rhetoric: "Just as [Muslims'] religiosity emerges from the matrix of Islam", Brubaker argues, "so 'our' secularity emerges from the matrix of Christianity (or the 'Judeo-Christian tradition') (Brubaker 2016)". In other words, secularism has become widely understood as a product—a unique product—of Christianity. But rather than describe Christianity as a religion, and thus a private faith without wider political and cultural dimensions, right-wing populists in North-West Europe describe Christianity as a civilization, or as the key element of Western civilization, which they describe as being created by unique Christian or Judeo-Christian values.

It is likely that civilizational populism does not end in North-Western Europe. Kaya and Tecmen (2019, 49), for example, demonstrate that the manifestos of five other European right-wing populist parties, "Alternative for Germany (AfD) in Germany, National Front (FN) in France, Party for Freedom (PVV) in the Netherlands, Five Star Movement (M5S) in Italy, and Golden Dawn (GD) in Greece), employ fear of Islam as a political instrument to mobilize their supporters and to mainstream themselves". They also argue that "right-wing populist party leaderships across Europe seem to be strongly capitalizing on civilizational matters by singling out Islam" and claiming that Christian or Judeo-Christian civilization is threatened by Islam (Kaya and Tecmen 2019, 61). Kaya and Tecmen restrict themselves to Europe, but as we discussed in the introduction, there is evidence that civilizational populism is a worldwide phenomenon.

What is civilizational populism? Scholars, including Brubaker (2017), Kaya (2021), Kaya and Tecmen (2019), and Yilmaz and Morieson (2021, 2022) have described the civilizational turn among populists, but not yet provided a succinct definition of the concept. Nor has civilizational populism been explored beyond Europe and, to some degree, North America. In this book, we argue civilizationalism is playing a similar role to other ideas and ideologies that can be adhered to populism to give its signifiers ('the pure people', 'corrupt elites', 'dangerous others') meaning. In the different forms of populism, thicker ideologies and ideas shape the boundaries of 'the people' 'elites' and 'others, and describe why 'the people' are pure, authentic and good and 'elites' and 'others' impure, bad, and inauthentic. Moreover, 'the people' in populism, are morally good and pure (Mudde 2017). However, 'elites' are perceived to be morally bad and impure, and to have betrayed 'the people' by acting against their interests, or even abandoning the culture and mores of 'the people' (Mudde 2017).

Civilizationalism is an idea which posits that the cultures and peoples of the world can be divided into 'civilizations', most of them defined by religion. When civilizationalism is adhered with populism, the result is a set of ideas that defines self and other not primarily in national terms, but in civilizational terms (Brubaker 2017). We argue that civilizational defines populism's signifiers first by categorizing people through civilizational identity (this may be self-imposed or imposed by populists). Second, by describing 'the people' as morally good because the civilization to which they belong is superior to all others, and the product of superior moral values derived chiefly from a religion. Conversely, civilizationalism adhered to populism permits populists to describe 'elites' as morally bad actors who betrayed and abandoned the values and culture of their own civilization. Equally, civilizational populism describes 'others' within the same society as morally 'bad' because they belong to a foreign civilization with inferior values, and which is the product of an inferior religion. The purpose of this book, then, is to clarify the concept 'civilizational populism' and work toward an operational definition. To do this, the book examines how populists in a variety of different religious, political, and geographic contexts, incorporate notions of 'civilization' into their respective discourses.

While there is literature on populism and civilizationalism in the European, North American, and Turkish contexts, and to a degree on American civilizationalism and populism, little is known of civilizationalism and its relationship with populism in South Asia, East Asian, South-East Asian, North African, and Sub-Saharan African contexts (Barton et al 2021; Filkins 2019; Yilmaz & Morieson 2022). We do not know, therefore, how civilizational populism operates in these crucial contexts, despite strong evidence that the phenomenon exists within them. Therefore we are uncertain as to whether all these civilizational populisms are generated by the same set political issues, or whether there are significant differences between them. Neither are we certain whether each civilizational populism attaches itself to a religion in the same manner, or whether the various religions influence civilizationalism in different ways.

Equally, we do not know how populists create demand for civilizational populism within these diverse political contexts. The relationship between civilizationalism and nationalism in different political and religious contexts is also little known, especially outside of Europe and North America. It is also not known whether civilizational populism leads to the establishing of transnational ties between populist movements or entire nations, or indeed whether there are forms of civilizational populism that move beyond the national paradigm. The impacts of civilizational populism on a society are also not well understood, and it is in particular not known whether civilizational populism is inherently violent, or whether rhetoric calling for violence is a common part of the phenomena.

The following chapters attempt to answer these questions by examining civilizational populism across the world. The following four questions are the focus of our investigation:

1. What is civilizational populism and how widespread has it become?
2. How do populists across the world, and in a variety of different religious, geographic, and political contexts, incorporate ideas of 'civilization' into their discourses?
3. What are the consequences of civilizational populism entering the political mainstream?
4. Is there a transnational dimension to civilizational populism?

Because civilizational identity is so closely linked with religion, we categorize the civilizational populisms by religion—Islamic, Christian,

Hindu, Buddhist, and Judaist—and examine these civilization populisms within a variety of polities. We begin with a study of the relationship between Islam and civilizational populism, and with case studies of two prominent Islamist civilizationalist movements: Indonesia's Islamic Defenders Front, and Turkey's ruling Justice and Development Party.

REFERENCES

Adamsky, Dmitry. 2022. "In the Kremlin, Faith and Force go Hand in Hand." *Foreign Policy*. https://www.foreignaffairs.com/articles/russian-federation/2022-03-05/russias-menacing-mix-religion-and-nuclear-weapons. (Last accessed September 21, 2022).

Ahmad, Eqbal. 1995. "The Clash of Civilizations: A Critical Analysis." *Strategic Studies* 18 (1): 120–128. http://www.jstor.org/stable/45182203.

Barr, Robert R. 2009. Populists, Outsiders and Anti-Establishment Politics. *Party Politics* 15: 29–48. https://doi.org/10.1177/1354068808097890.

Barton, Greg, Yilmaz, Ihsan, and Morieson, Nicholas. 2021. Religious and Pro-Violence Populism in Indonesia: The Rise and Fall of a Far-Right Islamist Civilisationist Movement. *Religions* 12 (6): 397. https://doi.org/10.3390/rel12060397.

Bjerre-Poulsen, N. 1986. Populism - A Brief Introduction to a Baffling Notion. *American Studies in Scandinavia* 18 (1): 27–36. https://doi.org/10.22439/asca.v18i1.1190.

Blackburn, Matthew. 2022. The persistence of the civic–ethnic binary: competing visions of the nation and civilization in western Central and Eastern Europe. *National Identities* 24 (5): 461–480. https://doi.org/10.1080/14608944.2021.2006169..

Bottici, Chiara, and Benoît Challand. 2010. *The Myth of the Clash of Civilizations* (1st ed.). Routledge: London. https://doi.org/10.4324/9780203848845.

Brubaker, Rogers. 2016, October 11. A New "Christianist" Secularism in Europe. *The Immanent Frame* https://tif.ssrc.org/2016/10/11/a-new-christianist-secularism-in-europe/.

Brubaker, Rogers. 2017. Between Nationalism and Civilizationism: The European Populist Moment in Comparative Perspective. *Ethnic and Racial Studies* 40 (8): 1191–1226. https://doi.org/10.1080/01419870.2017.1294700.

Canovan, Margaret. 1981. *Populism*. Harcourt Brace Jovanovich.

Canovan, Margaret. 1999. Trust the People! Populism and the Two Faces of Democracy. *Political Studies* 47: 2–16. https://doi.org/10.1111/1467-9248.00184.

Costello, Tim. 2022. "Vladimir Putin: Miracle Defender of Christianity or the Most Evil Man?" *The Guardian*. https://www.theguardian.com/commentisfree/2022/mar/06/vladimir-putin-a-miracle-defender-of-christianity-or-the-most-evil-man. (Last accessed September 21, 2022).

De Cleen, Benjamin, and Yannis Stavrakakis. 2017. "Distinctions and Articulations: A Discourse Theoretical Framework for the Study of Populism and Nationalism". *Javnost: The Public* 24: 301–19. https://doi.org/10.1080/13183222.2017.1330083..

De la Torre, Carlos. 2019. Is Left Populism the Radical Democratic Answer? *Irish Journal of Sociology* 27 (1): 64–71. https://doi.org/10.1177/0791603519827225..

Filkins, Dexter. 2019, December 2. "Blood and Soil in Narendra Modi's India". *The New Yorker* Available online: https://www.newyorker.com/magazine/2019/12/09/blood-and-soil-in-narendra-modis-india..

Fukuyama, Francis. 2006. *The End of History and the Last Man*. New York: Free Press.

Gidron, Noam, and Bart Bonikowski. 2013. "Varieties of Populism: Literature Review and Research Agenda." Weatherland Working Paper Series; Cambridge: Harvard University. https://scholar.harvard.edu/files/gidron_bonikowski_populismlitreview_2013.pdf.

Glaser, B. Linda. 2017, January 1. "Historian Offers Lessons from Antiquity for Today's Democracy." *Cornell Chronicle*. https://news.cornell.edu/stories/2017/11/historian-offers-lessons-antiquity-todays-democracy. (Last accessed September 21, 2022).

Hawkins, A. Kirk. 2010. *Venezuela's Chavismo and Populism in Comparative Perspective*. New York: Cambridge University Press.

Huntington, Samuel P. 1993. The Clash of Civilizations? *Foreign Affairs* 72 (3): 22–49.

Huntington, Samuel P. 1996. *The Clash of Civilizations and the Remaking of World Order*. New York: Simon & Schuster.

Ihsan, Yilmaz Nicholas, Morieson. 2022. Civilizational Populism: Definition Literature Theory and Practice. *Religions* 13 (11): 1026. https://doi.org/10.3390/rel13111026..

Interfax Religion. 2022. "Partriach Kirill Urges to Pray for Peace in 'Russian Lands'." http://www.interfax-religion.com/?act=news&div=16449.

Jack, Viktor. 2022. "Putin's European Pals Have to Eat Their Words." *Politico*. https://www.politico.eu/article/vladimir-putin-european-pals-eat-their-words-marine-le-pen-eric-zemmour-matteo-salvini-milos-zeman-alex-salmond-gerhard-schroder-boris-johnson-jean-luc-melenchon-francois-fillon-viktor-Orbán/.

Janjevic, Darko. 2018. "Vladimir Putin and Viktor Orbán's special relationship." *DW*.

Kaya, Ayhan. 2021. The use of the past by the Alternative for Germany and the Front National: heritage populism, Ostalgia and Jeanne D'Arc. *Journal of Contemporary European Studies* https://doi.org/10.1080/14782804.2021.1981835..

Kaya, Ayhan, and Ay.şe Tecmen. 2019. Europe versus Islam?: Right-wing Populist Discourse and the Construction of a Civilizational Identity. *The Review of Faith & International Affairs* 17 (1): 49–64. https://doi.org/10.1080/15570274.2019.1570759..

Kyle, Jordan and Gultchin, Limor. 2018, November 7. "Populists in Power Around the World." Tony Blair Institute of Global Change. http://institute.global/insight/renewing-centre/populists-power-around-world.

Laclau, Ernesto. 2005. *On Populist Reason*. London and New York: Verso.

Laclau, Ernesto. 2012. *Politics and Ideology in Marxist Theory: Capitalism, Fascism, Populism*. United Kingdom: Verso Books.

Madrid, R. L. 2008. The Rise of Ethnopopulism in Latin America. *World Politics* 60 (3): 475–508. http://www.jstor.org/stable/40060205.

Marzouki, Nadia, McDonnell, Duncan, and Olivier Roy. 2016. In *Saving the People: How Populists Hijack Religion*, edited by Nadia Marzouki, Duncan McDonnell, and Olivier Roy. London: C. Hurst & Co.

Mbete, Sithembile. "The Economic Freedom Fighters-South Africa's turn towards populism?" *Journal of African elections* 14 (1): 35–59.

Moffitt, Benjamin. 2016. *The Global Rise of Populism: Performance, Political Style, and Representation*. Stanford: Stanford University Press. http://ezproxy.acu.edu.au.ezproxy1.acu.edu.au/login?url=http://search.ebscohost.com/login.aspx?direct=true&db=nlebk&AN=1219467&site=ehost-live&scope=site.

Morieson, Nicholas. 2021. *Religion and the Populist Radical Right: Secular Christianism and Populism in Western Europe*. Delaware and Malaga: Vernon Press.

Mudde, Cas. 2004. "The Populist Zeitgeist." *Government and Opposition* 39 (4). https://doi.org/10.1111/j.1477-7053.2004.00135.x

Mudde, Cas, and Rovira Kaltwasser, Cristóbal. 2017, Feburary 23. Populism: A Very Short Introduction, Very Short Introductions online edn, *Oxford Academic* https://doi.org/10.1093/actrade/9780190234874.001.0001.

Mudde, Cas. 2017. "Populism: An Ideational Approach." In *The Oxford Handbook of Populism*, edited by Cristóbal Rovira Kaltwasser, Paul Taggart, Paulina Ochoa Espejo, and Pierre Ostiguy. Oxford: Oxford University Press.

Nicholson, Stephen P, and Segura, Gary M. 2012. Who's the Party of the People? Economic Populism and the U.S. Public's Beliefs About Political Parties. *Political Behavior* 34 (2): 369–389. https://doi.org/10.1007/s11109-011-9162-0..

Panizza, Francisco. 2005. Introduction: populism and the mirror of democracy. In *Populism and the Mirror of Democracy*, edited by Francesco Panizza, 1–31. Phronesis. London, UK: Verso Books. ISBN 9781859845233.

Ozzano, Luca, Bolzonar, Fabio. 2020. Is Right-wing Populism a Phenomenon of Religious Dissent? The Cases of the Lega and the Rassemblement National. *International Journal of Religion* 1 (1): 45–59. https://doi.org/10.33182/ijor.v1i1.1089.

Qureshi, Emran, and Michael Sells. 2003. *The New Crusades: Constructing the Muslim Enemy*. New York: Columbia University Press.

Ramirez, L.C. 2009. 'A New Perspective on Bolivian Populism', unpublished MA thesis, University of Oregon.

Roy, Olivier. 2013. Secularism and Islam: The Theological Predicament. *The International Spectator* 48: 5–19.

Roy, Olivier. 2016a. "Beyond Populism: The Conservative Right, The Courts, The Churches and the Concept of a Christian Europe." In *Saving the People: How Populists Hijack Religion*, edited by Nadia Marzouki, Duncan McDonnell and Olivier Roy. London: C. Hurst & Co.

Roy, Olivier. 2016a. "The French National Front: From Christian Identity to Laïcité." In *Saving the People: How Populists Hijack Religion*, edited by Nadia Marzouki, Duncan McDonnell and Olivier Roy. London: C. Hurst & Co.

Said, Edward W. 2001. The Clash of Ignorance. *The Nation*. https://www.thenation.com/article/archive/clash-ignorance/. (Last accessed September 21, 2022).

Satgar, Vishwas. 2019. Black Neofascism? The Economic Freedom Fighters in South Africa. *Canadian Review of Sociology/revue Canadienne De Sociologie* 56 (4): 580–605.

Sen, Amartya. 2006. "What Clash of Civilizations?" https://slate.com/news-and-politics/2006/03/what-clash-of-civilizations.html. (Last accessed September 21, 2022).

Shahi, Deepshikha. 2017. *The Clash of Civilizations Thesis: A Critical Appraisal*. E-International Relations. https://www.e-ir.info/2017/04/02/the-clash-of-civilizations-thesis-a-critical-appraisal/ (Last accessed September 21, 2022).

Shils, Edward. 1956. *The Torment of Secrecy: The Background and Consequences of American Security Policies*. Glencoe: The Free Press.

Silvius, Ray. 2015. Eurasianism and Putin's Embedded Civilizationalism. In *The Eurasian Project and Europe* edited by D. Lane, V. Samokhvalov, V. London: Palgrave Macmillan. https://doi.org/10.1057/9781137472960_5..

Snyder, Jack. 2011. *Religion and International Relations Theory*. Edited by Jack Snyder. New York: Columbia University Press.

Taggart, Paul. 2004. Populism and representative politics in contemporary Europe. *Journal of Political Ideologies* 9 (3): 269–288. https://doi.org/10.1080/1356931042000263528.

Taggart, Paul. 12 April 2021a. "Prof. Paul Taggart: I Do Not Agree Populists Will Inevitably Fail." *European Center for Populism Studies*. https://www.populismstudies.org/prof-paul-taggart-i-do-not-agree-populists-will-inevitably-fail/

Taggart, Paul. 2021b. "Prof. Paul Taggart: I Do Not Agree Populists Will Inevitably Fail." *European Center for Populism Studies*. https://www.populismstudies.org/prof-paul-taggart-i-do-not-agree-populists-will-inevitably-fail/.

Taguieff, Pierre-André. 1995. Political Science Confronts Populism: From a Conceptual Mirage to a Real Problem. *Telos* 103: 9–43. https://doi.org/10.3817/0395103009.

Vollaard, Hans J. P. 2013. Re-emerging Christianity in West European Politics: The Case of the Netherlands. *Politics and Religion* 6 (1): 74–100. https://doi.org/10.1017/S1755048312000776.

Weyland, Kurt. 2001. Clarifying a Contested Concept: Populism in the Study of Latin American Politics. *Comparative Politics* 34: 1–22. https://doi.org/10.2307/422412.

Yilmaz, Ihsan, and Nicholas Morieson. 2021b. A Systematic Literature Review of Populism, Religion and Emotions. *Religions* 12: 272. https://doi.org/10.3390/rel12040272.

Yilmaz, Ihsan, Nicholas Morieson, and Mustafa Demir. 2021a. Exploring Religions in Relation to Populism: A Tour around the World. *Religions* 12: 301. https://doi.org/10.3390/rel12050301.

Yilmaz, Ihsan, Erdoan Shipoli, and Mustafa Demir. 2021b. Authoritarian Resilience Through Securitization: An Islamist Populist Party's Co-Optation of a Secularist Far-Right Party. *Democratization* 1–18. https://doi.org/10.1080/13510347.2021.1891412.

Yilmaz, Ihsan, and Nicholas Morieson. 2022. "Civilizational Populism: Definition, Literature, Theory, and Practice." *Religions* 13 (11): 1026. https://doi.org/10.3390/rel13111026.

CHAPTER 3

Islam and Civilizational Populism

3.1 Introduction

The purpose of this chapter is to examine civilizational populism in an Islamic context. The chapter first surveys a variety of Muslim majority nations where populist leaders, movements, and parties have a significant presence, and examines whether civilizationalism also has a presence in their political discourses. The chapter finds a fusing of Islam and populism is common among Muslim majority democracies, leading at times to populist leaders attempting to construct a 'people' based on a shared identity as *ummah*, and portraying 'elites' and minority groups outside of the *ummah* as enemies of not merely the nation and Islam, but the civilizational bloc of Muslim peoples called *ummah*. It also describes how the Islam and populism nexus is closely related to the political form of Islam: Islamism. Islamism, which combines "material and cultural understandings of religion" and is "a multivalent religio-moral populism—a potentially explosive articulation of different class interests and religious cravings" (Tugal 2002, p. 86), is deeply wedded to Islamic ideas of justice, and for that reason can easily be attached to populism, which is itself based on notions of elites acting unjustly toward 'the people'.

Explicitly civilizational rhetoric, the chapter finds, is especially evident in Turkey, where it forms an important part of Erdoğan's Islamist, anti-Western and neo-Ottoman rhetoric. Thus, in the second section, the chapter discusses the civilizational populism present in Turkey under the rule of President Erdoğan and his Justice and Development Party. Following this, it examines the unusual case of Islamist populism in Indonesia in the form of the now banned, yet politically successful Islamic Defenders Front and its leader Muhammad Rizieq. While FPI do not use civilizational rhetoric as explicitly as the AKP, their Islamist populism incorporates a civilizational division between *ummah* and 'the West', and implies that the two are clashing. Each case study comprises an examination of the party's ideology, and the social, religious, and political context in which they operate, and an examination of the party's discourse, focusing on the civilizational discourse used by their respective leaders: Turkish President Tayyip Erdoğan and FPI leader Muhammad Rizieq Shihab.

The chapter shows that civilizationalism is a key element of the AKP's populism. Civilizationalism, when incorporated into the AKP's populism, gives content to populism's key signifiers: 'the pure people', 'the corrupt elite', and 'dangerous 'others'. For example, the AKP use a civilization-based classification of peoples to draw boundaries around 'the people', 'elites', and 'others', and declare that 'the people' are pure, good, and authentic because they belong to a civilization which is itself pure and good, and which created the nation and culture which populists claim to be defending. Conversely, Erdoğan describes the old secular nationalist elites as having betrayed 'the people' by abandoning the religion and/or values and culture that shaped and were shaped by their civilization. Equally, the AKP and Erdoğan frame religious minorities as 'dangerous' others who are morally bad insofar as they either belong to foreign civilizations or refuse to follow Islam correctly. Finally, the chapter describes how Erdoğan performs a civilization crisis in order to perpetuate his rule. In particular, Erdoğan attempts to keep supporters in a state of fear by claiming that the *ummah* is under constant attack from the West and ethnic and religious minorities within Turkey who collaborate with the West. Equally, he attempts to evoke feelings of anger toward these minorities and toward opposition political parties and activists who seek to defend the interest of minority groups including secularists, Gulenists, and Kurds. However, Erdoğan, the chapter shows, also seeks to tap into deep feelings of nostalgia for the glory of the Ottoman Empire, and feelings of hope that Turkey will return to its former greatness.

The chapter shows that Islam based civilizational populism has not been so successful in Indonesia. However, the chapter shows how the

FPI and their leader Muhammad Rizieq have incorporated *ummah*-based identity politics and in doing so have changed political discourse in Indonesia, injured its young democracy, and attacked pluralism. The chapter shows how Rizieq consistently portrays non-Muslims, LGBTQI people, and non-orthodox Sunni Muslims as civilizational enemies and threats to Islam. When incorporated into the FPI's populism, Civilizationalism gives content to its key signifiers: 'the pure people', 'the corrupt elite', and 'dangerous 'others'. Like the AKP, the FPI use a civilization-based classification of peoples to draw boundaries around 'the people', 'elites', and 'others', and declare that 'the people' are pure, good, and authentic because they belong to a civilization which is itself pure and good, and which created the nation and culture which populists claim to be defending. Conversely, FPI describes the liberal and secular Muslims—including 'moderate' President Joko Widodo—as having betrayed 'the people' by abandoning the true teachings of Islam and failing to improve the lives of poor Muslims. The FPI and Rizieq frame religious minorities such as Christians and Ahmadiyya as 'dangerous' others who are morally bad insofar as they either belong to foreign civilizations or refuse to follow Islam correctly. Like Erdoğan, Rizieq drew support by performing a civilization crisis. Rizieq, the chapter shows, keeps FPI members and supporters in a state of fear by claiming that the *ummah* is under constant attack from the West, secular and liberal 'elites', and ethnic and religious minorities within Indonesia. Equally, he attempts to evoke feelings of anger toward these minorities and toward opposition political parties and activists who seek to defend the interest of minority groups including secularists, liberals, Christians, Chinese, Shia Muslims, and Ahmadiyya Muslims. However, Rizieq, the chapter shows, also claims that by rejecting Western civilization and culture and returning to the authentic values of Islam Indonesia will become a morally good nation which looks after its poorest citizens.

3.2 Relationship Between Islam and Populism

The notion that Muslims ought to band together as a single civilization is not new to Muslim majority societies. In the early to mid-twentieth century, during the period of decolonization in the Middle East and South Asia, and the triumph of a number of freedom movements in these regions, pan-Islamic ideologies and movements became powerful political forces. These movements contained a populist element insofar as a key assumption of pan-Islamism was a transnational call for unification of the *ummah* under the banner of the shared Islamic identity (Formichi 2010; Aydın 2006; Lee 1942). The *ummah* is a body that is united and identified primarily by its faith, rather than by its shared ethnicity or geography (Formichi 2010; Aydın 2006; Lee 1942). Indeed, the *ummah*, owing to the non-national nature of Islam, is inherently multi-ethnic and multicultural, and can only be united by faith.

One early example of Islamic populism manifested in the form of the Khilafat (Caliphate) Movement in British India (1919–1924). An offshoot of the nationalist movement against colonialism in United India, the Khilafat Movement attempted to unite Muslims in the region to rally support for the Ottoman Empire, after it faced a precarious future in the aftermath of the First World War (Pernau-Reifeld 1999). The Ottoman Empire maintained a central position in affairs of the Sunni Muslim world for centuries, and therefore an existential threat to the Empire was a matter of concern for many Sunni Muslims inside and outside the Empire. Indeed, thousands of kilometers away from Anatolia, Muslims in British India rallied to save the "sacred" Caliphate (Pernau-Reifeld 1999; Trivedi 1981; 458–67). Yet the pan-Islamic movement did not end when the Caliphate was abolished by the Turkish Republic in 1924. Rather, merely pan-Islamic politics transformed from an Ottoman centered movement to one centered upon creating new Muslim superstates. For example, in Egypt populist leader Gamal Abdel Nasser attempted to form a union of Muslim states in the Middle East, and for a brief period appeared to have succeeded. Yilmaz (2020a) notes that Nasser "used nationalism, socialism, and pan-Arabism to usher Egypt into an era of great socio-economic improvement. Using his single-party-rule to establish the Arab Socialist Union (ASU), he instituted sweeping nationalization and the creation of the short-lived United Arab Republic with Syria". This pan-Islamic union was the manifestation of a populist ideology which sought to overcome all linguistic, ethnic, and national differences by insisting upon a common Islamic *ummah* identity (Lahouari and Roberts 2017, 210; Crabbs 1975).

A similar fusing of politics and Islam took place in Pakistan following the partition of India. Pakistan was formed in 1947 as a homeland for the Muslim peoples of South Asia who did not wish to live in the new Hindu-dominated independent state of India. Thus Pakistan, as a newly independent nation, sought to unite its citizens through a shared sense of Muslim identity, rather than on any ethnic or other cultural basis. As a political experiment, this initial *ummah* identity-based Pakistan came to an end in the early 1970s, when a civil war erupted between the Bengali majority in the East of the country, and the more powerful Western part of the country, leading to the separating of the two and the creation of Bangladesh out of the old East Pakistan in 1971 (Yilmaz and Saleem 2021). Ethnic and linguistic identity, no doubt exacerbated by the physical separation of West and East Pakistan, which were located on either side of India, was ultimately stronger than the pull of transnational Islam and an *ummah*-based national identity.

The failure of pan-Islamic states in the second half of the twentieth century did not, however, lead to the death of transnational Islamic politics and *ummah* based national identities. Indeed, deep into the Cold War era Islamic populism remained a part of the political discourse in a number of Muslim majority nations and regions (Casanova 1994). Post-revolutionary Iran, for example, has been cited as a key example of Islamic (or indeed Islamist) populism (Zúquete 2017, 449; Dorraj 2014, 134–40). Most recently, Islamist groups such as al-Qaeda, which calls for a 'global *Jihad*', have exhibited elements of populist discourse and ideology, insofar as they often claim to represent an oppressed and victimized transnational *ummah*, threatened by non-Muslim forces and secular Muslim 'elites' (Yilmaz et al. 2021a; Zúquete 2017, 449).

In Islamist populism, the social and economic justice concerns inherent in Islam can be instrumentalized by Islamic populists in order to serve their anti-elite and xenophobic agendas. Islamic populist parties, though all too rarely examined by scholars, have found a significant amount of electoral success in a number of Muslim majority nations in the twenty-first century (Hadiz, 2018: 567). Hadiz (2018, 567), for example, has examined Islamic populism in Indonesia, Egypt, Tunisia, and Turkey, and observes that for populism to succeed in these countries "cultural idioms associated with Islam are required… for the mobilisation of a distinctly ummah-based political identity in contests over power and resources in the present democratic period".

Islamic populists often identify themselves with "key religious figures from early Islamic history" (Yilmaz et al. 2021a), in an attempt to associate themselves with people trusted and loved by Muslims, and thereby evoking positive feelings and associations in the Islamic public. For example, as part of his nostalgic neo-Ottoman politics, Turkish President Erdoğan presents himself as an Ottoman Caliph. In a similar way, Pakistan's populist former Prime Minister Imran Khan (Shakil and Yilmaz 2021) speaks much about Osman the Great as part of an effort to identify himself with the founder of the Ottoman state, and often compares his own Islamist agenda to the political model and social examples provided by the Prophet and his companions (Ummid.com News Network 2018). Association with important Islamic figures and the use of religious imagery helps Islamic populists evoke religious rage in members of their respective publics, and assists in creating a feeling of belonging to an ingroup and 'heartland'. This heartland does not exist, of course, but is rather a utopian dream of a perfect land in which, after a glorious struggle, elites and 'others' are removed and the people govern themselves (Taggart 2004). Khan, for example, promises the creation of a "New Pakistan" modeled on the idealized and romanticized state of Medina (Bukhari 2018). Khan's populist instrumentalization of religion and Islamic history is designed to encourage 'the people' to hope that one day this 'heartland' of New Pakistan might become a reality, and to view the prime minister himself as a semi-religious figure, whose political agenda is legitimized by his connection with Islam.

As Yilmaz and Morieson (2021; 2022a) point out, while "religion can help sacralize 'the people' by tying them to an existing religious tradition" it can also be used to perpetuate an 'us vs. them' mentality. Thus the religion of 'the people' is framed positively by Islamist populists, while the religion (or lack of religion) of 'others' is demonized as an existential threat to 'us'. As part of this process, 'the others' or 'the elite' are highly stigmatized and turned into 'the enemy' and 'the people' are also shown as the 'victims' of the antagonists. This helps Islamist populists gain a position as 'saviours' of the *ummah*. The result of *ummah* based identity politics is a society intolerant of those who cannot be placed inside the *ummah*. However, because Islam is a global religion there is a necessary transnational element to Islamist populism. The Ummah, then, is not merely a group of Muslims within a nation, but rather a transnational group. Equally, when Islamist populists begin to rhetorically attack the West, and praise Islamic values as superior to Western values, and to blame the West for introducing immoralities into Islamic societies, a civilizational element is introduced into Islamist populism.

For example, the Iranian revolution of 1979 had a populist character linked to Shia Islam, especially insofar as the Ayatollah Khomeini's discourse during and after the revolution was itself populist in nature (Algar 1980). The revolution, which ended the corrupt rule of Mohammad Reza Shah, established a theocratic government with some democratic elements. Since the establishment of the Islamic

Republic of Iran, religious populism has often manifested in the country's politics (Maloney 2015; Dorraj and Dodson 2009; Ehsani 2006; Moghadam 1994). However, even before the revolution, Reza Shah attempted to consolidate his power by portraying himself as "an authentic Iranian hero framed within a monarchical tradition as well as a Zoroastrian one" (Dogru 2020). In a similar way his son, "Mohammad Reza Shah, linked divine monarchy with Iranian monarchical tradition and Shiite Islam", deepening the civilizational element within Iranian populism (Dogru, 2020). The blending of religion and politics in the personalized rule of a single leader was thus not new in Iran. The Ayatollah Khomeini, who emerged as a leading figure among Iranian dissidents after the death of Ali Shariati, was installed as Supreme Leader of Iran shortly after the Shah was removed from power. As Supreme Leader of a theocratic state, Khomeini wielded enormous religious and personal power over the lives of all Iranians. Like his predecessors, he blended nationalism and religion, forging a personalistic rule and personality cult. Since the revolution, and following Khomeini's death in 1989, nationalist and religious sentiments have remained a core part of Iranian politics and populism.

The revolutionaries called for the end of the Shah's rule on the basis that his regime was oppressing 'the people', and allowing foreign forces—especially the United States—to control Iran. This discourse, perpetuated by Khomeini, described two antagonistic groups 'the people' and 'elites'—the latter consisting of the regime and the oligarchs who benefitted from the Shah's corrupt and extravagant rule, and external 'enemies' such as the United States and Britain (Dogru 2020). The revolutionaries' discourse also created two other antagonistic enemies 'the people' (Shia Iranians who suffered oppression under the Shah's rule) and various 'others'; especially liberal and secular Iranians who opposed the transition to a theocratic hybrid regime. This resulted in the seizing of properties belonging to othered groups, and today extends to the harsh punishments given to anyone who publicly opposes the Shia Islamist regime or defies its laws (Amnesty International 2021; Dogru 2020).

Populism was especially prevalent in the rhetoric of Mahmood Ahmadinejad, president from 2005 to 2013 and now opposition leader. Ahmadinejad, aware of the growing disconnection between the regime, now ruled by Supreme Leader Ali Khamenei, and the people of Iran, promised to empower the people politically and economically, and to reconnect Iran with the ideals of the revolution (Jalili 2018; Maloney 2015; Ghiabi and Habibi 2014; Ehsani 2006). At first, Ahmadinejad's populist call for a return to revolutionary principles attracted the support of elements of the regime, including from Khamenei, the Islamic Republic Guard Corps (IRGC), and Basij (Dogru 2020). Ahmadinejad encouraged nationalist feeling and pride in Persia's civilizational history, and sought to reconnect the people of Iran with their heritage, which had been downplayed after 1979. But Khamenei eventually grew concerned about the power of Ahmadinejad's religious populism, particularly when the latter began to claim he could commune with the Mahdi, a claim which represented a threat to the regime's control over religion. By making this claim, and in his overall presentation as a man of the people, Ahmadinejad sought to portray himself as a religious figure and savior of the people, and who alone would return Iran to the principles set out in the revolution and make everything right again (Dogru 2020).

Growing enmity with the Khamenei regime, and Iran's increasing economic problems—which led to historic levels of inflation and an unemployment rate of 12.2 in 2012—hurt Ahmadinejad's popularity (Jalili 2018). Outmaneuvered by Khamenei, and with his supporters suffering heavy losses in the 2012 parliamentary elections, Ahmadinejad found himself out of office and in opposition for the rest of the decade. Populism made a powerful return to Iranian politics in 2021, in the figure of Ebrahim Raisi. Raisi emerged victorious in the 2021 Presidential election as the favored candidate of Supreme Leader Khamenei. Researcher Natasha Lindstaedt identified Raisi as a "populist", and "authoritarian" politician, not unlike Ahmadinejad, yet with one advantage over his fellow populist insofar as he possessed significant religious authority (Motamedi 2021) A Shia cleric and custodian of the Shrine of Imam Reza, one of the most revered and frequented shrines in the region, Raisi traces his heritage back to the Prophet Muhammad (Erdbrink 2017). His lineage and status as a cleric helped him overcome his ugly reputation, forged in the 1980s when he became known for his willingness to order the execution of the regime's enemies (Erdbrink 2017; Farmanfarmaian 2017).

Like his predecessors, and due to Iran's poor economic position (the result of harsh U.S. sanctions on the country), Raisi promised 'the people' cash handouts and subsidies to help them improve their lives. However, it is his religious authority that has given Raisi an advantage over his political opponents, and win power as a right-wing religious populist. Raisi has skilfully employed his religious position and coupled it with anti-West rhetoric and support for Shia Muslims and their interests across the region (Erdbrink 2017). His transnational interest in Shia interests does not conflict with his nationalism. For example, Raisi claims that Iranians need not look abroad for solutions because all the answers to the country's problems lay "inside the country" (Erdbrink 2017). He also asserted that one of the main reasons Iran is stable and secure is its military support for Shia fighters in Iraq and Syria" (Erdbrink 2017). A core part of his populist rhetoric involves the merging of conservative Islam and a call for social justice for the working class, or the "wronged" people (Erdbrink 2017; Farmanfarmaian 2017). Raisi's populist discourse reflects, of course, the post-revolution regime's political aspirations within the Middle East. Iran has long attempted to assert itself in the region by spreading its political influence among Shia Muslim communities. Iran has funded militia groups and, more broadly, portrayed itself as a protector of Shia Muslims across the region; at other times it has tried to assert itself in Sunni-dominated regions as part of the *ummah* (Dogru 2020; Gardner 2019; Middle East Institute 2020). Contemporary Iranian populism thus uses Iran's position as the dominant Shia power to encourage a sense of solidarity among Shia across the region in order to further Iranian interests.

Imran Khan, former prime minister of Pakistan, has incorporated a degree of Islamist civilizationalism into his populist discourse since his party won a majority in the 2018 elections. Pakistan was created in order to give the Muslim population of what was then British India a homeland (Jalal 2011). Despite this, Pakistan was not initially an explicitly Islamic state. Indeed, Pakistan's founder and first leader Mohammad Ali Jinnah "presented a patently secular idea of nation–building without mentioning the word 'secular'" (Ahmad 2010). Yet Pakistan was to become an Islamic Republic, and has become more Islamized and less secular, by and large, throughout its history. As a result, Islam has often been instrumentalized by Pakistan's politicians.

Following an electoral breakthrough in 2013, and securing a majority in the 2018 general elections, Pakistan Tehreek-e-Insaf (PTI) or the Pakistan Movement for Justice has become the face of Islamist populism in present-day Pakistan. As a result of his party's election victory, cricketer turned politician Imran Khan, who became chairman of the PTI in 1996, was elected prime minister of Pakistan in 2018. The PTI, a right-wing populist Islamist party, attacks Pakistan's political elite, calls for power to be returned to the people, and objects to 'Western interference' in the country's politics (Yilmaz and Shakil 2021a, b). "The people", in PTI's conception, are the Pakistanis wronged by elites and foreign powers and who deserve justice. Imran Khan, according to the PTI, is "the captain" who will sweep corrupt dynastic politics away, and return the stolen wealth from the "Swiss banks to the people" (Yilmaz and Shakil 2021a, b).

Islamism has become a profoundly important element of Khan's leadership of Pakistan. For example, Khan calls for Pakistan to be transformed into a utopian Islamic state based on the historical city-state of Medina; he teaches women to dress modestly to prevent rape, sends domestic violence bills for approval by the Council of Islamic Ideology (CII); he has encouraged parliament to Islamize the school syllabus under the Single National Curriculum, and in addition to funding and sheltering right-wing madrasas his party and its key ministers have an apologist attitude toward Taliban (Afzal 2021, 2019; BBC 2021; Yilmaz and Shakil 2021a, b; Hoodboy 2020). Thus in Khan's Pakistan, many members of civil society such as liberals, secularists, women's rights activists, and journalists critical of the government, are 'othered' and framed as enemies of 'the people' and Islam.

Islamist civilizationalism is a core part of PTI rhetoric, although it emerges on an inconsistent basis and may be used somewhat cynically. For example, Khan and his PTI ministers often speak of the injustices committed in Kashmir and Palestine, but refuse to talk about the Uyghur genocide (Yilmaz and Shakil 2021c). Moreover, the PTI often presents the Muslim *ummah*—not merely Pakistani Muslims but all Sunni Muslims—as 'victims' of the West, describes Western media as a tool for 'misleading the youth', promotes pan-Islamism, and labels Islamophobia a threat to Muslim civilization (Yilmaz and Shakil 2021a, b, d).

Islamist vigilantism, often encouraged by populist Islamist groups and politicians, also has a deep history in Pakistan. For example, from the 1970s *jamaties* (right-wing) youth groups have been active in violent politics, especially on university campuses across Pakistan (Hoodboy 2020; Baloch and Musyani 2018). One of the most significant of these groups is the ultra-right populist Islamist party Tehreek-e-Labbaik Pakistan (TLP) (Sabat et al. 2020). TLP came into existence as a nationwide anti-blasphemy movement in 2015. Led by cleric Khadim Hussain Rizvi and now his son Saad Rizvi, the two Rizvis use crude and aggressive language against Pakistani religious and government elites (Sabat et al. 2020, 370) coupled with religious references to attack the 'establishment', who they claim are 'puppets' installed by Western nations; indeed

"[TLP] feels Pakistan need to be a 'true Islamic state,' and wants to curb any form of expression that they deem as 'blasphemous'" (Yilmaz, 2020b). In this way, the Pakistani leadership appears to conceive of relations with the West through the prism of a clash of civilizations. TLP differ from most other Islamist populist groups, insofar as its leader Khadim Rizvi professed an exclusively religious agenda, and had no "political, social or economic vision to share with people" (Sabat et al. 2020, 376). Indeed, for Khadim, "the Barelvi-Sunni interpretation of Islam" offered a solution to the problems plaguing Pakistan but also all Muslims throughout the world (Sabat et al. 2020, 376).

According to the TLP, 'the people' are "pure" and "true lovers of the Prophet" who support the party's Barelvis Sunni interpretation of Islam and Islamic law (Sabat et al. 2020, 370). Using emotional religious rhetoric, they encourage their supporters to view themselves as a pure people pushed down by impure internal and external enemies. The anger created by the party is then expressed in violent acts committed by their supporters, such as vandalism and other forms of violent aggression. Indeed, according to the party, all non-Barevlis groups, including other Sunni Muslims, are enemy 'others' who must be overcome if 'the people' are to create the utopian 'heartland' they deserve, and where they will be freedom from corrupt religious and government elite oppression. After entering politics in 2018, the TLP became the first Islamic party to win significant representation in its first race. However, its nationwide campaign of violent vandalism led to its ban in 2021, and to the arrest of Saad Rizvi. While the fate of TLP is uncertain, there is no doubt that the members remained active and as radical as ever (Dawn 2021; Janjua 2021).

Islamist-based populism is also present in Tunisia. Since Tunisia won independence from France in 1956, Islamism has captured the imagination of many of its citizens. Governments have often sought to suppress Islamism; however, "the condemnation of Political Islamism in Tunisia historically backfired and led to the further underground radicalization of Tunisians, along with scores of human rights abuses by authorities" (Louden 2015). Tunisian governments' abuse of their own citizens only served to increase the popularity of Islamists, who drew support from people victimized by police and other government forces, and who portrayed Tunisian elites as enemies of the people controlled by foreign non-Muslim powers (Turner 2012).

For example, the Secular Ben Ali regime's attempts to destroy Islamism mostly aided the Islamists, who were able to portray themselves as victims of a corrupt, un-Islamic elite who violently suppressed any group which opposed their kleptocratic misrule (Louden 2015). Indeed, the populist Islamist Ennahda movement was among the political beneficiaries of the fall of the Ben Ali regime during the latter stages of the Arab Spring. Capitalizing on their 'outsider' status, and their longstanding opposition to the corruption and repression inherent in the rule of the Ben Ali regime, Ennahda became the largest political party in Tunisian parliament in 2011, winning government. Ennahda's rule over Tunisia has been described as post-Islamist and post-secular, suggesting that the movement has moved beyond simple religious politics and the religion—secularism dichotomy, and instead sought to "harmonize Islam and secular democracy" and incorporate Islam within the secular state (Lazreg 2021, 408). Ennahda, however, was unable to maintain power for long. While Ennahda first experienced electoral success by softening its Islamist image and forming coalitions with secular parties, Tunisian politics is today largely a battle between two factions: the Salafists and the secularists. Following the Arab Spring, calls for Sharia law or Sharia-inspired justice have become common in Tunisia, as part of a wider movement which calls for a "returning to the fundamentals offered by the scriptures and in emulating the behavior and appearance of the earliest Muslims, known as al-salaf al-salih, or the righteous predecessors" (Noueihed and Warren 2013, 267).

For example, Ansar al-Sharia (AST), a populist and militant Islamic party, dominates Islamist politics in the twenty-first-century Tunisia (Louden, 2015). AST and other Islamist movements have mobilized young people in coastal areas where poverty is rampant and these vigilante groups attack 'secularism' leading to attacks on popular tourist spots and even the American embassy (Crisis Group 2013). Furthermore, political assassinations of secular politicians and infighting between right-wing jihadist groups and security forces became common in Tunisia in the 2010s, destabilizing the country and making normal democratic politics difficult (Louden, 2015; Gartenstein-Ross 2014). As the 2010s drew to a close, complex power sharing agreements between disparate political parties in Tunisian parliament were beginning to break down and multiple populist movements and leaders emerged. Tunisia's populists, whether secular or Islamist, have generally framed their movements as centered around taking power from corrupt elites and returning it to the power. For example, independent candidate and eventual winner of the 2019 Presidential elections, Kaïs Saïed, promised to return to the 'power' of the Arab spring back to the people, portraying himself as an 'honest' man working for 'the people'. The charismatic media mogul was hardly the only populist vying for the Presidency in 2019. Nabil Karoui, businessman and leader of the populist-secularist Heart of Tunisia Party, positioned himself as an "outsider" and used his philanthropist activities to demonstrate his desire to raise 'the people' out of poverty and center Tunisian politics around their interests, rather than around the interests of the 'elite' (Grewal 2019). Karoui finished second in the Presidential elections, meaning that populists finished first and second in the 2019 elections.

While nominally an independent and secularist, Saïed is part of the majority Ennahda coalition government. Therefore, he has at times added an Islamic dimension to his populist discourse. For example, after becoming president, Saïed called for the imposition of capital punishment, and has introduced a Sharia-based interpretation of inheritance laws which disadvantages women. Saïed also rejected attempts to improve Tunisian–Israeli relations in order to please the Islamists. He attempted to create a sense of fear and crisis in the community by alleging that foreign countries were encouraging homosexuality in Tunisia. In addition, his government sought to antagonize the French government, as part of an effort to prove that the new Tunisia is no puppet of foreign powers (Brumberg 2021). However, it is the Islamist populist Dignity Coalition, the most popular Islamist party in the country, that most visibly incorporates religion and civilizationalism into their populist discourse. Combining "salafist Islam with a more radical jihadist ethos, the Dignity Coalition" has sought to create antagonistic politics in Tunisia by instigating conflict with secularists, Ennahda, human rights activists, French government officials, and President Saïed (Brumberg 2021). Dignity Coalition leader Rached Khiari created controversy when he appeared to defend the actions of a French *jihadist* who beheaded a schoolteacher accused of showing students caricatures of Islam's Prophet Mohammed. Khiari claimed on his personal Facebook page that "any attack on the Prophet is one of the greatest crimes and anyone who dares to do such a thing must bear the consequences, be it the state, an individual or a group" (Brumberg 2021). Khiari's defense of a foreign *jihadi* is a demonstration of his essential pan-Islamism, which does not necessarily conflict with his party's nationalist message but rather aids in the construction of their populist identity politics. For the Dignity Coalition, 'the people' are not merely the victims of a corrupt elite, but Muslim victims of a secularist elite. Thus, while the 'elite' remain the core enemy, non-Muslims, secularist Muslims, and liberal Muslims are also portrayed as dangerous and inauthentic elements within society who may harm 'the people'.

Throughout these brief studies of Muslim majority nations in which populism, and especially religious and ethnoreligious nationalist populism, has become a significant element of politics, we find several key similarities between each case. First, and most broadly, we find that religion is a powerful element of populist movements in each nation we studied. Thus even nominally secular populist parties, movements, and leaders in the majority Muslim world will incorporate, at times, religion into their discourse and political agenda. This is no doubt due to the cultural importance of Islam as a religious but also as an identity marker in the majority of Muslim nations we studied. Second, the instrumentalization of religion by the populist leaders, movements, and parties we have studied lends their respective discourses and ideology a civilizational and transnational character. This results in the identification of the constructed group 'the people' with the religion of Islam, and thus with Muslims elsewhere in the world, and Islamic civilization.

Third, *ummah*-based Islamist populism appears to be emerging as a reaction to the failure of dictatorship and secular nationalism, which populists describe—perhaps correctly—as the cause of a crisis within their respective polities. Islamist populism emerged in majority Muslim environments in which secular nationalist dictators and their supporters form or previously formed an oppressive and often corrupt elite. Nationalist dictators were never able to entirely secularize their territories or eliminate the civilizational bonds Muslims often felt across large distances. Therefore, when secular rule ended it was often Islamic parties which enjoyed the greatest support from the people, and to whom they looked for economic and social justice. Equally, given the large democratic deficit and the disillusionment many citizens felt toward their old ruling elite, it is not surprising that populism emerged as such a powerful force throughout the majority Muslim world, especially after the 2011 Arab Spring.

The most salient example of civilizational populism within Islamic context is undoubtedly that of the Justice and Development Party in Turkey. In the following section, we discuss in detail the civilizational populism of the ruling party of Turkey, and of its President, Recep Tayyip Erdoğan.

3.3 CASE STUDIES

3.3.1 *Turkey: Justice and Development Party (AKP)*

A Growing Space for Islamist Populism

Since 2002, Turkey has been ruled by the Justice and Development Party (AKP). The AKP, a populist and Islamist party, have governed in an increasingly authoritarian and repressive manner during the second part of their two decades in power. Initially, however, the AKP sought to portray themselves as a "Muslim democratic" (Yilmaz 2009) party supportive of pluralism, openness, and human rights. The AKP's decision to portray itself in this manner was prompted by the events surrounding Turkey's 1997 "postmodern coup", in which the right-wing Islamist government, led by the Islamist Prime Minister Necmettin Erbakan, was deposed by the Turkish 'deep state' and replaced by a secularist military establishment (Yilmaz and Bashirov 2018). The coup, which was intended to greatly diminish the role of Islam in Turkish politics and society, was in many ways a continuation of the Kemalist hegemony the country had experienced since it was put into place in the 1920s by Ataturk himself (Yilmaz 2021a, b, c, d; Yilmaz 2018).

In order to survive politically in the new military-dominated and ultra secular Turkish political environment, members of suppressed Islamist and socially conservative parties coalesced around a new party, the Justice and Development Party (AKP). The AKP portrayed itself as part of a "reformist younger generation of Turkish Islamists" which was broadly supportive of democracy, "universal human rights and other Western ideals" (Yilmaz and Bashirov 2018). The AKP, formed in 2001, sought to position itself as a religious conservative populist party that challenged the suffocating secular Kemalist order, which for decades suppressed Turkey's heterogeneous ethnic and religious communities (Yilmaz 2018, 2021a, b, c, d).

Capitalizing on the Turkish people's desire to liberate themselves from military tutelage and Kemalist repression, the AKP won power in 2002. The party at first governed as Muslim democrats, insofar as they pushed for greater democratization, initiated a reconciliation process with Kurds and other minority groups, committed to joining the European Union, and even began discussing the possibility of recognizing the Armenian genocide (Yilmaz 2021a, b, c, d; Yilmaz 2018; Yilmaz and Bashirov 2018). It is likely that the AKP's democratic turn was never entirely sincere, but rather a pragmatic act designed to help the party win power. Or as Yilmaz and Bashirov (2018) put it "scholars argued that AKP pragmatically embraced notions of democracy to survive in power, reframe its image as a democratic actor, and gain the support of the EU and those segments of society that previously did not vote for Islamist parties, such as Kurds, liberals and the Gülen movement" (Yilmaz and Bashirov 2018). Indeed, between 2007 and 2011 the AKP began to shed its democratic and pluralist image, and instead sought to capture the state and dominate Turkish politics and society. In this process, the AKP and particularly its leader Erdoğan alienated many of their allies in political and civil society, while simultaneously incapacitating the threat posed by the Kemalist-dominated judiciary and military (Yilmaz 2021a, 2018).

A referendum in 2017 saw Turkey become a Presidential republic, with Erdoğan installed as president. This change reduced the ability of parliament and the judiciary to check the power of the executive, and therefore gave Erdoğan and the AKP greater control over Turkish politics and society, and the ability to radically transform the country. The decline of Turkey's institutions after the 2017 referendum also allowed the AKP to use force to suppress civil and political opposition, and deflect attention from its corruption scandals, which surfaced for the first time in 2013 (Yilmaz 2021a). Initially, the AKP sought to portray themselves as the champion of 'the people' and enemy of 'elites'. However, as the AKP evolved in office, their increasing authoritarianism and Islamism altered their populist discourse. After 2013, in particular, the AKP invested much effort in portraying religious minorities, foreign governments, and even entire 'civilizations', as enemies of the people and of Islam in their quest to maintain power. The AKP's new strategy was built on an emotional populist campaign which exploited Turkish people's ontology security and feelings of trauma. The party exploited, in particular, the "Sèvres Syndrome" many Turkish people continue to suffer from, or their persistent fear that foreign powers wish to divide their territory, as they did after the Ottoman Empire collapsed in the closing stages of the First World War. When the now weakened Kemalist forces and their anti-AKP allies launched a coup in 2016, they quickly found themselves unable to remove the AKP and Erdoğan from power. In response, an emboldened AKP persecuted its enemies without mercy, throwing thousands into prison and driving others into exile. The party also began to re-engineer Turkish identity in an effort to demonize and dehumanize its enemies. Secularists and liberals, Gülenists, journalists, human rights advocates, and many ethnic and religious minorities were now portrayed by the party as threats to Islam and Turkish Sunni Muslims. The AKP also began to emphasize ever more the primacy of Sunni Islam in Turkish culture and identity, and the glory of the Ottoman Empire, the seat of the Caliphate for centuries. Thus, Erdoğan and the AKP set about creating a divisive and populist 'us vs them' politics in Turkey, in which Turkish Sunni Muslims were portrayed as an aggrieved yet innocent people, and the Kemalist secular elite and almost all other religious and ethnic minorities portrayed as threats to the people and their faith. The AKP thus used deep emotional insecurities to evoke feelings of victimhood in the majority population of the nation, who were said to be oppressed by "dark forces". These imagined "dark forces" range from foreign enemies to domestic foes of the AKP who are alleged to be working with foreigners to destabilize Turkey. Thus the AKP encourages Turkish Sunni Muslims to feel that they are under constant attack from "non-Turkish Muslims, such as Kurds and Lazes, ...and non-Muslims, such as Christians and Jews" (Yilmaz 2021a: 58; İnce 2012: 40; Yegen 2004; Bali 2003a, 2003b; Yıldız 2001). These minority groups are now essentially unwanted citizens in Turkey, a group which now includes members of the Gulen movement, journalists, academics, opposition leaders, human rights activists, and political opposition who have been critical of AKP regime all along (Yilmaz 2021a, c, d; 2020d; 2018). All these groups are now 'the other' in Turkey, and combined with xenophobia toward the West and Jews, all are portrayed by the AKP as internal "traitors" who do the bidding of external "dark forces" trying to "destabilize Turkey" (Yilmaz 2018, 2021a, c, d).

By encouraging their supporters to feel a sense of trauma, "humiliation, vengeance and hatred", the party is able to "trigger unconscious defence mechanisms which attempt to reverse these emotions" (Yilmaz 2021a: 11). The AKP's political ideology is based on three ideas: "Islamism, nationalism, and populism", which are merged together into a single ideology (Taş 2022: 2). By merging Islamism, Turkish nationalism, and populism, "Erdoğan has thus been presented as the voice of deprived 'real people' and the champion of their interest against old 'elites'", while at the same time "the party also pursued an Islamist, anti-secular project involving mandatory religious education of the young, and a "post-Kemalist neo-Ottomanist outlook in identity politics" that radically altered Turkey's sense of itself and elements of its foreign policy" (Yilmaz 2021a, 2018: 54–55). The AKP's Islamist populism has proven very potent, and has allowed the party to gradually Islamize Turkey over the two decades of their increasingly authoritarian rule.

Civilizationalism and the AKP
The triad of "Islamism, nationalism, and populism" creates a civilizational populist "programme involv[ing] Islamist elements such as Ottomanist nostalgia, Islamist conservatism, and growing Islamist generations" (Yilmaz 2021a, b, c; Yilmaz 2018: 54). Inside the AKP's conception of Turkey and Turkish identity, then, there are integrated concepts of nationalism rooted in Turkic glorification and the Ottoman pride, but also an added aspect of *ummatism*. This has become especially evident after the 2016 failed coup and the 2017 referendum, which gave Erdoğan unprecedented power to re-make Turkey in an image of his choosing. Post-2017 Erdoğan has "re-fashioned himself as a 'leader of the Muslim World' or 'the hope of the ummah'" (Yilmaz 2018). In re-making himself in this way, and by Islamizing Turkey and Turkish identity, Erdoğan moves his Islamism beyond the confines of Turkey's boundaries, making it a form of transnational religious populism (Yilmaz et al. 2017: 59; also see Yilmaz and Shakil 2021c, d). The transnational and civilizational element in the AKP's populist ideology is evident in the party's attempts to frame not merely Muslim Turkish people in Turkey, nor the wider Turkish Muslim diaspora, but rather all Sunni Muslims as victims of the Christian Crusader West and Israel. Sunni Muslims are thus 'pure' and pious victims of non-Muslim aggression, and are urged by Erdoğan to unite and struggle against their oppressors. In 2017, for example, Erdoğan remarked that exists a great gulf between the civilizations of Islam and the West insofar as "Islamic civilization" is based upon "help for all who need it, treating everyone, even stray animals with compassion", while "Western civilization directly focuses on the individual" (Hazır 2022). The superiority of "Islamic civilization" is evident, Erdoğan claims, in its "understanding comprising each area of social life" (Hazır 2022). On another occasion, Erdoğan claimed the Ottoman Empire was free of racism and ruled with the superior values of Islamic civilization, including "justice", "toleration", and "compassion", whereas the West ruled its empires through blind violence and racism (Hazır 2022).

Erdoğan, furthermore, claims Turkey to be the successor state of the defunct Ottoman Empire, and therefore responsible for the protection of Islam and Islamic civilization. Turkey, Erdoğan has said, is "heir to a civilization which, having flourished with various cultures, has left its mark on the history of humanity" (Erdoğan 2017). "Every vision of culture entails a vision of civilization as well", Erdoğan has claimed, "and thus one must also make efforts to build and revive the civilization while thinking over the culture". Thus, the Turkish people, he suggests, have a duty to revive Islamic civilization, a duty that stretches beyond the government and to general "society, the business world, NGOs, universities, people of arts and culture" (Erdoğan 2017). This is not mere rhetoric from Erdoğan. Indeed, in 2022 he opened a "Museum of Islamic Civilizations" in Istanbul inside a large mosque, and claimed that this museum "represent the thousand-year accumulation of Islamic civilization, which brought a brand new face to these lands" (Daily Sabah 2019).

These examples show how Erdoğan—to borrow a phrase from Brubaker (2017)—construes opposition between 'self' and the 'other' not in nationalist terms, but in civilizational terms, and as a battle between the 'Western' other and the Islamic and Ottoman 'self'. This categorization helps Erdoğan create in his supporters fear of 'others' and therefore a sense of crisis in the *ummah*, which Erdoğan consistently portrays as under attack from 'the West', Gulenists, and Kurdish rebels and activists. To create this sense of clashing civilizations and fear of the civilizational 'other', Erdoğan portrays issues such as the Palestine and Kashmir conflicts, as well as the displacement of the Burmese Rohingya, and incidences of Islamophobia in the West, as proof that immoral non-Muslims are attacking the *ummah* everywhere in an effort to destroy Islam (Yilmaz and Shakil 2021d). Erdoğan, however, is careful not to frame all attacks on Muslim peoples as attacks on Turkey and the wider *ummah*. For example, due to China's economic power and importance the Uyghur issue is rarely mentioned by the AKP regime, but swept under the carpet so as not to confuse AKP supporters who might be surprised that Turkey enjoys close relations with a country that suppresses Islam and places Uyghur Muslims in concentration camps.

Erdoğan and the AKP have used election victories to increase the power of the Directorate of Religions Affairs (Diyanet), Turkey's state sanctioned religious authority. Diyanet was created by the secular Kemalist regime in order to control religion in Turkey, and did so primarily through a social engineering program (involving education and control of the messages issued in Friday sermons and in *fatwas*) in which Turkish Muslims were encouraged to secularize and privatize their religious beliefs (Yilmaz 2005). According to Yilmaz (2021a, b, c, d, b, c, 23), the Kemalist regime sought to create an ideal citizen "Homo LASTus (the Laicist, Atatürkist, Sunni and Turkish people)", but used Diyanet to construct—out of the Muslim majority of Turks who did not wish to entirely privatize their faith—"Homo Diyanetus' (Yilmaz 2021a, b, c, d, b, c, 23). Homo Diyanetus was supposed to be a 'moderate' Sunni Muslim and a Turkish nationalist who supported the secular Kemalist regime. Under AKP rule, Diyanet was greatly empowered and staffed by AKP supporters, who sought—over time—to Islamize Turkey. Diyanet began to use its considerable authority, first, to support the AKP regime and portray its leader Erdoğan as a pious Muslim who was 'saving' Turkish people from Kemalist secular authoritarianism, and second, to assist the AKP in their social engineering program. The AKP sought to use Diyanet to create a new ideal citizen in Turkey—this time not a secular nationalist who practices Islam privately, but an Islamist who supports the populist neo-Ottoman ideology of the ruling party, and identifies as part of the *ummah*.

Under two successive pro-Erdoğan and Islamist leaders, Ali Erbaş and Mehmet Görmez, Diyanet played an important role in perpetuating Erdoğan's civilizational Islamist worldview, in which Christianity and secularism are foreign threats to the *ummah*. In his inauguration address, Erbaş outlined his opposition to secularism, remarking, "…we should work harder than ever to deliver the eternal and everlasting messages of the God and his Prophet to the humanity which flounder into the clamp of secularism and valuelessness" (Parlamento Haber 2017). During his sermon upon the re-conversion of the Hagia Sophia into a mosque, he spoke from the minibar with a sword in hand as if he were a conquering Ottoman leader, and in a deliberate affront to the Christian world and to Turkish secularists (Hurriyet 2020). Erbaş' predecessor in the role, Görmez, sought to defend Islam by declaring his opposition to Muslims partaking in Western traditions such as celebrating the new year. "No one can say it is right for the pagan culture and consumption culture, converging with hedonism, to create a corrupt culture over our children and teens", he remarked, "especially if all those are joined by things like Christmas, pine tree, gambling, drinking, lottery and such forth, that will move a human away from himself and his God to create a tradition that will corrupt the society" (Korkmaz 2014). Another Diyanet official echoed these sentiments instructing his followers "within the scope of all the activities related to the celebration of new year in our schools and institutions, you shall not use any ritual belongs to Christianity such as Christmas, Santa Clause, decorating a Christmas Tree etc. You shall stay away any social and cultural activity that are not associated with our national and religious values" (Korkmaz 2014). Through Diyanet, then, Erdoğan and the AKP attempt to Islamize Turkish society, and portray even secular Western celebrations as if they were closely connected with Christianity, and therefore as a foreign civilizational threat to Islam and the *ummah*.

Furthermore, the AKP transport their populist ideology globally through a variety of means, including hard and soft power collaboration. For example, it is not uncommon to see cooperation between Sunni majority countries and Turkey in matters of defense, the holding of joint conferences on various issues, and in strengthening economic ties between Muslim nations, all of which occur as part of the AKP regime's neo-Ottoman and Islamist populist ideology (Yilmaz and Shakil 2021c). Indeed, after nearly a decade of unprecedented economic, military, and cultural collaboration, Turkey and Pakistan supported Azerbaijan in its recent conflict with Armenia: "Not only did neighbouring Turkey lend support to "fellow Muslim" Azerbaijan but also Pakistan. Moreover, the American withdrawal from Afghanistan has also seen these two partners within the *ummah* take a leading role in negotiations with the Taliban and the Afghan government" (Yilmaz and Shakil, 2021c). The AKP's Islamist populist narrative is thus aimed at reconnecting the Muslim world, especially former Ottoman territories, and bringing them under the influence of the Turkish government. There is a violent aspect to this civilizational religious populism, insofar as "the faithful are encouraged to sacrifice their lives and, if needed, resort to violence" in order to protect the *ummah* from enemy civilizations and their domestic allies (Yilmaz 2021a; Yilmaz and Erturk 2021). The AKP's neo-Ottoman *Jihadism*, therefore, encourages 'the people' to sacrifice themselves in the struggle for the homeland and their faith. Death, in this conception of *jihad*, is not a failure but rather constitutes a victory for the *ummah*. As Yilmaz and Erturk (2021, 8) observe, in AKP ideology death does not belong only 'to the "Other", as is the case with a more traditional understanding of necropolitics. Rather, "death becomes the one and only condition to become 'oneself', shifting our understanding of necropolitical boundary-making'" (Yilmaz and Erturk, 2021: 8). The civilizational populism of the AKP therefore relies upon the exploitation and elicitation of the anxieties and fears of Muslim Turkish people, and encourages them to identify as an aggrieved yet innocent Sunni Muslim people, who must defend their homeland and religion from external and internal 'dark forces' threatening them.

Civilizational Populism in Erdoğan's Discourse
An AKP official has himself admitted that the party has carried out "emotional vampirism", making the party something of "a vampire that sucks emotions for sustenance rather than blood". (Yilmaz 2021a, 136). This suggests the AKP, or at least its leadership, is aware of how central the role of emotional exploitation has been in creating and sustaining the party's electoral success. The language used by President Erdoğan appears especially effective in creating an emotional response in his supporters, a response the party can subsequently exploit and turn into demand for their Islamist neo-Ottoman populism. Religion has proven especially useful to Erdogan, who has often sought to portray himself as a representative of not merely Turkish Muslims but a leader of the *ummah*. From reciting spirited Islamist poems that incite populist *jihadism*, to the recitation of the Qur'an at significant moments, Erdoğan has sought to instrumentalize Islam in an effort to galvanize support from Muslims inside and outside Turkey (Yilmaz 2021a, 149).

Erdogan has been adept at evoking fear in his supporters, particularly fear of mysterious 'dark forces' attacking Muslims in Turkey and abroad. The 2016 failed coup provided Erdoğan with an opportunity to exploit the fear and sense of crisis in the Turkish public. He claimed that Gülenists were behind the coup, labeled them terrorists who perverted Islam, and portrayed himself as a national savior whose supporters had protected 'the people' from a terrible fate when they prevented the coup from succeeding (Yilmaz 2021b, c; Yilmaz and Albayrak 2021). Erdoğan invoked religion by claiming that the coup was a "gift from God" that had explored the "traitors" and "collaborators" with foreign forces inside Turkish society, groups, and individuals which he, Erdoğan, would now purge (Gotev 2016; Yilmaz 2021b, c; Yilmaz and Albayrak 2022). Having created an atmosphere of fear and suspicion, Erdoğan declared that "every country needs a strong leader", again portraying himself as a protective 'savior' of the Turkish people, and inviting them to place their trust in him (Yilmaz and Shakil 2021d). Erdoğan's rhetoric appears to have proven electorally appealing. He emerged victorious following elections in 2018, having secured more than 52% of the vote, and winning 20% more votes than his nearest rival. This suggests the public was broadly responsive to his evocation of fear and crisis, and his self-portrayal as a protector and savior figure.

Erdoğan's talent for emotional vampirism and manipulation showed itself again when, following the coup, he sought to portray Sunni Muslims as victims of religious leader Fethullah Gülen and his supporters, who he held primarily responsible for the coup attempt. Gülen and Erdoğan had once been allies, however, after the coup the AKP and its clerical supporters began to refer to the Gülen movement as "FETO" or the Fethullah Gülen Terrorist Organization. It is interesting to note that the coup memory has been immortalized in Friday sermons, a national holiday is celebrated as well and Erdoğan on his foreign visits to countries such as Pakistan and Azerbaijan warns of the "malicious nature" of the proclaimed "FETO" (Duz and Berker 2021; Dawn 2016). On a trip a few days become the anniversary he said, "Recent events have once again revealed the bloody, dark, and ugly face of FETO. I hope we will overcome this threat together by standing shoulder to shoulder" and the Turkish nation has also been reassured that "Just as we carry out our fight against other terrorist groups without compromise and with determination, we will follow FETO until its last member is neutralized" (Avundukluoglu 2021; Duz and Berker 2021). In another quote from Erdoğan, we see how anti-AKP student protesters were delegitimized by associating them with negative connotations: "There is no difference between a terrorist holding a gun or a bomb and those who use their pen and position to serve their aim" (Yilmaz 2021c).

The purpose of this language was to, first, create a sense of fear and crisis, second, to encourage AKP supporters to consider themselves victims, and third, to turn these feelings of fear and victimhood into anger directed toward the Gülenists and anti-AKP student protestors. However, the language was also designed to dehumanize and delegitimize the AKP's opponents, thus creating an environment in which AKP violence against their enemies appeared necessary for the defense of 'the people' and Islam. These examples show how Erdoğan evokes in the Turkish public fear of "not only ...ethnic, religious and political minorities (non-Muslims, Kurds, Alevis, leftists, liberals, democrats)" but also those who oppose him in the political arena by portraying them as part of the "dark forces" attacking Turkey (Yilmaz 2021a).

Erdoğan has also instrumentalized Islam to distract the public when "mounting political and economic challenges" are encountered (Yabanci and Taleski 2018, 283). Poor economic policy is either rationalized as a "hardship" sent from God, making it an unavoidable "test" of the ummah, or it is simply seen as a ploy of the enemy to destabilize Turkey. For example, Erdoğan has repeatedly told the Turkish public that they should refrain from criticizing his economic management. Confronted by the plummeting value of the Turkish Lira, Erdoğan admonished the public, saying "don't forget, if they have their dollars, we have our people, our God. We are working hard. Look at what we were 16 years ago and look at us now" (Yilmaz 2021b, c).

According to Erdoğan, Islam is monolithic and its teachings are not open to interpretation. Thus he says "there is no moderate or immoderate Islam. Islam is Islam and that's it. […] The aim of using such terms is to weaken Islam" (RT 2017). In making this statement, he frames any divergence or different interpretation of Islam from his own as an attack on 'true' Islam, and in effect teaches his followers to fear and despise those who practice their faith differently. Islam is the defining element of the civilization to which Turkey belongs, according to Erdoğan, and therefore, he says, Turkish Muslims "should keep in mind that every civilization produces its own technology and every technology its own culture and value. Our ancestors constructed mosques with the aim of building the finest houses of prayer. And the techniques and technologies, employed in the construction of those mosques, reflect our civilization. Similarly, inns, caravansaries, bridges on trade routes are heritages of our civilization. If you do not produce your own technology and science, you cannot be determinative of its culture and value" (Presidency of the Republic of Türkiye 2017). The defense of Islamic civilization, then, is paramount for Erdoğan, and such a defense must be mounted in every sphere of endeavor: everything in Turkey must reflect the Islamic origins of the Turkish nation. Indeed, he suggests that any deviation from Islam is civilizational death.

For example, in order to defend the Islamic civilization to which Turkey belongs, Erdoğan encourages women to disregard feminist teachings which he claims runs contrary to the authentic values of Islamic civilization, and identify primarily as mothers. For example, according to Erdoğan, "Allah entrusted women to men. These feminists say 'how is that? It is an insult.' Then you have nothing to do with our religion and civilization. We look at the farewell sermon of the most beloved (Prophet Mohammed). He says 'women are entrusted by Allah to men. Take care of them. Don't hurt them" (Cumhuriyet 2015). Erdoğan, furthermore, seems to suggest that it is the primary if not sole duty of women to have children and thus create more Muslims to advance Islamic civilization within and outside Turkey. Thus, according to Erdoğan "we will multiply our descendants. They talk about population planning, birth control. No Muslim family can have such an approach. Nobody can interfere in God's work. The first duty here belongs to mothers" (Tharoor 2016).

Thus while Erdoğan is a Turkish ethnoreligious nationalist, civilizationalism is a key element of his populist rhetoric. Erdoğan's civilizationalism is connected to his Islamist worldview and desire to create a common cause with other Sunni Muslim majority nations, but also with his admiration for the Ottoman Empire. Erdoğan is skilled at drawing on Turkish people's feelings of nostalgia for the Ottoman Empire in Turkish citizens, and thus for the period in which the region which is today Turkey was at the center of the Muslim world, and also dominated the Mediterranean. Nostalgia for the Ottoman period is thus at the heart of Erdoğan's populist narrative, which posits that the *ummah* is the perennial victim of Western aggression, and that glory of the Ottoman Empire may be regained if Sunni Muslim nations unite under the banner of Islam—and under the leadership of Erdoğan and Turkey—to defy the West and pursue a common political agenda. For example, at a foreign summit Erdoğan declared "Unfortunately, the Islamic ummah lost the grounds of coming together, doing common business and producing common solutions to their problems. Even today, we see this deficiency in many of our issues, including Jerusalem, Palestine, anti-Islamism, anti-terrorism, justice and human rights […] Muslims look for solutions in the Western capitals for their problems, instead of reaching out to their Muslim brothers and sisters for help" (Daily Sahab 2019).

This call to unite Muslims against the Christian West was also made explicit during the re-conversion of the Hagia Sophia into a Mosque. The Hagia Sophia, a sixth-century Byzantine church in Istanbul, was converted into a mosque after the conquest of the Byzantine Empire, but later became a church under the secular rule of Attatürk. Erdoğan's decision to re-covert the building into a mosque was an explicit demonstration of his Islamist neo-Ottomanist civilizationalism. After the re-conversion, Erdoğan suggested that the re-conversion of the Hagia Sophia was an act of defiance against Western aggression, and marked a moment when Turkish Muslims were—at last—rising from a long slumber to regain their rightful place in the world. According to Erdoğan, "World War I was designed as a fight to grab and share Ottoman lands. In an era when the world order is shaken at the foundations, we will frustrate those who dream the same about the Republic of Turkey … We tear up those scenarios of those who want to siege our country politically, economically, militarily by realizing a much large vision … To those who are surprised by Turkey … rising again like a giant who woke up from its century old sleep, we say: 'it is not over yet!'" (Yilmaz 2021c).

On another occasion, at the pan-Islamist 'Kuala Lumpur Summit' in 2019, he was critical of Western hegemony at the United Nations, and angrily claimed that the United Nations Security Council ignored the interests of Muslims, saying "we [Muslims] depend on the words coming out from the mouths of the five permanent seat holders" (Povera 2019). First casting Muslims as victims of the world's great powers, Erdoğan then pivoted to religious sentiments, telling Muslims to feel hopeful that "regardless of the circumstance or how challenging the world might become, we can never question the bounty from Allah because every crisis will open window of opportunity" (Povera 2019). Here Erdoğan's Islamist civilizationalism is used to set up a dichotomy between 'us'—the pious and innocent Muslims—and 'them'—corrupt and violent Western civilization.

Based on this case study, it is possible to conclude that, in his discourse, Erdoğan separates society into two homogenous and antagonistic groups, 'the pure people' versus 'the corrupt elite' who collaborate with the dangerous others belonging to other civilizations that are hostile and present a clear and present danger to the civilization and way of life of the pure people. In this way, the Erdoğan construes opposition between 'self' and the 'other' not in a narrow, national manner, but in civilizational terms, and as a battle between the Islamic and Ottoman self and the Western other. Secular nationalist 'elites' are, in this conception of politics, working with Islam's civilizational other—the West—to dismember Turkey, corrupt Muslims with Western immorality, and weaken the resolve of the *ummah*. In response to the civilizational conflict, he claims is occurring within and outside Turkey, Erdoğan has sought to encourage nostalgia for the Ottoman Empire, and to associate himself and his party with its Golden Age. In doing so, Erdoğan is able to generate a sense of hope in his most ardent supporters, who may perceive him as a savior, and the only person capable of reversing the fortunes of Turkish Muslims, and restoring them to the rightful place at the center of Islamic civilization.

3.3.2 Indonesia: The Islamic Defenders Front (FPI)

The Rise of the Islamic Defenders Front

Turkey is of course not the only country in which civilizational populism exists within an Islamic context. In Indonesia, the now banned Islamic Defenders Front became politically consequential in the 2010s when it combined populism, Islam, and an *ummah*-based identity politics (Yilmaz and Barton 2021a; b). After gaining independence from the Dutch in 1945, Indonesia remained largely undemocratic up until the late 1990s. Under the 'Guided democracy' of independence leader Sukarno, and the 'New Order' of his successor General Suharto, Indonesia failed to develop a healthy political culture (Yilmaz 2020c; Barton et al. 2021a). Following the fall of Suharto in 1998, Indonesia began a swift and sometimes violent transition to democracy. This was an overwhelmingly positive transition, which opened up—after decades of dictatorship and political repression— a space within civil society in which politics could be discussed openly and political parties could organize. In this environment, a variety of political parties began to organize and compete for public attention and support. Religious parties emerged in this period, having previously been either suppressed entirely or incorporated into government approved coalitions. However, Islamist parties have failed to gain widespread electoral success in Indonesia post-Suharto. The moderating effects of Indonesia's non-sectarian constitution and strong civil Islamic groups Nahdlatul Ulama (NU) and Muhammadiyah have helped to engineer a society in which Islamist extremism is considered antithetical to the principles upon which Indonesia was founded (Barton et al. 2021a, b). As Azharghany et al. (2020, 240) note, "only two Islamic parties exist in the central parliament amongst the nine nationalist parties, namely the Partai Persatuan Pembanguan (PPP) and the Partai Keadilan Sejahtera (PKS) which have been further weakened by the entry of the PPP party in supporting the government".

Outside of parliament, however, Islamic groups and movements remain vital in Indonesian society, not only in the form of the civil society groups NU and Muhammadiyah, the official Islamic clerical body the Council of Indonesian Ulama (Majelis Ulama Indonesia), but also in the form of more radical and violent populist groups such as the Islamic Defenders Front (FPI) (Azharghany et al., 2020, 240). The MUI saw its influence grow during the Presidency of Susilo Bambang Yudhoyono (president from 2004 to 2014). Empowered by Yudhoyono, the body began to issue *fatwas* at odds with Indonesia's non-sectarian constitution.

For example, the MUI issued a *fatwa* which proclaimed secularism, pluralism, and liberalism incompatible with Islam (Van Bruinessen 2013), and another which declared the Ahmadiyya apostates (Barton et al. 2021a, b). These *fatwas* demonstrate the growing influence of Islamist radicals both within the MUI and within Indonesian society in general. Indeed, Islamist political movements have grown in importance in the 2010s and beyond. This is not to say that they are winning more seats in parliament, but rather that their social and overall political influence has increased. This was especially evident during and after the anti-Ahok protests of 2016, which were led and encouraged by Islamist groups including the FPI, but were supported by ordinary Indonesians, despite the disapproval of NU and Muhammadiyah leaders (Barton et al. 2021a, b). Islamist populism in Indonesia is more common among city dwellers than in rural areas. Rural Indonesians, some of whom practice their faith syncretically, are more likely to be influenced by the salvationist notions inherent in the traditionalist Islam taught by NU. Urban Indonesians, who have long been influenced by the Islamic modernism of Muhammadiyah and its calls for social and economic justice, have increasingly become drawn to Islamic populism, which incorporates many of the same political reformist messages (Azharghany et al. 2020).

During the period of democratization, the new space opened up for political discourse and public argument was quickly filled by Islamic groups. Some of these groups supported pluralism, such as the neo-Modernists and traditionalist Muslims who gathered around President Abdurrahman Wahid and his NU affiliated National Awakening Party. However, anti-pluralist Islamists—who conceived of Indonesian identity in a very narrow manner excluding all but Orthodox Sunni Muslims—began to fill the new space opened up by the fall of Suharto and democratization. Among the more extreme Islamist groups which grew in significance during this period and beyond was the FPI, an Islamist populist group with a militia wing. The FPI are not the only manifestation of populism in Indonesia. Since the fall of Suharto, Indonesia has witnessed the rise of technocratic nationalist and penal populism. For example, Penal populism is part of the discourse and political strategy of President Joko Widodo (Jokowi), while Islamist populism is evident in the discourse of Presidential candidate and former general Prabowo Subianto, who relies on alliance with Islamist groups (Barton et al. 2021a, b; Yilmaz 2020c; Arifianto 2019b; Hadiz, 2018; Mietzner 2018). The FPI, however, are the most prominent example of religious civilizational populism in Indonesia. The group was formed in 1998 by Salafi-inspired cleric Muhammad Rizieq Shihab, and quickly gained a reputation for street violence and encouraging communal strife (Barton et al. 2021a, b). The FPI's ideology is influenced by an "ultra-orthodox, Salafist understanding of the principles of Islam" (Barton et al. 2021a, b). The group was "founded for the purpose of amar ma'ruf nahi munkar, or 'commanding right and forbidding wrong'", and its militias were given the task of carrying out this task (Bamualim 270, 2011).

Thus according to the FPI and its leader Rizieq, the government of Indonesia is not sufficiently Islamic, and ought to base the country's laws on the Qur'an. The group desires therefore to implement Sharia law in Indonesia, as they understand it, and in doing so replace the somewhat secular or at least non-sectarian constitution of Indonesia with religious law (Barton 2021a, b, c; Mietzner 2018; Hadiz 2016, p. 112; Wilson 2015). However, they have not been primarily interested in gaining seats in parliament, but instead seek to influence sitting members and pressure them into adopting more extreme positions in line with the FPI's Islamism and populism.

The FPI claimed to be defending Islam, which it did through acts of vigilantism and intimidation of minorities including Shia Muslims and liberals. Because FPI members conceive of themselves as doing God's work on Earth, they and particularly their militia wing are comfortable defying the law and dismissing all government authority as un-Islamic, and therefore illegitimate (Barton et al. 2021a, b). As the movement grew throughout the 2000s and 2010s, it communicated a populist discourse in which the FPI and its supporters were part of a large Sunni Muslim victim group, oppressed by the Indonesian government and threatened by religious minorities. As part of this attempt to evoke a feeling of victimhood and fear, FPI "followers [were] kept constantly anxious about threats to their faith and way of life, and thus incentivized to hate "the Other" and at times manifest that hatred and insecurity in acts of intimidation, symbolic violence and hate speech toward out-group members" (Yilmaz and Barton 2021b).

The FPI, a hybrid vigilante and welfare group—and with Rizieq as its "Grand Imam" or Imam Besar—grew in relevance due to their grassroots work with the urban and rural poor of Indonesia (Jahroni 2004). This welfare work helped the group portray itself as a 'saviour' of the people on Earth, as well as in the afterlife. The group provided education, free meals, disaster relief, and jobs to marginalized Sunni Muslims (Hookway 2017). However, as Bamualim observes "the FPI has assembled a jemaah (community of followers) to manage religious activities and has mobilized laskars (soldiers) to enforce amar ma'ruf nahi munkar (commanding right and forbidding wrong)" (Bamualim 2011, 267). Pairing its philanthropy with Islamist notions of social justice, the FPI justified their vigilantism and attacks liberal establishments such as the night clubs and gambling places it labeled "dens of vice", and their violence against Ahmadiyya, Indonesian-Chinese, and communists, as a defense of Islam and Muslims (Barton et al. 2021a, b).

The FPI greatly increased its relevance during the mid-2010s when it became a driving force within the Defending Islam Movement (DIM) and the National Movement to Safeguard the Indonesian Ulema Councils Fatwa. DIM was formed by a coalition of Islamist groups including FPI and Hizbut Tahrir (HBT) in order to protest alleged 'blasphemous' remarks made by Christian Chinese governor of Jakarta Jasuki Tjahaja Purnama, known by his Hakka Chinese name "Ahok" (Maulia 2020; Nuryanti 2021; Adiwilaga et al. 2019; Fossati and Mietzner 2019; Hadiz 2018; Mietzner 2018). In 2016, Ahok was one of the most prominent non-Muslims in Indonesian politics. Already, governor of Indonesia's capital and largest city, Ahok was expected to act as running mate for Jokowi in the 2019 Presidential elections, and was considered a potential candidate for president himself in 2024 (Barton et al. 2021a, b; Mietzner 2018).

However, his career was destroyed when a video of him discussing the misuse of the Qur'anic verses by Islamists, who had claimed that Islam forbids non-Muslims ruling over Muslims, went viral on social media (Nuryanti 2021). Ahok's remarks were distorted and taken out of context, leading many who saw the video to conclude that the governor was himself distorting and insulting their holy texts (Nuryanti 2021; Mietzner 2018). Ahok was forced to apologize for his words, and despite clarifying that he was by no means insulting the Qur'an or Islam, public sentiment turned against him. Hundreds of thousands of Muslims took to the streets in protests, roused by Islamists who claimed they were defending Islam from Ahok's attacks. The Indonesian Ulema Council (MUI), an official Islamic body created in 1975 by Suharto in order to control religion and promote 'moderate' Islam, was perhaps intimidated by the size of the protests and their ferocity. They issued a statement declaring Ahok's remarks on the Qur'an blasphemous and offensive to Muslims (Nuryanti 2021; Mietzner 2018). Over the following months, several large-scale rallies organized by the FPI and other Islamist groups, and effectively sanctioned by the MUI, involving hundreds of thousands of Muslims, created the necessary pressure on Indonesia's government and police to ensure that Ahok was charged with blasphemy and put on trial for his 'crimes' (Nuryanti 2021). His political career destroyed, Ahok found himself imprisoned for blasphemy in a trial that demonstrated the newfound power of Islamist groups.

The FPI have never been an electorally successful group. Yet this does not mean they are not influential. Indeed, their role in the anti-Ahok rallies, which drew the support of 'moderate' Muslims who belonged to NU and Muhammadiyah, demonstrates their widespread influence. The power of FPI, however, began to disturb the government of Indonesia, which banned the group in 2020 on the somewhat spurious grounds that they were spreading Coronavirus (Maulia 2020). The group's power stems in part from their Islamist and populist division of Indonesian society—and beyond it the world—into two groups: '*ummah*' and non-*ummah*.

As Islamists, the FPI believe that Islam teaches the ideal way of living and political organization for all humanity. Islamism is therefore utopian, and urges its followers to try to build the perfect society ordered by the teachings of Islam. Their conception of politics—domestic and global—is thus influenced by their Islamist ideology. The combining of populism and Islamism in FPI ideology means the party does not merely divide society between the good and the evil, or Muslims (as they understand the term) and non-Muslims, but also between governing elites and the people they rule. Like all right-wing populists, the FPI attempt to construct an antagonistic relationship between 'the people' and their oppressors: 'elites' and various 'others'. However, the FPI distinguish between these groups according to their religious beliefs and practices. The FPI's populist ideology, while essentially nationalist, frames Indonesians as part of a transnational *ummah* (Barton et al. 2021a, b). This *ummah* is oppressed by non-Muslim and insufficiently Muslim forces both inside and beyond Indonesia. The FPI, therefore, portrays itself as the champion of pious Muslims who alone can overcome corrupt elites and threatening non-Muslim others, and rebuild Indonesia as a utopian society based on Sharia law.

For example, the FPI's capitalized on widespread antipathy toward Chinese, an economically successful community in Indonesia, during its successful anti-Ahok campaign by framing the Jakarta governor as both part of the 'elite' but also a threatening non-Muslim 'other'. The FPI could easily, therefore, 'other' Ahok, and portray him as an oppressor who insults and offends Muslims and therefore ought to be removed from power and jailed (Peterson 2020; Hadiz 2018: 571–72).

The anti-Ahok protests were cumulatively held by a collection of informal Islamic and Islamist groups under the banner of GNPF-MUI. However, the FPI was the face of the movement, and inspired protestors with the motto "defending Islam" (Fossati and Mietzner 2019: 774). The call to "defend" Islam was part of an FPI effort to portray Muslims as collective victims of a non-Muslim 'other' in Ahok. Moreover, "Rizieq Shihab positioned himself as the manifestation of the will of the people, and "[he] described himself as the "Great Leader of Indonesian Muslims", proclaiming a theologically grounded authority to voice the people's desire for a devout life and the removal of Islam's enemies" (Barton et al., 2021a, b: 6). In doing so, Rizieq constructed the Sunni Muslim majority in Indonesia as an aggrieved people, who had been insulted by a minority 'other', who had blasphemed and whose people dominated the economy. The FPI's evoking of a sense of victimhood in the majority population helped inspire approximately half a million people to attend the anti-Ahok rallies in Jakarta and elsewhere (Adiwilaga et al. 2019:169; Hutton 2018; Fealy 2016). In a unique instance, the FPI was able to create a successful populism based on hurt and victimhood, and unite it with an "asymmetric multi-class alliance" against a non-Muslim "enemy" (Adiwilaga et al. 2019; Hadiz 2016).

Prior to the protests, Rizieq had used a similar populist discourse, in which he attempted to create a sense of fear and feelings of rage in followers. For example, Rizieq called President Jokowi a "troublemaker" and "bringer of disasters" who opened the "Golden Entry Gate for non-Muslims to dominate and control the system" (Aspinall and Mietzner 2019). Thus the anti-Ahok protests were not random or isolated events, but the outgrowth of the FPI's Islamist populism and a demonstration of its increasing influence over middle-class urban Indonesians. The fall of Ahok and his subsequent imprisonment for blasphemy had a powerful impact on Indonesian politics and, in particular, on the 2019 Presidential elections.

The two major candidates in the 2019 elections, incumbent President Jowoki and challenger Prabowo Subianto, both responded to the anti-Ahok protests by aligning themselves with Islamic religious figures. Prabowo Subianto in particular sought to capitalize on the mainstreaming of populist Islamist influence in Indonesian society by allying himself with the FPI and the anti-Ahok protestors. He selected Sandiaga Uno, who had won the Jakarta governorship after Ahok's fall, as his running mate. Uno was a businessman like Ahok, but as a Muslim his economic success was not perceived as illegitimate or evidence of elite corruption (Setijadi 2017). In a campaign speech, Subianto excused Islamist terrorism, blaming poverty and foreign forces who exploited vulnerable Indonesians (Kennedy 2019). Jowoki, the eventual winner of the elections, picked NU cleric Ma'ruf Amin as his running mate, in an attempt to emphasize his Muslimness and perhaps downplay his relationship with the now jailed Ahok (Yilmaz 2020c; Arifianto 2019a, 2019b).

While the FPI did not enjoy good relations with Jowoki or his government, this does not mean that they had no influence over other important political figures. The FPI's rise saw the group begin to influence Indonesian politicians at the highest level of power, including former Vice President Jusuf Kalla, who allegedly helped return Rizieq from exile in Saudi Arabia to Indonesia in 2020 (Wirajuda 2020). Yet despite their impact on Indonesian politics and the 2019 elections, the FPI eventually met their downfall at the hands of the Jokowi government. Implicated in violence, mayhem, and murder, the FPI were banned in December 2020 by Jokowi, having broken COVID-19 restrictions by holding a mass rally during the pandemic. The FPI's decision to rally during the pandemic in defiance of the law provided the necessary pretext for the government to finally ban the group and imprison its members.

Curiously, Rizieq left Indonesia in 2017 after being charged with pornography offices and "insulting the official state ideology, Pancasila", though he claimed he was making a minor pilgrimage to Mecca (Karmini 2020) Rizieq remained in Saudi Arabia for three years. However, he returned to Indonesia in late 2020, where he was greeted at the airport by hundreds of supporters. (Karmini 2020). His comeback to politics coincided with the 2020 COVID-19 Pandemic. However, Rezieq was more interested in staging a "moral revolution" which would sweep non-Islamic influences from Indonesia (FR24 News 2020). He staged a series of large-scale rallies and presented the mounting problems facing the Indonesian economy, healthcare system, and society as part of a crisis created by non-Muslims, which could only be solved through Islamization (Barton et al. 2021a, b).

Rizieq, now a powerful Islamist presence in Indonesia, capitalized on sympathy among the *ummah* for a Muslim man in France who beheaded a teacher who had blasphemed by showing cartoons of Islam's prophet Muhammad. Rizieq reportedly approved of the killing, remarking, "If they [those accused of blasphemy in Indonesia] are not investigated, don't blame Muslims if their heads are found in the streets tomorrow" (FR24 News 2020). This shows how events occurring far from Indonesia but involving Muslims can be framed by Rizieq as part of a global conflict between the 'good' and 'pure' *ummah*, and the 'immoral' and 'impure' West. The popularity of Rizieq and the power of his rhetoric began to concern Jokowi and his government. To ban the group due to their extreme Islamist rhetoric was politically dangerous, and might inspire violence against the government. Yet when the 'grand imam' of the FPI refused to cooperate with medical authorities and be tested for COVID-19, and were later found to be transmitting the virus, the government found a pretext to ban the group. The Jokowi government had previously banned Hizbut Tahrir (HTI) in 2017 and it followed the same pattern for FPI by arresting Shihab following an "encounter" between its alleged militia and government forces (Kelemen 2021). Since the arrest and dismemberment of FPI members, Rizieq has been sentenced to six months in prison, leaving the movement leaderless with a sense of being "wronged" and "victimized" by the government's approach (Aljazeera 2021). Thus the FPI is now banned in Indonesia, but the movement's influence, however, is not so easy to vanquish. Having brought Islamist populism into mainstream Indonesian politics, the FPI—while they did not achieve their ultimate goal of a Sharia-inspired society—damaged pluralism in Indonesia and encouraged the growth of 'us vs them' politics based on a religious classification of peoples.

Civilizationism and the FPI

A key feature of the FPI is the classification of peoples according to their religious beliefs and practices. The party reinforces "cultural idioms associated with Islam" in order to mobilize "public support in contests over power and resources based on an ummah-based political identity" (Hadiz 2018). Thus while FPI is first and foremost a nationalist group, in essence, they practice a religion and civilization-based classification of peoples. This worldview heavily influences their populist ideology, and their antagonistic politics based on the division of society between the *ummah* and non-*ummah*. The party's civilizationalism, however, does not conflict greatly with their nationalism. Rather, civilizationism assists the party in their rhetorical construction of 'the people' and their supposed enemies, and assists the party in developing transnational links with other civilizationalist Islamist groups.

The notion that Indonesia is part of a transnational *ummah*, or brotherhood of Muslims, appears to have become more important to Indonesians since the fall of Suharto. The increasing significance of the MUI and its *fatwas* has opened an ever greater space for Islamists to promote civilizationalism in Indonesia. At the same time, pluralism has declined in Indonesia, as more Indonesians begin to identify their nation as Islamic, and its authentic 'people' as part of a global transnational *ummah*. Non-Muslims, secular and liberal Muslims, and non-Sunni Muslims are increasingly 'othered' by Islamist groups, and pushed out of the public sphere. This otherization has been extended to the state and its security forces at times, because when the government attempts to curb Islamic extremist activity the FPI and its allies frame national authorities as an un-Islamic "enemy state" oppressing 'the people' (Juoro 2019).

The group's civilizational categorization of peoples helps justify their vigilantism and mobilize their supporters to carry out attacks on 'others' and in defense of the pious *ummah*. For example, the FPI and its Islamist allies were able to mobilize so many Indonesians in anti-Ahok protests because they framed Ahok as a religious and civilizational enemy, whose position of power made him a danger to the *ummah*. Indeed, the FPI's leaders have long believed that the reformasi movement, which was responsible for the downfall of Suharto, led to "a general breakdown in the moral fabric of society" involving the "uncontrolled spread of ma'siat (immoral) businesses such as discos, bars, pornography, prostitution, and illicit drugs" (Bamualim 272, 2011). Significantly, Rizieq appears to think that ma'siat activities are the result of a conspiracy "by groups with a vested interest in the success of the businesses to bring about the gradual decline and moral decay of Islamic society" (Bamualim 272, 2011). Therefore, Chinese businessman such as Ahok appears particularly threatening to the FPI, and it is not surprising that they sought to remove him from power.

The FPI's ultimate goal is the Islamization of Indonesia. This utopian state will, the group claims, actualize the desires and interests of 'the people', but to achieve such a state radical acts are required, including a reinterpreting of Pancasila (Campbell 2017; Hookway 2017). It is an imperative, according to the FPI, that Indonesia's human made non-sectarian constitution be replaced with Islam's superior divine law (Barton 2021a, b, c; Mietzner 2018; Hadiz 2016: 112; Wilson 2015). "Do you want NKRI [Indonesia] to be Syariah [sharia]? Do you want Indonesia to be blessed? Do you want the State & Nation to be safe?" Rizieq asks his supporters, suggesting that to be saved from their enemies a transition to a Sharia-based state is required (CNN 2018). As part of this plan to create a heartland for pious Muslims in Indonesia, FPI wish to cleanse the country of non-Muslims and insufficiently orthodox Muslim elements, and build an Islamic society based upon their interpretation of Sharia law. The Islam of the FPI is not therefore entirely local or traditional to Indonesia, but belongs to the transnational Salafi movement which inspired other Islamist groups and militias. Indeed, an alarming aspect of the FPI's civilizationalism is manifested in its members' support for violent *jihad* and transnational civilizational terrorist groups such as al-Qaeda, ISIS, and local Indonesian groups Jemaah Islamiyah (JI) and Jamaah Ansharut Daulah (JAD) (MEI@75 2021; Idris 2018: 9 l Barton 2005, 2009, 2010, 2015, 2020a, 2020b).

Civilizational Populism in Rizieq's Discourse

FPI leader Rizieq, even when in exile or imprisoned, remained the most influential member of the group. Rizieq, "a qualified scholar in Islamic law who graduated from the Islamic University of Imam Muhammad ibn Saud" is known for his eloquent Arabic and personal charisma (Bamualim, 269, 2011). He portrays himself in his discourse as modest and pious, and as a man of the people who cares for the poor and marginalized (Bamualim 2011, 269). Rizieq's populist appeal relies upon his religious conception of good and evil, and its application to Indonesian society and the world. According to Rizieq, a Muslim must forbid evil and command good, or promote the good and prevent vice, whenever possible (al-amr bi al-ma 'ruf wa al-nahy 'an al-munkar) (Widiyanto 2017, 93). This phrase is found in several Quranic verses, perhaps most prominently 3:104 and 3:110, and is often interpreted as direction for Muslims to take action—including if necessary violent action—to prevent evil from occurring. Of course, there are complex questions around which acts might be categorized as evil, and when violence might be deemed necessary to combat this evil, and moreover who has the authority to use violence to prevent evil (Cook 2000). Rizieq argues "that al-amr bi al-ma 'ruf wa al-nahy 'an al-munkar is obligatory for Muslims", and bases his argument on "Islamic jurisprudence (usul al-fiqh)". According to Rizieq, then, evil must be destroyed as part of a Muslim's religious duty. Widiyanto describes Rizieq as conceiving of evil as a "social pathology" requiring "strict treatment (Widiyanto 2017, 105).

However, Rizieq does not call for mass violence against evildoers in Indonesia. He recognizes that the Qur'an and Hadith literature provide examples of Muslims correctly using violence against evil, but also examples of Muslims using a non-violent approach to combat evil (Widiyanto 2017, 103). Seeing no contradiction, Rizieq instead calls for Muslims to evaluate when violence is permissible to combat evil by applying "the standards of Shari 'ah, not merely rational consideration" (Widiyanto 2017, 104). He discerns between two types of violence: "praiseworthy" violence and "disgraceful violence" (Widiyanto 2017, 102). At the same time, Muslims, he argues, should not merely concern themselves with either commanding good or forbidding evil, but should rather balance the two in order that both occur. To illustrate his point Rizieq "compares 'commanding good' with planting rice, and 'forbidding evil with eradicating pests" (Widiyanto 2017, 104).

Rizieq has been careful to present the actions of the FPI in forbidding evil and commanding good as lawful. He claims that Indonesia's Jarkarta Charter of 1945, which suggests observing Sharia law as an obligation of all Muslims, provides justification for the FPI's sometimes violent actions against perceived 'evildoers' (Widiyanto 2017, 105–6). Rizieq, in a book on the charter, "asserts that reinserting the Jakarta Charter into the Indonesian constitution is a must: Muslims have the right to live by the Sharia, and it would apply exclusively to them and thus not discriminate against non-Muslims". In this way, he claims to be standing up for the right of Muslims to practice their faith, and to champion their rights in the face of hostile secularism and Western interference in Indonesia. Rizieq also claims that his group takes no action against evil until the group is certain that evil acts have taken place, and that they are against both Sharia and Indonesian secular law (Widiyanto 2017, 106). He also claims that when a local community does not welcome the FPI or is not "disturbed" by the evil taking place, the FPI will merely attempt to "enlighten" the community about the "noble message of Islam", and will not take violent action against them (Widiyanto 2017, 106). However, if a community welcomes the FPI and wishes to eliminate evil within their midst, the FPI—according to Rizieq—"is obliged to assist the local community" in the elimination of evil (Widiyanto 2017, 107). In this way, he portrays himself as a noble person, who fights evil but does so always within the boundaries of Islamic and Indonesian law, and always with the permission of 'the people'.

The FPI's conception of evil, however, has expanded over time. Where once it was confined to un-Islamic acts such as drinking alcohol, gambling, and involvement in prostitution, increasingly the group began to consider Ahmadiyyah and liberal Muslims as inherently evil (Widiyanto 2017, 109). Therefore, Rizieq and the FPI believe that, under the right circumstances, it is permissible to use violence to combat the evil presence of businesses that sell alcohol, permit gambling on their premises, or against people involved in prostitution, and also against members of religious movements they believe to be inimical to Islam. This desire to root out evil stems from Rizieq's belief that evil is a virus which cannot be eliminated merely "by curing the patient", but which also requires the destruction of the "nests" and "mosquitoes of evil" (Widiyanto 2017, 105). On this basis, the FPI justify their attacks on businesses, individuals, and faith groups which they hold responsible for the presence of evil in Indonesian society. The state, too, is held by the FPI to be partly responsible for the flourishing of evil in Indonesia. From the beginning, the FPI's leaders have declared their opposition to the "Western decadence, secularism, liberalism and immorality" permitted by Indonesian law (Bamualim 2011, 272). The FPI's leaders, including Rizieq, argue that democratic political reform has increased the presence of evil in Indonesia, "evidenced in the uncontrolled spread of businesses 'peddling in vice,' such as discos, bars, entertainment centers and other fronts for pornography, prostitution and illicit drugs" (Bamualim 2011, 272). Equally, the FPI claim that the state does too little to alleviate poverty, and therefore they attempt to attract the support of Indonesians who feel marginalized, and encourage them to reject "the present situation" and take radical action to improve their lives (Bamualim 2011, 272).

Rizieq and the FPI's conception of the world as a battleground between the forces of good (i.e. Islam and the pure and pious people who follow Islam and Sharia law) and the forces of evil (Non-Muslims and non-observant Muslims) provides the basis of their populism. For Rizieq, Islam is a liberating and revolutionary force which eradicates evil and promotes goodness everywhere. Moreover, he portrays himself as a representative of Islam and thus 'the good', and his FPI as protectors of 'the pure people'—orthodox Sunni Muslims. Anyone outside of this category is essentially, according to Rizieq's worldview, either a purveyor of evil or infected with evil. And because Rizieq believes that all evil must, one way or another, be rooted out, he and his supporters believe that it is permissible to eliminate—sometimes using force—groups and individuals who perpetuate evil. Thus non-Muslims and non-Sunni Muslims are othered by the FPI and framed as evildoers. Even the state is sometimes framed as an enemy other insofar as it remains neutral on religious matters, and does not prevent Muslims from drinking alcohol or involving themselves in other evil acts. For example, Rizieq has justified violence against evildoers acts by claiming that those who say his good for "commanding good and forbidding evil" leads to vigilantism "forget, or pretend to forget that evil itself is a kind of violence that does harm to people's morality, which is more valuable than property" (Widiyanto 2017, 103). In making this claim Rizieq attempts to legitimize attacks on 'othered' groups, while also portraying himself and the FPI as sufficiently knowledgeable about Islam and Islamic law that they may determine when violence may be used to forbid evil.

Rizieq's rhetoric is therefore an attempt to create a populist community which draws together marginalized and aggrieved Muslim Indonesians, disillusioned by government corruption and failure, and who may feel angry at the forces which they believe have led to their social and economic marginalization. Rizieq attempts to exploit these feelings of disappointment and resentment, and convert them into anger toward the state and elements within Indonesian society (non-Muslims, liberal and secular Muslims, ethnic minorities, businessmen) which he claims are responsible for the marginalization of Indonesia's authentic Muslim population. Rizieq claims that Indonesia's constitution prevents Muslims from living in a truly Islamic society, as is their right as the majority group within the nation. Therefore, he presents himself as the champion of 'the people', a pious and humble man who has taken it upon himself to help 'the people' overcome the non-Muslim forces which prevent them from achieving the utopian society envisaged by Islam. Islam, then, is the force which binds together the people, and which will solve the nation's economic and social problems.

Rizieq plays on people's religious beliefs and positive feelings toward Islam, describing himself as a Grand Imam and holy religious figure, therefore, giving him the appearance of religious authority and associating himself with Islam. Equally, by portraying Islam as the answer to the sufferings of 'the people', Rizieq encourages his supporters to feel hopeful for a happier future, and to be willing to struggle to create this future. He always plays on a deep and religious nostalgia for the early days of Islam, in which the Prophet Muhammad created such a utopian society, to be emulated by Muslims until the end of time. Thus by associating himself, the FPI, and 'the people' with Islam, Rizieq effectively sacralizes all three, and identifies them as inherently good. On the other hand, non-Muslims and people he deems insufficiently Muslim, are identified as on the side of evil, either because they actively promote evil, or because they attempt (like the Indonesian state) to remain neutral, and therefore refuse to forbid evil and promote the good.

Rizieq and the FPI combine populism within an Islamist conception of the world as a cosmic battle between good and evil. If Islam is on the side of the 'good' in this battle, then the West is the representation of evil. Rizieq and his allies have long argued that Islamic values are threatened by Western influences, and that 'the people' are suffering in Indonesia due to the decadent and immoral lifestyles encouraged by the West and permitted by the Indonesian law. For that reason, Rizieq called for the replacement of secular laws and the implementation of the Sharia, arguing that the former are Western in orientation and do not meet the needs of Indonesia's predominantly Muslim population, whose right to practice their faith and live in an evil free environment is constantly threatened by Western influences (Bamaulim 279, 2011). Rizieq has used his authority as a cleric and his forthright and somewhat crude manners to connect with the people as the man who is not afraid to attack evil. According to Rizieq, "true Mu'min [pious Muslim]must reject secularism, pluralism, liberalism, LGBT, apostasy, heresy, shamanism, corruption, khamr, drugs, gambling, prostitution, adultery, pornography, pornoaction, injustice, tyranny, immorality, evilness, and leadership of a kafir over Muslims, even when the constitution permits it because Qur'an and sunnah forbid it" (Sejati 2014).

This worldview made it impossible for Rizieq to accept Ahok—a Chinese Christian—in a position of authority over Muslims, despite the fact that the latter was democratically elected to the position of governor of Jakarta. For example, while addressing the anti-Ahok rallies he used populist Islamist rhetoric to other non-Muslims and portray them as too threatening to be allowed to participate in Indonesian politics, saying "once again I emphasize that it is haram to be a regional head in a Muslim-majority area, let alone a head of state in a Muslim-majority country. This is a non-negotiable stipulation of the scripture. And the scriptures are higher than the constitution" (Shihab 2016). The idea that civil law is flawed and manmade and should be replaced with "divine" law is also a theme that helps FPI portray themselves and their supporters as 'pure' and 'innocent' victims of secular oppression, and who only use violence when defending Islam. For example, following Ahok's election victory and subsequent swearing in as Governor of Jakarta, the FPI placed posters around Jakarta claiming "Civil law and customary law can never match Allah's laws" (Widjaja 2012). On another occasion, Rizieq reminded 'the people' that "the holy verses are a fixed piece, because it is a divine decree that cannot and should not be amended or revised. While the constitutional verse is only human, so at any time it can be amended or revised so that it is in line with the holy verses" (Shihab, last updated 2020). Rizieq has also attacked liberal and secular Muslims such as Prime Minister Jokowi, who he claimed was "a troublemaker and a source of disaster for Muslims" (Cikimm, last updated 2020d).

Indonesia's political leaders—and the state itself—are portrayed as a persistent danger to 'the people' because their neutrality on religious matters allows the faithful to be pushed into a sinful lifestyle, which the FPI then attempts to correct. Thus the call for *jihad* (or 'struggle') is a part of Rizieq's rhetoric, in which he urges the faithful to struggle for salvation in this life and the next, declaring that "from now on, it is obligatory for Muslim to unite themselves, to unite all potentials, this land cannot be taken by infidels!"(Cikimm, last updated 2020c). These infidels are charged by Rizieq with conspiring with each other to hurt Muslims, and with lying to Muslims in order to misdirect them away from the true path of Islam. For example, he warned supporters during an address that when "the enemy uses the weapons of lies" they must "use the weapon of honesty and truth" (Pinterest, last updated 2021). Equally, the struggle of the people, or the *ummah* against the West is consistently glorified in Rizieq's discourse. "Fighting is full of slander", he once remarked, "so strengthen your heart not to break easily, so that you say istiqomah fisabilillah" (steadfast in the cause of Allah) (Pinterest, last updated 2021). Rizieq claims that the *ummah* is under constant attack from the West and false Muslims, and asks his supporters "if the kuffar and hypocrites are so strong in attacking Islam, why are we afraid to defend Islam?" (Pinterest, last updated 2021). Curiously, he does not promise victory, but rather tells the faithful to "Remember!!!" that their "obligation to fight is not to win", but rather to "struggle", and that "to win or lose" is "a gift from Allah SWT" (Pinterest, last updated 2021).

Thus Rizieq does not wish to encourage his 'people' to fight merely to win, but to see something divine and purposeful in the struggle. This fight is not merely physical. Rather, Rizieq claims that "in a physical war, winning & losing is essentially a victory for the *mujahid*, but in a war of thought, winning is an absolute price, because if you lose, faith is at stake" (Arrahmah 2019). In one particular instance, he trivialized life itself and encouraged people to die for their faith, claiming "life is not long in this world, fight or not we will all die, and dying fighting for Allah is a beauty that is second to none" (Arrahmah 2019). In claiming that *jihad* or struggle itself is the goal, he legitimizes and rationalizes his own failures, and encourages his supporters to feel a powerful sense of belonging and purpose, which may have been lacking in their lives.

At the same time, Rizieq attempts to portray Islam as essentially peaceful, and to frame the violent actions of the FPI as necessary expressions of anger against corrupt and un-Islamic leaders. This displacement of responsibility is evident in another statement by Rizieq, in which he claimed, "Islam is a religion of peace but does not mean surrender to error, Islam is a religion of gentleness but does not mean silence against blasphemy and blasphemy" (Arrahmah 2019). Rizieq thus encourages his supporters to feel hatred toward the West and Muslims who fail to practice their religion in the manner prescribed by the FPI, and to justify their violence against non-Muslims, and liberal and secular Muslims, as necessary violence against evildoers and oppressors. Rizieq does not use explicit civilizational rhetoric. He does not call for a caliphate to be reestablished, or for a pan-Islamic state to be established. Rather, Rizieq is an Indonesian nationalist. However, his populism contains civilizational elements. First, insofar as Rizieq and FPI perceive Indonesia as a battleground in a wider war between Islam and the West, and between authentic and pure Sunni Muslims (*ummah*) on the one hand, and the forces of evil who hate Islam: corrupt and immoral 'elites' who have rejected Islam, Westernized Indonesians, and religious minorities. Thus while the FPI are primarily a nationalist movement, their Islamist ideology contains an inherent transnational and civilizational element insofar as Islamism places primacy upon religious identification over, for example, ethnic or national identification.

The FPI encourage Indonesian Muslims to conceive of their economic and social problems as created by elites and others who either oppose Islam or obstruct the development of an Islamic society. Islam is presented as the solution to these problems, and Islamic society is portrayed as a utopian heartland 'the people' must struggle to create. This narrative is perhaps designed to hijack the pain and shame ordinary Indonesian Muslims experience—a result of their nation's relatively poor governance—and turn it into feelings of anger and rage toward 'elites' and 'others'. At the same time, the FPI attempt to convince supporters that their group will lead Indonesians into a happier future when Sharia law is implemented and immoral people vanquished. Equally, the FPI tries to evoke in supporters a desire for 'struggle' or *jihad*. This desire for struggle is not synonymous with a desire for a political victory; rather, the struggle itself is the goal, and valorized as such. Death is a kind of victory for Muslims, then, because dying in a struggle to create an Islamic paradise on Earth is rewarded by Allah with gifts in heaven.

Rizieq is motivated by his hatred of Western culture and the decadence he believes it has brought to Indonesian society. He thus teaches his followers to regard Western culture, liberalism, and secularism as antithetical to Islam, and part of an oppressive foreign force that prevents the establishment of an Islamic society in Indonesia. Indonesia's elites are portrayed by the FPI as part of the Westernizing forces obstructing Islam, and who must be struggled against in order to win, either through a moral revolution or through the act of dying for Allah. In encouraging this necropolitics, or politics of death, Rizieq attempts to elicit deep feelings of love for Islam and the *ummah* from among his supporters, and hope for a better world either in heaven or—for the people left behind—on this Earth. Portraying himself as a wise and holy leader of Muslims, Rizieq created a powerful populist narrative in which he and his followers were fighting a battle against evil in the name of the people. In this cosmic battle between good and evil, 'the people' are innocent and pure victims of the Western decadence and immorality which had flooded the country in the Reformasi period and beyond. Once this narrative was established, Rizieq had the rhetorical material he required to build a movement which could justify at times extreme violence against evildoers. This language was thus marked as an attempt to delegitimize Indonesia's governing elites and dehumanize the FPI's civilizational and religious enemies, legitimizing and justifying violence against them.

3.4 Discussion of Case Studies

The Islamic Defenders Front and the Justice and Development Party differ in terms of their overall structure and position within their respective societies, yet share a number of features consistent with politically successful civilizationalist populist movements. While the FPI are a banned welfarist-militia group, and the AKP the ruling party of a powerful Islamic nation, both have achieved political success in their respective environments. Equally, the FPI's embrace of *jihadism* makes them rogue extremists in Indonesia, whereas the AKP's pro-*jihad* rhetoric and glorification of death in the service of the state and God are part of mainstream Turkish politics. Moreover, both are illiberal movements which have played an important role in reducing pluralism and the social acceptance of religious differences within their respective nations. Most importantly—and like the other Islamist groups we have discussed in this chapter—the AKP and FPI merge populism and a religious worldview in which Islam is threatened by the Christian West and other non-Muslim civilizations. Rizieq, a preacher, uses religious references more often than Erdoğan. Equally, while the FPI and the AKP each have a transnational dimension, the AKP's transnational populism is neo-Ottomanist and pan-Islamist, and covers a wide range of nations with both soft power and hard power exchanges. The FPI have educational exchanges with Salafist global educational institutions, however, they are small in number, and only a small number of *jihadis* from the FPI's militia have joined outfits such as ISIS (see Table 3.1).

Despite these differences, FPI and AKP have shared important attributes. As is often the case in populist movements, the leaders of each group have a central role to play as both the symbolic head, but also as a semi-divine figure who enjoys a direct connection with 'the people', and who is the only person capable of 'saving' 'the people' from the crisis which threatens their existence. Both leaders connect themselves with religion in order to portray themselves as saviors. Rizieq is already connected with Islam and enjoys a degree of religious authority due to his position as a cleric. Erdoğan, however, sought a connection with Islam by holding the Quran during speeches, and beginning his speeches with holy verses to show his piety and obedience to God.

In the populist narratives of the FPI and the AKP, religion is used to classify groups and individuals including entire civilizations. As a result, both the FPI and AKP construe opposition between 'self' and the 'other' not in national terms, but in civilizational terms, and as a battle between the Islamic 'self' and the Western and/or Christian 'other'. As Islamists, the Rizieq and Erdoğan recognize only Sunni Muslims as belonging to 'the people'. Non-elite citizens of Turkey and Indonesia, respectively, are not automatically included within 'the people'. Rather, Sunni Muslims are told that they are victims of a corrupt and immoral elite too beholden

Table 3.1 Comparison of Islamist populist case studies

	Pro-Violent Narratives	Links or Overlaps with the Far Right	Transnational Dimension, Diasporas
AKP	-Glorification of *jihadism* through necropolitics, education, and media/social media -Their "otherization" dehumanizes opponents and legitimizes violent narratives e.g. GM becomes "FETO" and university protestors are turned into "terrorist" and "deviants" -Anti-Western remarks by Erdoğan are aggressive and informed by his populist civilizationalism -Reclaiming and re-conversion of what was "stolen" from the ummah such as the Hagia Sophia, re-converted in 2020	-Supports right-wing clerics in Turkey for favorable *fatwas* -Transactional populist civilizationalism with other populist Islamist leaders -Collusion with MHP, an ultra-right Islamist party	-Clear transnational dimensions with other countries under the banner of ummahism. Exporting Islamist populism to other 'brother' countries and creating joint projects of defense and soft power experimenting -With the help of Diyanet and its expansive network, the Turkish diaspora is exposed to the AKP's Islamist populism. The body justifies and supports the AKP through its instrumentalization of Islamic scripture (see Yilmaz, 2021a; Yilmaz and Albayrak, 2022)
FPI	-Vigilantism violence toward "dens of sin" -Possesses a militant wing involved in anti-Ahmadi and anti-Chinese rioting -Uses faith to overtly legitimize violence (jihad) against "the others"	-Connection with MUI -Instances of exporting jihadists to the Syrian front	-Other than educational exchanges at Salafi institutes in the Middle East, there is no evidence of transnational cooperation -Informally, exporting jihadists to hotbeds of Islamist groups in regions such as Syria

to non-Islamic and Western ideas, and that they must come together in order to overcome their enemies. Victimhood is thus key to the populist narratives of Rizieq and Erdoğan; both claim that 'the people' are threatened by non-Muslim or 'false' Muslim enemies, and that only by coming together as *ummah* and placing their faith in God and—most importantly—the leader, can 'the people' triumph over the threats to their existence. To bring 'the people' together the AKP attempts to create alliances with right-wing, socially conservative, and Islamist groups in

Turkey, both inside and outside parliament (Yilmaz and Albayrak, 2022), and also instrumentalizes state institutions to affirm its populist narrative. The FPI, while not a political party per se, has at times allied itself with populist political forces such as Presidential candidate Prabowo and the MUI during elections. The FPI, before its banning in 2020, was at times successful in organizing protests and making alliances with other Islamist groups in order to create a national platform for its populist outreach (see Table 3.1).

Nostalgia for a religion-dominated past is another key aspect of the populist narratives of Rizieq and Erdoğan in which religion and civilization play a key role. Rizieq harkens back to Islam's initial period in which, under the rule of Muhammad and his companions (the *salaf*), Islamic civilization reached its purest form and early zenith. Erdoğan, however, encourages followers to remember the Ottoman Empire at its height, when it was the seat of the Caliphate (and thus the leader of Islamic civilization) and controlled much of the Mediterranean region. For both Rizieq and Erdoğan, these earlier periods show how 'the people' have lost their greatness and yet may return to that greatness, should they follow the teachings of Islam as propounded by the FPI and the AKP. Nostalgia is deeply connected with hope—indeed if the past was great, why should not the future also be made great if the conditions which created the glorious past were re-created? Yet the populist narratives of Erdoğan and Rizieq do not promise only happiness for 'the people'; rather, they promise the glory of struggle (*jihad*) and even death in the name of God. Portraying themselves as pious men who do the will of God on Earth, and protectors of 'the people', Rizieq and Erdoğan have constructed a necropolitical narrative in which those who fight and die for their respective Islamist movements are glorified and sanctified as religious martyrs.

Both Rizieq and Erdoğan and their respective political movements use religion to create a narrative in which the *ummah*—not merely 'the people' in a national context, but the entire body of practicing Sunni Muslims worldwide—are fighting on the side of God in a cosmic battle against the forces of evil. Religion and the defense of Islam and its civilization are also used inside this narrative to legitimize violence. Rizieq's and Erdoğan's narratives propose that the world is host to a cosmic battle between good and evil, and that Islam and the *ummah* represent the good, and non-Muslims, especially the Christian West and Westernized Muslims represent evil. However, Rizieq's narrative is built around the concept of 'evil', and the Islamic requirement to combat it. Rizieq finds evil in secular life, particularly in the practices introduced to Indonesia by the West such as drinking alcohol, and the selling and buying of pornographic material. Violence, according to Rizieq, is at times permitted against those who perpetrate these evils in order to protect Islam and 'the people'. Erdoğan, as President of Turkey, has at his disposal the police and security forces of a powerful nation. Therefore, his legitimation of violence results in not street thuggery but rather the mass jailing of critics of the regime and foreign military intervention. Erdoğan justifies his repression against opposition forces and, in particular, Gulenists, but claiming they are enemies of the people who either oppose Islam or attempt to pervert it in some way. Religion, then, is invoked throughout Erdoğan's and Rizieq's respective narratives, and is used to divide society between 'us' and 'them', to portray 'us' as victims of 'them', and to justify violence and repression against 'them'. At the same time, religion is often used to define not merely individuals within Indonesia and Turkey, respectively, but to define entire societies and civilizations. Thus inside Rizieq's and Erdoğan's narratives Indonesia and Turkey, respectively, are not merely nations with particular cultures, but part of Islamic civilization. Non-Islamic values, particularly Western values, are thus framed as foreign and threatening systems of thought which oppress Muslims and prevent them from returning to the glorious past. Moreover, their narratives both urge 'the people' to struggle against their civilizational enemies, and to glorify those who martyr themselves in the name of God.

Islamist populists claim that their society suffers from a number of serious social and economic issues which together threaten the livelihoods, culture, and identity of 'the people'. Therefore, the elite class must, the populists argue, be removed from power and replaced with a new government which understands and follows the will of 'the people'. Second, Islamist populists claim that certain 'others'—people who belong to foreign religions and Muslims who do not practice their faith correctly or at all—are either working with or permitted by elites to injure the people. Therefore, they argue these 'others' must be removed from society, either through violence or by pushing them out of the public sphere altogether.

Both Erdoğan and Rizieq conform to this pattern. Erdoğan, for example, came to power having framed the economic, social, and governance problems plaguing Turkey as a crisis created by the nation's secular nationalist elite. He has sustained his power by claiming that Turkey's enemies are continually attacking the country, and that he is devoting his life to protecting the nation. During the first two terms of AKP government, Erdoğan sought to improve ties with the West, and especially with the European Union, which Turkey attempted to join. Having been rebuffed by the EU, and with Turkey suffering from economic problems, Erdoğan began to claim the *ummah* was being attacked by the West. Erdoğan's new narrative framed Turkey's problems as part of a clash between the West and Islam, and portrayed Turkey as at the vanguard of Islamic civilization and Erdoğan himself as a brave protector of Turkey and the wider transnational *ummah*. Erdoğans domestic enemies were therefore accused of being controlled by foreign powers, "dark forces" which sought to destroy Turkey and Islam. Erdoğan successfully used events such as the 2016 failed coup to evoke feelings of deep fear for Turkey's future in the public, as well as anger toward the Gulenists and secularists held responsible for the coup. Beyond this, Erdoğan began to portray Western celebrations adopted by some Turkish people as threats to Islam and Turkish culture because they belonged to a foreign civilization, and to claim that Islamic civilization was superior to Western civilization.

In Indonesia, Rizieq did not seek electoral success for the FPI, but rather attempted to Islamize Indonesian politics and society by pressuring Indonesia's government, its official religious body the MUI, and other civil society actors to take action against perceived un-Islamic actors. He encourages his supporters to view the world through the lens of a cosmic war between good and evil, and to perceive themselves as a pure and innocent people oppressed by 'evil'. Rizieq thus divides Indonesia into two core groups: 'us'—the good Sunni Muslims—and 'them'—non-Muslims, Shia, Ahmadiyya Muslims, liberals, secularists, and 'Westernized' Indonesians. Having categorized the latter as 'evil', Rizieq encourages his followers to perceive non-Sunni Muslims as a threatening presence in Indonesia, which requires removal. In this way, he seeks to legitimize violence against non-Sunni Muslims by framing it as necessary part of the battle between good and evil, and part of Muslims' religious duty to combat evil. Equally, he frames the Indonesian government as corrupt and incapable or unwilling to carry out its duty to combat evil and promote goodness. In this way, Rizieq attempts to evoke feelings of anger in his supporters toward the government as well as toward non-Sunni Muslims, and to legitimize and sanctify anti-government violence.

The Ahok affair, in which the FPI portrayed Ahok as a blasphemer and threat to Islam and Muslims, was successful in pressuring Indonesia's politicians and judiciary to charge and imprison him. Rizieq staged and spoke at large-scale rallies in which Ahok's comments on the political use of the Quran were framed as attacks on Islam and Indonesian Muslims. Rizieq called for the people to force the government and judiciary to take action against Ahok, who was portrayed by the FPI leader as a dangerous foreign element threatening the *ummah*. Evoking feelings of religious rage toward Ahok, Rizieq and his Islamist allies encouraged a mob mentality among their supporters which appears to have frightened Indonesian authorities into investigating and later charging and imprisoning Ahok.

Rizieq's rhetorical war on Ahok was an extension of his belief that 'evil' must be combated. Indeed, Rizieq does not conceive of his enemies as being merely wrong, but rather as evildoers, and encourages his followers to perceive themselves as good Muslims who—following the teachings of Islam—must fight evil and promote goodness. By doing this, Rizieq is able to evoke feelings of religious rage in his followers which he directs toward a specific target (Ahok, businesses selling alcohol, nightclubs), legitimizing violence against his chosen targets as necessary acts intended to combat evil and promote goodness. Rizieq also encourages his followers to feel anger toward the Indonesian government and its business elites, who he claims are responsible for the evil gathering in Indonesia since the fall of Suharto. Elites, according to Rizieq, have permitted un-Islamic behavior to increase since 1998, and moreover have allowed Western values to spread across the archipelago.

The FPI do not encourage their followers to feel nostalgic for an earlier period of Indonesian history. Rather, they encourage FPI supporters to look to early Islam for inspiration, and to imitate the actions of Muhammad and his companions. However, like AKP leader Erdoğan, Rizieq encourages followers to believe that by fighting in the name of God they will either be part of the glorious triumph of Islam over 'evil', or die as a martyr and be sanctified and sent to heaven as a result. In making this claim, Rizieq and the FPI seek to elicit feelings of hope in followers that they will be victorious over their enemies in life or—if need be—in death. Both the AKP and FPI, then, promote a kind of necropolitics in which dying in the service of Islam is portrayed as the ultimate honor, and as something to be desired by the pious.

While Rizieq and the FPI succeeded in bringing about Ahok's downfall, their preferred candidate—General Prabowo Subianto—in the subsequent Indonesian Presidential election did not fare well. Having said that, there is little doubt that Rizieq and other Islamists have had a profound impact on Indonesian politics and society in the country's democratic era, and that the rise of Islamism has had a deleterious effect on pluralism in Indonesia. The banning of the FPI in 2020, while significant, came only after the group had won its most significant battles, and had played a significant role in destroying the career of the most prominent non-Muslim politician in Indonesia (Table 3.2).

Table 3.2 Narratives of AKP and FPI

	Identity narrative	Crisis narrative	Civilization narrative	Victimhood narrative
AKP	"The people": Sunni Muslims and ethnic Turks "The others": non-Muslims, non-Turks, "dark forces" outside and inside the country, human rights activists, academics, journalists, "FETO", and political opposition	An ontological crisis in which Muslim Turks are threatened from inside by "traitors" and by outside "dark forces" These threats range from geographical sovereignty to attacks on the moral (religious) fabric of society	A well-defined civilizationalism that goes beyond ethnicity and nationalism and takes a pan-Islamist form The AKP's neo-Ottomanism gives the party a transitional quality which is exported to other Muslim countries through economic, military, diplomatic, and cultural exchanges	Traumas—the result of the breakdown of the Ottoman Empire and its aftermath—are revived again and again, and given an Islamist coloring, where any non-Sunni Turk is an "other" harming "the people" In a populist transactional manner, the ummah is the victim of the West and non-Muslims that destroyed and later colonized the Ottoman Empire militarily, economically, and culturally

(continued)

Table 3.2 (continued)

	Identity narrative	Crisis narrative	Civilization narrative	Victimhood narrative
FPI	'The people': The oppressed poor who are ignored by government policies of development and growth. Sunni Muslims 'The others': The 'elite', politicians who are considered too liberal or friendly to non-Muslim countries such as China, or to the West. All non-Muslims in the country, especially Chinese	Moral breakdown of society, a falling away from Islam Political breakdown The lack of Sharia-based laws and inclusion of non-Muslims is an issue central to the FPI	Mostly limited to Indonesia. It features 'the people' who are Muslims are opposed to the Chinese or Westerns who are non-Muslim, and Christians FPI has ties beyond Indonesia's borders in terms of jihadist exporting, and sending students to the Saudi Arabia for further studies	A combination of economic, political, and social injustice felt by 'the people', who are oppressed by secularists, non-Muslims, and liberal Muslims

Winning elections is not the only kind of success possible for a political movement. Merely influencing political events or changing social attitudes in a particular manner may also be considered forms of political success. In this respect, the FPI is a successful populist group, insofar as it achieved at least two of its political aims, removing Ahok from Indonesia's political scene, and having him charged and later imprisoned for blasphemy. Equally, the FPI's activism has forced Indonesia's mainstream parties and leaders to adopt at least the Islamist rhetoric—if not the political substance—of the FPI. In this way, the FPI has helped to Islamize Indonesian politics, and push the country away from its non-sectarian constitution and instead a narrow Indonesian identity based on religious affiliation and practice.

The primary consequence of the rise of the AKP in Turkey has been the death of Turkish democracy, and the creation of an authoritarian populist regime in its place, a regime which has destroyed pluralism, and replaced it with a monolithic idea of the ideal citizen: a Sunni Muslim Turk loyal to the Erdoğan regime, and who perceives Turkey to be the defender of Muslims the world over. Islamist populists have achieved little electoral success in Indonesia. However, the chapter shows how the FPI and its leader Rizieq have impacted Indonesia. Although FPI are now banned, in their lifetime the group contributed to the worsening of community relations between the majority and minority groups, and pushed Indonesia in an overall conservative direction in which tolerance of minority religious practices was diminished.

Throughout the democratic Muslim majority world, Islamist and Islamic populism has found an increasing amount of support over the past two decades. Islamist populists have enjoyed electoral victories in Pakistan, Iran, Turkey, and Tunisia. At the same time, Islamist populist groups have succeeded in affecting social and political change in Indonesia, using their power to pressure governments into de-secularizing their societies and attacking pluralism.

References

Adiwilaga, Rendy, Mustabsyirotul Ummah Mustofa, and Muhammad Ridha Taufik Rahman. 2019. "Quo Vadis Islamic Populism? An Electoral Strategy". *Central European Journal of International and Security Studies* 13: 432–53. https://cejiss.org/quo-vadis-islamic-populism-an-electoral-strategy. Last accessed September 21, 2022.

Afzal, Madiha. 15 January 2021. "Terrorism in Pakistan has Declined, but the Underlying Roots of Extremism Remain". *Brookings*. https://www.brookings.edu/blog/order-from-chaos/2021/01/15/terrorism-in-pakistan-has-declined-but-the-underlying-roots-of-extremism-remain/. Last accessed September 21, 2022.

Afzal, Madiha. 14 October 2019. "Imran Khan's Incomplete Narrative on the Taliban". *Brookings*.https://www.brookings.edu/blog/order-from-chaos/2019/10/14/imran-khans-incomplete-taliban-narrative/. Last accessed September 21, 2022.

Ahmad, Ishtaq. 2010. "The Pakistan Islamic State Project: A Secular Critique". In *State and Secularism*: Perspectives from Asia. Edited by Michael Siam-Heng Heng and Chin Liew Ten. Singapore: World Scientific. https://doi.org/10.1142/9789814282383_0012.

Algar, H. 1980. *Constitution of the Islamic Republic of Iran*. Berkeley: Mizan.

Aljazeera. 2021. "Indonesia: Rizieq Shihab Jailed for Concealing COVID Test Result." *Aljazeera*. Available online https://www.aljazeera.com/news/2021/6/24/indonesia-rizieq-shihab-jailed-for-concealing-covid-test-result. Last accessed December 29, 2022.

Amnesty International. 2021. "IRAN 2020". https://www.amnesty.org/en/countries/middle-east-and-north-africa/iran/report-iran/. Last accessed September 21, 2022.

Arifianto, R. Alexander. 25 April 2019a. "Is Islam an Increasingly Polarizing Political in Indonesia?" *Brookings*. https://www.brookings.edu/blog/order-from-chaos/2019a/04/25/is-islam-an-increasingly-polarizing-political-cleavage-in-indonesia/. Last accessed September 21, 2022.

Arifianto, Alexander R. 2019b. What the 2019 Election Says about Indonesian Democracy. *Asia Policy* 26 no. 4: 46–53. https://doi.org/10.1353/asp.2019.0045.

Arrahmah. 15 July 2019. "10 Pearls Of Habib Rizieq's Struggle". https://www.arrahmah.id/10-mutiara-perjuangan-habib-rizieq/. Last accessed September 21, 2022.

Aspinall, Edward, and Marcus Mietzner. 2019. Southeast Asia's Troubling Elections: Nondemocratic Pluralism in Indonesia. *Journal of Democracy* 30, no. 4: 104–118. https://doi.org/10.1353/jod.2019.0055.

Avundukluoglu, Emin. 14 July 2021. "Turkey vows to continue fighting FETO terrorism with determination". *AA*. https://www.aa.com.tr/en/turkey/turkey-vows-to-continue-fighting-feto-terrorism-with-determination/2304253. Last accessed September 21, 2022.

Aydın, Cemil. 2006. "Beyond Civilization: Pan-Islamism, Pan-Asianism and the Revolt against the West." *Journal of Modern European History / Zeitschrift Für Moderne Europäische Geschichte / Revue D'histoire Européenne Contemporaine* 4, no. 2, 204–223. www.jstor.org/stable/26265834.

Azharghany, Rojabi, Siahaan, Hotman and Muzakki, Akh. 2020. "Alliance of Ummah in Rural Areas: A New Perspective on Islamic Populism in Indonesia". *Religious: Jurnal Studi Agama-Agama dan Lintas Budaya* 4, no. 4, 239–250. DOI : https://doi.org/10.15575/rjsalb.v4i4.10476.

Bamualim, Chaider S. 2011. Islamic Militancy and Resentment against Hadhramis in Post-Suharto Indonesia: A Case Study of Habib Rizieq Syihab and His Islamic Defenders Front. *Comparative Studies of South Asia Africa and the Middle East* 31, no. 2: 267–281. https://doi.org/10.1215/1089201X-1264226.

Baloch, Shah Meer and Musyani, Zafar. 16 November 2018. "Pakistan's Dark History of Student Extremists". *The Diplomat*. https://thediplomat.com/2018/11/pakistans-dark-history-of-student-extremists/. Last accessed September 21, 2022.

Bali, Rıfat N. 2003a. *Cumhuriyet Yıllarında Türkiye Yahudileri: Bir Türkleştirme Serüveni (1923–1945)*. İstanbul: İletişim Yayınları.

Bali, Rıfat N. 2003b. *Aliya: Bir Toplu Göçün Öyküsü*. İstanbul: İletişim Yayınları.

Barton, Greg. 2005. *Jemaah Islamiyah: Radical Islamism in Indonesia*. Singapore: Singapore University Press.

Barton, Greg. 2009. "The Historical Development of Jihadi Islamist Thought in Indonesia". In *Radical Islamic Ideology in Southeast Asia*. Edited by Scott Helfstein. New York: The Combating Terrorism Center atWest Point. https://www.hsdl.org/?view&did=718972.

Barton, Greg. 2010. *Indonesia*. In *Guide to Islamist Movements*. Edited by Barry Rubin. New York: M.E. Sharpe, Inc.

Barton, Greg. 2015. "Islamic State, Radicalisation and the Recruitment of Foreign Fighters in Australia: Making hijrah from Lucky Country to God's Nation". In *Panorama—From Desert to World Cities—The New Terrorism*. Singapore: Konrad Adenaeur Stiftung. https://www.kas.de/en/web/politi kdialog-asien/panorama/detail/-/content/from-the-desert-to-worldcities-the-new-terrorism. Last accessed September 21, 2022.

Barton, Greg. 2020a. "The Historical Context and Regional Social Network Dynamics of Radicalisation and Recruitment of Islamic State Foreign Terrorist Fighters in Indonesia and Its Southeast Asian Neighbours". In *United by Violence, Divided by Cause: A Comparison of Drivers of Radicalisation and Violence in Asia and Europe*. Edited by La Toya Waha. Baden-Baden: Nomos/KAS, pp. 117–140. https://www.nomos-elibrary.de/10.5771/978 3748905738.pdf.. Last accessed September 21, 2022.

Barton, Greg. 2020b. "Salafist-jihadism in Southeast Asia." In *Counterterrorism Yearbook 2020b*. Edited by Issac Kfir and John Coyne.Canberra: Australian Strategic Policy Institute, chp. 8. pp. 43–51. https://www.aspi.org.au/rep ort/counterterrorism-yearbook-2020b. Last accessed September 21, 2022.

Barton, Greg, Ihsan Yilmaz, and Nicholas Morieson. 2021. Religious and Pro-Violence Populism in Indonesia: The Rise and Fall of a Far-Right Islamist Civilisationist Movement. *Religions* 12: 397. https://doi.org/10.3390/rel 12060397.

Barton, Greg. 2021. "Contesting Indonesia's Democratic Transition: Laskar Jihad, the Islamic Defenders Front (FPI) and Civil Society". In *Security, Democracy, and Society in Bali*. Edited by Andrew Vandenberg and Nazrina Zuryani. Singapore: Palgrave Macmillan, Chapter. 13. pp. 305–31. https://www.springerprofessional.de/en/contesting-indonesia-s-democr atic-transitionlaskar-jihad-the-is/18440394.

Barton, Greg, Ihsan Yilmaz, and Nicholas Morieson. 2021a. "Authoritarianism, Democracy, Islamic Movements and Contestations of Islamic Religious Ideas in Indonesia" Religions 12, no. 8: 641. https://doi.org/10.3390/rel120 80641

BBC. 28 July 2010. "Najib Razak: Malaysian ex-PM gets 12-year jail term in 1MDB corruption trial". https://www.bbc.com/news/world-asia-53563065. Last accessed September 21, 2022.

BBC. 7 April 2021. "Imran Khan Criticised for Rape 'Victim Blaming'". https://www.bbc.com/news/world-asia-56660706. Last accessed September 21, 2022.

Brubaker, Rogers. 2017. Between Nationalism and Civilizationism: The European Populist Moment in Comparative Perspective. *Ethnic and Racial Studies* 40, no. 8: 1191–1226. https://doi.org/10.1080/01419870.2017.1294700.

Brumberg, Daniel. 28 January 2021. "As 2021 Begins, Rival Populisms Menace Tunisia's Democracy". *Arab Center Washington DC*. http://arabcenterdc.org/policy_analyses/as-2021-begins-rival-populisms-menace-tunisias-democracy/. Last accessed September 21, 2022.

Bukhari, Gul. 2018. "Imran Khan Wants to Create a Medina-Like Pakistan but He Is No Sentinel of Human Rights". *In Print*. https://theprint.in/opinion/imran-khan-wants-to-create-a-medina-like-pakistan-but-he-is-no-sentinel-of-human-rights/104903/. Last accessed September 21, 2022.

Campbell, Charlie. 2017. "ISIS Unveiled: The Story Behind Indonesia's First Female Suicide Bomber". *Time*. https://time.com/4689714/indonesia-isis-terrorism-jihad-extremism-dian-yulia-novi-fpi/. Last accessed September 21, 2022.

Casanova, José. 1994. *Public Religions in the Modern World*. Chicago: University of Chicago.

Cikimm. (last updated 2018). https://www.cikimm.com/2018/09/kata-kata-habib-rizieq-tentang-cinta.html. Last accessed September 21, 2022.

Cook, Michael. 2000. *Commanding Right and Forbidding Wrong in Islamic Thought*. Cambridge: Cambridge University Press.

CNN. 2018. "Support Prabowo, Rizieq Shihab Throws the Issue of the Unitary Republic of Indonesia". *CNN Indonesia*. https://www.cnnindonesia.com/nasional/20180917142559-32-330808/dukung-prabowo-rizieq-shihab-lempar-isunkri-bersyariah. Last accessed September 21, 2022.

Crabbs, Jack. 1975. "Politics, History, and Culture in Nasser's Egypt". *International Journal of Middle East Studies* 6: 86–420. http://www.jstor.org/stable/162751.

Crisis Group, 2013. "Tunisia: Violence and the Salafi Challenge: Middle East and North Africa Report" No. 13713. https://www.crisisgroup.org/middle-east-north-africa/north-africa/tunisia/tunisia-violence-and-salafi-challenge. Last accessed September 21, 2022.

Cumhuriyet. 17 February 2015. "Erdoğan: Bu feministler falan var ya...." *Cumhuriyet*. https://www.cumhuriyet.com.tr/haber/erdogan-bu-feministler-falan-var-ya-216282. Last accessed December 29, 2022.

Daily Sabah. 28 November 2019. "President Erdoğan decries divide in the Muslim world." *Daily Sabah.* https://www.dailysabah.com/politics/2019/11/28/president-erdogan-decries-divide-in-the-muslim-world. Last accessed December 29, 2022.

Dawn. 17 November 2016. "'Feto a threat to Pakistan's security': Turkey's Erdoğan rails against 'coup plotter' Gulen in Islamabad". https://www.dawn.com/news/1296907. (Last accessed September 21, 2022).

Dawn. 18 December 2019. "Muslim leaders gather in Malaysia for summit shunned by Saudi". https://www.dawn.com/news/1522976. Last accessed September 21, 2022.

Dawn. 14 July 2021. "Twitter sees jump in govt demands to remove content of journalists, news outlets". https://www.dawn.com/news/1635058/twitter-sees-jump-in-govt-demands-to-remove-content-of-journalists-news-outlets. Last accessed September 21, 2022.

Dawn. 16 April 2021. "Ban is no answer". https://www.dawn.com/news/1618522/ban-is-no-answer. Last accessed September 21, 2022.

Dogru, Ahmet. 22 December 2020. "Iran". *European Centre for Populism Studies.* https://www.populismstudies.org/tag/iran/. Last accessed September 21, 2022.

Dorraj, M. and Dodson, M. 2009. "Neo-Populism in Comparative Perspectives: Iran and Venezuela". *Comparative Studies of South Asia, Africa and the Middle East* 29, no. doi https://doi.org/10.1215/1089201x-2008-049

Dorraj, Manochehr. 2014. Iranian populism: Its vicissitudes and political impact. In *The Many Faces of Populism: Current Perspectives*, ed. Dwayne Woods and Barbara Wejnert, 127–142. Emerald Books: Bingley.

Duz, N. Zehra, and Merve Berker. 2021. "FETO threatens national security of Turkey, Kyrgyzstan: Turkish leader". *AA.* https://www.aa.com.tr/en/turkey/feto-threatens-national-security-of-turkey-kyrgyzstan-turkish-leader/2268749. Last accessed September 21, 2022.

ECPS. 11 October 2020. "Malaysia". https://www.populismstudies.org/tag/malaysia/. Last accessed September 21, 2022.

Ehsani, Kaveh. 2006. "Iran: The Populist Threat to Democracy". *MERIP*, 241. https://merip.org/2006/12/iran-the-populist-threat-to-democracy/. Last accessed September 21, 2022.

Erdbrink, Thomas. 18 May 2017. "Iran Has Its Own Hard-Line Populist, and He's on the Rise". *The New York Times.* https://www.nytimes.com/2017/05/18/world/middleeast/iran-ebrahim-raisi-president-election.html. Last accessed September 21, 2022.

Erdoğan, Recep Tayyip. 2017. "We should Set New Cultural Goals for Ourselves in Accordance with the 2023 Vision". *Presidency of the Turkish*

Republic. https://www.tccb.gov.tr/en/news/542/72201/we-should-set-new-cultural-goals-for-ourselves-in-accordance-with-the-2023-vision. Last accessed September 21, 2022.

Farmanfarmaian, Roxane. 10 May 2017. "Iran's presidential election puts populism to the test". *Al Jazeera*. https://www.aljazeera.com/opinions/2017/5/10/irans-presidential-election-puts-populism-to-the-test. Last accessed September 21, 2022.

Fossati, Diego, and Marcus Mietzner. 2019. Analyzing Indonesia's Populist Electorate. *Asian Survey* 59: 769–794. https://doi.org/10.1525/AS.2019.59.5.769.

Formichi, Chiara. 2010. "Pan-Islam and Religious Nationalism: The Case of Kartosuwiryo and Negara Islam Indonesia". *Indonesia*, no. 90, 125–146. www.jstor.org/stable/20798235.

FR24 News. 2020. "Rizieq Shihab, Back in Indonesia, Calls for 'Moral Revolution'". https://www.fr24news.com/a/2020/12/rizieq-shihab-back-inindonesia-calls-for-moral-revolution.html. Last accessed September 21, 2022.

Gardner, Frank. 7 November 2019. "Iran's network of influence in Mid-East 'growing'". *BCC*. https://www.bbc.com/news/world-middle-east-50324912. Last accessed September 21, 2022.

Gartenstein-Ross, Daveed, Bridget Moreng, and Kathleen Soucy. 2014. "Raising the Stakes: Ansar al-Sharia in Tunisia's Shift to Jihad." International Centre for Counter-Terrorism—The Hague. https://www.icct.nl/app/uploads/download/file/ICCT-Gartenstein-Ross-Moreng-Soucy-Raising-the-Stakes-ASTs-Shift-to-Jihad-Feb-2014.pdf. Last accessed September 21, 2022.

Ghiabi, M and Habibi, N. 2014. "Tumbling oil prices a challenge to Iranian economy as it tries to come in from the cold". *The Conversation*. https://theconversation.com/tumbling-oil-prices-a-challenge-to-iranian-economy-as-it-tries-to-come-in-from-the-cold-33518. Last accessed September 21, 2022.

Gotev, Georgi. 18 July 2016. "Erdoğan says coup was 'gift from God' to reshape country, punish enemies". *Euractiv*. https://www.euractiv.com/section/global-europe/news/Erdoğan-says-coup-was-gift-from-god-to-reshape-country-punish-enemies/. Last accessed September 21, 2022.

Grewal, Sharan. 16 September 2019. "Political outsiders sweep Tunisia's presidential elections". *Brookings*. https://www.brookings.edu/blog/order-from-chaos/2019/09/16/political-outsiders-sweep-tunisias-presidential-elections/. Last accessed September 21, 2022.

Guardian. 20 January 2011. "Islamic scholar attacks Pakistan's blasphemy laws". https://www.theguardian.com/world/2011/jan/20/islam-ghamidi-pakistan-blasphemy-laws. Last accessed September 21, 2022.

Hadiz, R. Vedi. 2014. "A New Islamic Populism and the Contradictions of Development". *Journal of Contemporary Asia* 44, no. 1, 125–143. https://doi.org/10.1080/00472336.2013.832790

Hadiz, Vedi R. 2016. *Islamic Populism in Indonesia and the Middle East*. Cambridge: Cambridge University Press.

Hadiz, Vedi R. 2018. Imagine All the People? Mobilising Islamic Populism for Right-Wing Politics in Indonesia. *Journal of Contemporary Asia* 48: 566–583. https://doi.org/10.1080/00472336.2018.1433225.

Hazır, Ümit Nazmi. 2022. Anti-Westernism in Turkey's Neo-Ottomanist Foreign Policy under Erdoğan. *Russia in Global Affairs* 20, no. 2: 164–183. https://doi.org/10.31278/1810-6374-2022-20-2-164-183.

Hoodboy, Pervaiz. 18 July 2020. "Education: PTI's plan exposed". *Dawn*. https://www.dawn.com/news/1569679. Last accessed September 21. 2022.

Hoodbhoy, Pervez. 19 December 2020. "Pakistan has damaged its universities beyond repair by rewarding professors with phoney achievements". *Scroll.In*. https://scroll.in/article/981252/pakistan-has-damaged-its-universities-beyond-repair-by-rewarding-professors-with-phoney-achievements. Last accessed September 21. 2022.

Hookway, James. 13 September 2017. "Curfews, Obligatory Prayers, Whippings: Hard-Line Islam Emerges in Indonesia." *The Wall Street Journal*. Available online https://www.wsj.com/articles/indonesia-once-a-model-of-moderate-islam-slides-toward-a-harder-line-1505311774. Last accessed December 29, 2022.

Hurriyet. 24 July 2020. "First Muslim prayers held in Hagia Sophia after 85 years." *Hurriyet*. https://www.hurriyetdailynews.com/first-friday-prayers-held-in-hagia-sophia-after-mosque-reconversion-156812. Last accessed December 29, 2022.

Hussin, Rais. 21 January 2018. "Unmasking the recalcitrant Hadi." MalaysiaKini. https://www.malaysiakini.com/news/409460. Last accessed September 21. 2022.

Idris, Iffat. 2018. "Youth Vulnerability to Violent Extremistgroups in the Indo-Pacific". *GSDRC*. https://gsdrc.org/wpcontent/uploads/2018/10/1438-Youth-Vulnerability-to-Violent-Extremist-Groups-in-the-Indo-Pacific.pdf. Last accessed September 21. 2022.

İnce, Başak. 2012a. *Citizenship and identity in Turkey: From Atatürk's Republic to the Present Day*. London and New York: I.B. Tauris.

Jalal, Ayesha. 2011. *The Sole Spokesman Jinnah, the Muslim League and the Demand for Pakistan*. Columbia University, New York: Cambridge University Press.

Jalili, Saeed. 6 March 2018. "Iran's Ahmadinejad: From populist president to oppositionist". *Al Jazeera*. https://www.aljazeera.com/features/2018/3/6/irans-ahmadinejad-from-populist-president-to-oppositionist. Last accessed September 21. 2022.

Janjua, Haroom. 15 April 2021. "Pakistan protests: Why the Islamist TLP party is now a major political force". *DW*. https://www.dw.com/en/pakistan-protests-why-the-islamist-tlp-party-is-now-a-major-political-force/a-57214719. Last accessed September 21. 2022.

Jati, R. Wasisto. 2013. "Radicalism in the Perspective of Islamic-Populism: Trajectory of Political Islam in Indonesia". *Journal of Indonesian Islam* 7, no. 2. DOI: https://doi.org/10.15642/JIIS.2013.7.2.268-287.

Jahroni, Jajang. 2004. "Depending the Majesty of Islam: Indonesia's Front Pembela Islam (FPI) 1998–2003". *Studia Islamika* 11.

Johnson, P. 1972. "Egypt Under Nasser". *MERIP Reports*, no.10, 3–14. https://doi.org/10.2307/3011223

Juoro, Umar. 29 November 2019. The Rise of Populist Islam in Indonesia. *Turkish Policy Quarterly* 18: 27–33.

Karmini, Niniek. 2020. "Firebrand Indonesian Cleric returns from 3 year Saudi exile". *AP*. https://apnews.com/article/international-news-virus-outbreak-saudi-arabia-jakarta-indonesia-7caf5b3b8beaaa8a798c877c7587fb54. Last accessed September 21. 2022.

Kelemen, Barbara. 2021. "COVID-19 Fuels the Return of Islamism in Indonesia." *MEI@75*. Available online https://www.mei.edu/publications/covid-19-fuels-return-islamism-indonesia. Last accessed December 29, 2022.

Kennedy, S. Edward. 18 January 2019. "Presidential Debate: How Can Prabowo Call Terrorists Sent by Foreign Countries?" *Trito*. https://tirto.id/debat-capres-kok-bisa-prabowo-sebut-teroris-dikirim-negara-asing-deEH. Last accessed September 21. 2022.

Khalid, Muhammed Abdul, and Yang, Li. 2019. "Income Inequality and Ethnic Cleavages in Malaysia Evidence from Distributional National Accounts (1984–2014)". *WID.world WORKING PAPER N° 2019/09*. https://wid.world/document/9231/. Last accessed September 21. 2022.

Korkmaz, Özgür. 31 December 2014. "Happy 'illicit' New Year." *Hurriyet*. https://www.hurriyetdailynews.com/opinion/ozgur-korkmaz/happy-illicit-new-year-76336.

Lahouari, Addi, and Anthony Roberts. 2017. *Radical Arab Nationalism and Political Islam*. Washington, DC: Georgetown University Press. http://www.jstor.org/stable/j.ctt1rfzxkc.

Lazreg, B. Houssem. 2021. Post-Islamism in Tunisia and Egypt: Contradictory Trajectories. *Religions*. 12: 408. https://doi.org/10.3390/rel12060408.

Lee, Dwight E. 1942. "The Origins of Pan-Islamism." *The American Historical Review* 47, no. 2, 278–287. www.jstor.org/stable/1841668.

Lipka, Michael. 9 August 2017. "Muslims and Islam: Key findings in the U.S. and around the world". *Pew Research Centre.* https://www.pewresearch.org/fact-tank/2017/08/09/muslims-and-islam-key-findings-in-the-u-s-and-around-the-world/. Last accessed September 21. 2022.

Lodhi, Maleeha. 2012. *Pakistan Beyond the Crisis State.* Karachi: Columbia University Press.

Louden, Sarah, R. 2015. "Political Islamism in Tunisia: A History of Repression and a Complex Forum for Potential Change". *Journal of Islamic and Middle Eastern Multidisciplinary Studies* 4, no. 1. https://doi.org/10.17077/2168-538X.1060.

Maloney, Suzanne. 2015. "Populism, Version 2.0: The Ahmadinejad Era, 2005–2013". In *Iran's Political Economy since the Revolution*, 315–367. Cambridge: Cambridge University Press. https://doi.org/10.1017/CBO9781139023276.007.

Maulia, Erwida. 2020. "Indonesian Firebrand Cleric Habib Rizieq Faces Arrest in Jakarta". *Nikkei Asia.* https://asia.nikkei.com/Spotlight/Islam-in-Asia/Indonesian-firebrand-cleric-Habib-Rizieq-faces-arrest-in-Jakarta. Last accessed September 21. 2022.

Motamedi, Maziar. 2021. "Who is Ebrahim Raisi, Iran's next president?" *Aljazeera.* https://www.aljazeera.com/news/2021/6/19/who-is-ebrahim-raisi-irans-next-president. Last accessed September 21. 2022.

MEI@75. 2021. Jihadi Recruitment and Return: Asian Threat and Response. https://www.mei.edu/publications/jihadi-recruitment-and-return-asian-threat-and-response. Last accessed September 21. 2022.

Mietzner, Marcus. 2018. "Fighting Illiberalism with Illiberalism: Islamist Populism and Democratic Deconsolidation in Indonesia". *Pacific Affairs* 91: 261–82. https://paca2018.sites.olt.ubc.ca/files/2019/04/pdfHollandshortlist2018Meitzner.pdf. Last accessed September 21, 2022.

Middle East Institute. 20 April 2020 "Understanding Iranian Foreign Policy". https://www.mei.edu/publications/understanding-iranian-foreign-policy. Last accessed September 21. 2022.

Mohamad Shukri, S.F., and A. Smajljaj. 2020. Populism and Muslim democracies. *Asian Politics & Policy* 12: 575–591. https://doi.org/10.1111/aspp.12553.

Moghadam, V. 1994. "Islamic Populism, Class, and Gender in Post- revolutionary Iran." In: A Century of Revolution: Social Movements in Iran. Ed. John Foran. Minneapolis: University of Minnesota Press.

Noueihed, Lin and Warren, Alex. 2013. *The Battle for the Arab Spring: Revolution, Counterrevolution 6 and the Making of a New Era.* New Haven: Yale UP.

Nuryanti, Sri. 2021. Populism in Indonesia: Learning from the 212 Movement in Response to the Blasphemy Case against Ahok in Jakarta. In *Populism in*

Asian Democracies. Edited by Sook Jong Lee, Chin-en Wu and Kaustuv Kanti Bandyopadhyay. Boston: Brill.

Parlamento Haber. 18 September 2017. "Yeni diyanet isleri baskani ilk mesajinda laikligi hedef aldi." *Parlamento Haber*. https://www.parlament ohaber.com/yeni-diyanet-isleri-baskani-ilk-mesajinda-laikligi-hedef-aldi/. Last accessed December 29, 2022.

Pernau-Reifeld, Margrit. 1999. "Reaping the Whirlwind: Nizam and the Khilafat Movement". *Economic and Political Weekly* 34, 2745–51. http://www.jstor.org/stable/4408427.

Peterson, Daniel. 2020. *Islam, Blasphemy, and Human Rights in Indonesia: The Trial of Ahok*. London: Routledge.

Pinterest. Last updated 2021. "Habib Muhammad Rizieq Syihab". https://id.pinterest.com/aqielabdurrani/habib-muhammad-rizieq-syihab/. Last accessed September 21, 2022.

Povera, Adib. 19 December 2019. "Erdoğan calls on Muslim nations to strategise policies". *Stratis Times*. https://www.nst.com.my/news/nation/2019/12/549266/Erdoğan-calls-muslim-nations-strategise-policies. Last accessed September 21, 2022.

Presidency of the Republic of Türkiye. 2017. "Every Civilization Produces its own Technology and Every Technology its own Culture and Value." *Presidency of the Republic of Türkiye*. https://www.tccb.gov.tr/en/news/542/70882/her-medeniyet-kendi-teknolojisini-her-teknoloji-kendi-kultur-ve-degerini-uretir. Last accessed December 29, 2022.

Repucci, Sarah and Slipowitz, Amy. 3 Mach 2021. "Democracy under Siege". Freedom House. https://freedomhouse.org/report/freedom-world/2021/democracy-under-siege. (Last accessed September 21, 2022).

RT. 11 November 2017. "Erdogan rejects 'moderate Islam' as a Western tool to weaken Muslims." *Russia Today*. https://www.rt.com/news/409532-erdogan-rejects-moderate-islam/. Last accessed December 29, 2022.

Sabat, A., M. Shoaib, and A. Qadar. 2020. Religious populism in Pakistani Punjab: How Khadim Rizvi's Tehreek-e-Labbaik Pakistan emerged. *International Area Studies Review* 23 (4): 365–381. https://doi.org/10.1177/2233865920968657.

Sejati, Mukmin. 19 November 2014. *FPI*. https://web.archive.org/web/20150206121208/http://fpi.or.id/157-Mukmin-Sejati.html. Last accessed September 21, 2022.

Setijadi, Charlotte. 2017. "Ahok's Downfall and the Rise of Islamist Populism in Indonesia." *ISEAS* no.38. https://www.iseas.edu.sg/images/pdf/ISEAS_Perspective_2017_38.pdf. Last accessed September 21, 2022.

Shakil, Kainat, and Ihsan Yilmaz. 2021. "Religion and Populism in the Global South: Islamist Civilisationism of Pakistan's Imran Khan." *Religions* 12, no. 9: 777. https://doi.org/10.3390/rel12090777.

Singh, Amarjit. 23 October 2020. "Pakistan Fighting War in India's Hinterland Without Weapons. That's sixth-Generation Warfare". *The Print*. https://theprint.in/opinion/pakistan-fighting-war-in-indias-hinterland-without-weapons-sixth-generation-warfare/529243/ Last accessed September 21, 2022.

Taggart, Paul. 2004. Populism and Representative Politics in Contemporary Europe. *Journal of Political Ideologies* 9: 269–288.

Taş, Hakkı. 2022. The Chronopolitics of National Populism. *Identities* 29, no. 2: 127–145. https://doi.org/10.1080/1070289X.2020.1735160.

Tharoor, Ishaan. 31 May 2016. Muslim Families Should not use Birth Control, says Turkey's Erdogan. *The Washington Post*. https://www.washingtonpost.com/news/worldviews/wp/2016/05/31/muslim-families-should-not-use-birth-control-says-turkeys-erdogan/. Last accessed December 29, 2022.

The News. 14 February 2020. "Watchdog Slams PTI Government on New Social Media Measures". https://www.thenews.com.pk/latest/613904-watchdog-slams-pti-government-on-new-social-media-measures. Last accessed September 21, 2022.

Trivedi, Raj Kumar. 1981. "Mustafa Kemal and the Indian Khilafat Movement (to 1924)". *Proceedings of the Indian History Congress* 42: 458–67. http://www.jstor.org/stable/44141163.

Tugal, Cihan. 2002. "Islamism in Turkey: Beyond Instrument and Meaning". *Economy and Society* 31: 85–111. https://sociology.berkeley.edu/sites/default/files/faculty/tugal/Islamism_in_Turkey.pdf. Last accessed September 21, 2022.

Turner, John. 2012. "Untangling Islamism from Jihadism: Opportunities for Islam and the West After the Arab Spring." *Arab Studies Quarterly* 34, no. 3, 173–90. https://www.jstor.org/stable/41858701.

Ummid.com News Network. 2018. "My inspirations are Prophet Muhammad, The City of Medina that He Founded: Imran Khan." https://ummid.com/news/2018/July/26.07.2018/imran-khan-in-first-speech-my-inspiration-is-prophetmuhammed-and-ideal-state-madinah-munawwera.html. Last accessed September 21, 2022.

Van Bruinessen, Martin. 2013. "Contemporary Developments in Indonesian Islam: Explaining the "Conservative Turn"". Singapore: ISEAS–Yusof Ishak Institute.

Widjaja, Henky. 11 August 2012. "Convenient thugs". https://www.insideindonesia.org/convenient-thugs-2. Last accessed September 21, 2022.

Widiyanto, Asfa. 2017. "Violence in Contemporary Indonesian Islamist Scholarship: Habib Rizieq Syihab and 'enjoining good and forbidding evil'". In Shadi H. (Ed.), *Islamic Peace Ethics: Legitimate and Illegitimate Violence in Contemporary Islamic Thought* (pp. 87–112). Baden-Baden, Germany: Nomos. http://www.jstor.org/stable/j.ctv941t4z.8.

Wilson, Ian. 2015. *The Politics of Protection Rackets in Post-New Order Indonesia: Coercive Capital, Authorityand Street Politics*. London: Routledge.

Wirajuda, Tunggul. 2020. "Former Indonesian VP Denies Bringing FPI Head Back to Indonesia". *Kompas*. https://go.kompas.com/read/2020/12/09/032404574/former-indonesian-vp-denies-bringing-fpi-head-back-to-indonesia?page=all. Last accessed September 21, 2022.

Yabanci, Bilge, and Dane Taleski. 2018. Co-opting Religion: How Ruling Populists in Turkey and Macedonia Sacralise the Majority. *Religion State and Society* 46, no. 3: 283–304. https://doi.org/10.1080/09637494.2017.1411088.

Yegen, Mesut. 2004. "Citizenship and Ethnicity in Turkey". *Middle Eastern Studies* 40, no. 6, 51–66. https://www.jstor.org/stable/4289952.

Yıldız, Ahmet. 2001. *Ne Mutlu Türküm Diyebilene: Türk Ulusal Kimliˇginin Etno-Seküler Sınırları (1919–1938)*. Istanbul: İletişim Yayınları.

Yılmaz, Ihsan. 2005. "State, Law, Civil Society and Islam in Contemporary Turkey." *The Muslim World*, 95, no. 3: 385–411.

Yilmaz, Ihsan. 2009. Muslim Democrats in Turkey and Egypt: Participatory Politics as a Catalyst. *Insight Turkey* 11, no. 2: 93–112.

Yilmaz, Ihsan. 2014. Pakistan Federal Shariat Court's Collective Ijtihād on Gender Equality, Women's Rights and the Right to Family Life. *Islam and Christian-Muslim Relations* 25 (2): 181–192. https://doi.org/10.1080/09596410.2014.883200.

Yilmaz, Ihsan. 2018. "Populism, Erdoganism and Social Engineering Through Education in Turkey". *Mediterranean Quarterly* 29, no. 4, 52–76. https://ssrn.com/abstract=3252356.

Yilmaz, Ihsan. 9 October 2020a. "Egypt". *European Center for Populism Studies*. https://www.populismstudies.org/tag/egypt/. Last accessed September 21, 2022.

Yilmaz, Ihsan. 9 October 2020b. "Pakistan". *European Center for Populism Studies*. https://www.populismstudies.org/tag/pakistan/. Last accessed September 21, 2022.

Yilmaz, Ihsan. 21 October 2020c. "Indonesia". *European Center for Populism Studies*. https://www.populismstudies.org/tag/indonesia/. Last accessed September 21, 2022.

Yilmaz, Ihsan. 2021a. *Creating the Desired Citizen: Ideology, State and Islam in Turkey*. Cambridge and New York: Cambridge University Press.

Yilmaz, Ihsan. 2021b. 5 February 2021b. "The AKP's Authoritarian, Islamist Populism:Carving out a New Turkey". *European Center for Populism Studies*. https://www.populismstudies.org/the-akps-authoritarian-islamist-populism-carving-out-a-new-turkey/. Last accessed September 21, 2022.

Yilmaz, Ihsan. 2021c. 14 February 2021c. "Erdoğan's Political Journey: From Victimised Muslim Democrat to Authoritarian, Islamist Populist". *European Center for Populism Studies*. https://www.populismstudies.org/Erdoğans-political-journey-from-victimised-muslim-democrat-to-authoritarian-islamist-populist/. Last accessed September 21, 2022.

Yilmaz, Ihsan. 18 February 2021d. "Turkey". European Center for Populism Studies. https://www.populismstudies.org/tag/turkey/. Last accessed September 21, 2022.

Yilmaz, Ihsan, and Galib Bashirov. 2018. The AKP after 15 years: Emergence of Erdoğanism in Turkey. *Third World Quarterly* 39. https://doi.org/10.1080/01436597.2018.1447371.

Yılmaz, Ihsan, Greg Barton, and James Barry. 2017. "The Decline and Resurgence of Turkish Islamism: The Story of Tayyip Erdogan's AKP". *Citizenship and Globalisation Research Papers* 1, no. 1, 48–62. https://doi.org/10.21153/jcgs2017vol1no1art1061.

Yilmaz, I., and Greg Barton. 2021a. Political Mobilisation of Religious. *Chauvinist and Technocratic Populisms in Indonesia and Their Activities in Cyberspace, Religions* 12 (10): 822. https://doi.org/10.3390/rel12100822.

Yilmaz, Ihsan, and Greg Barton. 2021b. "Islamic Defenders Front: The Face of Indonesia's Far-Right Islamism". ECPS. https://www.populismstudies.org/the-islamic-defenders-front-the-face-of-indonesias-far-right-islamism/. Last accessed September 21, 2022.

Yilmaz, Ihsan, and Ismail Albayrak. 2022. Demonization and De-Humanisation of AKP's Opponents. In *Populist and Pro-Violence State Religion*. Palgrave Studies in Populisms. Singapore: Palgrave Macmillan. https://doi.org/10.1007/978-981-16-6707-7_7.

Yilmaz, Ihsan, and Morieson, Nicholas. 18 May 2021. "How Are Religious Emotions Instrumentalized in the Supply of and Demand for Populism?". *European Center for Populism Studies*. https://www.populismstudies.org/how-are-religious-emotions-instrumentalized-in-the-supply-of-and-demand-for-populism/. Last accessed September 21, 2022.

Yilmaz, Ihsan, and Morieson, Nicholas. 2022a. "Civilizational Populism: Definition, Literature, Theory, and Practice". *Religions*.

Yilmaz, Ihsan, Nicholas Morieson, and Mustafa Demir. 2021a. Exploring Religions in Relation to Populism: A Tour around the World. *Religions* 12: 301. https://doi.org/10.3390/rel12050301.

Yilmaz, Ihsan, and Omer F. Erturk. 2021. "Populism, Violence and Authoritarian Stability: Necropolitics in Turkey". *Third World Quarterly*.

Yilmaz, Ihsan, and Saleem, A. M. Raja. 2021b March 2021b. "A Quest for Identity: The Case of Religious Populism in Pakistan".*European Center for Populism Studies*. https://www.populismstudies.org/a-quest-for-identity-the-case-of-religious-populism-in-pakistan/. Last accessed September 21, 2022.

Yilmaz, Ihsan, and Saleem, Raja M. Ali. 2021. A Quest for Identity: The Case of Religious Populism in Pakistan. Populism & Politics. *European Center for Populism Studies (ECPS)*. https://doi.org/10.55271/pp0007.

Yilmaz, Ihsan, and Shakil, Kainat. 3 February 2021a. "Pakistan Tehreek-e-Insaf: Pakistan's Iconic Populist Movement". *European Center for Populism Studies*. https://www.populismstudies.org/pakistan-tehreek-e-insaf-pakistans-iconic-populist-movement/. Last accessed September 21, 2022.

Yilmaz, Ihsan, and Shakil, Kainat. 10 February 2021b. "Imran Khan: From Cricket Batsmanto Populist Captain Tabdeli of Pakistan". *European Center for Populism Studies*.https://www.populismstudies.org/imran-khan-from-cricket-batsman-to-populist-captain-tabdeli-of-pakistan/. Last accessed September 21, 2022.

Yilmaz, Ihsan and Shakil, Kainat. 15 April 2021c. "Transnational Islamist Populism Between Pakistan and Turkey: The Case of Dirilis—Ertugrul". *European Center for Populism Studies*. https://www.populismstudies.org/transnational-islamist-populism-between-pakistan-and-turkey-the-case-of-dirilis-ertugrul/. Last accessed September 21, 2022.

Yilmaz, Ihsan and Shakil, Kainat. 26 June 2021d. "The Silence of the Khans: The Pragmatism of Islamist Populist Imran Khan and his Mentor Erdoğan in Persecuting Muslim Minorities". *European Center for Populism Studies*. https://www.populismstudies.org/the-silence-of-the-khans-the-pragmatism-of-islamist-populist-imran-khan-and-his-mentor-Erdoğan-in-persecuting-muslim-minorities/. Last accessed September 21, 2022.

Zúquete, Jose Pedro. 2017. "Populism and Religion". In *The Oxford Handbook of Populism*. Edited by Cristóbal Rovira Kaltwasser, Paul Taggart, Paulina Ochoa Espejo and Pierre Ostiguy. Oxford: Oxford University Press.

CHAPTER 4

Christianity and Civilizational Populism

4.1 Introduction

Christianity is the most widespread faith across the world, with the highest number of adherents in the Americas, Europe, and Sub-Saharan Africa, although significant numbers of Christians also live in the Asia–Pacific region (Vaughan 2021; Kuzoian 2015). Far from monolithic, the Christian world is divided between several denominations, including Roman Catholicism, Protestantism, and the Eastern Orthodox Church (Vaughan 2021; Kuzoian 2015). This makes discussing the relationship between Christianity and politics somewhat complex; there are many forms of Christianity, and Christians themselves have differing opinions on the role religion ought to play in the public sphere. Indeed, the relationship between Christianity and the state has varied greatly over time throughout the Christian majority world (Asad 1993).

One difficulty Christians have faced when attempting to govern is the absence of a political doctrine in the Christian scriptures. The New Testament is not a guide to building a society. Largely confined during its first two centuries to lower-class Jewish and later non-Jewish Roman citizens, the early Christians could not conceive of a society ruled by Christians. Indeed, Jesus possessed no Earthly power, did not encourage their followers to seek political influence, and according to the Gospel of

© The Author(s), under exclusive license to Springer Nature Singapore Pte Ltd. 2023
I. Yilmaz and N. Morieson, *Religions and the Global Rise of Civilizational Populism*, Palgrave Studies in Populisms, https://doi.org/10.1007/978-981-19-9052-6_4

John claimed his kingdom was "not of this world". However, when Christianity spread throughout the Roman upper classes, eventually becoming the de facto state religion under Constantine the Great, there was a fusion of Christianity and the state which must have appeared unimaginable to the early Christians. After the fall of the Western Roman Empire Christianity and the Church remained a powerful politics force across Western Europe, while much of Eastern Europe and, before the rise of Islam, North Africa, remained under the rule of the Christian Byzantine Empire. The Church thus held a central position in the politics of early Christian empires such as the Byzantine, medieval Holy Roman Empire, and the Carolingian empire (Stefon et al. 2020). For example, traditionally the Papal States maintained a close relationship between the state and Church, where the political domain was seen as the 'kingdom of god' that ought to be run by divine decree, and where the Pope was God's representative.

The two great schisms in Christianity, the East–West schism of 1054 C.E. and the Protestant Reformation of the sixteenth century, ended the world of 'Christendom' and any genuine possibility of a significant portion of Europe becoming united in a single Christian superstate dominated by the Church. The Reformation, moreover, led to the rise of modern nation-states in Europe, the weakening of the political power of the Catholic Church in Rome, and the enlarging of secular spaces in European public life. Indeed, the rise of Protestantism appears to have played an important role in the privatization of faith, and to the growth of secularism which, over time, has played in increasingly important role in defining the boundaries of religion.

During the eighteenth century European Enlightenment intellectuals began to reject religious explanations for phenomena, and embrace non-theistic interpretations of reality. At the same time, the exploration and colonization of the Americas—and indeed the expansion of the Western world into Africa and parts of the Asia–Pacific—demonstrated to Europeans new manifestations of religion which did not conform to their understandings or expectations. This led to a larger questioning of faith, and a mental repositioning of Christianity as a 'religion'—one among many—rather than absolute truth. In a world where Christianity had been separated into different denominations, and where Europeans now ruled over non-Christians (often for the first time), it became imperative to accommodate people with varying and sometimes conflicting religious beliefs and practices. One solution to the problem of religious difference was to insist on a secular public sphere. (Goldberg 2021; Dreisbach

2002). Thomas Jefferson, a deist, argued in favor of such a model when he declared "I contemplate with sovereign reverence that act of the whole American people which declared that their legislature should 'make no law respecting an establishment of religion, or prohibiting the free exercise thereof,' thus building a wall of separation between Church and State" (Dreisbach 2002). Post-revolutionary France, in a more dramatic way, sought to end the power of the Roman Catholic Church in France by insisting on a new constitution based on the principles of *laïcité*. *Laïcité*, which remains a core part of the French constitution, was designed to subordinate religion under state authority and to secularize the public sphere.

While Christianity increased its adherents in Asia and Africa during the twentieth century, European states secularized throughout the same period, particularly after the Second World War. By the nineteenth century the axiomatic belief in the Christian God was beginning to break down. This caused much consternation among European intellectuals, who sometimes celebrated—as Nietzsche did—the 'death' of God, or bemoaned—as Arnold did in his poem 'Dover Beach'—the loss of moral and spiritual certainty that necessarily accompanied the vanishing of the "sea of faith'. By the mid-twentieth century it appeared that the process of modernization caused societies to secularize, and either conceive of religion as a form of 'belief' or embrace non-religion and at times outright atheism. However, as the twentieth century drew to a close, it was becoming clear that modernization need not always lead to a privatization of religion. Rather, outside of Europe and its settler societies, societies were modernizing yet maintaining a public role for religion.

There is, therefore, a special relationship between our concepts of 'religion' and 'secularism' and the development of Christianity in Europe. Moreover, the rise of secularism may not mark a simple 'break' from religion, as it has often seemed, but may be a continuation of certain Western European understandings of the boundary between religion and the secular. This is perhaps what José Casanova (2009, 1054) had in mind when he wrote that "the function of secularism as a philosophy of history, and thus as ideology, is to turn the particular Western Christian historical process of secularization into a universal teleological process of human development from belief to unbelief, from primitive irrational or metaphysical religion to modern rational postmetaphysical secular consciousness". Thus, Casanova writes (2009, 1054), "even when the particular role of internal Christian developments in the general process of secularization is acknowledged, it is in order to stress the universal significance of the uniqueness of Christianity as, in Marcel Gauchet's expressive formulation, 'the religion to exit from religion'".

This is an important point to bear in mind when considering the arguments made by European populists, who often stress the 'Europeanness' of secularism, and argue that only Christian societies can secularize, and that therefore non-Christians cannot be trusted to integrate into European cultures, but will always seek to religionize the secular European public sphere. Having said that, the 'secular' nature of European states, their settler societies, and especially the United States, is more ambiguous than it may first appear. While the constitutions of many Christian nations have been secularized, the role of Christianity in electoral politics has often remained present. Yet while Christianity has sometimes been secularized into 'culture' and 'heritage' in Europe, this is not always the case elsewhere in the Christian majority world (Yilmaz et al. 2021). While we find the secularization of Christianity into culture occurring in Australia, in the United States and across Africa and Latin America, Christianity remains a somewhat public religion, sometimes despite official secularism and separation of church and state.

4.2 Civilizational Populism in Christian Majority Nations

Across Europe and in the United States populists have achieved varying, but often significant, degrees of political success portraying themselves as defenders not merely of their nation, but of Judeo-Christian heritage, values, and civilization (Kaya 2021; Kaya and Tecman 2019; Haynes 2020; Marzouki et al. 2016a, b; Yilmaz and Morieson 2021; Morieson 2021; Yilmaz and Morieson 2022). The body of literature on European and North American 'Christian identity' populism is large and growing, and describes how right-wing populists incorporate a civilization-based classification of peoples into their populism in order to portray Muslims as 'evil' invaders threatening the 'good' and 'pure' people of Europe and their Christian or Judeo-Christian heritage, values, and culture (Brubaker 2017; Vollaard 2013; Marzouki and McDonnell 2016; Roy 2013, 2016a, b; Apahideanu 2014; van Kessel 2016; Brubaker 2017; Ozzano and Bolzonar 2020; Yilmaz and Morieson 2022). For example, sociologist Rogers Brubaker (2017, 1193) describes how a number of right-wing populist parties in North-West Europe have made a civilizational turn, and now perceive "opposition between self and other not in narrowly national but in broader civilizational terms". This civilizational turn, he writes, is the product of a reaction to mass immigration to Europe from people from Muslim majority nations, and the subsequent higher visibility of Muslims and Islam, and the fear it creates among many Europeans. The growth of Islam in Europe, which has admittedly occurred quickly and at the same time as a collapse in birth rates among ethnic Europeans, appears to create a sense of unease and fear that Muslims are inevitably going to become the majority populism in a large number of European nations, and in the process Islamize the continent. Right-wing populists in North-West Europe are especially disturbed by this because they perceive Islam and its civilizations to be inferior to the West and its Judeo-Christian values (Kluveld 2016). Growing fears of a Muslim takeover has led, according to Brubaker, to the merging of secularism and Christianity in the populist imagination: "Just as [Muslims'] religiosity emerges from the matrix of Islam", Brubaker argues, "so 'our' secularity emerges from the matrix of Christianity (or the 'Judeo-Christian tradition') (Brubaker 2016)". The civilizational turn in populism in North-West Europe is not a particularly religious phenomenon, at least when compared with the civilizational populism of much of the Muslim majority world, but incorporates a form of Christian identity politics. Indeed, according to Brubaker, despite populists' emphasis on defending the 'Judeo-Christian' or 'Christian' or at times "Judeo-Christian and Humanist' values from Islam, European right-wing civilizational populism remains a form of nationalism, rather than an anti-nationalist or even transnational ideology (Brubaker 2017). Thus, rather than perceiving in Christianity a system of ethics and form of religious practice, civilizational populists in North-West Europe instead use 'Christianity' or 'Judeo-Christianity' as "sacred code" words "to denote a secular, liberal order distinct from Islam, reflecting the culturalization of Christian religion in Europe" (Vollaard 2013, 94). The Dutch Party for Freedom (PVV) exemplifies the Christian-based civilizational populist trend in North-West Europe. PVV leader Geert Wilders describes Dutch culture as the product of the "Judeo-Christian and Humanist' civilization of the West, and Islam as a "totalitarian" political tradition wholly at odds with the liberal humanism of the Judeo-Christian West.

A similar example might be found in France, where the Marine Le Pen led National Rally party also draws on Christian identity to construct a 'people' based on shared Christian heritage (though not belief) and a Muslim 'other'. The French National Front, now known as *Rassemblement National* (National Rally), became increasingly successful after 2011 when it turned away from the conservative Catholicism of its founder Jean-Marie Le Pen, and toward Christian-based civilizationalism under the leadership of his daughter Marine Le Pen. The party had long had an association with Catholicism, and under Jean-Marie Le Pen's leadership frequently used Catholic imagery and promoted traditionalist Catholicism, even holding a traditional Latin Mass during a campaign event (Davies 2010, 577). Yet under Marine Le Pen's leadership the party secularized and moved toward the center of French politics, abandoning its previous anti-Semitism, and instead embracing Gaullism and *laïcité* (Roy 2016a). Marine Le Pen did not, however, entirely abandon her father's pro-Christian rhetoric and anti-establishment and anti-immigration politics. Instead, she began to identify French culture with both *laïcité* and Christianity, asserting that France was both a Christian nation, but also entirely secular (Roy 2016a; Morieson 2021). This allowed her to portray Muslims as doubly threatening; not merely did they threaten the practice of Christianity in France, but also the secular differentiation between religion and politics.

In Le Pen's rhetoric, 'elites' are immoral insofar as they have abandoned the Christian-based culture and identity that made French culture special, and she declares them to be unpatriotic "globalists" who have weakened French sovereignty and permitted the mass immigration of Muslims into France, Islamizing the country against the will of the people (Morieson 2021). Indeed, Le Pen's strongest criticisms are often not of Muslims and Islam, but rather of French elites who have introduced neoliberalism and the worship of money into the country, and in doing so have diluted French culture, making the Islamization of France all but inevitable (Morieson 2021). At the same time she claimed that Islam threatened France's Christian heritage and contemporary secular culture, declaring the religion could not be secularized (RFI 2011). She thus encouraged her supporters to fear Muslims, and to perceive Islam as a dangerous imported religion foreign to French civilization, and inherently hostile to its joint Christian and secular traditions. In making these arguments Le Pen portrays France as a nation experiencing a civilizational crisis, in which it is being invaded and Islamized by Muslim migrants, who are aided and abetted by greed-driven elite politicians who care little for the country. Le Pen portrays herself as a savior of the nation who will end the crisis and protect France's Christian and secular culture. In a nation badly shaken by multiple Islamist terror attacks and a growing Muslim population, Le Pen found it relatively easy to exploit the fears of a large minority of French people, many of whom appear to feel anxious about the demographic changes the nation is experiencing.

In 2017 the National Front broke into mainstream French politics. During campaigning, the party demanded that *laïcité* and women's rights be defended in the face of attacks by Islamic fundamentalists, and claimed that France's core values, 'Liberty, Equality, Fraternity', proceed "from a secularization of principles stemming from our Christian heritage" (Morieson 2021, 105). While she remains a deeply loathed figure on the French left, partly due to her association with her anti-Semitic and xenophobic father Jean-Marie Le Pen, Marine Le Pen won the second largest share of votes in the 2017 French Presidential elections, strongly suggesting that a large segment of the French public responds to her claims that she is 'saving' France from the deleterious effects of globalization including Islamization. The National Front's rhetoric is reminiscent of the Austrian Freedom Party, which has also used a civilizationalist discourse. Emphasizing the need to protect "cultural Christianity ...which is based on the separation of the church and the state" from Islam and Muslim immigrants to Austria, the party seeks to prevent the alleged imminent Islamization of Austria (Weidinger 2017, 58–59; Hadj-Abdou 2016, 37–38).

While Marine Le Pen is unlikely to become French president, the rise of Éric Zemmour in 2021–2022 suggests that Christian-based civilizationalism is likely to remain an important part of French politics into the future. In an interview with a Hungarian publication Zemmour describes his worldview, claiming that "French intellectual René Girard, writes in one of his last books, Achever Clausewitz, that today we are entering a spirit of the age where we are closer to Charles Martell and the Crusaders than to the French Revolution and the consequences of the Second Empire's industrialization. Today we are living through the same struggles between Islam and Christianity, East and West. This struggle never came to an end. One of the basic elements is demography" (Szocs 2021).

Brubaker and others have found civilizationalism in the populism of North-West Europe, and exemplified by the Dutch Party for Freedom and its leader Geert Wilders. Kaya and Tecmen (2019, 49), however, show civilization in the manifestos of five European right-wing populist parties, "Alternative for Germany (AfD) in Germany, National Front (FN) in France, Party for Freedom (PVV) in the Netherlands, Five Star

Movement (M5S) in Italy, and Golden Dawn (GD) in Greece)", all of which "employ fear of Islam as a political instrument to mobilize their supporters and to mainstream themselves". Their paper also shows that "right-wing populist party leaderships across Europe seem to be strongly capitalizing on civilizational matters by singling out Islam", and furthermore claim that Europe's Judeo-Christian cultures are threatened by Muslim immigrants and ultimately by the 'elites' who encourage mass immigration (Kaya and Tecmen 2019, 61). Thus, they find civilization being incorporated into populism across the continent. For example, Poland's ruling Law and Justice Party (PiS) co-founder and de facto leader, Jarslaw Kaczyński, describes Europe as a civilization based on Christianity which is threatened by left-wing secularists and Muslim immigrants. PiS, which won national elections in 2016, has promised to protect Christianity and Christian-based civilization in Poland, and made bold claims that it will try to "re-Christianize" Europe (Mazurczak 2019). In a similar way, Hungarian Prime Minister Viktor Orbán portrays himself as protecting Christian "civilization" in Europe, which he claims to be defending from Islam, globalists, and secular left-wing activists (Ádám and Bozóki 2016a, b).

The populist radical right Italian party Lega (League; previously Lega Nord) is "a clear example of a right-wing populist party that has used religion to define both 'the people' and 'the others'" through its relationship with Catholicism (McDonnell 2016, 13). Once a regional party representing Northern Italy, Lega has become a powerful and electorally successful party throughout Italy in the 2010s and into the 2020s. Lega discourse instrumentalizes religion to create an ingroup based around "culturally Catholic northern Italian" identity, and to 'other' Muslims and other Italians who oppose the social conservatism espoused by the party (McDonnell 2016, 13). Muslims, in particular, and portrayed in party discourse as an invader group "seeking to dominate the native population" (McDonnell 2016, 13). At the same time, the Lega attacked "secular elites at national and supranational levels who do not respect the traditions or identities of the people and instead privilege the rights of 'others'" (McDonnell 2016, 13).

It is important to note that Catholic identity is more important to the League than the performance of Catholic practice or obedience to the Pope. Indeed, the League does not always find itself in perfect accord with the Vatican. Rather, the party is often critical of the Church, which it accuses of siding "with elites and 'the others' against the people, leaving the party as the sole constant defender (and savior) of ordinary northern Italians" (McDonnell 2016, 13). Thus while defending Catholic identity in Italy, the League often opposes official Vatican positions on refugees, immigration, and racism (Yilmaz et al. 2021). Party leader Matteo Salvini claims he is a "devout Catholic", yet his reinvention as a Catholic politicians came after his initial attachment to neo-pagan mythologies (Molle 2019). Salvini's religious sounding rhetoric his unusual in contemporary Italian politics, and may signal a "reemerging" of faith in the "political arena" (Molle 2019, 151). Yet the Lega's discourse contains only a shallow religiosity, and is largely identitarian and civilizationalist, with 'Catholic' signifying not so much the religion but Italian identity.

The Lega, like other similar right-wing populist parties, weaponizes notions of a European Christian tradition, real and imagined, threatened by Islam in order to portray Italy's centrist parties and the European Union as out of touch 'elites' who are permitting the destruction of Western civilization via Islamization (Molle 2019, 151–52). Yet Christianity is important to the Lega. As Molle points out, in Lega discourse "the perception of Muslim immigration as a threat is maximized by the salience of implicitly religious cultural customs in public life" (Molle 2019, 158). Furthermore, he observes, "the success of [the Lega] lies in its ability to use an adaptive mythology that plays on pre-existing religious norms to stoke fears of a decline of cultural homogeneity and a loss of political and economic power" (Molle 2019, 151). Salvini and his party are masters of emotional manipulation, then, exploiting the demographic decline of ethnic Italians and promising to 'save' Italy from Islamization and cultural oblivion. Having won the largest share of seats in the 2018 Italian general election, the Lega became part of a coalition government alongside the eclectic populist *Movimento 5 Stelle* (Five Star Movement). Once in power, the Lega imposed hefty fines on NGOs assisting migrants—Muslims and Christian—and directed discriminatory language toward the Roma community, which the party perceives to be lacking in "Italian-ness" due to their cultural practices (ECPS 2021b).

While most significant in Europe, Christian identitarian populism has a small but significant presence in Australia, especially in the form of Pauline Hanson's One Nation Party, which pivoted from ethnic chauvinism and toward anti-Muslim Christian identity populism in the post-9/11 environment (Sengul 2022; Poynting and Mason 2007; Morieson 2016). The feeling among many Australians that Muslims posed a threat to Australian values due to Muslims' alleged religiosity, conservatism, and backwardness, was exploited by One Nation in the post-9/11 environment (Yilmaz 2020). Indeed, the early 2000s saw Hanson "transition from anti-Asian and anti-Arab racism to anti-Muslim racism, reflected in and responding to changes in the identities and cultural politics of the minority communities" (Poynting and Manson 2007). Where Hanson's populism once identified two enemies of 'the people', 'corrupt elites', and 'Asian immigrants', she later shifted toward North-Western European style 'Judeo-Christian' civilizationalism. 'The people' of Australia were no longer defined by their skin color or ethnic heritage, but by their Christian heritage or Christian-derived values. According to the One Nation website current in 2016, "Australia is a country built on Christian values. Our laws, way of life and customs enforced in the Australian Constitution were based on a secular society. Secularism is asserting the right to be free from religious rule and teachings or, in a state declared to be neutral on matters of belief, from the imposition by government or religion or religious practices upon the people" (Morieson 2016). This curious passage appears to blend together secularism and Christianity as if they were the same thing, or as if secularism was a simple extension of Christianity, or entirely compatible with Christian teachings. Here again we see evidence of a 'clash of civilizations' mentality, in which Muslims are held to be incompatible with and by nature a threat to Australia's 'Christian' values and heritage.

In the United States, Republican Party Presidential candidate Donald Trump used civilizational rhetoric during his 2016 campaign. As Brubaker notes, Trump did not dwell strongly on civilizational politics as many European populist parties, (Brubaker 2017, 1207). However, he described the United States as a Judeo-Christian nation, and promised to protect American from Islam, which Trump claimed "hates us" (Haynes 2020). As a candidate for President Trump, like his European populist counterparts, singled out Islam as an enemy civilization, and did not claim that other religious minorities belonged to incompatible cultures. For example, speaking to a largely Hindu audience Trump exclaimed that he was a "big fan of Hindu" (sic) (Haberman 2016).

Beyond Europe, the United States, and Australia, there is evidence of Christian-based civilizational populism, though little scholarship on the subject. Berntzen and Bjune (2012, 15), for example, describe how "the relation between religion and politics" has for decades "manifested itself in a certain tendency towards religious populism" across Latin America. Perhaps the key example of populism incorporating civilizationalism is that of Brazil's right-wing leader Jair Bolsonaro. Bolsonaro has long found support inside "Brazil's conservative religious groups, such as the Neo-Pentecostal churches and Charismatic Catholics (those who pledge formal allegiance to Rome but adopt Pentecostal-style worship practices (Knoll 2019, 227)". 'Bolsonarismo', Feltran argues, "seeks a major shift away from modern politics", away from "party mediation", "law", "pluralism", "the constitution", and toward "mass movement …male honour …identity …the gospel" (Feltran 2020). He has furthermore described Brazil as belonging to Judeo-Christian civilization, a language he has perhaps used to construct a 'people' from Brazilians of different ethnic backgrounds together, and also to construct an 'other' from religious and sexual minorities (Garcia 2020; Pachá 2019).

To further test our hypothesis, we conduct two in-depth case studies of three of the most significant populist movements in the Western world: Hungary's Fidesz party, the Netherlands' Party for Freedom, and the Trump Administration in the United States. The case studies begin with an outline of the movement and a discussion of the political and religious context in which they operate. This is followed by discourse analysis of the party leader's statements and discussion of the party's policy agenda.

4.3 Case Studies

4.3.1 *Hungary: Victor Orbán and Fidesz*

Fidesz (Fiatal Demokratak Szovetsege—Alliance of Young Democrats) began as a liberal, anti-communist student-led movement in 1980, and entered formal politics in the early 1990s, when Hungary was experiencing its first free elections (Ádám and Bozóki 2016a, b, 132). Before 1995 Fidesz "advocated liberal reforms and were quick to condemn nationalist and antisemitic undercurrents in the governing coalition" (Kenes 2020). In 1995 the party turned toward the right, and remained itself Fidesz—Magyar Polgari Part, or Fidesz, the Hungarian Civic Party, aligning itself with the center-right European People's Party (EPP). The party's rightward turn was reflected in the personal life of its leader, Viktor Orbán, who after 11 years of legal marriage reaffirmed his vows in a church ceremony, marking the beginning of the merger of religion and politics in Hungarian society (Kenes 2020). Equally, Orbán and his party began to assert, after 1995, the importance of maintaining the Magyar traditions of the homeland, family values, faith, and emphasized themes of respectability and morality in party discourse (Lendvai 2019).

When Fidesz first won government in 1998 it was under the leadership of Viktor Orbán, who solidified the party's center-right, social conservative orientation. During subsequent years in opposition (2002–2010) and in the party's return to power (2010–) Fidesz has become increasingly nationalist, socially conservative, populist, and illiberal, cementing itself as the dominant political force in Hungary (Ádám and Bozóki 2016a, b, 130–131; Buzogány 2017).

Fidesz reached a turning point in 2006, when the party turned toward right-wing populism in the wake of a political scandal involving then Hungarian Socialist Party Prime Minister Ferenc Gyurcsány. Gyurcsány had been caught on tape admitting that he was willing to lie to the public in order to achieve a set of reforms he desired. In the wake of the scandal, which appears to have led to a loss of confidence in Gyurcsány's leadership and the Hungarian Socialist Party, Orbán capitalized on growing public dissatisfaction with the government by embracing populist ideas and rhetoric (Lendvai 2019; Buzogány 2017). Following the 2008 financial crisis, and as public confidence in the Hungarian Social Party further declined, Fidesz was able to take advantage of the public mood. The party "successfully combined social paternalism with the promise of large-scale tax reductions and a pro-market orientation. Thus, Orbán strengthened his claim on power, calling for an overhaul of the political system" (Kenes 2020).

Winning government in 2010, Fidesz turned toward a nationalist conservatism which relies heavily on Christian identitarian and civilizationalist rhetoric (Fekete 2018). Since 2010, Fidesz has so thoroughly ensconced itself in power that it has successfully implemented illiberal policies aimed at defending perceived traditional Hungarian Christian values, including the closing of university departments teaching subjects such as Gender Studies (Szubori 2018). By the time of the 2018 elections, Fidesz dominated Hungarian politics, winning just under 50% of the national vote, and gaining more than twice the votes of its closest rival, the more extreme populist radical right party Jobbik.

Fidesz Merges Civilizationalism and Populism

Fidesz first won power by capitalizing on the anger felt by many Hungarians toward the Socialist-led government, which was blamed for Hungary's economic decline during the 2008 global financial crisis. The party began to attack globalization during this period, and claimed the government had deceived and failed the people of Hungary, and allowed the country to fall into an economic crisis. After winning a supermajority of 57% of the votes in the 2010 elections, Orbán enjoyed enormous political capital. He instigated a "revolution at the ballot box" that led to a 'revolution' in the constitution, and ultimately to the 'Fundamental Law of Hungary' (Lendvai 2019). The new constitution allowed Fidesz to increase its power of Hungary's institutions, and assert greater control over the judicial system, media, the universities, and the film industry (Kenes 2020; Fabry and Sandbeck 2019; Lendavi 2019). The new constitution also permitted Fidesz to begin to re-engineer Hungarian identity. According to Kenes, the "constitutional discourse of Orbán's party recalled the Christian and national traditions that were prevalent in Hungary prior to the communist era" (Kenes 2020). At the same time, "the Hungarian nation is defined in an ethnocentric way in the Fundamental Law, which not only symbolically embraces the ethnic Hungarians of neighbouring countries in the constitution, but enfranchises them to participate in Hungarian general elections through a newly introduced dual-citizenship scheme" (Kenes 2020; Illés et al. 2018).

In the 2010–2015 period Fidesz used its institutional and cultural influence, and the lack of checks and balances on its power, to attack the previous government and the European Union, claiming they were corrupt and did not act in the best interests of the Hungarian people. Fidesz also added an ever increasing Christian civilizationalist subtext to its nationalist rhetoric. The use of Christianity in Fidesz' populist discourse can be observed in the party's complex relationship with the European Union and neo-liberal economics. Orbán has on numerous occasions attacked the European Union, calling it a threat to "Christian freedom" (MTI-Hungary Today 2019). According to Orbán, Christian freedom means "patriots instead of cosmopolitans, patriotism instead of internationalism, marriage and family instead of promoting same-sex relationships, protection of the children instead of drug liberalisation, border protection instead of migration, Hungarian children instead of migrants and Christian culture instead of a multicultural mishmash". (MTI-Hungary Today 2019) Equally, the party claims that Orbán is protecting Hungarians from the deleterious effects of economic liberalism spread by the European Union. In a 2014 speech, Orbán claimed that "Hungarian voters expect from their leaders to figure out, forge and work out a new form of state-organization that will make the community of

Hungarians competitive once again after the era of liberal state and liberal democracy, one that will of course still respect values of Christianity, freedom and human rights. Those duties and values that I enumerated should be fulfilled and be respected" (Orbán 2014). Yet these claims are hollow. Hungary has a market-based economy, and is a major recipient of the European Union money (Fabry & Sandbeck 2019). Fidesz, therefore, is reliant on the very economic policies to which it claims to object in the name of protecting Christian values.

Yet Fidesz' Christian-based civilizationalism is most evident in Orbán's anti-immigration rhetoric, which is based upon notions of Hungary as a Christian society with Christian values, and Islam as fundamentally incompatible with these values. This became especially evident during the 2015 refugee crisis, during which the Fidesz-led government refused Muslim refugees entry into Hungary (Haraszti 2015, 39). Moreover the party has attempted to boost fertility within Hungary through a set of 'family friendly' policies, in order to create a stable population that does not require immigrants to facilitate economic growth (Walker, 2019). According to Orbán, Western powers have "opened the way for the decline of Christian culture and ... Islamic expansion" (Boffey 2018). Fidesz, however, has "prevented the Islamic world from flooding us from the south" (Boffey 2018). Yet Orbán does not believe that secular political power is enough to stop Islamisation. Rather, he says, "Europe's last hope is Christianity" (Macintyre 2018). Religion is thus a core part of Fidesz' populist rhetoric. Under Fidesz' rule, non-Hungarians and non-Christians were increasingly portrayed as threatening 'others'. For example, Illés et al. (2018) note that "Christianity has become one of the key state-building elements in Hungary, along with culture and language". Therefore, they argue that "the influx of immigrants – largely Muslim – is unequivocally interpreted as a threat to the existence of the state" (Illés, Körösényi and Metz 2018). Fidesz' Christianity is not the "mainstream, universal form of Christianity as a religion of love" (Ádám and Bozóki 2016a, 115). It is a political Christianity which perceives the nation-state, and European civilization, to be the product of Christian values and culture. Therefore, just as Orbán categorizes European civilization and Hungarian nationalism as intrinsically Christian, so anything which appears to threaten these things is categorized as 'anti-Christian'. Thus Orbán is able to sacralize secular things and concepts—nationalism, the European 'race', Hungarians as an ethnic group—by linking them with Christianity. Having categorized these secular things and ideas as

'Christian', Orbán is free to frame his anti-immigration and anti-Muslim rhetoric and policies as a defense of Christianity. Indeed, as Ádám and Bozoki have noted, the Fidesz constitution states that the party recognizes "the role of Christianity in preserving nationhood" (Ádám and Bozóki 2016a, 108).

Orbán has attempted to bridge the divide between Christianity and the pagan and secular aspects of Hungarian culture, bringing together in his speeches Christian symbols such as the Holy Crown of Hungary's first King St Stephen and ethnic Hungarian pagan symbols such as the Turul Bird. All are brought into a sacred matrix containing nation, Christianity, Hungarian ethnicity, and European civilization, and declared to be 'Christian'. Indeed, Orbán claims that when Hungarians "draw the boundaries of our identity, we mark out Christian culture as the source of our pride and sustaining strength. Christianity is a culture and a civilisation. ...The essence is not how many people go to church, or how many pray with true devotion" (Székely 2017). Moreover, he claims that "Christian culture shows us the way. It determines our understanding of justice and injustice, the relationship between men and women, family, success, work and honour" (Székely 2017).

In this way, as Orbán himself has stated, Christianity becomes the "unifying force of the nation" giving "the inner essence and meaning of the state" (Ádám and Bozóki 2016a, b, 137). And thus Orbán says that "Hungary will either be Christian or not at all" (Halmai 2019, 308). To this end, Fidesz has created a greater institutionalized role for Christianity within Hungary by financing Church-run universities, hospitals, and through their program of compulsory religious studies in elementary schools (Ádám and Bozóki 2016a, b, 142–143). At the same time, while Fidesz's Christian message is ultimately shallow and identitarian, it is not secularist or liberal. Fidesz is by no means a secular Christianist party. Rather, Fidesz' Christianity represents the social conservative values which have increasingly been swept away by secular liberalism in Europe. Thus is it not merely Muslims who are othered by Fidesz Christianist rhetoric, but also liberals and progressives (ECPS 2020; Kenes 2020). Moreover, Orbán has fashioned his party as the defender of the 'old Europe' and 'traditional' European values, and thus he portrays the liberalism and open borders promoted by the European Union, as well as progressive attitudes toward gender and sexuality, as a threat to traditional 'Christian' values.

Fidesz' civilizational scheme also displays transnational attributes. For example, in a statement on family values Orbán demonstrates a transnational narrative, explaining that there "exists a dividing line that begins in the Baltics and runs all the way along the western borders of Poland, Czech Republic, Slovakia, Hungary and Slovenia. To the west of this line lie countries that, for example, have already abandoned family protection; everywhere to the east of the line, on the other hand, family-friendly policy has prevailed and nowhere is same-sex marriage accepted". Here Orbán defines the boundaries of the liberal world, and where illiberal, socially conservative Europe begins. Fidesz, moreover, has sought to find a common purpose with other socially conservative parties in the region, creating a bloc in European parliament which represents the Visegrad nations and their social values (Poland, Czech Republic, Slovakia, and Hungary).

Moreover, soon after coming to power Fidesz created a Ministry of Foreign Affairs and Trade was formed. This body is led by Orbán's protégé Péter Szijjártó, who is focused on an "Eastern opening" that seeks diplomatic and trade ties beyond the European Union (Mészáros 2021; Paszak 2021; Kenes 2020). In this context Hungary has developed close ties with centrally controlled autocratic governments in Russia (suspended after the invasion of Ukraine), China, and Turkey (Kenes 2020). These autocratic nations are unlikely to attempt to coerce Hungary into undertaking liberalizing reforms, or pursuing socially progressive policies on women's rights or homosexuality. Fidesz' decision to deepen engagement with autocratic, non-liberal nations appears to be an attempt to create strong trade relationships outside the European Union and the American-dominated liberal democratic world, in order to prevent the body from using its influence and power to liberalize (if not Americanize) Hungarian culture, and the country's legal and political systems. At the same time, Orbán has gained followers and allies in the United States among Republicans and Christian conservatives, who are inspired by his ability to prevent his country from embracing American style liberal values, and who in 2021 traveled to meet Orbán in Hungary and discuss politics (Thorpe 2021). Conservative journalist Ross Douthat (2021), reflecting on the growing relationship between American conservatives and Orbán, observed that it is not merely the Hungarian leader's "anti-immigration stance or his moral traditionalism", that embattled conservatives in culturally liberal societies find appealing. Rather, it is

Orbán's ability to intervene in "Hungarian cultural life" to disrupt "liberal academic centers" and spend money on "conservative ideological projects" which most inspire American conservatives, and which they believe are "examples of how political power might curb progressivism's influence" (Douthat 2021).

In order to further 'defend' 'traditional' culture and values from the liberal democratic world's incursions into Hungary, and to further sacralize the party, its leader, and the Hungarian people, Fidesz has attempted to integrated Christian churches into the state. However, it is noteworthy that churches that indorse the politics of Orbán have been bestowed with privileges whereas the "politically less obedient" churches in Hungary, however, "have been stripped" of official status (Ádám and Bozóki 2016a, b, 116). In this way, perhaps, Fidesz use state power to grant legitimacy to certain churches, while in return gaining legitimacy from the support of those same churches. Fidesz's religious populism, then, may not contain a "spiritual" element, nor is it grounded in belief in God, but it does involve a close connection with religious organizations that it uses to "other" Muslims and defend traditional sexual relations and gender roles. Fidesz' Christian populism is strongly identitarian, though unlike its Northern European counterparts it does not conflate liberal social values and Christianity. Rather, by combining ethnonationalism with a call to preserve traditional social values, the party has created a "surrogate religion" which "offers a nationalist and paganized understanding of Christianity and elevates the concept of ethnically defined nation to a sacred status" (Ádám & Bozóki 2016a, b, 98).

Civilizationalism in Orbán's Discourse
Orbán was born in 1963 in Hungary, and thus in a time when the country was under communist rule. He grew into a young activist who demanded political change and the liberalization of Hungarian society. Since the late 1980s, Orbán has used his oratory skills to captivate audiences. Yet his message has not been wedded to one particular ideology, leading some commentators to suggest he is more of a political opportunist than an ideologue (Kenes 2020). Indeed, initially Orbán claimed that the governing elites of the Hungarian Socialist Party had acted corruptly and incompetently throughout their time in office, and led the country to the brink of economic destruction. Later Orbán would increase his attack on the European Union, arguing that the body was undemocratic and that its growing power was undermining Hungary's sovereignty and ability to

govern itself. Orbán argued that the European Union was destroying the Hungarian people's freedom.

Orbán's crisis began to take on an increasingly civilizational shape, even as he called for Hungarian sovereignty to be respected, and portrayed his government as Hungarian nationalists and patriots. Religion, though largely absent of Christian spirituality or theological or ethnical concerns, began to play an increasingly important role in Orbán's civilizational discourse and policies. For example, Orbán's revised constitution, which became law in 2012, begins with a preamble that declares Hungarians "are proud that our king Saint Stephen built the Hungarian State on solid ground and made our country a part of Christian Europe one thousand years ago" (Fundamental Law of Hungary 2011). Equally, the preamble acknowledges "the role Christianity has played in preserving our nation", though it also claims to "respect all our country's religious traditions" (Fundamental Law of Hungary 2011).

Christianity, in the preamble to the Hungarian constitution, is therefore not conceived as a spiritual tradition, or private faith, but rather an aspect of Hungarian culture. Christianity is to be valued as a source of Hungarian values and identity, and as a force which has helped to prevent its destruction, particularly during the communist period. According to Orbán, Christianity is the foundation of "human rights", a concept which may not, he thinks, be exported to civilization built on non-Christian "foundations" (Székely 2017). This Christianity therefore encompasses secularism and even atheism, which are understood as products of Christianity itself. For example, addressing Hungarians at Christmastime, Orbán claimed that "we Europeans live in a culture ordered in line with the teachings of Christ. Here I can quote the well-known words of an earlier Hungarian prime minister, the late József Antall: In Europe, even an atheist is Christian" (Székely 2017).

It is also important to note how the concept of freedom is understood in Orbán's Hungary. Orbán's freedom does not signify the right to live an utterly individualistic existence, or give a person the right to break taboos. Rather, as the preamble to Hungary's constitution puts it, "individual freedom can only flourish through cooperation with others" (Fundamental Law of Hungary 2011). The constitution therefore proclaims "that the family and the nation provide the fundamental framework for community, in which the pre-eminent values are loyalty, faith and love" (Fundamental Law of Hungary 2011). In Orbán's discourse, then, family, nation, and religion are bound together and form a sacred matrix.

Hungary itself is portrayed as defending this sacred matrix, though not merely within the nation, but also within Europe. Moreover, in the preamble to the constitution, the people of Hungary are said to have spent centuries defending "Europe in a series of struggles and enriched Europe's common values with [their] talent and diligence" (Fundamental Law of Hungary 2011). Therefore the leaders of bodies such as IMF and the EU, which Orbán claims wish "to take Europe into a post-Christian and post-national era", are portrayed in his discourse as enemies of Christianity and thus the people of Hungary (Visegrad Post 2018). Thus Orbán's has remarked that in 'his' Hungary "foreign banks and bureaucrats are not telling us what to do", and that his government is fighting for its people's freedom (*szabadságharc*) by reducing external "influences" and strengthening the culture of "the people" (Buzogány 2017). This language serves to encourage Hungarians to feel threatened by outside forces, and to develop a siege mentally, but also to perceive in Orbán a savior who will spare them from outside threats.

Orbán frames issues related to LGBTQ rights within the civilizational conflict he claims he is waging against the European Union, and other liberal secularist powers and transnational bodies, on behalf of Christianity and the people of Hungary. For example, when faced with EU criticism over a law perceived as anti-LGBT, and which made the promotion of homosexuality among children illegal, Orbán framed this criticism as an attack on Hungary's children by decadent foreign powers. According to Orbán, "Brussels has clearly attacked Hungary in recent weeks regarding the law […] The future of our children is at stake, so we cannot cede ground in this issue" (Radio Free Europe 2021). Previously, in 2016, Orbán told the people of his country that they "must decide whether there will still be nations or if we want a united Europe? Do we want families and children or can we not even determine who is a man and who is a woman?" (Orbán 2016a). This emotional language, which portrays the EU as a threat to the nation's children, and moreover its future, is designed to further evoke fear in Hungarians. At the same time, by framing the EU's criticism of Orbán's new laws as an attack on children, Orbán appears to be attempting to create a feeling of anger or rage in Hungarians, or a sense of outrage that their children should be threatened by foreign powers.

Orbán has also accused the EU of limiting Hungarian's freedom of speech, claiming that "Europe is not free […] because freedom begins with speaking the truth. …it is forbidden to say that those arriving are not refugees, but that Europe is threatened by migration. It is forbidden to say that tens of millions are ready to set out in our direction. It is forbidden to say that that immigration brings crime and terror to our countries" (Orbán 2016a). Yet even here Orbán's framing is chiefly civilization insofar as he claims that it "is forbidden to point out that the masses arriving from other civilizations endanger our way of life, our culture, our customs, and our Christian traditions" (Orbán 2016a). Orbán furthermore claims that it is "the duty of the freedom-loving people of Europe is to save Brussels from becoming Sovietized", linking the EU to the atheist, anti-Christian Soviet Union, which dominated Hungarian society for much of the second half of the twentieth century (Orbán 2016a). Here, perhaps, we see the core of Orbán's civilizational populism, which perceives Muslim immigrants to Europe as an existential threat to Hungarian nationhood and to Christian civilization. Yet the greater enemy in Orbán's rhetoric is not Muslims themselves, but the European Union and the liberal democratic nations of Western Europe, which he claims have "regularly mocked Hungary" and Hungarian's "Asian origins" (Orbán 2013). Here Orbán attempts to create a sense of victimhood among Hungarian people by encouraging them to believe they are mocked in Europe due to their immutable characteristics. Yet Orbán assures Hungarians that this mockery will be turned on Western Europeans, because "the center of gravity of the world economy is moving from the West toward the East" (Orbán 2013).Orbán thus encourages Hungarians to become "successful" in a vindicative fashion to "show" Western Europeans the talent and superiority of Hungarian culture and ethnicity, telling 'the people' to fight for them "homeland" (Visegrad Post 2018). Orbán has also invoked Hungary's experience under Ottoman domination in order to increase Hungarians sense of victimhood and anger toward Muslims, remarking "I have to say that when it comes to living together with Muslim communities, we are the only ones who have experience because we had the possibility to go through that experience for 150 years" (Orbán 2015).

In a call for Hungarians to join his fight against the EU and to protect Hungary, Orbán claims that while Jesus, in the Gospel of Mark, commands people to "love your neighbor as yourself", those who accuse Hungarians of breaking this commandment by refusing Muslim refugees entrance into Hungary are incorrect (Székely 2017). Orbán claims "they have forgotten the second part: we must love our neighbor, but we must also love ourselves. Loving ourselves means that we love our country, our nation, our family, Hungarian culture and European civilization. Within these contexts, our freedom – Hungarian freedom – has unfolded, and can unfold, time after time" (Székely 2017). In Orbán's crisis-driven emotional rhetoric, the "fundamental elements of European life" are being attacked by Muslims and Western European liberals, who would force Hungarians—regardless of whether they practice their faith or not—to "celebrate Christmas behind drawn curtains to avoid hurting the feelings of others" (Székely 2017). He encourages religious and non-religious Hungarians alike to feel angry at immigrants and liberals who would try to eliminate or change Hungarian culture. "Every right-thinking European citizen bristles with anger" when Europe's Christian festivals are altered or banned, according to Orbán (Székely 2017). "This is also true of those for whom Christianity …is 'just paganism with holy water', Orbán has said, and "true of those like Oriana Fallaci, who feared for Europe as 'an atheist Christian'".

Orbán has encouraged his supporters to perceive Muslim immigrants as a virus, claiming that "Europe's immune system is being deliberately weakened", and that social liberals and globalists "do not want us to be who we are. They want us to mix together with peoples from another world. …In return for the life we have lived up to now they are promising one which is new and more enlightened" (Székely 2017). Dehumanizing immigrants by calling them "terrorists", Orbán claims that "the factual point is that all the terrorists are basically migrants" (Pearso, 2018), and furthermore claims that social liberals and leftists would "parallel societies" within Hungary, "because Christian and Muslim society will never unite" (Pearson 2018). Muslim immigration, he says, must cease before it causes the "destruction of Europe" (Orbán 2015).

Orbán's populist discourse consists of ethnoreligious nationalism and civilizational rhetoric, the promotion of traditional Christian sexual and gender norms, and the framing of 'freedom' as a form of group rights belonging to national majorities rather than as individual rights. His civilizational turn has manifested in a populism that defines national belonging in civilizational and not narrowly national terms. In it, 'the people' are defined as ethnic Hungarian and culturally Christian, and heirs to a glorious Christian civilization. This Christian civilization contains values superior to those of the liberal secularism of European 'elites', and the Islamic values of Muslim immigrants, both of whom are portrayed in his discourse as inauthentic and impure 'others' who do not belong in Hungary or Christian civilization. Worse, elites are framed as being of the people, yet turning against their interests and attempting to destroy the traditions of the superior 'Christian' civilization.

This discourse has, over the last decade, had a profound effect on Hungarian society, turning it inward and creating a sense among its people of perpetual crisis and fear. The key to Orbán's political success lies in his ability to evoke in Hungarians a persistent fear of losing their culture, whether at the hands of the European Union, Western liberals, Muslim immigrants, or all three. Orbán has proven adept at exploiting these fears, and converting public anxiety into feelings of victimhood and ultimately anger toward those who threaten the Hungarian people and their culture. Christianity—as a civilization and culture, rather than a spiritual and ethnic tradition or private faith—plays an important role in defining the ingroup and outgroup in Orbán's populism. The power of this discourse has played an important role in the creation of vigintile groups such as "National Legion", a paramilitary offshoot of the Our Homeland Movement, which harasses immigrants, Roma people, and anyone deemed a "threat" to Hungarian civilization (TRT 2019; Bozoki 2016). While the group has no formal ties to Orbán or his party, it is Fidesz that has produced an environment in which the anti-immigrant activities of vigilante groups are legitimized, and portrayed as a defensive act necessary to protect the nation.

4.3.2 Netherlands: Party for Freedom

Growth of Christian-Based Civilizational Populism in the Netherlands

The presence and political significance of Christian identitarian populism in the Netherlands, one of the most secularized and socially liberal nations on Earth, may at first appear puzzling. The Netherlands was the first country to legalize same-sex marriage in 2001, and is widely recognized as having championed women's rights during the twentieth century (Damhuis 2019; Ignazi 2003). Despite the secularization of the country in the post-war period, there remain several Christian parties operating in the Netherlands. The Christian Democratic Appeal (CDA) is the largest, but though it is the product of the merger of several Christian democratic parties, the CDA is today a centrist and secularist party, and could not be described as religious in orientation. The Christian Union (CU), however, is a self-described 'Christian social party', and claims to base its political platform in part on Christian principles. The Reformed Political Party (SGP), a small party which represents the interests of deeply religious Calvinists but maintains a parliamentary alliance with the CU, is genuinely hostile toward secularism and liberalism, and possesses a political ideology based upon a conservative interpretation of Christian principles and beliefs. However, the SGP is neither populist nor does identify Dutch culture as a continuation of Christian civilization. Thus neither the SGP nor the CU could be described as Christian identitarian parties.

Yet since the 1990s, Christian-based civilizational populism has had a significant growing presence in the Netherlands. The rise of Christian identitarian is visible in the increasing use of the term 'Judeo-Christian' within Dutch parliamentary debates. Between 1814 and 2000 the term was used on only 33 occasions, yet in the 2000–2011 period it was used 143 times in speeches and debates (van den Hemel 2014, 91). Among the first Dutch politicians to use Christian identitarian discourse was Frits Bolkestein, leader of the center-right People's Party for Freedom and Democracy (VVD) throughout most of the 1990s. Bolkestein was an important figure in Dutch politics. In 1991 Bolkestein, describing the difficulty many Muslims appeared to experience when attempting to integrate into Dutch society, claimed that this difficulty was created by a fundamental difference between Dutch culture—based upon "Rationalism, humanism and Christianity", and Islamic culture, which was based upon non-rational, non-humanistic religious principles (van den Hemel 2014, 53; (Ignazi 2003). In 1994, Bolkestein suggested Christianity and humanism would "offer the moral guidelines and unity for a political community facing a growing influx of migrants" (Vollaard 2013, 90). Bolkestein also criticized emerging moral relativism "because it denied the superiority of Western values", and encouraged the VVD to amend their political platform and identify Christianity as a source of Dutch culture and identity (Vollaard 2013, 90).

Bolkestein's concerns about Islam appear to be related to the increasing number of Muslims in the Netherlands, but also the surprise he and other Dutch people felt when Muslim immigrants did not immediately privatize their faith, or adopt the seemingly secular customs of the Dutch. When Muslims began arriving in the Netherlands in the 1970s, there were few Mosques in the country. Yet by 2010 450 mosques were in operation, as well as dozens of Islamic schools (Morieson 2021–). Due to its colonial past, the Netherlands has long permitted the arrival of migrants from the Antilles, Indonesia, and Suriname, among other places. Many of these people were originally brought to the country as "guest workers", who later became Dutch citizens (Damhuis 2019). Many Muslims initially arrived in the Netherlands as "guest workers" in the 1970s, mostly from Turkey and Morocco, but more recent Muslim immigrants have settled in the country after fleeing war in Yugoslavia and Syria. Today nearly six percent of the population in the country identities as Muslims out of which nearly 4.7% are either "guest workers" or their children or grandchildren (Central Bureau of Statistics 2016). Yet despite being a small minority of Dutch, Muslims are a highly visible group. Indeed, the Dutch tend to wildly overestimate the number of Muslims in the Netherlands (Morieson 2021). The presence of Islam, and the perception that Muslims are a threat to the 'rational' Christian and Humanistic culture of the Netherlands, appears to have played an important role in the development of Christian-based civilizationalism in the country. Muslims' visibility is the result of their often different appearance and different forms of religious practice, and of the manner in which Dutch culture is both secularized and suffused with Christianity. Supposedly secular aspects of Dutch culture—the official celebration of Christmas and Easter—are of course Christian in origin. Therefore when Muslims do not enjoin these activities they are perceived as not assimilating into Dutch society. Equally when they do not privatize their faith, but remain publicly religious, they may be accused of refusing to secularize, or being unable to separate their private religious beliefs from their public behavior. Muslims may be confused by these accusations, and may perceive in official holidays for Christmas and Easter celebrations, and the use of public funds to repair aging churches and cathedrals, as the Dutch state permitting Christianity to penetrate into the secular, and thus religiously neutral, public sphere. In an environment in which Christianity is privileged among religions, yet this privilege is ubiquitous and therefore often invisible, and in which there has been a breaking down of the old division between the secular and sacred, allowing Christianity to be secularized into 'Dutch culture', it is hardly surprising that Muslims should be so visible in the Netherlands. And thus it is not surprising that Islam is singled out by populist radical right parties as a uniquely political religion.

Frits Bolkestein was not a right-wing populist, yet his Christian-based civilizationalism and call for the protection of Christianity and humanism in the Netherlands inspired two significant right-wing populist leaders in the Netherlands: Pim Fortuyn and Geert Wilders. Neither Fortuyn nor Wilders possessed any previous affiliations with extreme right or fascist movements. Rather, both were secular liberals who claimed to despise religious fanaticism. Fortuyn, a gay man, based his populist ideology on the idea that the socially liberal and open-minded Dutch people were threatened by religious fanatics who hated gay people and women, and wished to oppress them (Morieson 2021). Fortuyn also accused Dutch political leaders of failing to follow Bokestein's example and fight to protect the "Judeo-Christian" values that lay at the heart of the Netherland's liberal and open culture, and moreover made the Enlightenment itself possible (Morieson 2021; Koopmans and Muis 2009). Thus Fortuyn combined populism with Judeo-Christian civilizationalism, in which 'we' are Judeo-Christian, secular, socially liberal, and rational, and 'they' are the fanatical, illiberal, and irrational Muslims who want to impose their ideology upon 'us', or 'elites' who permit the Islamization of Dutch society.

A gay man with liberal views on sexuality and culture, Fortuyn appears to have perceived in Islam a backward religion which would, if it were more widely supported in the Netherlands, criminalize his own sexual proclivities. According to Fortuyn, Islam was a backward and dangerous religion incompatible with the secularism that emerged out of Judeo-Christianity (Kolbert 2002). Islam was therefore more dangerous than even fundamentalist Christianity, because out of Christianity emerged the social values that allowed Fortuyn to enjoy a successful political career despite his own homosexuality. Perhaps for Fortuyn, then, "Islam was not only a reminder of the religious conservatism which had been overcome or transformed into secular liberalism, but something far more insidious: a religious tradition which could not overcome itself and secularise" (Morieson 2021, 42). Fortuyn had shown that there was a growing constituency in the Netherlands for an anti-Muslim, socially liberal, Christian identitarian populist party. Thus when Fortuyn was murdered by a left-wing activist in 2002 his death opened up a space for a new populist leader and movement to emerge.

Geert Wilders, a member of Dutch parliament and the VVD, emerged as the most significant right-wing populist and Christian identitarian following Fortuyn's murder. Wilders was something of a protégé of the older Bolkestein, with whom he shared an antipathy toward Islam as well as—in the 1990s and early 2000s—a preference for free market liberal economics (Mass 2014, 71). When Bolkestein left the VVD and entered European Parliament, Wilders began a political shift toward populism, although he remained within the VVD until 2004. Perhaps reacting to the 9/11 attacks, Wilders shifted away from classical liberalism and toward a robust neoconservativsm after 2001, embracing "market liberalism, traditional values and aggressive democratic interventionism against chosen adversaries" (Pauwels 2014, 117). Wilders supported the Bush Administration's so-called War on Terror, advocated regime change across a variety of Muslim nations, and called for the arrest of suspected Islamic radicals (Morieson 2021). He grew increasingly critical of his own party, and more broadly the other parties of the political center, who he alleged were permitting the Islamization of Dutch society. According to Wilders, Islam was an especial threat because it was not really a religion, but rather a totalitarian ideology whose adherents were seeking to conquer the Western, and whose values were antithetical to Judeo-Christian values (Pauwels 2014, 117; Morieson 2021).

In 2004 Wilders resigned from the VVD and formed the Party for Freedom, an explicitly anti-Muslim populist party. The PVV contested its first election in 2006, running on a platform which called for the cessation of Muslim immigration and the strengthening of Dutch sovereignty in order to prevent the EU from controlling the country's immigration and economic policies (Pauwels 2014 115). The party received only 6% of the vote in the 2006 elections. Yet Wilders was undeterred. After 2006 he reoriented the party toward welfare chauvinism, nativism, and populism, and away from aggressive neoconservativism (Morieson 2021, 44). Wilders also increased his attacks on Muslims, producing a film—*Fitna*—which denigrated Islam and portrayed ordinary Muslims as an existential threat to Dutch society. The PVV grew in popularity in the second half of the 2000s, and emerged from the 2010 elections as the third largest party, winning 15% of the vote (Morieson 2021, 45).

Emboldened, Wilders entered the 2012 elections with a more radical set of proposals. He called for a vote on Dutch membership of the EU, the abandoning of dual nationality, the forcing of immigrants to learn to speak Dutch, laws preventing the construction of mosques and Islamic schools, and a ban on the wearing of Islamic clothing in government buildings (Vossen 2011). Dutch voters largely rejected Wilders' radical plans, and the PVV subsequently lost nine seats, receiving a mere 10% of all votes.

Yet Wilders was to make a remarkable political comeback in 2016, which saw his party briefly rise to become the most popular, according to polls, in the Netherlands. Perhaps the key reason behind Wilders' rise in popularity was the refugee crisis in the Middle East and North Africa, which saw over a million mostly Muslim people seek refuge in

Europe from a series of wars and conflicts. The PVV capitalized on Dutch fears of a Muslim 'invasion', and using incendiary and alarmist language claimed the Netherlands was on the brink of Islamization, and promise to "de-Islamize" the country (Wilders 2017). The party also promised to ban all Muslim asylum seekers from entering Dutch territory, ban the construction of Mosques, ban headscarves at "public functions", and arrest suspected Islamic radicals (Wilders 2017). This time the PVV's radical program struck a chord with voters, and though the party failed to win government, they emerged as the second largest party in Dutch Parliament, winning 20 seats (though well behind the VVD, which one 33 seats) (Morieson 2021, 47). 2017 saw a second anti-Muslim, Christian identitarian populist party contest elections, the Forum for Democracy (Fvd). Party leader Thierry Baudet portrays himself as a lover of European culture and defender of the continent's Judeo-Christian culture and heritage, which he claims is threatened by the traditional governing parties of the Netherlands and by Islam (Faber 2018; Morieson 2021). The PVV lost support during the 2021 election, perhaps because the perceived threat of Muslim invasion via the refugee crisis had not materialized. However the PVV and FvD won 25 seats between them in 2021, a demonstration of the significant power of Christian civilizationalism and right-wing populism in the Netherlands. Indeed, though the center-right VVD continues to dominate Dutch politics, after 2021 right-wing Christian identitarian populist parties possessed more seats than at any previous time (Damhuis 2021).

Civilizationalism in Party for Freedom Discourse
A key element of the populism in the Netherlands is civilizationalism. This civilizationalism is most prominent in the discourse of the PVV. It may appear paradoxical that the PVV, a nationalist party which demands Dutch sovereignty be strengthened and which calls, at times, for a Dutch exit from the European Union, should also use civilizational rhetoric within its discourse. Yet, as Brubaker has observed, the PVV define 'self' and 'other' not in nationalist terms, but in civilizational terms, and moreover claim that Islam and the Judeo-Christian and Humanist Western are locked in an existential battle (Brubaker 2017).

Perhaps, then, the key to understanding the PVV's civilizationalism is to consider their description of the major players in the clash of civilizations. According to PVV leader Geert Wilder, the West is characterized by its "Judeo-Christian" heritage, identity, and values. 'Judeo-Christian' may sound like a religious term, but it appears to be empty of genuinely religious content, and appears to be used as a description of Europe's contemporary secular culture (Kluveld 2016, 150). 'Judeo-Christian' is therefore best understood as a vague term without a real connection with religious faith or Christian or Jewish theology, used to define European culture as the sole product of a single tradition, and therefore portray other traditions—particular Islam—as foreign and threatening. Therefore we might understand the civilizationalism of the PVV as a response to the perceived threat of Islam, which has caused the party—and before them Fotruyn and Bolkestein—to emphasize "Christianity as a cultural and civilization identity" (Brubaker 2017, 1193).

Civilizationalism is the key element in the crisis the PVV performs in order to create demand within the Dutch public for their variety of populism. In order to create a sense of crisis the party claims that Judeo-Christian-based Western civilization is under threat in the Netherlands from Islam, and that Dutch and European Union 'elites' are permitting the destruction of their own society and, ultimately, their civilization. The construction of Mosques and Islamic schools are, for the PVV, signs of the Islamization of the Netherlands, and prefigure the death of Judeo-Christianity and secular humanism in the country. Muslims and 'elites' are the primary antagonists in the civilizational conflict posited by the PVV, and therefore constitute the main outgroups—along with left-wing 'cultural relativists'—the party constructs in its discourse. Equally, the party constructs an ingroup consisting of secular ethnic European Dutch who are either nominally Christian or post-Christian in the sense that they may no longer believe in God, but feel either a sense of Christian belonging or alternatively believe their liberal secular values are in some way derived from the Netherlands' Christian or Judeo-Christian heritage. The PVV does not appear to attract many genuinely religious voters, who are more likely to vote for the Netherlands' Christian parties. Thus the PVV uses civilizationalism to classify Dutch citizens as either part of a "Judeo-Christian and Humanist" ingroup, or part of a series of outgroups into which they place Muslims, leftists, and the centrist-left and center-right parties that dominate Dutch politics. Additionally, as part of their welfare chauvinism, the PVV claims Dutch political elites have failed 'the people' by failing to provide adequate funding for police forces, pensions, and health care for vulnerable people (NL Times 2021; Dutch News 2010).

The Judeo-Christian and Humanist ingroup (or 'the people), according to the PVV, are oppressed by Dutch and European Union elites and the Netherland's growing Muslim population. Yet this group are also framed by the PVV as supreme in all moral matters due to their progressive social beliefs and Judeo-Christian derived 'humanism'. Wilders uses the example of the Dutch Golden Age, a time in which the Dutch were colonizing non-European societies, and during which the Dutch mastered the art of painting and contributed to various scientific fields, as proof of the superiority of the Dutch people (Damhuis 2019). Wilders uses this example to support his argument for a Dutch exit from the European Union, and an end to immigration, especially immigration from outside the Western world. "Unfortunately", Wilders has claimed, "Dutch political elites suffer from the fatal arrogance of thinking they know better than the people" (Waisbord 2019, 222). Islamist attacks across Europe are further proof of the arrogance of 'elites', and Wilders claims that by refusing to cease Muslim immigration "Europe simply hasn't learned her lesson" (Confino 2020). The PVV, however, the party claims, has learned the hard lessons taught by Islamist terrorism, and promises to instead represent the interests of the "fictitious Henk and Ingrid", the "'typical' Dutch couple that are the 'heart' of Dutch society" (Hawkins 2019, 57). Thus the PVV call for the state to protect all things Dutch, and to reject the cultural relativism inherent in multiculturalism, which the party claims have a deleterious effect on the lives of ordinary Dutch people (Vink 2007).

The party's civilizationalism has led it to seek out transnational alliances. Despite its opposition to the European Union and strong nationalism and nativism, the PVV is an active participant in European parliament, and in which its representative, Marcel de Graaff, is a member of the right-wing, Christian identitarian and anti-Muslim Identity and Democracy bloc. Beyond Europe, the PVV has attempted to create alliances—if only informally—with other Christian identitarian populist and anti-Muslim parties. Wilders celebrated the victory of Donald Trump, claiming it was the beginning of a populist "revolution" in the world (de la Torre and Anselmi 2019, 469). Equally, he has visited Australia and the United States and entered into dialogue with parties and movements within both nations, respectively, in order to build alliances and further their shared anti-Muslim, Christian civilizationalist, and populist agendas (Demir and Shener 2021). At the same time, Wilders draws a distinction between his secular and socially liberal (at least on sexual matters) party and the European far-right. "My allies are not [France's Jean-Mari] Le Pen or [Austria's Jorg] Haider. We'll never join up with the fascists and Mussolinis of Italy, Wilders has said, adding that he is "very afraid of being linked with the wrong rightist fascist groups" (BBC 2010). Indeed, Wilders has expressed admiration for the centrist French President Emmanuel Macron, praising him for "doing something" to combat Islamic radicalism in France (Confino 2020). The PVV's civilizational rhetoric is thus constructed in such a way so as to buttress, rather than to diminish, Dutch culture, and to increase nationalist feeling. It is a form of civilizationalism created out of a sense of Muslim difference, which has collapsed the secularism vs Christianity binary, but which ultimately demands not a return to Christendom but to a stronger Dutch nationalism. Thus when the PVV seeks international allies it prefers to partner with other nationalist parties and movements.

Civilizational Populism in the Discourse of Geert Wilders
Wilders claims Muslim immigration to the Netherlands is but a front in a larger war between Islam and the Judeo-Christian and Humanist West. Wilders' thus tells his followers to fear Muslims, who he claims are an invading force which will, if permitted, destroy the Judeo-Christian culture of the Dutch people. According to Wilders, the center-right VVD government "has destroyed our country with its austerity policies and has allowed our country to be colonized by Islam" (Wilders, 2016). In this way, Wilders blames Dutch 'elites' for bringing about a civilizational crisis in the Netherlands, by permitting Muslims to settle in the country. Wilders does not claim that all Muslims are a threat, but rather claims that while "there are many moderate Muslims …there is no such thing as a moderate Islam. There is only one Islam and it is a dangerous ideology. It is intolerant, it is violent. It should not be tolerated, but should be contained" (Wilders 2012). Islam is so dangerous, he says, that by allowing Muslims to settle on the continent "Europe made a fatal mistake" (Wilders 2012). Furthermore, Wilders claims, "so many people rooted in a culture entirely different from our own Judeo-Christian and humanist tradition have entered Europe that our heritage, our freedoms, our prosperity and our culture are in danger" (Wilders 2012). Once again, Wilders does not claim that every Muslims is a threat to Europe. Rather, he tells his followers, "Islam says it wants to kill us. The Koran leaves no doubt about that" (Wilders 2016). Yet at the same time he claims that Muslims are giving Dutch people "the middle finger", and are parading through the streets of The Hague with "IS flags" and through Rotterdam with the flag of Turkey (Wilders 2016). Calling for something akin to

direct democracy, Wilders claims that the Netherlands' "political system is …ruled by the same arrogant political elites with their false promises and hypocritical apologies" (Wilders 2016). "If the mess created by Mark Rutte has taught us one thing", Wilders claims, "it is this: the people should be able to pull the emergency brake when the political elites violate their will" (Wilders 2016).

Wilders seeks to convert Dutch fears about the growth of Islam in the Netherlands into anger toward elites and Muslim immigrants themselves. Comparing Islam to Nazism, Wilders claims that "…our Western leaders today are making the same mistake that the European leaders made in the 1930s. They are appeasing Islam and refuse to see it for what it really is: dangerous and evil" (Wilders 2015). Islam, then, is an evil and dangerous totalitarian political religion which poses an existential threat to the Dutch people and their Judeo-Christian—and therefore freedom loving—culture. Thus Islam must be stopped, according to Wilders, who claims that a "choice has to be made …between Islam and freedom" (Wilders 2015). "One million immigrants", he claims, "mostly Islamic, are waiting in North Africa to cross into Europe. If we do not stop them, we will be facing a catastrophe" (Wilders 2015). Like other right-wing politicians, Wilders is concerned with the demographic changes occurring in Europe, which are likely to see Muslims become an ever larger minority, and perhaps even the largest single religious group, in a number of Western European nations. "The growth rate of Islam is more than double that of Christianity", Wilders (2015) tells his followers. The menace of Islam, he says, is unique, for "if Christianity or Buddhism were to become dominant in the world, there would hardly be a problem for freedom of speech. But when Islam becomes the major force, it is going to be hell for everyone …churches and Christian schools will be closed down by Islam and women and homosexuals will be treated badly" (Wilders 2015). Wilders' solution to this problem is to show Islam the door, and prevent Muslims exercising their right to practice their religion by forbidding the construction of Mosques, Islamic schools, and preventing Muslim women from wearing Islamic clothing in public places (Wilders 2016). Wilders' attempts to win support for his campaign to deny Muslims their rights by encouraging Dutch people to perceive Islam as an existential threat, and to believe that they must pre-emptively attack Islam before it destroys their culture and heritage. Cognizant that he may be called a hypocrite for advocating free speech yet calling on the government to "ban the Koran and close down mosques and Islamic schools",

Wilders defends his position by claiming that he is merely acting to defend the West from an aggressive foreign power (Wilders 2015). "Islam is a totalitarian ideology aimed at establishing tyrannical power over non-Muslims", Wilders claims. The "West has a concrete identity…not Islamic but based on Judaism, Christianity and humanism. Our freedoms result from this identity" (Wilders 2015). Therefore by "depriving Islam of the means to destroy our identity", Wilders (2015) argues, "we are not violating freedom; we are preserving our identity and guaranteeing freedom".

Encouraging his supporters to feel a sense of victimhood is an important part of Wilders' emotional populism. In Wilders' discourse 'we' are victims of 'their' oppression. Moreover, 'they' threaten 'our' values, heritage, and even our lives with their violence. 'They' are invading 'our' lands, and 'their' religion is wholly antithetical to our own, and may not even constitute a true religion, because it is too public and political. 'We' however, does not always mean merely the Dutch people; rather it can sometimes, in Wilders' discourse, refer to all 'Judeo-Christian' peoples. For example, using the language of victimhood, Wilders (2012) told an audience in Denver Colorado in 2012 that he had "been marked for death for criticizing Islam", a religion, he says, which is not a true religion but "predominantly a totalitarian ideology striving for world dominance. I believe that Islam and freedom are incompatible". On the other hand, he told his overseas audience, "faith, family and freedom are the pillars of our Judeo-Christian civilization and need to be defended". He knows this, he claims, because the "Islamization of our society is undermining our Western Judeo-Christian values" (Wilders 2012). Therefore he warns his American audience that "Islam is also coming for America. Indeed, it has already arrived. Your country, too, is facing a stealth jihad" (Wilders 2012). In a later speech Wilders claims that Muslims have "destroyed" the Netherlands, and that elites who permit Muslim immigration have created an environment in which terrorists "can just cross the border at Hazeldonk", and where women, Jews, homosexuals, and critics of Islam such as Wilders himself are constantly threatened with violence and murder (Wilders 2016).

The threat of terrorism in the Netherlands played an important role, at times, in Wilders' narrative of Dutch and Judeo-Christian victimhood. After the 9/11 attacks, the Netherlands and much of Europe suffered from a number of Islamist terror attacks, in which mostly young Muslim men attacked individuals and public spaces in order to punish—directly or indirectly—European society for 'insulting' their religion (Reinares 2015; Voortman 2015). In 2004 Theo van Gogh, a filmmaker who had recently worked on a film highlighting fundamentalist Islam and its repercussions on women's rights, was murdered in the street by Mohammed Bouyeri, a young Dutch citizen of Moroccan descent. Van Gogh's film featured women wearing translunar fabrics with Quranic verses tattooed on their skin. Bouyeri apparently believed this film to be blasphemous, and in response he stabbed, shot, and tried to decapitate van Gogh in broad daylight on a Dutch street (Peters 2020). This incident, and others like it, have made the Dutch public fearful of Muslims, and created an environment in which the fears of the public have been exploited by Wilders and other civilizational populists, and in which populists have been able to portray Islam as a civilization which creates terrorists (Welten and Abbas 2021). Islamist terror attacks and the subsequent rise of civilizational populism have had a deleterious effect on the lives of many Muslim Dutch citizens, who have struggled in an environment in which fear of Muslims, and a sense of victimhood, are among the main "reasons why citizens and activists mobilize in support of populist politicians, parties and movements" (Hawkins 2019, 57).

Wilders, indeed, used the killing of van Gogh as an example of Dutch victimhood, and sought to create a sense of victimhood among his supporters by describing reasons behind his killing, telling them that "Twelve years ago, Theo van Gogh was murdered. He gave his life for the freedom that lies at the heart of our Dutch identity" (Wilders, 2016). Wilders attempts to turn these feelings of victimhood into anger toward Muslims, but perhaps just as importantly toward 'elites' who allow Muslims to settle in the Netherlands. He demands the Dutch defend their identity, telling followers that they "must not allow those who want to destroy our freedom to abuse freedom in order to take ours away. We must stop being naive and defend ourselves. Because this is our country. ...the elite wants to abolish the word 'allochtoon' (foreigner), but it is the native people who are losing their country" (Wilders 2016).

Dutch far-right groups have received threats from *jihadist* groups, and at times these threats have been enacted. In 2018, a man of Pakistani origin was tired and sentenced to ten years in jail for plotting a terror attack targeting Wilders (Confino 2020). This attacker had planned to send Wilders to "hell" after he had launched anti-Islamic cartoon drawing competition, which asked participants to draw Islam's prophet (DW 2019). Wilders and the PVV have maintained that they are using their right of freedom of expression when expressing their views on Islam, and that they are not provoking Muslims; rather it is the intolerance of faith itself that surfaces in the form of violent outbursts of anger in these terror attacks. By blaming terrorist attacks on Islam itself, and not on individual Muslims angered by the actions of the PVV, Wilders portrays himself as a peaceful freedom fighter, and Muslims are inherently violent and dangerous. "A tolerant society is not a suicidal society" Wilders said while defending himself from accusations of bigotry, "I am on trial, but on trial with me is the freedom of expression of many Dutch citizens. I have spoken [...] nothing but the truth" (BBC 2010). After being forced to appear before a court following his remarks denigrating Dutch-Moroccans, Wilders claimed that the Netherlands has, "become a corrupt banana republic where the leader of the opposition is sentenced in a political trial [...] while Moroccans who set our cities on fire usually get away with it and never see the inside of a court" (ECPS 2021c). "A politician like me", Wilders, claims, "who speaks the truth about a huge problem many Dutch are confronted with every day – yes, I am talking about the terror of Islam and the Moroccan problem – is dragged to court ...while imams can preach all the hatred they want and the political elites keep silent". The Dutch, according to Wilders, are victims of an elite who give Muslims special privilege to preach hatred, while refusing Wilders the right to speak "the truth".

The Dutch people are 'victims' of a foolish elite and "evil" Muslim immigrants, yet Wilders calls upon them to defend themselves by becoming more patriotic, and to assert their Judeo-Christian heritage (Wilders 2015). He calls on all Judeo-Christian peoples of the West to defend their civilization and its "superior" values (Wilders 2012). Mimicking the language of Jesus, Wilders claims acknowledging the superiority of the Judeo-Christian West and abandoning "cultural relativism" will "set us free" (Wilders 2012). In a message to his supporters in the Netherlands, he calls upon his fellow Dutch to feel pride in their particular national heritage. "Pim Fortuyn was right", Wilders says, "nothing is impossible for us. We are Dutch ...the only people in the world living in a country which for the largest part we created ourselves" (Wilders 2016). The Dutch, he reminds his audience, "founded New York and discovered Australia. Sometimes, it seems like we have forgotten it all" (Wilders 2016). Portraying himself as a national savior, he claims he will "protect" and "de-Islamize" "our beautiful country" and its values "based on the Judeo-Christian and humanist civilization" (Wilders 2016). In doing this,

Wilders encourages his supporters to feel nostalgic for and proud of the Dutch Golden Age, when the country was exploring and colonizing the world, and the Netherlands was at the center of world affairs. He also appears to suggest that such a world might return if the elites that allow Muslims to immigrate to the Netherlands were removed from power, and he and his Party for Freedom installed in their place.

Curiously, despite all his references to 'Judeo-Christian values' and the need to defend them from Islam, "fear of Islamic immigrations in the Netherlands is not based in fears of ethnic or religious competition, but is rather veiled in the defence of secularist and liberal values" (Vodegel 2018, 15). Instead, Wilders' performance of crisis is based upon exploiting fears among the Dutch that their secular identity will soon be lost and their culture Islamized (Brubaker 2017). In PVV's narrative, the crisis is mainly focused on the imminent Islamization of the Netherlands via a "tsunami of refugees", and the threat this poses to the freedom and socially liberal culture of the Dutch people. PVV voters fear becoming a minority within their own country, and see in Islam a force which will destroy their secular, liberal gender and sexual mores, and end their freedom to behave as they wish (Vodegel 2018: 43–44). Wilders is adept at tapping into these fears, and also the concomitant sense among many Dutch that Christianity or Judeo-Christianity is the ultimate source of Dutch secularism, democracy, and freedom. For example, Wilders claims that "if we do not oppose Islam, we will lose everything: our freedom, our identity, our democracy, our rule of law, and all our liberties" (Demir and Shener 2021).

It is not surprising, given the extreme nature of Wilders' language, that vigilantism has found itself a permanent home in Netherlands. These vigilante groups have not been endorsed by Wilders or the PVV. They are a microlevel community-based collective where neighbors band together to safeguard society from criminals and terrorists. These groups, which are perhaps filled with well-meaning individuals, become hotspots of Islamophobia and xenophobia. Attacks on veiled women following the partial ban on Muslim clothing may have occurred as a result of the legitimizing of anti-Muslim feelings by politicians such as Wilders. Moreover, Wilders' calls for Dutch people to feel pride in and protect their Judeo-Christian and Humanist culture may also have led to the formation of vigilante groups that do this by searching for illegal immigrants and attacking those they view as "suspicious" (Morel 2020; Dettmer 2019).

4.3.3 USA: The Trump Administration

The Rise, Fall, and Rise Again of Christian-Based Populism in the United States

Civilizationalism and populism in the United States did not originate in the Trump Administration. Indeed, Trump's rhetoric when campaigning for president in 2016, which incorporated ideas of America as a Judeo-Christian civilization at war with Islam, can be traced back to the George W. Bush Administration. Moreover, populism as a set of ideas has very old roots in the United States. Thus, to comprehend the Trump Administration's civilizationalism we must begin by examining historical and more recent ideas of civilization in the United States. Equally, it is important to investigate the influence of Huntington's 'Clash of Civilizations' thesis on twenty-first-century American politics and foreign policy, and the manner in which it may have encouraged the United States to engage in military interventions in the Muslim majority world in the aftermath of the September 11, 2001 terrorist attacks on New York and Washington.

Christianity and populism have often had a close relationship in the United States. The Constitution of the United States insists upon the separation of church and state, yet this does not mean that religion is not an important part of American politics. A 2020 survey found that one in five American adults feel that it is "very important" that the president has strong religious beliefs, while 14 percent felt that the head of state should share their belief system (Lipka 2020). Christianity has long held an important place in American society and politics. For example, the preference for Protestantism throughout American history is evident in the fact that it took nearly sixty years for America to vote for its second Catholic President, Joe Biden, in 2021. The election of the first Catholic President, John F. Kennedy, in 1960 was itself evidence of the diminishing anti-Catholic feeling which was once pervasive across American society (Carroll 2015).

It should not be surprising, then, that populists in America have often incorporated religious, and especially Protestant, themes, and symbolisms into their respective discourses. As Yilmaz and Morieson point out, "since the beginning of populism in America, then, populism in the United States has often expressed itself in terms blending Christian language and patriotic sentiments, and has found support among different Christian denominations, particularly among evangelical Christians" (Morieson 2021, 11; Creech 2006, XVIII–XIX). For example, the original 'populist' party, the United States People's Party, was founded in 1892 and built upon earlier anti-bank, anti-elite agrarian movements. At the same time, the party sought to "reignite the lost connection with America's God-given inalienable rights, freedoms, and values that were under assault by the elites" (Zúquete 2017, 447). Moreover, religious notions "shaped the way Populists understood themselves and their movement, they wove their political and economic reforms into a grand cosmic narrative pitting the forces of God and democracy against those of Satan and tyranny" (Creech 2006, XVIII–XIX).

Religion played an important albeit somewhat different role in later populist movements. While Huey Long is rarely recognized as a religious figure in American life, the populist politician of the 1930s was, before his assassination, fond of using religious allusions in his rhetoric (Hogan and Williams 2004). For example, Hogan and Williams (2004, 162) find that Long claimed his populist 'Share our Wealth' plan was "approved by the law of our Divine Maker" and "prescribed by the Bible". Long, they find, also interpreted Leviticus and the Book of James to dictate that wealth be "scattered among the people" (Hogan and Williams 2004, 162). Long's use of religious rhetoric appears to have been part of his 'folksy' persona, and attempt to portray himself as a common man who followed the word of God (Hogan and Williams 2004). Long also used religious language as part of his overall emotional appeal to voters, which was widely considered "legendary" in his day, with one critic describing long as a "past master" of emotional rhetoric (Hogan and Williams 2004, 150). In the 1930s Depression era America, a "time of fear and uncertainty, Long cast himself as a charismatic" religious leader, and in this way he sought to associate himself and his political with "the metaphysical, the transcendent" (Hogan and Williams 2004, 163). Moreover, Long appears to have successfully created a close relationship between himself and his audience—much like a preacher does with his 'flock'. Indeed, as Hogan and Williams (2004, 163) point out, after Long's death his movement was not able to sustain itself, suggesting that Long's religious emotionalism played a key role in creating support for his movement.

Civilizationalism in the United States is may be linked to notions of American exceptionalism, and to what Robert Bellah (1967) called the civil religion of the United States. The American Revolution, though it was in some senses a conservative revolution which preserved English customs, was in many respects a "fundamental, world-changing" shift for Americans, leading them from a weak position within the British Empire to rulers of a powerful republic (Onuf 2012). Two decades after the signing of the declaration of independence, differences between Americans and Europeans were considered so large that Alexander Hamilton argued that European immigrants to the United States must shed their Europeanness when they settled in the country, and suggested that if they kept their old culture they would ruin the United States in the same manner that barbarians had ruined Ancient Rome (Alexander Hamilton on the Naturalization of Foreigners 2010). Of course, whatever cultural differences white Americans had with Europeans, they were small compared to their cultural differences with non-Europeans, including the black population of the United States, who were largely enslaved in a number of southern states until the civil war.

Until the late twentieth century, the United States remained a culturally European and Protestant society. The nation's 'civil religion' (Bellah 1967) merged together American nationalism with Protestant Christianity, making other identities somewhat marginalized in the country, although in the 1960s and 1970s, the political and cultural power of White Anglo-Saxon Protestants (WASPS) began to decline (Schrag 1971). Following the Second World War, the government of the United States made an effort to expand American identity to include Jews and Catholics. Thus the notion of America as a 'Judeo-Christian' society was born. This may have begun as a positive development which sought to end anti-Semitism, but as we shall see, the concept was later used to 'other' Muslims, who were portrayed as being incompatible with Judeo-Christian culture and values. The 'othering' of Muslims increased following the September 11, 2001 terror attack perpetrated by al-Qaeda, but the groundwork was, in certain respects, already laid by Samuel P. Huntington. Huntington argued (1993, 1996) that Islam was set to become an enemy of not merely the United States, but the civilizational bloc which was centered around the core state of the United States. This idea influenced a generation of American politicians and policymakers, including members of the George W. Bush Administration. Following Huntington's clash theory, politicians and commentators characterized the September 11, 2001 attacks as strong evidence that a clash of civilizations was occurring between the West and Islam (Haynes, 2020). The subsequent "War on Terror" was perhaps also influenced by Huntington's clash thesis, and was a misguided attempt to transform Islam from an enemy civilization into a 'friend' of the West.

Following the election of Barack Obama and in the wake of the 2008 financial crisis, the Tea Party, essentially a faction of the Republican Party, emerged. The Tea Party, a right-wing, anti-government populist movement which drew large-scale support in the 2000s and 2010s, also possessed a significant religious dimension. The Tea Party marked a "convergence of libertarianism and fundamentalist religion" that "coalesced into the Tea Party's concept of American exceptionalism" (Montgomery 2012, 180–81). Where Huey Long argued that the Bible called for the redistribution of wealth, the Tea Party claimed that the American Constitution, "which restricts the powers of government …[was] divinely inspired" (Montgomery 2012, 180–81). If the Constitution itself was a divinely inspired document, then it naturally followed that an interpretation of America's founding documents which permitted an expanded role for government" were "not only un-American but are also ungodly and unchristian" (Montgomery 2012, 180–81). Tea Party ideology was closely linked to the "gospel of Christian free enterprise" widely espoused by Southern evangelical churches and certain Republican representatives (Dochuk 2012, 19).

An important part of Tea Party rhetoric was their reverence for "Judeo-Christian values" (Braunstein 2021). Tea Party leaders largely ignored racial language when describing the core features of American identity, but instead defined Americanness in cultural-religious terms: as Judeo-Christian (Braunstein 2021). The Tea Party argued that American failure and decline were closely related to the nation moving away from its Judeo-Christian roots (Braunstein 2021). While the language used by the Tea Party appears civilizationalist, it is important to recognize that the movement is fundamentally nationalist, and links Judaism and Christianity to the United States, its culture, people, and the documents which created and shaped the nation. Therefore if the Tea Party may be considered in any way a civilizationalist group, then the civilization they are trying to protect is the exceptional Judeo-Christian civilization of the United States. The Tea Party fell into decline during the 2010s. However, many of its supporters were later absorbed into the more significant, though somewhat less religious, Trump movement. While Trump himself does not appear to be a committed Christian, he enjoyed the support of the Christian evangelicals who were generally supportive of the Tea Party, perhaps in part because he ran as a Republican, but also because he picked Evangelical conservative Christian Mike Pence to be his running mate (and eventual Vice President) in 2016. Indeed, "81 percent of white evangelicals voted for Trump" according to one estimate (Pally 2020, 405). Building on previous iterations of American Christian influenced populism, Donald Trump's rhetoric when campaigning for president in 2016 incorporated notions of America as a Judeo-Christian civilization at war with Islam.

Civilizationalism and the Trump Administration
Trump, despite running as a Republican, discarded the free trade rhetoric common to his party, and indeed to the Tea Party faction within the Republican Party, and embraced economic protectionism and a degree of nativism, although he retained the populist anti-elite rhetoric of the Tea Party (Young et al. 2019). As a candidate he initially retained much of the clash of civilizations and anti-Islam rhetoric common to the Tea Party, although he also ran as an anti-war candidate and was critical of the Bush Administration's wars in Iraq and Afghanistan (Haynes 2021). Trump's 'America First' foreign policy was based on the idea that the United States ought to take care of its own citizens first, and force other nations into defending their own territories rather than relying on the United States. However, Trump did not cease demonizing Muslims, even if he called for the American military to begin leaving Afghanistan. Rather, Trump increased, as a candidate for president, the demonization of Muslims as a civilizational 'other', hostile to America's Judeo-Christian culture.

Trump, according to Haynes (2021), continued to repeat the Huntington-esque 'clash of civilizations' rhetoric common to many Republicans, although he added a dangerous new dimension insofar as he did not identify 'radical' Muslims as a threat to the United States, but all Muslims. Using belligerent and divisive language, Haynes (2021) says, Trump insinuated that there was a clash of civilizations between Islam and Judeo-Christian America, and did not distinguish between genuinely dangerous Islamist terrorists who might wish to attack the United States and its people, and ordinary Muslims. Trump was not alone in his campaign team, and later in his administration, in demonizing Muslims by suggesting they hated America. Steve Bannon and Sebastian Gorka, two close Trump advisors, also encouraged the demonization of Muslims, at least before Trump sacked them from his administration in 2017 (Haynes 2021).

Once Trump became president, the demonization of Muslims as an enemy 'other' became a matter of policy. For example, in Executive Order

13,769, often (if unfairly) called as the "Muslim ban", the Trump Administration made substantial changes to the immigration system which targeted citizens from a number of Muslim majority nations. Making good on a promise to reduce the number of refugees accepted into the United States and end the terrorist threat to the country, Executive Order 13,769 banned entry to the United States for people from Iran, Iraq, Somalia, Sudan, Syria, and Yemen (Executive Order 13,769 2017). It is important to note that the ban did not, perhaps for political reasons, extend to citizens of Pakistan, Egypt, or Saudi Arabia, American 'allies' which had previously exported terrorism or had themselves experienced terror attacks, indicating the presence of a terror threat. Nor did the ban extend to citizens of Afghanistan, where the United States was fighting a war against Islamist radicals. Thus Executive Order 13,769 was not a wholesale, so to speak, 'Muslim ban'. However, it was clearly aimed at stopping Muslims from a variety of countries from entering the United States, and was part of a larger effort by the Trump Administration to demonize Muslims and frame Muslims as a threatening 'other'.

Trump's foreign policy was influenced by nations of America as a Judeo-Christian power. This was evident in the administration's religious freedom agenda (Haynes 2020). Religious freedom is protected by the U.S. constitution, and the U.S. State Department has an Office of International Religious Freedom which seeks to globalize religious freedom, a mission the Office claims is a "core objective of U.S. foreign policy" (Office of International Religious Freedom 2022). The American state department's conception of religious freedom has been categorized as "Judeo-Christian" in the sense that, whether or not the authentic values of the United States are a product of Judaic and Christian thought, the department believes that "fundamental values of Western society …come from both Judaism and Christianity" and that the U.S. foreign policy out to reflect these values (Altshuler 2016; Hurd 2010). Religious freedom is said to be one of the core values of 'Judeo-Christian' culture and civilization, although it is obvious that religious freedom has not always been a core value of Christian or Jewish-dominated societies (Office of International Religious Freedom 2022). The Trump Administration did not cease promoting religious freedoms around the world; rather, during Trump's presidency a "privileging of Judeo-Christian values …replaced a more flexible Christocentric approach, which characterized the three prior administrations". This new approach "was contoured by ideological commitment to a Judeo-Christian" moral and ethnical worldview, though one based on conservative evangelical Christianity (Haynes 2020). For example, the Trump Administration increased efforts to highlight the suffering and persecution of Christian communities, and refused to fund health and humanitarian agencies that performed or funded abortions in foreign countries (Haynes 2020).

The Trump Administration's exceptionally strong support for the nation of Israel, and its recognition of Jerusalem, not Tel Aviv, as the capital of Israel, may demonstrate Trump commitment to the idea of America as a Judeo-Christian nation, or of America as belonging to a wider Judeo-Christian civilization which includes Israel (Schake 2017). Speaking in 2016 to the pro-Israel lobby group AIPAC, Trump promised that, if elected, he would "move the American embassy to the eternal capital of the Jewish people, Jerusalem", an act which would "send a clear signal that there is no daylight between America and our most reliable ally, the state of Israel". (Time 2016) In the same speech he warned Palestinians that, under his administration, they would be forced to "come to the table knowing that the bond between the United States and Israel is absolutely, totally unbreakable" (Time 2016). Furthermore, the idea that the United States and Israel are core states of a broader Judeo-Christian civilization appears to have played an increased role, at least according to Raphael Greenberg, an Israeli archeologist and academic, in American foreign policy under the Trump Administration. Greenberg (2021) observes the use of the term "Judeo-Christian" by "the American right" since the 1980s "to highlight its support of right-wing activism in Israel and its opposition to "secular liberals" and the Islamic Other". He finds an extreme example of this in the visit of Mike Pompeo, secretary of State in the Trump Administration from 2018 to 2021, to Israel in November 2020. Pompeo, Greenberg writes (2021), visited the "high-profile, settler-run antiquities site of "the City of David" in Israeli-annexed East Jerusalem, in and beneath the Palestinian neighborhood of Wadi Hilweh (Silwan), less than two hundred yards away from the Temple Mount and the Al-Aqsa mosque". A long discussion of this disputed site is included in this book's chapter on civilizational populism in Israel. It will suffice to say here that the site claimed by some Israeli Archeologists and the settler-run Ir David Foundation (or Elad) as the 'City of David' is the centerpiece of an archeological park in Jerusalem. According to Elad, which manages the park, the 'City of David' excavations prove that Jewish people were the earliest inhabitants of the region, which therefore belongs to their descendants (City of David 2022). According to the Trump Administration's press release, Mike Pompeo's visit to the 'City of David' archeological site highlighted "the more than 3,000 years of Jerusalem's heritage upon which the foundations of both the US and Israel rest" (Kempinski 2020). Greenberg describes the visit and this particular language as "a clear demonstration of a religious-political ideology that continues to reverberate in Israel and Palestine, even after the end of the Trump years" (Greenberg 2021).

Shortly before Pompeo's visit to the City of David, the American embassy installed a plaque in the city of David's evacuation tunnels shortly before Pompeo's visit, which reads "The spiritual bedrock of our values as a nation comes from Jerusalem. It is upon these ideals that the American Republic was founded, and the unbreakable bond between the United States and Israel was formed" (Greenberg 2021). Greenberg considers this further evidence that "Pompeo and the Christian right" believe "the elevation of Donald Trump to the presidency" was "part of God's plan", and furthermore that "in the words of Mike Evans", a prolific author and evangelical advisor to President Trump, "Israel has received a gift from God in an evangelical Secretary of State, an evangelical Vice President and a President who is the most pro-Israel, pro-evangelical President in American history" (Greenberg 2021). This may or may not be true. Either way, it suggests that the incorporation of Israel and America into a single Judeo-Christian tradition is important to the Trump Administration, and may be related to both a desire to demonize Muslims as a civilizational 'other' outside of the Judeo-Christian tradition, and to please the administration's Christian Zionist supporters.

Civilizational Populism in the Discourse of Donald Trump
Trump's populist civilizationalism was especially evident when he was campaigning for president, and in the first year of his presidency. When campaigning for president, Trump claimed that American 'elites'—exemplified by Democratic Party Presidential Candidate Hilary Clinton—were unwilling to protect America from Muslim terrorists, but had instead allowed "thousands upon thousands" of Muslims to immigrate to America, increasing the terror threat (Time 2016). This Trump used as evidence of the corruption of America's elite, and their betrayal of 'the people' and their interests. Indeed, when running for President Trump claimed that Muslim refugees from the Middle East ought to be stopped from entering the country, and used what Hall (2021) describes as "clearly existential tones" to pronounce "that taking in refugees from

Syria (who he assumed to be potential terrorists) would lead to 'the destruction of civilization as we know it!'. When a Muslim man who had sworn allegiance to Islamic State, Omar Mateen, murdered 49 people at a gay nightclub in Orlando, Florida in June 2016, Trump used the massacred to highlight the dangers of "radical Islam" (Time 2016). Trump claimed that then President Obama was ultimately responsible for the terrorist atrocity insofar as he had presided over a foolish immigration policy that allowed Muslims to migrate to America (Time 2016). According to Trump, America's "dysfunctional immigration system" was bringing in Muslims who possessed "the same thought process" as the "savage killer" Mateen (Time 2016). Muslim thought processes, Trump furthermore claimed, were the product of religion and culture "incompatible with Western values and institutions" (Time 2016). According to Trump, "radical Islam is anti-woman, anti-gay and anti-American", and "enslaves women" (Time 2016). If elected president, he said in a 2016 speech, he would not "allow America to become a place where gay people, Christian people, Jewish people are targets of persecution" (Time 2016). Moreover, he would, he promised his audience, take power away from self-interested elites, and make certain that America's immigration policies reflected the interest of the American people (Time 2016). Portraying himself as a savior, and drawing deeply on feelings of nostalgia for a past American golden age, Trump promised that his administration would, if elected, defeat Islamic radicalism and make America great again (Time 2016).

In an interview with an evangelical Christian magazine during which he was asked whether the United States was created based on Judeo-Christian values, Trump affirmed that "it was ... to a large extent". Trump added that when he sees "football coaches being fired because they held a prayer on the field, like yesterday, I think it's absolutely terrible, I think it's a terrible thing. I see so many things happening that are so different from what our country used to be. So religion's a very important part of me and it's also, I think it's a very important part of our country". (Blue 2016). It is unlikely that religion was particularly important to Trump, a man who when asked for his favorite Bible verse, replied with a straight face "an eye for an eye" (ABC News 2016). However, his remarks demonstrate a desire to portray himself as a defender of Christian practices and the notion of America as a Judeo-Christian nation.

Trump's chief advisors during his campaign for president, Steve Bannon and Sebastian Gorka, made stronger remarks about Islam and its incompatibility to America's Judeo-Christian culture. Gorka, who later became Deputy Assistant to the President of the United States in the Trump Administration, claimed that Islam is an "enemy ideology" at war with America. Gorka furthermore claimed that Muslim terrorists were motivated by hatred of America's Judeo-Christian traditions, and that a "nuanced" explanation for Islamist terror was not required (Haynes 2017). Earlier, in 2014, Steve Bannon that "the Judeo-Christian West" faced an existential war with Islam, which were the West to lose would "completely eradicate everything that we've been bequeathed over the last 2,000, 2,500 years" (Hirsh 2016). Mike Flynn, who became national security advisor in the Trump Administration, claimed on Twitter that "Fear of Muslims is RATIONAL", characteristically making no distinction between violent radicals and ordinary Muslim people, and thus exacerbating the civilizational conflict rhetoric common to several members of the administration including Trump himself. (Hirsh 2016).

Following his election victory in 2016, Trump traveled to Poland where he gave a speech which described the right-wing Law and Justice Party government as a model for others to follow, insofar as it was protecting the West through its anti-immigration policies that prevented Muslims from immigrating to the country. Trump's civilizationalism—and belief in the clash of civilizations between the Judeo-Christian West and Islam—reveals itself no better than in his Poland speech, in which he remarked that "the fundamental question of our time is whether the West has the will to survive. Do we have the confidence in our values to defend them at any cost? Do we have enough respect for our citizens to protect our borders? Do we have the desire and the courage to preserve our civilization in the face of those who would subvert and destroy it?" (Time 2017). Historian Stephen Wertheim described Trump's speech as having outlined a new "civilizational framework", which was in part a continuation of Obama and Bush era justifications of America's occupations of Afghanistan and Iraq, but which added a new element in which America's "forever wars" were framed as part of a policing of the "enemies of civilization" (Wertheim 2017). This was perhaps a mischaracterization, given that Trump sought to end those wars. However, Wertheim is right to point out the essential civilizationalism of Trump remarks.

Later in his presidency, as Trump sought to further wind down the 'War on Terror' and end the war in Afghanistan, he ceased using civilizational rhetoric against Muslims (Hall 2021). Having overseen the "territorial defeat of ISIS and the relative decline of 'lone wolf' attacks in the West", and having fired Bannon and Gorka, "Trump ...changed the primary target of his crisis rhetoric from terrorists to immigrants" (Hall 2021, 58). According to Hall, when a caravan of at least 5000 people was found to be headed toward the U.S. southern border with the intention of seeking asylum, Trump claimed that it constituted an "invasion" of the United States by "criminals and unknown Middle Easterners" among others (Hall 2021, 57). Thus, Trump's populist rhetoric shifted somewhat during his presidency, insofar as his claims that elites were permitting the destruction of Judeo-Christian values and civilization by allowing the mass immigration of Muslims to the West gradually disappeared. However, as Hall (2021) points out, Trump continued to argue that elites were ignoring the interests of 'the people' by refusing to police the border, and prevent criminals from invading the United States. It appears, then, that as the War on Terror became increasingly perceived as a failure, and when few Islamist terror attacks occurred during his presidency, Trump no longer felt compelled or saw any political advantage in framing Muslims as a civilizational threat to the West or to America's Judeo-Christian values, or in framing elites such as former President Obama and Hilary Clinton as immoral and for allowing Muslims to immigrate to America.

4.4 Discussion of Case Studies

This chapter has described how Christianity is today incorporated into the populist agendas of a wide variety of populist movements the world over. Throughout the cases we how Christian identity plays a vital role in civilizational populism among both religious and secular political parties and movements. Most Christian populism, however, draws little from Christian ethics, literature, spirituality, or theology, and must therefore be considered primarily identitarian. This is true even when there is a mixing of secular and religious power, such as occurs in Hungary, Brazil, and Italy, where elements within various churches and religious communities support the Fidesz and Lega parties, respectively. Yet it has emerged not as an authentic expression of Christian religious belief, ideas, or practices, or a desire to re-create 'Christendom'. In Europe, Christian civilizational populism appears to have emerged in reaction to Muslim immigration. This is not true, however, of all Christian-based populisms. In the United States, Protestant Christianity was an important element in the populism of the People's Party and the movement centered on

Huey Long. The Tea Party and Trump movement sought support from American Christians, and used Christian identitarian language at times, but their language was rarely civilizational, but was instead nationalist. The anti-Muslim feeling appears to have played a role in strengthening the United States' Christian identity, but unlike in Western Europe, this identity had not been subsumed by secularism; nor has Muslim immigration itself become a primary animating force behind the rise of populism. In Brazil, Muslim immigration plays no role in the rise of the Christian populism of Bolsonaro. Instead, Bolsonaro seeks the support of Christian churches, who see him as a social conservative ally, and appears to be attempting to create an large 'ingroup' based on shared Christian values and identity. Bolsonaro's populism is reliant, in particular, on Pentecostal churches and Charismatic Catholics to construct populist-civilizational divisions within Brazilian society.

In Europe, however, Christian identitarian populism is inseparable from anti-Muslim rhetoric and civilizationalism. Fear of a Muslim invasion plays a key role in the discourse of all the European Christian identitarian populist parties we studied, including the two parties we selected for our longer case studies. Orbán and Wilders lead two very different parties. Fidesz has been the ruling party of Hungary for two decades, and has been able to re-shape Hungarian identity and consolidate control over several important Hungarian institutions including the universities. Wilders' Party for Freedom has never won government in its own right, and has suffered from being placed within a *cordon sanitaire* due to Wilders' controversial statements. Yet the PVV remains one of the largest parties in the Netherlands, and Wilders' influence nationally—and internationally—has made him something of a figurehead of right-wing populism the world over.

Our findings suggest that Europe is home to the most significant Christian populist movements and parties. The identitarian populism of radical right populist parties such as the French National Rally, and the Geert Wilders led Party for Freedom in the Netherlands, for example, differentiates between peoples on the basis of the religion-defined civilizations to which they are supposed to belong, i.e. Islamic civilization, Western (Judeo-)Christian civilization. Yet, these parties, because they take nothing from Christian ethics, theology, or tradition, and are merely concerned with using Christian identity to oppose the entry of Muslims into Western civilization and protecting secularism, cannot be called religious. For these 'Christianist secular' populist parties, Christianity is identified as the progenitor of Western Europe's secularism and liberalism (Brubaker 2017), and Islam as a civilizational threat to European culture, secularism, and identity.

Another group of radical right populist parties in Europe, toward the East, remain broadly identitarian, but also link their political program to the traditional or conservative values of the Catholic Church or the various Orthodox Churches. Hungarian Prime Minister Viktor Orbán's governing Fidesz party reinterpreted and "re-framed" Christianity in a "non-universalistic, nationalist way to legitimize [Fidesz] rule" (Ádám and Bozóki 2016a, b, 98). Fidesz, while not a deeply religious party, has consistently portrayed itself and Orbán as socially conservative, Christian, nationalist and thus close to the Church. Moreover, the "Orbán regime demonstrates that radical right-wing populism employs a quasi-religious ideological construction through which it attempts to mobilize a wider social spectrum: ethnonationalism" (Ádám and Bozóki, 2016a, b, 98).

How, then, do Trump, Orbán, and Wilders incorporate religion and civilizationalism into their populist narratives? There are instructive similarities and differences between the two men's discourses. Orbán's discourse posits that Hungary is a historically Christian nation, and that its culture and values are based on Christianity. He does not claim that there is no other influence; indeed, he acknowledges Hungarians' Asian and pagan origins. Nor does he claim that Hungarians are a uniquely religious people, or that Christian belief and practice is an essential element of Hungarian culture. An atheist, according to Orbán, remains a Christian in Europe. What, then, is a Christian in Orbán's rhetoric? A Christian is someone who identifies as a Christian in a cultural sense, and who lives according to the socially conservative values Orbán and Fidesz foster and encourage in Hungary. An atheist or agnostic person, then, can be a Christian in Hungary, because Christianity has been secularized into Hungarian culture and its traditional values, leaving the two inseparable. Orbán performs a crisis in which Muslim immigrants, the European Union, and social progressives, present an existential threat to Hungarian—and European—identity and culture. Muslims, according to Orbán, are poised to invade Hungary and Europe and destroy their Christian culture and values. The European Union's permissive immigration policies, according to Orbán, by allowing millions of Muslims to enter Europe, facilitate the death of Christian culture in Europe. Thus when Orbán calls for the defense of Christianity or Christian civilization, he is also calling for the defense of European culture and traditional European values as he understands them. Christianity, then, is used to define the identity and values of 'the people' of Hungary, and to 'other' those who oppose or reject Orbán particular vision of Hungarian nationality. Orbán's civilizationalism, therefore, is constructed in opposition to Islam and liberal progressivism. He identifies socially conservative 'Christian' values as the authentic values of Hungary and Europe, and by doing so portrays Muslims and social progressives as inauthentically European and non-Christian.

Wilders, too, claims that Muslims and the European Union threaten Western civilization. However, Wilders' conception of European values and cultures is profoundly different to Orbáns'. Where Orbán connects Christianity with social conservatism and 'traditional' values, Wilders describes Western values as Judeo-Christian and humanist. In making this claim, Wilders links Christianity with the secular liberal values possessed by the majority of Dutch. Wilders' conception of Judeo-Christianity appears to be largely constructed in reaction to the immigration of tens of thousands of Muslims to the Netherlands, and the impact the presence of Islam has had on Dutch self-identity. He posits that the Judeo-Christian and Humanist West faces an existential threat from Islam. Moreover he does not consider Islam a true religion, like Christianity and Judaism, because it does not respect, he claims, the boundary between religion and politics. The key feature of Christianity, for Wilders, is its inherently secular nature, or Christianity's ability to 'render to Caesar that which is Caesar's'. Christianity, according to Wilders', is the ultimate source of the West's freedom. Islam, he claims, is a "totalitarian" belief system which is antithetical to Western values. Islam would, he says, destroy women's rights and gay rights, oppress Jews and ex-Muslims, and ultimately create an unfree society in the Netherlands.

When Wilders identifies centrist and left-wing parties, and the European Union, as civilizational enemies, he does so not because he believes they are attempting to destroy socially conservative Christian or 'traditional' values, but because he believes the European Union's lax immigration rules—which are broadly supported by the Dutch center and left-wing parties—will ultimately be responsible for the Islamization of the Netherlands and the destruction of its socially liberal values and culture. Curiously, Wilders—an ostensible liberal—becomes very illiberal when speaking about the need to restrict the ability of Muslims to practice their religion in the Netherlands. He defends the paradox by claiming that in order to preserve social liberal values and mores, Muslims—who he alleges wish to oppress women, homosexuals, Jews, etc....—must themselves be censored and prevented from carrying out their plans. Therefore Wilders calls for the defense of Judeo-Christian civilization by demanding that no further mosques being constructed in the Netherlands, and that Muslim women be forbidden from wearing headscarves in government buildings. Yet if Wilders is waging a civilizational war on behalf of Judeo-Christian and Humanist Western Civilizational against Islam, there is little Christianity or Judaism in his conception of Western civilization. Instead, his conception of Western civilization appears to be constructed in order to 'other' Muslims, and to frame Muslims as fundamentally different to the Dutch and incompatible with their culture.

It is instructive to observe that Trump also claimed that Muslims were too conservative, misogynist, homophobic, and Judeophobic to assimilate into Western civilization. Yet Trump's civilizational rhetoric appears to have largely dissipated once Muslim terrorism ceased in the United States, and when the Trump Administration was attempting to withdraw soldiers from Afghanistan. Equally Trump's 'Judeo-Christian' religious freedom policies, and his strong support for Israel, were probably the result of his reliance on electoral support from evangelical Christians than from a deeply held belief that Judeo-Christian values and the protection of Jews and Christians above all other people ought to be core values upon which the United States builds its foreign policy. Yet Trump, especially when campaigning for president and, in his speech in Poland in 2016 as president, incorporated civilizationalism within his populist discourse, framing 'the people' as innocent victims or corrupt 'elites', who had betrayed the people they governed by allowing Muslims to immigrate in large numbers to the West, where—according to Trump—they threatened to destroy the Judeo-Christian values of Western civilization.

Orbán, on the other hand, associates his government with churches and is himself a participant in Christian rituals. However, while he claims his ultimate aim is to re-Christianize Europe, his idea of re-Christianization does not appear to require belief in God. Moreover, neither Orbán nor Wilders desires a pan-Christian government or any kind of rule by religious authorities. Yet while they use civilizational rhetoric and seek out transnational relationships, these relationships tend to be political in nature, and with other anti-Muslim right-wing parties and movements. Both are nationalists, and hostile toward the European Union, although Orbán appears content for Hungary to remain an

EU member. Their Christian civilizationalism, then, is not an attempt to create a new form of transnational Christian government; it is a method of othering their core enemies: Muslims, the European Union, and centrist and left-wing politicians who support open borders and the free movement of peoples, multiculturalism, globalism. Their civilizationalism, while important, is always subordinate to nationalism within their respective populist ideologies; civilizationalism is a method of differentiating between the ingroup and outgroups. Moreover it is used to help create a belief that an existential crisis is descending upon Europe, that European culture is on the brink of being obliterated by a Muslim invasion, and that only Wilders and Orbán, respectively, have the courage to prevent the death of (Judeo-)Christian Europe.

Trump, Orbán, and Wilders alike portray the increasing presence of Islam in the West as part of a wider civilizational crisis brought about by elite corruption, globalization, multiculturalism, and open borders. In this shared civilizational populist discourse Islam is portrayed as a dangerous foreign ideology antithetical to the West's native (Judeo-)Christian values and culture, yet also as something of an unstoppable force which cannot be contained, or at least not within a political environment dominated by multiculturalism and globalism. Orbán, Trump, and Wilders also attempt to frame their supporters as victims of elite corruption, arrogance, and indifference. It may appear strange that presidents and prime ministers should portray themselves as outsiders and part of the non-elite 'people'. However, because populists distinguish between 'the people' and 'elites' primarily through morality, and perceive 'the people' as pure and moral and elites as immoral insofar as they have abandoned the culture and religion of 'the people', then anyone—despite their wealth and power—can become part of the people if they share the people's values and moral beliefs.

Orbán, for example, portrays Muslims as a threat which he personally keeps at bay, despite the best efforts of the EU to force him to admit Muslims into Hungary, something which he claims would precipitate the death of Christian culture in Hungary. Wilders also claims that the Dutch are victims of Muslims, who are terrorists, criminals, and totalitarians who will destroy Dutch culture and the Judeo-Christian and humanist values of Western civilization. Yet the Dutch, according to Wilders, are also victims of the centrist parties of the Netherlands, which have permitted Muslims to destroy the country and its culture and values. By evoking a sense of victimhood in their electorates, Orbán and Wilders, respectively, seek to justify their anti-Muslim agenda, which includes the cessation of Muslim immigration, and restrictions of Islamic practice, by framing it as a form of self-defense against Muslim aggression. Equally, the elicitation of feelings of fear and victimhood also helps Orbán and Wilders create feelings of anger in their supporters. In this case, angry and hateful feelings toward the 'elites' who permit Muslims to immigrate to Europe and destroy the continent's native (Judeo-)Christian culture and values, but also Muslims themselves.

Trump, Wilders, and Orbán all draw on nostalgia for a partly imagined past in which life was superior. Wilders, for example, encouraged his supporters to reflect on the glory of the Dutch Golden Age, in which rather than receiving Muslim immigrants, the Dutch colonized Muslim lands and spread their culture across south-east Asia. He calls for Dutch people to feel pride in their cultural achievements, and their reclaiming of the lowlands from the sea, and to believe that if Muslims were removed from the country the Netherlands might reclaim its former greatness. Orbán, on the other hand, cannot point to a time in which Hungarians were conquering foreign peoples on the other side of the world. However, he encourages the Hungarian people to feel pride in their ability to preserve their culture during Ottoman occupation, and throughout the brutal twentieth century. He also claims that Hungarians played a vital role in protecting Europe from Ottoman invasion, and calls upon 'the people' to feel proud of their contributions to European culture. Trump, on the other hand, promised to make America great again, but was ambiguous about when this period of greatness was, although he claimed he would be able to restore America's greatness.

Yet while Orbán, Trump, and Wilders share the same civilizational conception of the world and seek to construct, in their discourse, similar outgroups (Muslims, 'elites', globalists, the European Union) they frame the ingroup and outgroups in a different manner. Trump and Wilders frame Muslims as a conservative and regressive force in Western society, and a threat to liberal individualism, freedom, women's rights, and gay rights. In Wilders' discourse "we" are liberal, open, free, and respect women and homosexuals, but Muslims do not. Equally, he portrays the European Union as a threat to the Dutch people's ability to control their borders, and prevent the Islamization of their society. Wilders' ostensible liberalism, secularism, and Christian civilizational rhetoric is thus described by Brubaker as "Christianist Secularism" insofar as it combines Christian identity with a defense of secularism (Brubaker, 2017). Orbán, however, does not combine his Christian identity rhetoric with a defense of liberal values. Instead, he seeks to defend traditional values as he understands them. Orbán's civilizational populism has two distinct aspects. First, an ethnic dimension, which allows Orbán to portray himself and his party as representing and protecting ethnic Hungarians. Second, a civilizational aspect, which allows Orbán to 'other' Muslims and progressive 'elites' by portraying them as enemies of Hungary (and Europe's) Judeo-Christian cultural traditions. Orbán portrays the European Union as a political body which is aggressively interfering in Hungarian affairs in order to force the nation to adopt progressive, liberal values which, he claims, are antithetical to the authentic Christian values Hungarians have traditionally held. Equally, he does not appear to portray Muslims as a regressive and socially conservative people. Instead, according to Orbán "we" have held fast to traditional Christian values in the face of European Union and globalist elites' pressure to adopt progressive values, and the persistent threat of Muslim invasion. Thus Orbán and Wilders may attempt to construct similar ingroups and outgroups with their discourse, but they frame the ingroup and outgroups in a very different manner (see Table 4.1 These differences are part of a regional divide in Europe, between the more liberal and secularist Christian civilizationalist parties of North-Western Europe, and the socially conservative 'traditionalist' populist parties of a number of Central and Eastern European nations, especially Poland's Law and Justice Party and Hungary's Fidesz.

Civilizationalism was less important, overall, in Trump's discourse. However, his policies on religious freedom and Israel might be understood as reflecting a belief in the superiority of Judeo-Christian values and civilization, and the inferiority of all other religions and cultures. Trump portrayed Muslims as both a physical threat to the American people, but also as a less tangible threat to Judeo-Christian values. Yet these values do not appear to be especially religious, but rather incorporate women's rights, gay rights, and the protection of Jewish citizens from anti-Semitism. However, at other times Trump portrays Judeo-Christian values as essentially evangelical Christian values. This suggests that there is no core to Trump's conception of Judeo-Christianity, and that it is an empty term which can be whatever required of it at a given moment. The one constant is that it is always used to exclude other Muslims.

An important difference between the three leaders is the transnational links each has attempted to foster. Trump appears to have been largely uninterested in transnational links with other right-wing populists,

Table 4.1 Narratives of Christian populist parties

Party	Identity narrative	Crisis narrative	Civilizational narrative	Victimhood narrative
Party for Freedom	- "The people" are Judeo-Christian ethnic Europeans - "The others" are the political elite who fail to stop immigrants, and non-European, non-Judeo-Christian immigrants, especially Muslims	- "Threat" of Islam to the Dutch value system - Fear of Islamist jihadism - Fear of losing financial and territorial control of the EU - Need to preserve the Judo-Christian civilizational identity	- A secularized Judo-Christian identity - Love for the Dutch nation and a fixation of the "Golden Age" - Identifying with the Western ethos of transnational Western civilization	- "The people" are victims of elite-driven globalization and mass immigration -Islam is "taking over" the Netherlands and destroying its Judeo-Christian and Humanist values - "The people" are victims of the European Union elite
Fidesz	- "The people" are the "rightful" Hungarian and Christian owners of the land - "The others" are the political elite who encourage immigration and globalization immigrants, progressives, and Muslims -Immigrants are a cultural and security threat to "the people"	- Loss of Hungarian culture - Threat Islamist jihadism and Islamization - Disapproval of Roma people and their lifestyle - Judo-Christian civilization is threatened and traditional values are threatened by gender fluidity, feminism, and the broader progressive agenda	- Judo-Christian identity is rooted in Catholicism - Hungarian ethnic and national identity is emphasized -Islam is a civilizational threat -Western progressivism is a civilizational threat	- The Hungarian people are victims of fundamentalist Islam and *jihadi* terror - Victims of elite attacks on traditional family values -Hungarian people are treated as "outcasts" by elites

Party	Identity narrative	Crisis narrative	Civilizational narrative	Victimhood narrative
Trump Administration	- "the people" are morally good American Judeo-Christians - "Muslims" are portrayed as threats to the Judeo-Christian people of America - "Elites" are corrupt and immoral, and have abandoned the Judeo-Christian culture of "the people" and ignore their interests by allowing Muslims to "invade" America	"Muslims" are committing violent terrorist attacks, and threaten women, homosexuals, and Jews "Elites" are ultimately responsible for the crisis threatening America and its Judeo-Christian foundational values	Islam is waging a war again the Judeo-Christian civilization of the West to which America belongs	Judeo-Christian Americans, particularly white, working-class Americans, are victims of an elite that doesn't care about them, and of Muslims who threaten to exterminate their way of life and core beliefs

and pursued an 'America First' foreign policy based largely on transactional arrangements between nations. The only exception was Israel, with which Trump sought closer ties based on shared interests. Orbán, on the other hand, has sought an "Eastern opening", in order to establish close ties with autocratic, collectivist, anti-liberal polities such as China and Russia, which he believes to share "common interests" with Hungary. Wilders, however, has sought closer ties with Christian-based civilizational populists in the supposedly freedom loving Judeo-Christian world, especially in the United States, Western Europe, and Australia. His transcontinental tours designed to form alliances with right-wing conservatives, and his use of social media to disseminate English language videos, are examples of how Wilders' civilizational populism is exported to a wider audience. (See Tables 4.1 and 4.2).

Based on this survey, we find that the relationship between Christianity and populism is complex and multifaceted, and often more connected to identity than religion. What the Christianity-based civilizational populisms have in common, however, is that they often place Christianity within a sacred matrix of ethnos, nation, and civilization, in which (Judeo-)Christianity acts as a signifier of all three. Equally, we find that the reason Europe—in particular—is home to so many politically and electorally successful Christian populist parties is because the growing presence of Islam creates a sense of fear all too easily exploited by populists. In an environment in which religious belief and practice have declined to the point where atheism is unremarkable, and secular differentiation of church and state is considered normal, the perceived and real religiosity of Muslim immigrants may itself appear to constitute a threat to secular arrangements. Moreover, the presence of Islam may alter Western European self-perception, leading Europeans to feel that secularism is not merely a neutral space between religions, but a specific product of the West's Christian or Judeo-Christian heritage. Thus secular Europeans may perceive Islam as a religion unable to produce secularism, and therefore a threat to their Christian yet secularized culture and values. In a sense, believing that 'we' are returning to our traditional 'Judeo-Christian' values may also be a way of increasing European societies' ontological security in an age defined by rapid change. In what Bauman (2000) identified as 'liquid modernity', in which nations are no longer solid objects with impermeable borders, and in which the old solid categories of 'race' and 'ethnicity' have been exploded by science, it is impossible to define a nation by anything other than its cultural heritage. Therefore it

4 CHRISTIANITY AND CIVILIZATIONAL POPULISM   167

Table 4.2   Comparison of Christian populist case studies

	Pro-violent narratives	*Links or overlaps with the far right*	*Transnational dimension, diasporas*
Fidesz	- Portrays immigrants, Roma, liberal values, and Muslims as a "danger" to Hungarian society. Legitimizes the anger and paves way for violence to defend the "victimized" "people"	- Known for tolerating and funding far-right online social media groups - Not officially linked to far-rights groups but maintains transnational ties with authoritarians and other Christian populists in Eastern Europe	- Maintains transnational ties with authoritarian states in China and Russia; links with American conservatives - Uses Hungarian ethnicity to construct an ethnoreligious connection with Eastern European states and to a degree Central Asia
PVV	- Demonization of Muslim immigrants as terrorists and uncivilized "threats" to Dutch society - Deflection of blame toward the EU, aggressive civilizationalist rhetoric	- Within the EU parliament, gives support and creates coalitions with right-wing parties such as Identity and Democracy (ID) and Europe of Nations and Freedom (ENL) - Creates transnational connections with right-wing parties and alliances in Australia and North America	- Transatlantic connections with right-wing parties and alliances in Australia and the North America; praises identitarian European right-wing leaders - Transmission of populist ideas via English video on internet, and spreading anti-immigration and anti-Muslim content on digital media outlets
Trump Administration	- Describes all Muslims as dangerous radicals who "hate" America and wish to destroy Western civilization	- Trump called upon all Western nations to follow Poland's lead and restrict Muslim immigration, and defend Judeo-Christianity	-Not applicable

is not surprising that right-wing populist parties across the West should combine, to differing degrees and in different ways, civilizationalism and populism.

REFERENCES

ABC News. 2016. "Donald Trump: My Favorite Bible Verse is 'Eye for an Eye'." https://abcnews.go.com/Politics/donald-trump-favorite-bible-verse-eye-eye/story?id=38416270. (Last accessed September 21, 2022).

Ádám, Zoltán, and András Bozóki. 2016a. State and Faith: Right-wing Populism and Nationalized Religion in Hungary. *Intersections EEJSP* 2: 98–122. https://doi.org/10.17356/ieejsp.v2i1.143.

Ádám, Zoltán, and András Bozóki. 2016b. "The God of the Hungarians." In *Saving the People: How Populists Hijack Religion*, edited by Nadia Marzouki, Duncan McDonnell and Olivier Roy. London: C. Hurst & Co.

Altshuler, George. 2016, December 1. "What Are 'Judeo-Christian' Values? Analyzing a Controversial Term." *Washington Jewish Week*. https://www.washingtonjewishweek.com/judeo-christian/. (Last accessed 30 December, 2022).

Apahideanu, Ionut. 2014. Religious Populism: The Coup De Grâce to Secularisation Theories. *South-East European Journal of Political Science* II (1, 2): 71–100. (1) (PDF) Populism and Religion. https://www.researchgate.net/publication/321805689_Populism_and_Religion (Last accessed December 30, 2022).

Asad, Talal. 1993. *Genealogies of Religion: Discipline and Reasons of Power in Christianity and Islam*. United Kingdom: Johns Hopkins University Press. https://muse.jhu.edu/book/16014.

BBC. 2010, October 4. "In quotes: Geert Wilders." https://www.bbc.com/news/world-europe-11469579. (Last accessed September 21, 2022).

Bellah, Robert N. 1967. Civil Religion in America. *Daedalus* 96 (1): 1–21. JSTOR. http://www.jstor.org/stable/20027022.

Berntzen, Einar, and Maren Christensen Bjune. 2012. Introduction: Religion and Politics in Latin America. *Iberoamericana. Nordic Journal of Latin American and Caribbean Studies*. 42: 15–20.

Boffey, Daniel. 2018. "Orbán Claims Hungary is Last Bastion Against 'Islamisation' of Europe." *The Guardian*. https://www.theguardian.com/world/2018/feb/18/Orbán-claims-hungary-is-last-bastion-against-islamisation-of-europe. (Last accessed September 21, 2022).

Bozoki, Andras. 2016. "Mainstreaming the Far Right Cultural Politics in Hungary." *RECEO*.https://www.cairn.info/revue-revue-d-etudes-comparatives-est-ouest1-2016-4-page-87.htm. (Last accessed September 21, 2022).

Braunstein, Ruth. 2021. "The "Right" History: Religion, Race, and Nostalgic Stories of Christian America." *Religions* 12: 95. https://doi.org/10.3390/rel12020095.

Brubaker, Rogers. 2016, October 11. "A new "Christianist" secularism in Europe". *The Immanent Frame*. https://tif.ssrc.org/2016/10/11/a-new-christianist-secularism-in-europe/. (Last accessed 30 December, 2022).

Brubaker, Rogers. 2017. Between Nationalism and Civilizationism: The European Populist Moment in Comparative Perspective. *Ethnic and Racial Studies* 40 (8): 1191–1226. https://doi.org/10.1080/01419870.2017.1294700.

Buzogány, A. 2017. "Illiberal democracy in Hungary: Authoritarian diffusion or domestic causation?" In *Democratization: Clusters of Authoritarian Diffusion and Cooperation: The Role of Interests vs. Ideology?* Guest Editors: André Bank and Kurt Weyland 24 (7): 1307–1325. https://doi.org/10.1080/13510347.2017.1328676.

Carroll, Rory. 2015, September 12. "America's Dark and Not-Very-Distant History of Hating Catholics." *The Guardian*. https://www.theguardian.com/world/2015/sep/12/america-history-of-hating-catholics. (Last accessed September 21, 2022).

Casanova, José. 2009. The Secular and Secularisms. *Social Research* 76 (4). https://www.jstor.org/stable/40972201.

Confino, Jotam. 2020, December 11. "Europe's Most Provocative Far-Right Politician is Looking to Israel for Answers." *Haaretz*. https://www.haaretz.com/israel-news/.premium-europe-s-most-provocative-far-right-politician-is-looking-to-israel-for-answers-1.9363024. (Last accessed September 21, 2022).

Creech, Joe. 2006. *Righteous Indignation Religion and the Populist Revolution*. Champagne: University of Illinois Press.

Damhuis, Koen. 2019, July 24. "The Biggest Problem in the Netherlands": Understanding the Party for Freedom's Politicization of Islam." *Brookings*. https://www.brookings.edu/research/the-biggest-problem-in-the-netherlands-understanding-the-party-for-freedoms-politicization-of-islam/. (Last accessed September 21, 2022).

Damhuis, Koen. 2021. "Dutch Elections: Mark Rutte Wins Another Term but Fragmented Results Mask Continuing Popularity of the Far Right." *The Conversation*. https://theconversation.com/dutch-elections-mark-rutte-wins-another-term-but-fragmented-results-mask-continuing-popularity-of-the-far-right-156993. (Last accessed September 21, 2022).

de la Torre, Carlos and Anselmi, Manuel. 2019. "Epilogue: Further Areas of Research." In *Routledge Handbook of Global* Populism, edited by Carlos de la Torre. New York: Routledge.

Davies, Peter. 2010. The Front National and Catholicism: From *intégrisme* to Joan of Arc and Clovis. *Religion Compass* 4 (9): 530–587. https://doi.org/10.1111/j.1749-8171.2010.00237.x.

Demir, Mustafa, and Omer Shener. 2021, March 9. "Populist International (II)—Geert Wilders, an Agent of Anti-Islam Populist International Alliance." *European Center for Populism Studies.* https://www.populismstudies.org/populist-international-ii-geert-wilders-an-agent-of-anti-islamist-populist-international-alliance/. (Last accessed September 21, 2022).

Dettmer, Jamie. 2019, August 8. "Dutch Headwear Ban Sparks Vigilantism Fears." *Voice of America.* https://www.voanews.com/europe/dutch-headwear-ban-sparks-vigilantism-fears. (Last accessed September 21, 2022).

Dochuk, D. 2012. Tea Party America and the Born-Again Politics of the Populist Right. *New Labor Forum* 21: 15–21. https://doi.org/10.4179/NLF.211.0000004.

Douthat, Ross. 2021. "Why Hungary Inspires So Much Fear and Fascination." *The New York Times.* https://www.nytimes.com/2021/08/07/opinion/sunday/hungary-Orbán-conservatives-free-speech.html. (Last accessed September 21, 2022).

Dreisbach, Daniel. 2002. *Thomas Jefferson and the Wall of Separation Between Church and State.* New York, USA: New York University Press. https://doi.org/10.18574/9780814785324.

Dutch News. 2010, April 23. "Geert Wilders' PVV is Ready to Rule on Behalf of Henk and Ingrid." https://www.dutchnews.nl/news/2010/04/geert_wilders_pvv_is_ready_to/. (Last accessed September 21, 2022).

DW. 2019, December 29. "Dutch Far-Right Politician Geert Wilders Holds Muhammad Cartoon Contest." https://www.dw.com/en/dutch-far-right-politician-geert-wilders-holds-muhammad-cartoon-contest/a-51823840. (Last accessed September 21, 2022).

ECPS. Last updated 2020. "Hungary." https://www.populismstudies.org/tag/hungary/. (Last accessed September 21, 2022).

ECPS. Last updated 2021a. "Greece." https://www.populismstudies.org/tag/greece/. (Last accessed September 21, 2022).

ECPS. Last updated 2021b. "Italy". https://www.populismstudies.org/tag/italy/. (Last accessed September 21, 2022).

ECPS. 2021c, January 2. "Dutch Appeals Court Clears Far-Right Leader Wilders of Inciting Hatred." https://www.populismstudies.org/dutch-appeals-court-clears-far-right-leader-wilders-of-inciting-hatred/. (Last accessed September 21, 2022).

Faber, Sebastiaan. 2018. "Is Dutch Bad Boy Thierry Baudet the New Face of the European Alt-Right?" *The Nation.* https://www.thenation.com/article/world/is-dutch-bad-boy-thierry-baudet-the-new-face-of-the-european-alt-right/. (Last accessed 30 December, 2022).

Fabry, A., and S. Sandbeck. 2019. Neoliberalism, Crisis and Authoritarian-Ethnicist Reaction: The Ascendancy of the Orbán Regime. *Competition & Change* 23 (2): 165–191. https://doi.org/10.1177/1024529418813834.

Fekete, Liz. 2018. Alt-America: The Rise of the Radical Right in the Age of Trump. *Race & Class* 60 (1): 107–109. https://doi.org/10.1177/0306396818771235.

Feltran, Gabriel. 2020. "Centripetal Force: A Totalitarian Movement in Contemporary Brazil: What are the Foundations of the Mass Movement that has Been Driving Bolsonaro Forward?" *Soundings* 75, 95–110. https://link.gale.com/apps/doc/A638610937/AONE?u=anon~235dd3ac&sid=googleScholar&xid=1ca47afa.

Fundamental Law of Hungary. 2011. https://lapa.princeton.edu/hosteddocs/hungary/Hungarian%20Constitution%20English%20final%20version.pdf. (Last Accessed September 21, 2022).

Garcia, Raphael Tsavkko. 2020. "Is Brazil Becoming an Evangelical Theocracy?" *Sojourners*. https://sojo.net/articles/brazil-becoming-evangelical-theocracy. (Last Accessed September 21, 2022).

Goldberg, George. 2021. "Church, State, and the Constitution." In *Christianity and Modern Politics*, edited by Louisa S. Hulett, 165–179. Berlin, Boston: De Gruyter. https://doi.org/10.1515/9783110847710-014

Greenberg, Raphael. 2021. "Pompeo in Silwan: Judeo-Christian Nationalism, Kitsch, and Empire in Ancient Jerusalem." *Forum Kritische Archäologie* 10: 55–66. https://refubium.fu-berlin.de/bitstream/handle/fub188/31216/2021_10_5_Greenberg.pdf?sequence=1. (Last Accessed September 21, 2022).

Haberman, Maggie. 2016. "Donald Trump Says He's a Big Fan of Hindus." *The New York Times*. https://www.nytimes.com/2016/10/16/us/politics/trump-modi-indian-americans.html. (Last Accessed September 21, 2022).

Hadj-Abdou, Leila. 2016. "The Religious Conversion of the Austrian Freedom Party." *Saving the People: How Populists Hijack Religion*, edited by Nadia Marzouki, Duncan McDonnell and Olivier Roy. London: C. Hurst & Co.

Halmai, Gábor. 2019. Populism, Authoritarianism and Constitutionalism. *German Law Journal* 20: 296–313. https://doi.org/10.1017/glj.2019.23.

Haraszti, Miklós. 2015. Behind Viktor Orbán's war on refugees in Hungary. *New Perspective Quarterly* 32 (4): 37–40. https://doi.org/10.1111/npqu.12008.

Hawkins, A. Kirk. 2019. "The Ideational Approach." In *Routledge Handbook of Global Populism*, edited by Carlos de la Torre. New York: Routledge.

Haynes, Jeffrey. 2020. Right-Wing Populism and Religion in Europe and the USA. *Religions* 11 (10): 490. https://doi.org/10.3390/rel11100490.

Haynes, Jeffrey. 2017. Donald Trump, 'Judeo-Christian Values', and the 'Clash of Civilizations. *The Review of Faith & International Affairs* 15 (3): 66–75. https://doi.org/10.1080/15570274.2017.1354463.

Hirsh, Michael. 2016, November 20. "Team Trump's Message: The Clash of Civilizations is Back." *Politico.* https://www.politico.eu/article/president-donald-trump-team-message-clash-of-civilizations-back/. (Last accessed 30 December, 2022).

Hogan, J. Michael, and Glen Williams. 2004. The Rusticity and Religiosity of Huey P. Long. *Rhetoric and Public Affairs* 7 (2): 149–171. JSTOR. http://www.jstor.org/stable/41939906.

Hurd, Elizabeth Shakman. 2010. What Is Driving the European Debate about Turkey? *Insight Turkey* 12 (1): 185–203. JSTOR. http://www.jstor.org/stable/26331150.

Ignazi, Paolo. 2003. "The Netherlands: A Fleeting Right Extremism." In *Extreme Right Parties in Western Europe.* Oxford: Oxford University Press.

Illés, G., A. Körösényi, and R. Metz. 2018. Broadening the Limits of Reconstructive Leadership: Constructivist Elements of Viktor Orbán's Regime-Building Politics. *The British Journal of Politics and International Relations* 20 (4): 790–808. https://doi.org/10.1177/1369148118775043.

Kaya, Ayhan. 2021. The Use of the Past by the Alternative for Germany and the Front National: Heritage Populism, Ostalgia and Jeanne D'Arc. *Journal of Contemporary European Studies.* 1–14. https://doi.org/10.1080/14782804.2021.1981835.

Kaya, Ayhan, and Ayşe Tecmen. 2019. Europe Versus Islam?: Right-Wing Populist Discourse and the Construction of a Civilizational Identity. *The Review of Faith & International Affairs* 17 (1): 49–64. https://doi.org/10.1080/15570274.2019.1570759.

Kenes, Bulent. 2020, August 2. "Viktor Orbán: Past to Present." *European Center for Populism Studies.* https://www.populismstudies.org/viktor-Orbán-past-to-present/. (Last accessed September 21, 2022).

Kluveld, Amanda. 2016. "13. Secular, Superior and, Desperately Searching for Its Soul: The Confusing Political-Cultural References to a Judeo- Christian Europe in the Twenty-First Century". In *Is there a Judeo-Christian Tradition?: A European Perspective*, edited by Emmanuel Nathan and Anya Topolski, 241–266. Berlin, Boston: De Gruyter. https://doi.org/10.1515/9783110416596-014.

Knoll, Travis. 2019. "Seeking Liberation in Brazil: Though Growing Right-Wing Religious Groups Helped Pave Jair Bolsonaro's Path to Power, Brazil's Faith Community Has at Other Times Driven Progressive Social and Political Change. Can Liberation Theology Stage a Comeback?" *NACLA Report on the Americas* 51: 227–31. https://www.tandfonline.com/doi/abs/10.1080/10714839.2019.1650483.

Kolbert, Elizabeth. 2002. "Beyond Tolerance." *The New Yorker.* https://www.newyorker.com/magazine/2002/09/09/beyond-tolerance. (Last accessed September 21, 2022).

Koopmans, R., and C.J. Muis. 2009. The Rise of Right-Wing Populist Pim Fortuyn in The Netherlands: A Discursive Opportunity Approach. *European Journal of Political Research*. https://doi.org/10.1111/j.1475-6765.2009.00846.x.

Kuzoian, Alex. 2015, July 29. "Animated Map Shows How Christianity Spread Across the World." *Business Insider*. https://www.businessinsider.com/how-christianity-spread-around-world-animated-map-2015-7. (Last accessed September 21, 2022).

Mészáros, R. Tamás. 2021, May 12. "As Hungary Lauds its 'Eastern Opening' Policy, Statistics Fail to Show Benefits." *EURACTIV*. https://www.euractiv.com/section/economy-jobs/news/as-hungary-lauds-its-eastern-opening-policy-statistics-fail-to-show-benefits/. (Last accessed September 21, 2022).

Lendvai, Paul. 2019. "The Transformer: Orbán's Evolution and Hungary's Demise." *Foreign Affairs* 98 (5): 44–54. https://www.foreignaffairs.com/articles/hungary/2019-08-12/transformer. (Last accessed September 21, 2022).

Lipka, Michael. 2020, February 27. "Most Americans Don't See Democratic Candidates as Very Religious." *Pew*. https://www.pewresearch.org/fact-tank/2020/02/27/most-americans-dont-see-democratic-candidates-as-very-religious/. (Last accessed September 21, 2022).

Macintyre, James. 2018. "'Christianity is Europe's Last Hope Against Rise of Islam' Claims Hungarian PM." *Christianity Today*. https://www.christiantoday.com/article/christianity-is-europes-last-hope-against-rise-of-islam-claims-hungarian-pm/126015.htm. (Last accessed September 21, 2022).

Mass, Willem. 2014. "The Netherlands." In *Controlling Immigration: A Global Perspective*. Third Edition, edited by James Hollifield, Phillip L. Martin, Pia Orrenius. Stanford: Standford: University Press.

Mazurczak, Filip. 2019. "How Catholic is Poland's 'Law and Justice' Party?" *The Catholic World Report*. Available online: https://www.catholicworldreport.com/2019/10/21/how-catholic-is-polands-law-and-justice-party. (Last accessed 30 December, 2022).

McDonnell, Duncan. 2016. "The Lega Nord: The New Saviour of Northern Italy." In Saving the People: How Populists Hijack Religion, edited by Nadia Marzouki, Duncan McDonnell and Olivier Roy. London: C. Hurst & Co.

Molle, Andrea. 2019. Religion and Right-Wing Populism in Italy: Using 'Judeo-Christian Roots' to Kill the European Union. *Religion, State & Society* 47: 151–168. https://doi.org/10.1080/09637494.2018.1532266.

Morel, Pierre. 2020, March 23. "Vigilante Groups in Europe: Taking the Law into Their Own Hands." *Euro News*. https://www.euronews.com/2020/01/31/vigilante-groups-in-europe-taking-the-law-into-their-own-hands. (Last accessed September 21, 2022).

Morieson, Nicholas. 2016, December 8. "By Framing Secular Society as a Christian Creation, Hanson's Revival Goes Beyond Simple Racism." *The Conversation*. https://theconversation.com/by-framing-secular-society-as-a-christian-creation-hansons-revival-goes-beyond-simple-racism-67707. (Last accessed 30 December, 2022).

Morieson, Nicholas. 2021. *Religion and the Populist Radical Right: Secular Christianism and Populism in Western Europe*. Delaware and Malaga: Vernon Press.

Montgomery, Douglas. 2012. *Design and Analysis of Experiments*. Hoboken: Wiley.

MTI-Hungary Today. 2019. "Orbán: 'Agreement between Two Parts of Europe Conditional on the West'." *Hungary Today*. https://hungarytoday.hu/orban-christian-freedom-v4-west/. (Last accessed 30 December, 2022).

NL Times. 2021, January 9. "PVV Releases Election Program: "Country Without Headscarfs, But with Traditional Dutch Coziness"." https://nltimes.nl/2021/01/09/pvv-releaseselection-program-country-without-headscarfs-traditional-dutch-coziness. (Last accessed September 21, 2022).

Onuf, Peter S. 2012. American Exceptionalism and National Identity. *American Political Thought* 1 (1): 77–100. JSTOR. https://doi.org/10.1086/664594.

Orbán, Viktor. 2013, February 12. Hungarian-Chinese Business Forum in Beijing During an Official Visit to the People's Republic of China. https://444.hu/2014/02/12/ugye-maganak-is-elege-volt-abbol-hogy-europaban-gunyoljak-az-azsiai-szarmazasunk-miatt/. (Last accessed September 21, 2022).

Orbán, Viktor. 2014. "Full text of Viktor Orbán's speech at Băile Tuşnad (Tusnádfürdő) of 26 July 2014." *The Budapest Beacon*. https://budapestbeacon.com/full-text-of-viktor-Orbáns-speech-at-baile-tusnad-tusnadfurdo-of-26-july-2014/. (Last accessed September 21, 2022).

Orbán, Viktor. 2015, March 15. Speech by Prime Minter Commemoration in Budapest of the Outbreak of the 1848 Hungarian Revolution. https://theorangefiles.hu/notable-quotes-prime-minister-viktor-Orbán-by-subject/. (Last accessed September 21, 2022).

Orbán, Viktor. 2016a, October 23. Budapest Commemorating the 1956 Hungarian Revolution. https://theorangefiles.hu/notable-quotes-prime-minister-viktor-Orbán-by-subject/. (Last accessed September 21, 2022).

Orbán, Viktor. 2016b, September 11. Anual Civil Picnic in Kötcse, Hungary. https://index.hu/belfold/2016b/09/13/Orbán_es_az_orosz_foideologus_egymasra_talalt/. (Last accessed September 21, 2022).

Ozzano, Luca, and Fabio Bolzonar. 2020. "Is Right-Wing Populism a Phenomenon of Religious Dissent? The Cases of the Lega and the Rassemblement National." *International Journal of Religion* 1: 45–59. https://doi.org/10.33182/ijor.v1i1.1089.

Pally, Marcia. 2020. Why is Populism Persuasive? Populism as Expression of Religio-Cultural History with the U.S. and U.S. Evangelicals as a Case Study. *Political Theology* 21: 393–414. https://doi.org/10.1080/1462317X.2020.1740145.

Pachá, Paulo. 2019. "Why the Brazilian Far Right Loves the European Middle Ages." https://psmag.com/ideas/why-the-brazilian-far-right-is-obsessed-with-the-crusades. (Last accessed September 21, 2022).

Paszak, Pawel. 2021, March 8. "Hungary's "Opening to the East" Hasn't Delivered." *CEPA*. https://cepa.org/hungarys-policy-of-opening-to-the-east-is-more-than-a-decade-old-but-it-hasnt-delivered-much-chinese-investment/. (Last accessed September 21, 2022).

Pauwels, Teun. 2014. *Populism in Western Europe: Comparing Belgium, Germany and the Netherlands*. Abingdon: Routledge.

Pearson, Alexander. 2018, September 1. "Viktor Orbán's Most Controversial Migration Comments." *DW*. https://www.dw.com/en/viktor-Orbáns-most-controversial-migration-comments/g-42086054. (Last accessed September 21, 2022).

Peters, Rudolph. 2020. "Dutch Extremist Islamism: Van Gogh's Murderer and His Ideas." In *Shariʿa, Justice and Legal Order*. https://doi.org/10.1163/9789004420625_035. (Last accessed September 21, 2022).

Poynting, Scott, and Victoria Mason. 2007. The Resistible rise of Islamophobia. *Journal of Sociology* 43 (1): 61–86. https://doi.org/10.1177/1440783307073935.

Radio Free Europe. 2021, July 21. "Hungary's Orbán Calls For Referendum Amid Outrage Over Controversial 'Anti-LGBT' Law." https://www.rferl.org/a/hungary-Orbán-lgbt-referendum/31370082.html. (Last accessed September 21, 2022).

Reinares, Fernando. 2015. "How to Counter Jihadist Appeal Among Western European Muslims." *The Wilson Center*. https://www.scribd.com/document/292111073/How-to-Counter-Jihadist-Appeal-Among-Western-European-Muslims. (Last accessed September 21, 2022).

RFI. "Le Pen: Islam not Compatible with Secular Society." 2011. http://en.rfi.fr/france/20110128-le-pen-says-islam-not-compatible-secular-society. (Last accessed September 21, 2022).

Roy, Olivier. 2016a. "Beyond Populism: The Conservative Right, The Courts, The Churches and the Concept of a Christian Europe". In *Saving the People: How Populists Hijack Religion*, edited by Nadia Marzouki, Duncan McDonnell and Olivier Roy. London: C. Hurst & Co.

Roy, Olivier. 2016a. "The French National Front: From Christian Identity to Laïcité." In *Saving the People: How Populists Hijack Religion*, edited by Nadia Marzouki, Duncan McDonnell and Olivier Roy. London: C. Hurst & Co.

Roy, Olivier. 2013. Secularism and Islam: The Theological Predicament. *The International Spectator* 48: 5–19. https://doi.org/10.1080/03932729.2013.759365.

Schake, Kori. 2017, December 13. "Religious Bias Is Distorting American Foreign Policy." *The Atlantic*. https://www.theatlantic.com/international/archive/2017/12/middle-east-christians-vp-pence/548216/. (Last accessed 30 December, 2022).

Schrag, Peter. 1971. *The Decline of the WASP*. Simon and Shuster.

Sengul, Kurt Adam. 2022. Performing Islamophobia in the Australian Parliament: The Role of Populism and Performance in Pauline Hanson's "burqa stunt". *Media International Australia* 184 (1): 49–62. https://doi.org/10.1177/1329878X221087733.

Stefon, Matt, Martin E. Marty, Linwood Fredericksen, John Hick, Ernst Wilhelm Benz, Paul A. Crow, Jaroslav Jan Pelikan, Sidney Spencer, Lawrence E. Sullivan, Bernard J. McGinn, Geoffrey Wainwright, Henry Chadwick, Carter H. Lindberg, and William Richey Hogg. 2020 November 26. "Christianity". *Encyclopedia Britannica*. https://www.britannica.com/topic/Christianity. (Last accessed September 21, 2022).

Székely, Tamás. 2017. "'We Shall Do Our Utmost To Ensure That Europe Remains European'—Hungarian PM Viktor Orbán Christmas Message In Full." *Hungary Today*. https://hungarytoday.hu/shall-utmost-ensure-europe-remains-european-hungarian-pm-viktor-Orbán-christmas-message-full-30520/. (Last accessed September 21, 2022).

Szocs, Laszlo. 2021. "Zemmour: This is the 'era of the struggle for civilization between Islam and Christianity'." *Magyar Nemzet*. https://magyarnemzet.hu/english/2021/09/zemmour-this-is-the-era-of-the-struggle-for-civilization-between-islam-and-christianity. (Last accessed 30 December, 2022).

Szubori, Anna. 2018. "Gender Studies Banned at University—The Hungarian Government's Latest Attack on Equality." *The Conversation*. https://theconversation.com/gender-studies-banned-at-university-the-hungarian-governments-latest-attack-on-equality-103150. (Last accessed September 21, 2022).

Thorpe, Nick. 2021. "Tucker Carlson: What the Fox News Host is Doing in Hungary." *BBC*. https://www.bbc.com/news/world-europe-58104200. (Last accessed September 21, 2022).

Time. 2016, March 21. "Read Donald Trump's Speech to AIPAC." *Time*. https://time.com/4267058/donald-trump-aipac-speech-transcript/. (Last accessed 30 December, 2022).

Time. 2017, July 6. "Read President Trump's Remarks on 'Defending Civilization' in Poland." *Time*. https://time.com/4846924/read-president-trumps-remarks-on-defending-civilization-in-poland/. (Last accessed 30 December, 2022).

TRT World. 2019, June 1. "Despite Far-Right Lurch, Hungary's Fidesz Rides High in Europe and at Home." https://www.trtworld.com/magazine/despite-far-right-lurch-hungary-s-fidesz-rides-high-in-europe-and-at-home-27162. (Last accessed September 21, 2022).

van den Hemel, Ernst. 2014. "(Pro)claiming Tradition: The 'Judeo-Christian' Roots of Dutch Society and the Rise of Conservative Nationalism." In *Transformations of Religion and the Public Sphere*, edited by R. Braidotti, B. Blaagaard, T. de Graauw and E. Midden. Palgrave Macmillan: London. https://doi.org/10.1057/9781137401144_4.

Vaughan, Don. (Last updated 2021). "What is the Most Widely Practiced Religion in the World?" *Britannica*. https://www.britannica.com/story/what-is-the-most-widely-practiced-religion-in-the-world. (Last accessed September 21, 2022).

Vink, Maarten. 2007. Dutch 'Multiculturalism' Beyond the Pillarisation Myth. *Political Studies Review* 5 (3): 337–350. https://doi.org/10.1111/j.1478-9299.2007.00134.x.

Visegrad Post. 2018. "'The West Will Fall, as Europe is Occupied Without Realising it,' said Viktor Orbán. 'Christianity is the last hope' – Full Speech." *Visegrad Post*. https://visegradpost.com/en/2018/02/20/the-west-will-fall-as-europe-is-occupied-without-realising-it-said-viktor-orban-christianity-is-the-last-hope-full-speech/. (Last accessed 30 December, 2022).

Vodegel, Jasper. 2018. "Populism in the Netherlands: Framing a Crisis." *Masters Thesis*. Radboud University, Nijmegen. https://theses.ubn.ru.nl/bitstream/handle/123456789/5584/Vodegel%2c_J_1.pdf?sequence=1. (Last accessed 30 December, 2022).

Vollaard, Hans J.P. 2013. Re-Emerging Christianity in West European Politics: The Case of the Netherlands. *Politics and Religion*. 6 (1): 74–100. https://doi.org/10.1017/S1755048312000776.

Voortman, Aude. 2015. "Terrorism in Europe. Explaining the Disparity in the Number of Jihadist Foreign Fighters between European Countries." Student Paper Series, 20. https://www.ibei.org/ibei_studentpaper20_71964.pdf. (Last accessed September 21, 2022).

Vossen, Koen. 2011. Classifying Wilders: The Ideological Development of Geert Wilders and His Party for Freedom. *Politics* 31 (3): 179–189. https://doi.org/10.1111/j.1467-9256.2011.01417.x.

Walker, Shaun. 2019. "Viktor Orbán: No Tax for Hungarian Women with Four or More Children." *The Guardian*. https://www.theguardian.com/world/2019/feb/10/viktor-Orbán-no-tax-for-hungarian-women-with-four-or-more-children. (Last accessed September 21, 2022).

Waisbord, Silvio. 2019. "Populism as Media and Communication Phenomenon." In *Routledge Handbook of Global* Populism, edited by Carlos de la Torre. New York: Routledge.

Weidinger, Bernhard. 2017. "Equal Before God, and God Alone: Cultural Fundamentalism, (Anti-)Egalitarianism, and Christian Rhetoric in Nativist Discourse from Austria and the United States." *Journal of Austrian-American History* 1 (1): 40–68. https://www.jstor.org/stable/10.5325/jaustamerhist.1.1.0040.

Welten, Liselotte, and Tahir Abbas. 2021. "We are Already 1–0 Behind": Perceptions of Dutch Muslims on Islamophobia, Securitisation, and De-Radicalisation. *Critical Studies on Terrorism* 14 (1): 90–116. https://doi.org/10.1080/17539153.2021.1883714.

Wertheim, Stephen. 2017, July 22. "Donald Trump's Plan to Save Western Civilization." *The New York Times.* https://www.nytimes.com/2017/07/22/opinion/sunday/donald-trumps-plan-to-save-western-civilization.html. (Last accessed 30 December, 2022).

Wilders, Geert. 2012. "Speech Geert Wilders at the Western Conservative Summit, Denver, 30 June, 2012." *Geert Wilders Weblog.* https://www.geertwilders.nl/index.php/87-english/news/1795-speech-geert-wilders-at-the-western-conservative-summit-denver-30-june-2012. (Last accessed September 21, 2022).

Wilders, Geert. 2015. "Speech Geert Wilders, Bornholm, Denmark. June 13, 2015." Party for Freedom Website. https://www.pvv.nl/index.php/36-fj-related/geert-wilders/8411-speech-geert-wilders-bornholm-danmark-june-13-2015.html. (Last accessed September 21, 2022).

Wilders, Geert. 2016. "Wilders Plan: Time for Liberation." *Geert Wilders Weblog.* https://geertwilders.nl/index.php/94-english/2015-wilders-plan-time-for-liberation. (Last accessed September 21, 2022).

Wilders, Geert. 2017. "The Netherlands Ours Again!" *Geert Wilders Weblog.* https://www.geertwilders.nl/94-english/2007-preliminary-election-program-pvv-2017-2021. (Last accessed 30 December, 2022).

Yilmaz, Ihsan. 2020, October 6. "Australia." *European Center for Populism Studies.* https://www.populismstudies.org/tag/australia/. (Last accessed September 21, 2022).

Yilmaz, Ihsan, and Nicholas Morieson. 2021. A Systematic Literature Review of Populism, Religion and Emotions. *Religions* 12 (4): 272. https://doi.org/10.3390/rel12040272

Yilmaz, Ihsan, and Nicholas Morieson. 2022. "Civilizational Populism: Definition, Literature, Theory, and Practice." *Religions.*

Yilmaz, Ihsan, Nicholas Morieson, and Mustafa Demir. 2021. Exploring Religions in Relation to Populism: A Tour around the World. *Religions* 12 (5): 301. https://doi.org/10.3390/rel12050301.

Young, Clifford, Katie Ziemer, and Chris Jackson. 2019. Explaining Trump's Popular Support: Validation of a Nativism Index. *Social Science Quarterly* 100: 412–418. https://doi.org/10.1111/ssqu.12593.

Zúquete, Jose Pedro. 2017. "Populism and Religion." In *The Oxford Handbook of Populism*, edited by Cristóbal Rovira Kaltwasser, Paul Taggart, Paulina Ochoa Espejo and Pierre Ostiguy. Oxford: Oxford University Press.

CHAPTER 5

Hinduism and Civilizational Populism

5.1 Introduction

India's founding father Jawaharlal Nehru spent almost sixteen years, from the partition of India 1947 till his death, attempting to modernize and democratize India. It was the Nehruvian spirit that allowed for the country's constitution to not only act as the world's largest democracy but also enshrine secularism in its constitution (Desai 2021; Habib 2016). However, the momentum set some seven decades ago seems to have reversed itself in the last twenty years. For example, in 2014, India elected a populist government which appears to increasingly incorporate religion into its political discourse and agenda, and has in certain respects begun a process of de-secularization. Religious populism is especially dangerous in India, a densely populated nation and one of the most diverse religious and ethnic nations of the world, and therefore highly vulnerable to divisional politics.

At the same time, populism flourishes in a divided political and social environment, so it is not surprising that the Hindu Populist Bharatiya Janata Party (BJP), led by incumbent Prime Minister Narendra Modi, has achieved sustained political and electoral success in India. The BJP's Hindu populism and instrumental use of Hindutva ideology has de-democratized India, deepened religious divides, and facilitated populist vigilantism and constitutional/legal discrimination (Freedom

House 2021; The Economist Intelligence Unit 2021). This chapter explores both political and non-political populist groups to observe the key role religion plays in shaping the populism of India.

The chapter begins by differentiating between Hinduism and Hindutva, two concepts that are sometimes used interchangeably, a differentiation that helps us understand the true nature of Hinduism's role in shaping populism in the Indian context. The second section begins with a history of Hindu nationalist politics, and describes the manner in which nationalism, religion, and civilizationalism are blended together in Hindutva. The chapter shows how Hindutva adherents consider Buddhism, Jainism, and Sikhism as offshoots of the Hindu culture and religion, but view Christianity, Islam, and Parsi religions as "outside" religions, and therefore seek to bring former Hindus and their offspring who converted to "alien religions" back to Hinduism (Ramachandran 2020, 22; Human Rights Watch 2020a).

Hindutva has been used as a tool by political parties in India to consolidate a singular identity for nationalistic purposes (Saleem et al. 2022). Thus, the chapter examines the birth of the first Hindu identarian political party during the colonial era, and maps its transition during the independence struggle and beyond. In this subsection, a detailed overview of religion in politics also aids in establishing that pre-independence and early post-1947 political parties in India were not populist but primarily secular nationalist. This leads us to a discussion of the BJP and its journey from nationalism to Hindutva influenced populism. The second section also discusses the role of the Rashtriya Swayamsevak Sangh (RSS) and its various affiliates in shaping the politics of the BJP.

The third section examines the relationship between the RSS and Hindutva to understand the political use of religion in Indian politics. This examination contributes to our understanding of not only our case study of the BJP but also the limits of Hindutva itself. In this section, then, we show how the narrative of the RSS and the populism of its leaders aid in supporting civilizationalism and pro-violence narratives and their physical manifestation. We also discuss the ways in which the two parties attempt to engage with their audiences, and to compel them to engage in violent and aggressive behaviors toward religious minorities, especially Muslims. This chapter concludes with a case study of BJP, tracing the party's journey from Hindutva and religiously rooted nationalism, to its transformation into a mainstream Hindu populist party. We examine and discuss what a *hindu rashtra* (Hindu kingdom) means to the BJP and its supporters, and investigate its civilizational construction of 'the people' and 'others'. In this process, the chapter explores the BJP's call for "cleansing" the once lost "homeland" of the enemies of Hindu civilization, and the BJP's role in inciting violence against 'the others'.

5.2 Relationship Between Hinduism and Populism

5.2.1 Understanding Hinduism

It is noteworthy that while Hinduism is the third largest religion in the world, its followers term their devotion as *Sanatana Dharma* (translated as eternal order, way, or duty) rather than classifying themselves simply as Hindus. Muslims, Jews, and Christians largely follow prescribed rituals, and their texts provide clear descriptions of how to live and behave in public and private. Thus there is a certain sense of permeance and rigidity to the Semitic faiths. On the other hand, it is debatable if there is strictly speaking a Vedic dharma or even Hindu civilization. The Hindu 'religion' has no clear founder or origin story; rather there is immense flexibility that makes this complex religion highly fluid. In a sense, Hinduism's beauty lies in its pluralism (Jacobs 2010, 6–7).

Human beings, according to our own nature, like to categorize identities, and therefore there are certain attributes and behaviors that can be linked with Hindu identity. Ideas such as karma (causality of good actions/ideas leading to good and bad consequences), *samsara* (cycle of life death and rebirth, usually referring to the seven cycles until the final stage of release), veganism, cow-worship, and idol worship are often believed to be key features of what it means to be a Hindu. However, this is not necessarily the case (Flood 1996, 5–8). Contrary to popular belief, unlike Semitic monotheistic faiths Hinduism does not center itself around a god or gods, which means that its followers are better able to adapt to different philosophies and absorb their ideas and faith into their 'religion'. There are no parameters set by the faith itself or even the government of India that make one a Hindu based on the customs and traditions being practiced. Under the statute of personal laws, a Hindu citizen is one who is born of Hindu parents or who does not identify with other local religions such as Christianity, Islam, or Zoroastrianism. Thus if an Indian citizen is not an explicit member of one of those religions, they are automatically classified by the state as a Hindu. While most of the Indian population, according to these guidelines, is "Hindu", the country has no official religion and is officially secular. Frawley (2018), due to this diversity notes, "the very beauty of Hinduism is that it cannot be defined in a simplistic manner. It contains all the mystery and complexity, magic, wonder and enigma of life itself".

This openness makes India one of the most diverse places on the planet, and a region that has historically allowed for various religions to be imported, but also acted as an incubator for the development of indigenous religions such as Jainism, Buddhism, and Sikhism (Tharoor 2018). Wilberg (2009, 30) comments on this plural and tolerant feature which is 'modern' compared to the Abrahamic faiths exclusivism, noting that "'Hinduism' is not an ethnically exclusive religion, and it understands itself as inclusively embracing the partial truths of other religions from within a higher, holistic perspective. In contrast, Judaism is both an ethnically and doctrinally exclusive religion, whereas Christianity and Islam are ethnically inclusive but doctrinally exclusive faiths". This pluralist aspect of Hinduism leads to the question of how such a fluid belief system can be turned into a vehicle for populism? We now proceed to discuss what sort of populism exists in India and the role played by Hindutva in creating Hindu populism.

5.2.2 *Variants of Populism in India*

Literature has shown that populism cannot succeed unless it is grafted onto another 'thick' ideology, which means that autocrats, democrats, reformers, and religious leaders have all relied on this merger to support their agendas (Yilmaz and Morieson 2021; Yilmaz et al. 2021; Yilmaz and Saleem 2021; de la Torre 2019, 7; Gidron and Bonikowski 2013). Populism in India, therefore, has different faces owing to the various 'thick' ideologies populism is meshed with, or onto which it is grafted. Politicians and social reformers advocating for social class equity, political and social reform, neo-liberalism, secular nationalism, and socialism have all used populist discourse to divide 'the people' from 'the elite" in Indian political discourse over the last seventy years. This leads Jaffrelot and Tillin (2017) to classify India's populism into three categories. The first two are leader-centered populisms, for example the populist movements centered on former Prime Minister Indira Gandhi, Nehru's daughter and leader of Congress; the second type includes the Hindutva populist movement centered on incumbent Indian Prime Minister Narendra Modi. This third category encompasses political movements in the Southern Indian states of Tamil Nadu and Andhra Pradesh. Indira Gandhi's populism dates to the 1960s where, using an autocratic leadership style, she reinvented Nehruism to consolidate power. Her populism used notions of populist securitization, welfarism, and protectionist economic policies to legitimize her undemocratic rule. Indira Gandhi also experimented with the idea of courting Hindu religious factions to prolong her rule, especially during a period of targeted violence toward the Indian Sikh community (Jaffrelot and Tillin 2017; Sahgal 2013; Subramanian 2007).

The second type of populism identified by Jaffrelot and Tillin (2017) is the Hindu populism of Prime Minister Modi, which is Hindutva rather than Hindu. We will discuss this type of Indian populism in the following section. Jaffrelot and Tillin's third type of populism is more ideological rather than leader centric. In southern India, welfare-populism mixed with religious identity has maintained a stronghold. Examples of this type of populism include the movements associated with M. G. Ramachandran in Tamil Nadu and N. T. Rama Rao in Andhra Pradesh, who use regional politics to 'otherize' the 'elite' politics of the Congress Party from Northern India. Simultaneously, these groups practice pseudo-socialism merged with populism that has led their leaders to not only dichotomize society but to present themselves as the solution to their respective regions' political problems, by benevolently promising free electrical appliances and monetizing domestic work for stay-at-home women (Chandrababu 2021). In the capital city of Delhi, the Aam Aadmi Party/Common Person's Party (AAP) has mixed the ideas of welfarism, class equity, anti-corruption, and reformism to promise the real empowerment of "the people" (Lama-Rewal 2019; Nikore, 2014). Kaustuv Chakrabarti and Kaustuv Kanti Bandyopadhyay (2021) point out that in most cases populist rhetoric is a key element of election rhetoric, which fades away in the post-voting time. However, we exempt the BJP from this case, as the party—as we shall shortly discuss—maintains its use of populist discourse beyond election campaigns.

5.2.3 *Hindu Nationalism: The Birth of Hindutva*

It is important that we recognize the difference between nationalism and populism in India. Hindu nationalism or Hindutva is an ideology that promotes the idea that Hinduism is the authentic religious and cultural identity of the Indian people. This classification of Hinduism by Hindutva adherents frames all other religious identities within the country as foreign and inauthentic. For Hindutva adherents, then, the removal of inauthentic and foreign religions can be perceived as a 'cleansing' of India, and a way of returning the nation to its civilizational roots. Hindu nationalism and in its present form of Hindutva therefore promotes a highly antagonistic perception of Muslims and Christians, who are framed by the ideology as 'outsiders', whereas Jainism, Sikhism, and Buddhism are seen as members, so to speak, of the Hindu family (Jaffrelot 2007).

Mahatma Gandhi himself used language reminiscent of populist rhetoric during his campaign against British rule. For example, his appeal for *Swaraj* (self-rule) was inspired by the anti-colonialism struggle that divided the society between 'the elite' and 'the people'. Within this narrative was coupled a romanticized image of ancient India and its traditions (Gandhi 2021). While there was not an explicit renunciation of other religions in Gandhi's discourse, through his lifestyle Gandhi promoted a syncretic brand of Hinduism. His Hindu monk image and practices "articulated his views in a thoroughly Hindu style" (Jaffrelot 2007). This preference for Hindu-driven ideals manifested when the Indian National Congress party won a majority in elections held under the Government of India Act in 1935. During 1935–1939 Congress introduced the Vidya Mandir Scheme in elementary schools that mandated the use of the Hindi language and Deva Nagri script, while *Vande Mataram* (I praise thee, Mother) along with the worship of Gandhi's portraits in schools were made morning rituals in schools (Oesterheld 2016; Samanta 2011; Kaura 1975). Congress's pro-Hindu innervations naturally alienated Muslims, the largest minority of India, and this feeling of alienation shaped the future Pakistan movement in the late 1930s and early 1940s (Dhulipala 2014).

Chakrabarti and Bandyopadhyay (2021) discuss Mahatma Gandhi's Swadeshi movement and raise a key question, "was Mahatma Gandhi a populist or a Hindu populist?" Gianolla (2020) disagrees with the idea that Gandhi was a Hindu populist, and observes that Gandhi had an intercultural quality to his politics that improved democratic discourse, and lacked the de-democratizing quality common to populism. Sajjan Kumar (2019) agrees but notes that the Gandhi's "charismatic-popular-populist pitch doesn't automatically transcend into populism. It requires demagoguery wherein hitherto suppressed but popular desires get articulated by a mesmerizer who emerges as the savior. Both Mahatma Gandhi and Jawaharlal Nehru were charismatic but not populist as they assumed a guiding role vis-à-vis the people rather than getting subsumed by their worldview. Gandhi didn't hesitate to withdraw the non-cooperation movement in the aftermath of Chauri Chaura when it gained momentum, and Nehru stood for secularism and scientific rationality in the midst of Partition's mass frenzy". In essence, then, Gandhian philosophy was about an introverted self-exploration of the good and bad within, rather than the populist construction of 'the people' as 'good' and enemy 'elites' and 'others' as 'bad'.

Rather, it was V. D. Savarkar who Semitized Hinduism and enabled Hindutva. Like Gandhi, Savarkar's worldview was a reaction to colonialism, but his Hindutva was also a reactionary movement responding to the growing influence of pan-Islamism in the Indian Subcontinent. Savarkar was perhaps influenced by earlier Hindu reform movements, such as Brahmo Samaj and Arya Samaj, that sharped the future of Hindu nationalism. Savarkar wrote a book in the early 1920s titled *Hindutva: Who is a Hindu?* in which he claimed that Hindu identity is connected to land, culture, and language: "Hindu, Hindi, Hindustan" or the 3Hs (Jain 2012; Bhosale 2009; Heredia 2009). V. D. Savarkar helped shape a form of Hindu nationalism that constructed "the people" the rightful owners of the 'holy land' (*punyabhumi*) that belonged to their forefathers (*pitribhumi*). This conception of Hinduism was different to Gandhi's inclusive nationalism, and cast migrant groups and other faiths as 'outsiders' or 'intruders' who had damaged Hindu civilization.

Hindutva is therefore not a religion, but rather a political movement in which religion plays an important role. For example, Savarkar himself wrote that "Hinduism is only a derivative, a fraction, a part of Hindutva" (Devare 2013, 195–196). According to Savarkar, then, Hindutva encompasses 'Hinduism', and also the Hindu people as a race, culture, and when all these things are combined a civilization. Savarkar believed that "failure to distinguish between Hindutva and Hinduism has given rise to much misunderstanding and mutual suspicion between some of those sister communities that have inherited this inestimable and common treasure of our Hindu civilization… It is enough to point out that Hindutva is not identical with what is vaguely indicated by the term Hinduism. By an "ism" it is generally meant a theory or a code more or less based on spiritual or religious dogma or system. But when we attempt to investigate into the essential significance of Hindutva, we do not primarily—and certainly not mainly—concern ourselves with any particular theocratic or religious dogma or creed…' (Hindu Rashtra Darshan 2021, Section 31). Rather, according to Savarkar, "Hindus are bound together not only by the tie of the love we bear to a common fatherland and by the common blood that courses through our veins and keeps our hearts throbbing and our affections warm, but also by the tie of the common homage we pay to our great civilization—our Hindu culture" (Savarkar 2009, 94–95).

Savarkar's civilizational-based categorization framed the British, the Indian National Congress party, and Muslims the 'enemies' of the people, and as people who belonged to intrinsically foreign civilizations. Moreover, in Hindutva there was an immense focus on Hindu "spiritualists and social reformers" that made "the people" a "single distinct people" who were encouraged to feel a strong sense of being victimized by "powerful foreign elites" (McDonnell and Cabrera 2019, 485–86). Of course, this only made early Hindutva nationalist and not populist in orientation. A pragmatic movement, the Hindutva and Savarkar inspired Hindu Mahasabha (MS) party formed collations with the Indian Muslim League, and boycotted the anti-colonial Civil Disobedience Movement of 1930 and the Quit India Movement (Visana 2020; Tharoor 2018, 40–50; Bapu 2013, 26–43; Gondhalekar and Bhattacharya 1999). MS and other Hindutva movements, and indeed Gandhi's own activism, were to an extent influenced by Hinduism and nationalism. Yet there were not themselves populist movements. In time, however, Hindu nationalists began to incorporate populism into their ideology.

5.3 Case Study: Hindutva Nationalism to Populism

In this section we examine the discourse of the BJP, and consider the role civilizationalism plays in the party's rise to power and sustained electoral success. Before this, however, we examine the history of the party, and its origins in the Rashtriya Swayamseval Sangh movement.

5.3.1 *Rashtriya Swayamsevak Sangh (RSS) and its Affiliates*

Hindutva ideology has been flourishing outside of politics since 1925 in the form of Rashtriya Swayamsevak Sangh (RSS), and its various affiliated bodies known as the *Sang Parivar* (SP) (Anderson and Damle 1987; 2019). Founded by K. B. Hedgewar in Nagpur, the RSS focused on welfare activities and communal training programs in rural and urban communities, and sought to encourage "proper young Hindus" to shun polluted ways of living and embrace old "Hindu" traditions mostly centered on the Vedic texts (Chatterji et al. 2020). Military training has been a core part of their training since the 1940s, activities that the RSS portray as a way of creating healthy young people ready to defend Hindu virtues (Anderson and Damle 2005, 29–35). The RSS was initially rooted in right-wing nationalism, and their "Hindutva ideology" was a "means to further build a nationalistic identity that sought ways to remove any non-Hindu socio-religious elements from South Asia" (Yilmaz et al. 2021, 8). The RSS calls its supporters *swayamsevaks* (members), and they number nearly 6 million people in India according to estimations (Friedrich 2020).

Under the leadership of M. S. Golwalkar, the organization strongly encourage its followers to live and experience the "Hindu way of life" (Anderson and Damle 2005, 29–35) but also preserve it, creating a civilizational dimension which defined Hinduism as a civilization, and Indian people who belonged to other religion as intrinsically foreign to India. Golwalker, who was rather radical in his ideals, admired Hitler's Nazi ideology and claimed that to "keep up purity of the nation and its culture, Germany shocked the world by her purging the country of the Semitic races, the Jews. National pride at its highest has been manifested here. Germany has also shown how well-nigh impossible it is for races and cultures having differences going to the root, to be assimilated into a united whole, a good lesson for us in Hindustan to learn and profit by" (Patwardhan 2014). Golwalker's influence is still felt in India, where the civilizational divide between Hindus and non-Hindus remains strong, and where it is not the Hindu faith but rather the "Hindu way of life" which defines Hindu-ness for many Hindutva adherents (Sarkar 1993).

Indeed, RSS has selectively selected elements from the Hindu faith to create the basis of its "Hindu" civilizational identity. For example, it uses Manusmriti laws of *Dharmaśāstras*[1] penned down in the *Manusmriti*[2] as "the basis of the spiritual and divine march of the nation" (Patwardhan 2014). Given its timebound reference it is a highly ethnocentric text that portrays ancient Vedic Hindu customs as supreme to others. This legitimizes archaic notions of social class, skepticism toward non-Hindus, and supports antiquated gender roles (Sawant 2020; Shantha 2020). Sawant (2020) notes that their principles are deeply embedded within the RSS

---

[1] Sanskrit theological texts.

[2] An Indian text dating back to 100 ce as major source of Hindi law (Britannica 2015).

ideology. RSS uses this notion to justify its call for "cleansing" and the creation of a 'pure Hindu society' that is inspired by its imaginings of the Indian golden age (Anderson and Damle 2019; Jha 2016).

At present, RSS is not entirely following Golwalker's radical right-wing ideas word-for-word, as it is open to non-Hindus who are willing to embrace the Hindutva way of life (Andersen 2018). Yet discriminatory beliefs are deeply embedded in its philosophy. Ramapada Pal, a preacher in the organization, while addressing the inclusion of non-Hindus, argued "the superiority of the Hindu kingdom" is a matter of fact he stressed and "If a Muslim living in India chooses their god before India, then why should he be allowed to live in our country? This country belongs to Hindus first" (Reuters 2015). This ultra-nationalist sentiment is also present in the official RSS booklet which reads, "Non-Hindus must be assimilated with the Hindu way of life. The words 'Muslim' and 'Christian' denote a religious phenomenon, while the word 'Hindu' is synonymous with the nation. Even in the United States, it is emphasized that non-Americans should be assimilated into 'Anglo-Saxon' culture" (Anderson and Damel 2019).

The RSS has a clear vision of India as the product of Hindu civilization. The movement, however, is not populist but is strongly civilizationalist. Its members long for a lost glorified Hindu age, and feel "a nostalgic yearning for a glorified Vedic period, or Hinduism's 'Golden Age'" which came to an end due to "tyrant invaders" such as Muslim and later the British (Leidig 2016). There is little historical validation of these ideas, and RSS is known to blur the lines between fact and fiction when it comes to history. As Sawant (2020) points out, RSS logic traces the Hindu people's roots back to the Aryans coming to India, yet fails to see themselves as invaders in the land of the Dravidian people of the Indus Valley civilization. The RSS thus conveniently picks and chooses who are the "original" or rightful residents of the region. The *Sangh Parivar* union has pushed for "a pro-Hindutva agenda in the name of cultural nationalism" that makes the Hindu "golden age" the root of all scientific and philosophical knowledge that has ever been produced by humans (Thapar 2020; Jain and Lasseter 2018; Leidig 2016). At present the 'loss' of the knowledge the Hindus once possessed is blamed on "invaders", and primarily on the Muslims who allegedly destroyed the region and led to its downfall, instilling a vindictiveness and narrative of victimhood in RSS members (Thapar 2020; Jain and Lasseter 2018; Leidig 2016).

The RSS's size and capacity to influence popular conceptions of Hinduism and Indian civilization has helped make Hindutva a commonplace notion in Indian society in a span of a century. However, there is nothing inherently populist about the RSS, which is a right-wing nationalist rather than a populist organization. We will now discuss how the BJP, and its leader Narendra Modi, took the Hindutva of the RSS and successfully merged it with populism.

5.3.2   BJP: From Right-Wing Nationalism to Populism

The RSS formed the Bharatiya Jana Sangh (BJS) 1951–1977 as a political arm to find an avenue for the political presentation of the interests of Hindus (Carothers and O'Donohue 2019; Lahiry 2005). Under the Indra Gandhi imposed 'Emergency', it merged with the Janata Party and eventually detached itself from the RSS, ultimately forming the BJP in 1980 as an independent party. There is little evidence of populism in the early BJP, or under the leadership of Atal Bihari Vajpayee, who later twice became Prime Minster of India (between 1996 to 2004). While trained as a youth within the RSS system, and sympathetic to Hindutva, he always kept RSS away from politics and his BJP maintained a conservative but not populist course during this period (Yilmaz et al. 2021; Nag 2015).

At the same time, Vajpayee sometimes gravitated toward populist 'us vs them' conceptions of society. For example, he was at times a Hindutva apologist at a time when communal divides between Muslims and Hindus were deepening in India; and on one occasion claimed "Wherever Muslims live, they don't like to live in co-existence with others, they don't like to mingle with others; and instead of propagating their ideas in a peaceful manner, they want to spread their faith by resorting to terror and threats. The world has become alert to this danger" (*Hindustan Times* 2018; Varadarajan 2018). In the latter period of his leadership, Vajpayee began to observe greater RSS influence within the party, yet could do little about it. BJP member and Hindutva adherent Narendra Modi, then chief minister of Gujrat, permitted deadly rioting and the killing of Muslims in Gujrat and refused to step down or apologize (Nag 2015). Noting the changing political landscape in India represented by Modi, Vajpayee termed this "new" Hindutva worrying, "I accept the Hindutva of Swami Vivekananda" he said, "but the type of Hindutva being propagated now is wrong and one should be wary of it" (Varadarajan 2018). By 2003, people within BJP and the SP increasingly disapproved of Vajpayee. Giriraj Kishore, the leader of VHP, called him a "pseudo Hindu" for his tolerance of non-Hindus and for opening diplomatic engagement with Pakistan in efforts such as the Lahore Pact[3] (Nag 2015).

Others have argued that the Lal Krishna Advani and Vajpayee duo performed the respective roles of "good cop" and "bad cop" duo, where the former was drawing in RSS deeper in BJP politics while the latter was the soft-line democrat in comparison (Subrahmaniam 2009). Leidig (2020) notes that while the late 1990s and 2000s saw the rise of conservative right-wing politicians, "yet Hindutva was not truly 'mainstreamed' until the election of the current prime minister, Narendra Modi, in 2014. In order to construct a narrative that furthered Hindu insecurity, Modi mobilized his campaign by appealing to recurring themes of a Muslim 'threat' to the Hindu majority. The result is that Hindutva has become synonymous with Indian nationalism".

It was under Modi's leadership that the dominant political narrative turned from right-wing nationalist to populist while maintaining a reliance on the Hindutva narrative of Hindu victimhood and nostalgia for the lost golden age of Hindu civilization. Narendra Modi rose to prominence after winning an election in the state of Gujrat in 2002. Growing in stature despite many controversies attached to his leadership, he became Indian prime minister in 2014. Like Advani and Vajpayee, Modi was educated in the RSS system and quickly climbed ranks in the organization. Unlike his predecessors, Modi unapologetically and openly embraced the Hindutva ideology, and he brought it to the center stage of BJP politics. For example, he refused to nominate any Muslim BJP candidates in the Gujrat elections in 2012, appeared to care little about the violence propagated by SP members in communal riots, and refused to wear clothes given by Muslim leaders in order to demonstrate his Hindu-ness (Jaffrelot 2016; Chakrabortty 2014).

The Modi led BJP uses the classic populist appeal of attacking the Indian National Congress party, calling them the political 'elite' as opposed to the BJP which is the 'real voice' of the people of India (Yilmaz et al. 2021; Human Rights Watch 2020a; Jaffrelot and Tillin 2017, 184). There is also in Modi's rhetoric the promise of neo-liberal reforms, and

---

[3] The Lahore Pact is a bilateral agreement between India and Pakistan to curb the use and proliferation of nuclear arms in South Asia and paved ways to easing tensions between the two countries (UN 1999).

to boost the country's international competitiveness through a 'Made in India' campaign (Filkins 2019; Jaffrelot 2016). Yet the lynchpin of Modi's discourse is civilizational populism driven by Hindutva. The manifestation was represented in billboards from the 2014 general electoral campaign. On this board we see a picture of Modi covered in photoshopped saffron hues boasting, "I am a Patriot. I am Nationalist. I am Born Hindu" (Ghosh 2013). This wording and imagery of the electoral campaign was the beginning of what is termed as the "saffron tide" that has swept India (Bhattacharjee 2017; Nag 2014). Rooted in the RSS's Hindutva ideology, the BJP called for the building of a society for Hindus and run by Hindus, justifying their agenda through the Hindutva call for the "cleansing" of "impurities" from society. In this narrative of crisis, Modi was the "born Hindu" and "ideal Indian" who would lead the country as a "strongman" and revive the glory of the *hindu rashtra* (Hindu kingdom) (Lefèvre 2020).

However, under the BJP's classification of peoples and religions, McDonnell and Cabrera (2019) observe, "the people" and the "others" are not always categorized as Hindus and non-Hindus, respectively. Rather, Indian citizens are also judged according to the degree to which they love the Indian nation and its culture. This idea is embodied in the words of Manohar Lal Khattar, the BJP chief minister of Haryana, who explained that "Muslims can live here, but in this country, they will have to stop eating beef" (McDonnell and Cabrera 2019, 493). Of course, because the BJP frame Indian culture and the nation as the product of Hindu civilization, to love India and its culture is—according to the BJP—to either love or at least respect and obey the rules of Hindu culture. Or as Irfan Ahmad (2017) puts it, "Hindutva defined Indianness exclusively in religious terms: an Indian is someone who considers India as their holy land". The BJP's populism is not, therefore, entirely pro-Hinduism or anti-Muslim, but rather the embodiment of the civilizationalist Hindutva ideals transmitted from the RSS into the party. This civilizationalism is reflected in the party's "abrogation of article 370, the ban on cow slaughter and the construction of a Ram temple in Ayodhya", which the BJP claims are necessary acts to revive and protect Hindu culture (Ammassari 2018, 8). These actions are also framed as attempts to invalidate "invasion" of India, and to purify it in order that Hindu civilization may regain its lost glory (Ammassari 2018; Jain and Lasseter 2018).

The BJP frames itself as the voice of the people, and accordingly attacks 'elites' such as Congress leader Rahul Gandhi, who they call "a shahzada (princeling) of the Delhi Sultanate" (Peker 2019, 32). At the same time, the party portrays its leader Modi as a true man of the people, making much of his blue-collar job as *chaiwala* (tea stall boy) and his simple RSS background, and largely represents him as a "humble yet anointed Hindu leader" (Peker 2019, 32). From the clothes Modi chooses to wear to his routines of yoga and visiting temples, his actions are carefully "choreographed" to create a 'Zen' or 'woke' tolerant face of Hindutva, and to portray Muslims as intolerant fanatics and terrorists (Lakshmi 2020). At the same time, the BJP often presents Modi as a religious figure, "sacralised with a halo indicating Hindu symbolism of gods who glow like surya (the sungod)", to consolidate his position as "the leader" for "the people" (Peker 2019, 32). Chacko (2018) notes that even the call for neo-liberal reforms to boost the economy is framed by religious Hindutva populism rather than simple nationalism. In Modi's calls for neo-liberal reforms in India, he stresses the importance of regaining the lost Hindu homeland, and on overcoming the hurdles placed in front of this goal by elites, internal non-Hindu enemies, and external antagonists such as Pakistan.

5.3.3 Legislative Changes

Since assuming power, the BJP has legislated to "safeguard" Hindu culture, framing Hindu people as victims and encouraging them, at times, to act with vindictiveness in order to revive 'lost homeland' of Hindu civilization. Where once the party had quietly mobilized SP members to attack minorities, increasingly the BJP government has simply created legislation which oppresses minorities and empowers Hindu nationalists. For example, the Citizenship Amendment Act (CAA) targets Bengali Muslims, who were mostly displaced after the Pakistani civil war in the early 1970s, and leaves them potentially stateless (Amnesty International 2021; Sharma 2020). In 2019, the abrogation of Articles 370 and 35a stripped India held Kashmir of its special status, and led to the forceful unification of the region with India. Kashmir's parliament has been suspended, with massive lockdowns in place in the region since August 5, 2019, communication blackouts, civil liberties suspended—including the right to congregate for prayers—countless arbitrary arrests, and the killings of 'suspected terrorists' (Human Rights Watch 2020b, c, d). Aggression toward 'others' is deeply embedded in the BJP's actions in Kashmir. For example, BJP lawmaker Vikram Saini remarked that the abrogation of the special status of Kashmir allowed Muslim party workers to "go and marry fair-skinned Kashmiri girls", treating Muslim women as if they were the spoils of war (Siddiqui 2018).

At the other end of the spectrum, the chastity of the Hindu women demands legal protection, in view of the BJP. For example, the BJP has framed inter-faith marriages between Hindu women and Muslim men as a "love jihad" in which Muslims attempt to reduce the overall number of Hindus in India. The party's attacks on the supposed "love jihad" being waged by Muslims on Hindus have paved the way for communal targeted attacks by SS on inter-faith couples (Asthana 2021; Pradhan 2020; *The Indian Express* 2020). The BJP are now considering a birth control program involving voluntary sterilization in states with the highest Muslim populations, in the form of a bill that has been floated in the Uttar Pradesh province (Quraishi 2021). Under BJP rule there has been an overall tolerant attitude toward vigilantes that attack people suspected of butchering cows. This is led to an increase in 'cow/beef lynching', a phenomenon which generally targets Muslims (Human Rights Watch 2020a). India's relationship with Pakistan has also soured under Modi's leadership, reaching a new low in which highly toxic commentary is present on both sides, and which has prevented diplomatic and civil society led efforts to normalize the relationship (Pandey 2019). All of these actions have been justified as defensive measures taken to preserve Hindu culture and revive Hindu civilization, deepening social divides along civilizational lines.

5.3.4 *Reshaping History*

Like contemporary populists in Turkey and Pakistan, India's BJP has also pushed for a change in the school curriculum that promotes civilizational populism by restructuring history and cultural identity (Yilmaz 2021; Yilmaz and Shakil 2021). Post-2014, the Hindutva version of Indian history has increasingly blurred the lines between culture and history, fact and fiction. These changes were justified by RSS's Manmohan Vaidya, who claimed "the true colour of Indian history is saffron and to bring about cultural changes we have to rewrite history" (Jain and Lasseter 2018). The BJP written syllabus uses history to set a "Hindu first" narrative, in which other cultural influences are depicted as products of invader Muslim and Christian cultures. Prakash Javadekar, Minister of Human Resource Development, claims these changes are courageous, saying "Our government is the first government to have the courage to even question the existing version of history that is being taught in schools and colleges" (Jain and Lasseter 2018). This fictional narrative of history is also promoted outside the classroom. Modi himself has claimed that all scientific interventions can be traced back to Vedic India. In this regard he has claimed that the appearance of Ganesh, the deity with a boy's body and an elephant head, was the result of plastic surgery, and further suggested that ancient Hindus were possibly highly skilled genetic scientists (Rahman 2014). Adding to this glorification of Vedic India, Modi has used the Hindu epic of Mahabharat to claim that the chariot of the Hindu God Rama was in fact the world's first aeroplane, and other BJP leaders such as Biplab Deb, chief minister of Tripura, have attributed the invention of the internet to ancient Indians (BBC 2018; Rahman 2014).

5.3.5 BJP Leadership: Beyond Modi

Notions of a "clash of civilizations" in India occurring between Hindus and Muslims, and of the ultimate superiority of the Hindu people over all others, have a dark history in India and played an important role in the shaping BJP and RSS ideology. BJP and RSS leaders, in return, have played a key role in shaping and mainstreaming civilizational populism in India, a process that eventually led to the election of Narendra Modi as prime minister in 2014. Violent and aggressive civilizationalism in India can be traced back to 1990's Ram Rath Yatra, a national rally at the site of the Babri Mosque/Ram Temple at Ayodhya and headed by BJP member L. K. Advani. This rally resulted in the unlawful demolition of the Mughal era mosque, and communal rioting along its pathways in 1992 (Filkins 2019; Chakrabortty 2014). The demolition of the mosque created a never-ending cycle of violence. On the 10th anniversary of the event Muslim fanatics set fire to a train containing mostly RSS and SS members, who were on their way to Faizabad to visit the Ayodhya site. In response, violence in Gujrat erupted in 2002 which left hundreds dead, most of them Muslims (Filkins 2019; Chakrabortty 2014). In both instances violence sprang from one location and spread like wildfire around the country, leading to the widespread perpetration of religious hate crimes.

This momentum has now found permanence in the form of the populist politics of key BJP figures. Their actions, politics, and rhetoric embody the aggressive Hindutva civilizationalism that has formed the core of the BJP's populist approach.

The BJP's 'poster boy' is Yogi Adityanath, a monk-politician and chief minister of Uttar Pradesh (UP) (Gupta 2018). He represents the younger and more aggressive face of Hindutva. His title of 'yogi' or spiritual leader is accompanied by his styling of himself in saffron robes in classic Vedic fashion. Now in his 50s, the monk is unmarried in yogi tradition, and divides his time between temples and running India's most populated state (and the state with the highest Muslim population). Despite the 1.2 million people in his state following a different faith Yogi has openly pushed for the establishment of a *Hindu Rashtra* (Hindu polity) that he claims to be the right "way of life" (*Hindustan Times* 2017). Adityanath likes to present himself as a peace-loving preacher. His god, Kalu, is an internet sensation in his own right, and he also follows the Hindutva way by abstaining from eating meat and living on a milk and roti (South Asian flat bread) diet (*Hindustan Times* 2019).

The Yogi has not been shy to legitimize the use of violence against 'others'. He has argued that those who try to hinder the *Hindi Rashtra* dream will be "taught" a lesson "in the language they understand (violence)" (*Hindustan Times* 2017). At the same time, he has no problem when Hindus disrespect the sacred places of non-Hindu 'others' because they are seen as rightfully belonging to the Hindus: "If given a chance, we will install statues of Goddess Gauri, Ganesh and Nandi [Hindu deities] in every mosque" (*Hindustan Times* 2017). The District of Faizabad (now renamed Ayodhya since Yogi assumed office) is the home to the Ram Temple/Babri Mosque site. The Yogi has pressured the courts to declare the desecrated mosque site a viable location for rebuilding the Hindu temple he and his supporters claim once stood there, despite no archaeological proof of the Ram Mandir temple having existed in that loaction, and under his rule the state of Uttar Pradesh has heavily invested in *yatries* (pilgrims) and Hindu religious tourism (Sikander 2020; The Wire 2020; Sharma 2018).

Perhaps as a result of the BJP's aggressive Hindutva populism, cow-lynching has become a problem in Uttar Pradesh, a situation made worse by the chief minister who claims that "Hinduism is a lifeline and a rich tradition that cannot flow in the veins of those who justify killing cows and eating beef" (Human Rights Watch 2020a; Gupta 2018). Additionally, the "fear" that Muslims will, in time, outnumber Hindus in India is also instrumentalized by the Yogi. Not only is the state parliament mulling over a two-child policy for Uttar Pradesh, it has already approved a "love-jihad" law preventing interfaith marriages between Muslim men and Hindu women (Apoorvanand 2021; Pradhan 2020). Adityanath, on the occasion of passage of the bill, warned Muslims in the following words, "I warn those who conceal identity and play with our sisters' respect. If you don't mend your ways your '*Ram naam satya*' (a chant associated with Hindu funerals) journey will begin" (Asthana 2021; Pradhan 2020; *The Indian Express* 2020). He has justified gendered violence toward Muslim women by saying, "if they [Muslims] take one Hindu girl, we will take 100 Muslims girls [...] if they kill one Hindu, there will be 100 that we..." and waited for the crowd to chant "kill" (Crabtree 2017). These words have only empowered the Hindutva adherents to feel a dangerous sense of victimhood, accompanied by a feeling of anger and desire for vengeance, feelings that can be used to justify violence against Muslims.

Another prominent political figure behind the growth of civilizational populism is Amit Shah. Unlike the Yogi, Shah is not a religious scholar or preacher. He was trained in the RSS system and belongs to the Modi cohort, and is therefore much older than Yogi and began his career around the time of the Indra Gandhi imposed a state of emergency. He has framed the CAA as an attempt to "protect" Hindu civilization and to ensure that India remains "Hindu by character, by culture" (Human Rights Watch 2020a; McDonnell and Cabrera 2019, 488). Rationalizing the CAA, Shah claimed it was necessary because "infiltrators are like termites in the soil of Bengal. A Bharatiya Janata Party government will pick up infiltrators one by one and throw them into the Bay of Bengal" (Al Jazeera 2018). Acting as the Home Minister, Shah was also the force behind Articles 370 and 35A. In justification of these changes, Shah assured that they were required to "root out terrorism in Kashmir" (Dey 2019). In reality, the changes further pushed Kashmir into the hands of insurgents who saw India's increasingly aggressive conduct as legitimizing their jihadism. The abolition of the articles is the larger part of the Hindutva call for an *Akhand Bharat* (Greater India) that seeks to restore the territorial configuration of India to its "golden age", that expanded from Afghanistan to Sri Lanka (Rashid 2020; PTI 2019). The BJP has thus moved Hindutva beyond right-wing nationalism and toward a civilizational struggle between Hindus and 'others'.

5.3.6 Political Affiliates: Shiv Sena (SS)

In its two successive governments the BJP has won overwhelming majority, but in various states it requires coalitions to govern. Shiv Sena (SS) is one such partner. SS was founded in 1966 and entered into a collation with the BJP in 1998, lasting until 2018 (Roychowdhury 2018). An ideologically right-wing party in its own right, the politics of SS revolves around the protection of Marathi ethnicity blended with Hindutva. Its attachment to the BJP in 1998 led to a phase in which the SS used civilizational rhetoric.

The regional party was formed in 1966 within the city of Mumbai (then Bombay). Led by Bal Thackeray, it was formed to protect the Marathi *manoos* (person/s) interests when this indigenous population felt left out by the economic progress that benefited the non-Marathis (Annamalai 1987). Much like the RSS, the party's *sainiks* (workers) formed a "family" led by the unapologetic and charismatic Thackeray, who called them his "children" (Gupta 1982, 97). SS involvement in politics increased throughout the 1960s thanks to Congress support, and the larger party's use of SS *sainiks* to counter Bombay's communist trade unions (India Today 2019; Gupta 2010; Shaikh 2005). To draw support, party officials went to *sainiks* from *ashrams, shakhas* (Vedic/religious schools), and religious schools (Shaikh 2005; Palshikar 2004). This religious influence gave SS a Hindu-Marathi right-wing ideology. Additionally, like the RSS founders Thackeray also "eulogized Hitler in his speeches, public gatherings, writings and interviews, thus following in the footsteps of RSS chief Golwalkar" (Gupta 2010, 1025).

Much like the RSS *karyakartas* (functionaries), the *sainiks* during the 1990s and 2000s were involved in communal rioting during the Ayodhya land dispute (Gupta 2010; Heuze 2000). Perhaps due to its close collaboration with the BJP, the party embraced the slogan "*Garv se kaho hum Hindu hain*, (say with prid that we are Hindus)" (Roychowdhury 2018). After the national election victory of the BJP in 2014, SS was emboldened to use more anti-Muslim rhetoric. The same traumas, notions of victimhood, and anxieties were evoked by the SS, and the subsequent feelings of anger among their supporters were harvested by the party and converted into feelings of anger to be directed toward secular 'elites' and non-Hindus (especially Muslims). For example, the SS called for a Hindu Rashtra by abolishing the secular foundations of the Indian

Constitution and at the same time called for bans on burkas, used anti-Muslim/Pakistan rhetoric, and promised monetary rewards for Marathi Hindu families who have more than five children in order to counter the Muslim demographic "threat" (Roychowdhury 2018; *Indian Express* 2015; *Times of India* 2015).

Eventually, the SS-BJP coalition fell apart. In 2017 the two split over ethnic-regional issues, and the two parties came into conflict with the SS perceiving the situation as one involving "Hindutva versus Marathi *manoos*" (Rawal 2021; PTI 2017). The SS leadership has even criticized the BJP for its studied ignorance bordering on approval of cow-lynching. SS's Marathi *manoo* identity is now paramount; however, it remains a right-wing Hindutva party.

5.3.7 Grass Roots Organizations: RSS and the SP

Vishva Hindu Parishad/Universal Hindu Council (VHP) and Bajrang Dal/Brigade of Hanuman (BD) are the militant wings of the RSS. The former is a uniform platform for Hindutva supporters formed in 1964, while the latter is the student/youth wing formed in 1984, and fashioned after the monkey god Lord Hanuman (Friedrich 2020; Doniger 2018; Nair 2009). Both of these groups practice military training in order to be ready to 'defend' the Hindutva way of life, and take the form of militant vigilantes (Jaiswal 2019; Nair 2009; Lochtefeld 1994). Due to their notorious role in communal rioting, inciting hate speech targeting Muslims and Christians, and repeated acts of vandalism along with harassment, both groups were categorized as "militant religious organizations" by the CIA in 2018 (Friedrich 2020). Some scholars and commentators even term these activities as ethnoreligious terrorism (Lefèvre 2020).

Significant support for these groups comes from Hindu religious bodies/groups across India, and accordingly the groups have cultivated relationships with various sages to gain a foothold in *ashramas* (Jha 2019; Jaffrey and Slater 2017). This has led to the transfer of Hindutva civilizationalism to thousands of these *ashramas* spread throughout India. S. S. Apte, co-founder and early leader of the VHP, in one meeting with these religious sanctuaries described Hindutva victimhood in the following words, "The world has been divided into Christian, Islamic and Communist, and all three consider Hindu society as a very fine rich food on which to feast and fatten themselves. It is therefore necessary in this age of competition and conflict to think of, and organize, the Hindu world to save itself from the evil eyes of all the three" (Jha 2019). Instilling these ideas has led *bhaktis* (followers) of various orders to embrace the Hindutva victimhood narrative and subsequently volunteer for these organizations (Friedrich 2020; Jha 2019; Frayer and Khan 2019).

For example, Advani might have led the Hindutva crowds to the mosque site in 1992, but it was the *kar sevaks* (temple volunteers) from BD and VHP that illegally demolished the mosque and triggered events leading to the death of 2,000 mostly Muslim people (Lefèvre 2020). These volunteers have pressured the legal system to vote in favor of the construction of the Ram Mandir temple at the location of the former mosque, and have been calling for the handover of Banaras and Mathura mosques on the same grounds.[4] Even in times of peace the groups target Muslims and Christians with violence. A horrific example, from 1999, was the killing of a Muslim trader, whose arms were amputated and body set on fire in front of 400 people who watched it occur (Human Rights Watch 1999).

The BJP has been very tolerant of the violent activities of the BD and VHP, and benefits from their call to end the influence of the "invader Muslims" (Singh 2020; The Wire 2020). Supporting the BJP's neo-liberal agenda, the two groups have also acted as striker breakers, attacking human rights groups, and Muslim-led protests in Uttar Pradesh and other locations (*Indian Express* 2020; Mahmood 2020). BD is known for targeting and harassing Kashmiri Muslim youth in campuses around India, and these actions are justified as a means of teaching "the students a lesson so that no one can ever dream of doing what had happened in Pulwama[5]" (Mishra and Jha 2019). While BJP politicians facilitated legislation that leads to discrimination based on religious civilizational lines, on the ground it is the SP organizations such as BD and VHP that carry out 'cow-lynching' and 'love jihad' (Friedrich 2020; Ahuja 2019; Mishra and Jha 2019; PTI 2016). Thus the BJP and BD

---

[4] A number of mosques are built on old temple sites. However, most RSS claims of Hindu ownership of Mosque land are not rooted in fact but on assumptions. For instance, archeological excavations have never been able to find evidence of a temple underneath the hotly contested Babri Mosque (The Wire 2020).

[5] An attack on an Indian military post in 2019 that killed several officials in India's part of Kashmir.

and VHP work hand in hand to oppress Muslims and to revive, as they understand it, Hindu Civilization.

In a more subtle form of violence, SP militant groups have policed popular culture. For example, BD and VHP supporters pressured not only local media but also Netflix to remove "anti-Hindu" content such as *Leila*, a dystopic series,[6] from Indian screens, claiming the show was "propaganda" and "lies" that damaged the Hindu dharma (News18 2020). VHP and BD members regularly target Muslim actors in Bollywood (Pandey and Krishna 2020). The interfaith marriages of some Bollywood celebrities have, in particular, captured the VHP's attention (Pandey and Krishna 2020). All these activities conducted by SP's militant wings are a manifestation of the Hindutva victimhood-nostalgia narrative, which encourages adherents to perceive themselves as the victims of a Muslim invasion, and to re-create the "golden age" on Hindu civilization.

5.3.8 Online Populism

The online space is a critical part of BJP political mobilization, and the party uses social media to rally support during election campaigns and fuel divisional politics. Moreover, the BJP has used laws to curb space for opposition online, and has used this space to propagate its civilizational populism.

Modi's online presence is unparalleled in world politics. His Facebook official page alone has 45 million 'likes' (PTI 2020). Other BJP leadership figures such as Yogi Adityanath and Amit Shah also have millions of followers, giving these leaders immense power and representation on these platforms (PTI 2020). Their mammoth online presence allows the BJP to monopolize space and propagate its agendas online. For example, Modi has used social media to promote the Hindutva way of living as superior by posing on yoga mats and practicing chants, giving Hindutva a "peaceful face". The BJP also attempts to create viral trends and hashtags that have aided its popularity and play a key role in electoral success (Tewari 2019). Furthermore the party has a highly synchronized social media wing that disperses messages on platforms such as WhatsApp, some of which is pro-BJP propaganda disguised as news (Bansal 2019).

---

[6] The series feature an Orwellian or Atwood styled world where fundamental Hindutva-like norms are in practice (News-18).

To support the CAA, the BJP uses click-baiting to attract citizens adding the "'promise of sex', 'jobs', 'free mobile data' and 'Netflix accounts' as part of the 'missed call campaign'" that linked audiences to a video by Hindu sage Jaggi Vasudev (Sadhguru). In this video Sadhuguru defends the CAA and accuses university youth of unjust rioting without really reading or fully understanding the legislation (Halder 2020). The religious figure's stature combined with his deep conviction was further backed by Modi who tweeted, "Do hear this lucid explanation of aspects relating to CAA and more by Sadhguru Jaggi Vasudev. He provides historical context, brilliantly highlights our culture of brotherhood. He also calls out the misinformation by vested interest groups" (Halder 2020). Modi thus began the aggressive #IndiaSupportsCAA campaign (Halder 2020). The large amount of money and energy pumped into the campaign helped to legitimize the BJP's civilizational populism among the Indian public, who were bombarded with propaganda online promoting the BJP's agenda and legislation.

RSS, BJP leaders, and even common citizens in India have incited riots using social media applications such as WhatsApp. Hate speech rooted in Hindutva civilizational populism is a key force behind the spillover of digital hate into real-life violence (Bhatnagar 2022; Nizaruddin 2022). Mirchandani's (2018) study of freedom of expression and hate speech on social media shows that in India majoritarian hate speech is common on online platforms, and at times triggers events that display majoritarian violence. For example, in Indian villages communities have been provoked through online propaganda and lies to act in violent ways when they have received rumors about Muslims or 'untouchables' slaughtering cows, leading to cow-lynching murders and attacks (Asrar 2018; Anand and Raj 2017). The platforms' widespread nature and unchecked content undoubtedly play a powerful role in propagating civilizational-inspired populist violence with or without the BJP's direct involvement.

While the BJP is comfortable using social media to promote its civilizational agenda, it has consistently failed to combat lies and misinformation about minorities groups, and has at times restricted minorities' freedom of expression online. It has frequently demanded various Silicon Valley technology companies such as Facebook, Google, and Twitter block connect contrary to its Hindutva victimhood-nostalgia narrative (Singh 2019). Modi, for example, has termed any opposition directed toward his policies as "dirt" which ought not to be spread around (*The Print* 2018). The BJP government is today drafting a law to ensure the monitoring of social media and digital space, which many fear would be used to further shrink the space available online for freedom of speech in India (Saaliq and Pathi 2021).

5.4 Discussion of the Case Study

Our survey of India shows Hindutva has found a permanent home in the country, and that it has been successfully merged, in the form of the BJP, with populism. What began as a response to colonialism and the rise of pan-Islamism has transitioned from a peripheral ideology to the heart of mainstream Indian politics within a century. We have found that, in one significant respect, Hindutva is unlike Hinduism. Unlike Hinduism, Hindutva is not divisive in nature and opposes plural understandings of religion and religious practices. Moreover, when merged with populist ideation, Hindutva provides populists with a powerful tool through which they can define populism's key signifiers in primarily civilizational terms.

While Hindutva predates modern India, it did not manifest in a populist-civilizational form until the turn of the last century, and did not become electorally successful until 2014, when the BJP became India's ruling party and Narendra Modi Indian Prime Minister. The BJP began as a conservative right-wing party unfriendly, but not yet violently hostile, toward Muslims. However, an aggressive Hindutva, alive in grassroots organizations, would eventually become more influential within the BJP. RSS and its SPs groups over many years penetrated ashrams, cultivating relationships with their leaders, and by combining forces managed to politicize the ashrams and religionize the RSS and its militant wings. Thus by the 1990s, the RSS the BJP with many politicians and activists, but was also at the forefront of a civilizational struggle against 'others' to preserve the authentic values of the Hindu culture and civilization. Following the violent communal rioting of 1992 and 2002, Modi and the BJP sought to embrace more openly than before the RSS and its Hindutva ideology, and to position itself as an anti-elite, anti-secular nationalist party which instrumentalized Hindutva in order to exploit the ontological insecurities felt by many Indian Hindus (see Tables 5.1 and 5.2).

Our study of RSS and its SP groups not only reveals RSS's impact on politics, but its sheer street power, which it has gained by inciting violence. The mutualistic relationship between RSS and the BJP online and in real space has proven highly efficacious for both groups. Having the backing of RSS benefits the BJP insofar as it helps the party prolong and perform a crisis, while at the same time helping their followers to

Table 5.1 Hindutva populist case study

	Pro-violent narratives	Links or overlaps with the far right	Transnational dimension, diasporas
BJP	– Belief that region is rightfully theirs and "the others" have displaced the "real" culture, thus the aggrieved victimhood narrative justifies calls for the "cleansing" the 'homeland' of "the others" and their culture – BJP members periodically use derogatory terms to justify their actions against Muslims, e.g. Shah calling Bengali displaced people "termites" or treating Kashmiri women as spoils of wars – BJP tolerance toward RSS and SP rioters and use of brute force against Muslims, liberals, and secularists – Use of school syllabus and cyberspace to propagate division creating social disharmony – Use of the legal system to help construct populist divisions within society based on religious adherence	– Core leadership has been RSS members such as the BJP elected Prime Minister and Home Minister – SP organizations which are militant in nature are largely left unchecked and even glorified for their efforts – Collaboration with SS in Maharashtra another Hindutva-ethnicity-inspired society for 25 years – The BJP draws support from local ashrams and religious leaders within the Hindu faith. Pro-BJP yogis such as Adityanath entering parliament	– Not clear as India is the only country with a majority Hindu population – RSS has branches overseas but their impact is unclear in the Indian diaspora

Table 5.2 Populism at Present in India

	Populist divide/Identity	Crises	Civilizationalism	Victimhood
BJP	– "The people" are defined as Hindus and descendants of the Aryan race, whose culture is supreme – "The others" are those who fail to follow the Hindu way (Hindutva), including Muslims and Christians, "the elite" and human rights activists, opposition parties. Pakistan is an external "other"	– The Hindutva way of life is in danger of disappearing – Hindus have been subjected to centuries of oppression by "outsiders" – The dharma and the homeland are both under "threat" and require defending	– Defines Hindutva as the ideal and authentic way of life for all Indians – Laws and street violence are used to protect symbolic identity markers – Hindu identity is based on a mix of fiction and Vedic scripture which romanticizes a lost "homeland"	– Hindus are losing their "homeland" – Hindus are victims of periodic "oppression" by British colonization and Muslim "invaders" and economically exploited by parties such as Congress – Anger toward Muslims and fear of terrorism, conversions, and demographic change creating a larger Muslim population – Legislation such as the CAA and love jihad laws are seen as means to protect the "historically oppressed" – The violence tolerated by BJP and carried out by SP vigilantes is a channel to express this victimhood and "defend" Hindu civilization

feel less like victims and more like empowered conquerors kicking out 'invaders' and restoring Hindu civilization. Most worrying, perhaps, is the new generation of BJP leaders showcased by Yogi Adityanath, who represents the Hindutva marriage between RSS, ashrams, and the BJP. With faith, politics, and street power combined, civilizational populism takes a highly violent turn where the core goal is the establishment of a Hindu 'homeland' at all costs. The detaching of the SS from the BJP provides one ray of hope, however, and suggests a totalizing Hindu-based civilizationalism will always find resistance in diverse India. At the same time, the case of the SS shows that political parties in India often opt for particular ideologies and types of rhetoric in order to win votes and elections, and may thus cease their association with an ideology or type of rhetoric if it is not successful. For Shiv Sena, Marathi *manoo* identity supersedes the Hindutva identity. However, the BJP is unlikely to find an identity wider and more personally significant to large numbers of Indians than 'Hinduism', with which it can construct populist antagonistic relationships.

The most successful Hindutva populism in India is associated with Narendra Modi and the BJP. Modi and the BJP combine populism with Hindutva, and through this combination identify the Hindu people of India as the pure, moral, and authentic people of the land. The combining of Hindutva and populism permits the BJP to portray secular Congress Party 'elites' as corrupt and immoral insofar as they have abandoned Hindu culture and beliefs for a 'foreign' system in secularism, and Muslims as inauthentic foreigners who belong to a wholly different and incompatible cultural tradition (i.e. Islam). The merging of Hindutva and populism permits Modi—and other populists in India—to access deep emotions in the Hindu majority, feelings related to a sense of India as a sacred land polluted and defiled by 'invaders' (Muslims, British Christians), and which must be restored. Such feelings can lead to a sense of personal and communal violation, leading to anger which has, at times, been directed toward these invader groups, particularly Muslims. Hindutva thus provides Modi and the BJP with the means to create a civilizational dichotomy between those who follow the 'Hindu way of life', and who thus belong in India, and those who do not, and must be cast out of society. At the same time, this civilizational classification of peoples permits populists to portray anyone who does not follow the 'Hindu way of life' (as understood by Hindutva adherents) as threat to Indian culture. Thus when Muslims have more children, these children can be framed as an existential threat to the Hindu majority by BJP chief ministers in regions of India with large Muslim populations regardless of whether these fears are justified.

Fear of the civilizational 'other' is a key element of Hindutva discourse, and is often paired with a narrative based around the notion that Hindus are the victims of foreign aggression, and that only by defeating the Muslim 'invaders' and their allies can Hindu civilization rise again and attain the heights Hindus enjoyed during the Vedic period. This victimhood-nostalgia narrative contains a powerful civilizational dimension insofar as it not only constructs 'the people' as the innocent, pure, and authentic Hindu people, but Muslims and secular elites as betrayers and immoral and inauthentic enemies of the Hindu people, and gives the Hindu people a goal to achieve (the restoration of Hindu civilization), and a set of 'others' to blame for India's 'backwardness' and socioeconomic problems. The victimhood-nostalgia narrative also helps Modi and the BJP create a populist crisis, in which the India is being held back and suffering under Muslim-secular elite oppression. Equally, Modi and the BJP portray themselves as the only group capable of 'saving' India from its internal and external civilizational enemies, and restoring the Hindu people to their former greatness.

The *saffronisation* of India comes at a huge cost. Modi's Hindutva political narrative has eroded democracy and the secular state, and given the power to Hindu vigilantes who are attempting to reestablish a civilization rooted in largely fictitious tales of glory. Its impossibility and farfetched nature do not seem to bother the BJP and its most ardent supporters, who use violence to construct their ideal homeland, and to purify it of the 'invaders' who have allegedly prevented the flourishing of Hindu civilizational. The Hindutva victimhood-nostalgia narrative evokes a sense of hope, nostalgia, and anger in adherents that excites and invigorates them, and helps Modi and the BJP mobilize support for the party. The result is an India less tolerant, riven by civilizational divisions, and in which the secular democracy of the Indian National Congress—however flawed—is being replaced by a new system in which Hindutva is merged with the state.

REFERENCES

Ahmad, Irfan. 2017. "Modi's Polarising Populism Makes a Fiction of a Secular, Democratic India". *The Conversation*. https://theconversation.com/modis-polarising-populism-makes-a-fiction-of-a-secular-democratic-india-80605. Last accessed September 21, 2022.

Ahuja, Juhi. 2019. "Protecting Holy Cows: Hindu Vigilantism Against Muslims in India". In *Vigilantism Against Migrants and Minorites*, edited by Tore Bjørgo and Miroslav Mareš. New York: Routledge. https://library.oapen.org/bitstream/handle/20.500.12657/23655/9781138493803_text.pdf?sequence=1&isAllowed=y.

Al Jazeera. 24 September 2018. "BJP Chief Slammed for Calling Bangladeshi Migrants 'Termites'". https://www.aljazeera.com/news/2018/9/24/bjp-chief-slammed-for-calling-bangladeshi-migrants-termites. Last accessed September 21, 2022.

Ammassari, Sofia. 2018. "Contemporary Populism in India: Assessing the Bharatiya JanataParty's Ideological Features". *IBEI*, Students Papers Series 48. https://www.semanticscholar.org/paper/Contemporary-populism-in-India-%3A-assessing-the-Ammassari/70aebdce34835d6920b5cb28ad7c740572936efd. Last accessed September 21, 2022.

Amnesty International. Last updated 2021. "INDIA 2020". https://www.amnesty.org/en/countries/asia-and-the-pacific/india/report-india/. Last accessed September 21, 2022.

Anand, Geeta, and Suhasini Raj. 25 May 2017. "Rumors on WhatsApp Ignite 2 Mob Attacks in India, Killing 7". *The New York Times*. https://www.nytimes.com/2017/05/25/world/asia/india-vigilante-mob-violence.html. Last accessed September 21, 2022.

Anderson, Walter, and Damle, Shridhar D. 1987. *The Brotherhood in Saffron: The RSS and Hindu Revivalism*. New Delhi: Vistaar Publications.

Anderson, Walter, and Damle, Shridhar D. 2019. *Messengers of Hindu Nationalism: How the RSS Reshaped India*. London: Hurst & Company.

Annamalai, E. 1987. "Language Movements in India: The Samyukta Maharastra Movement (1946–1960)". http://www.ciil-ebooks.net/html/langMove/samyukta. Last accessed September 21, 2022.

Andersen, Walter. 4 August 2018. "RSS Is a Lot More Diverse Than It Used to Be: Author Walter Andersen". *Economic Times*. https://economictimes.indiatimes.com/news/politics-and-nation/rss-is-a-lot-more-diverse-than-it-used-to-be-author-walter-ndersen/articleshow/65273543.cms?utm_source=contentofinterest&utm_medium=text&utm_campaign=cppst. Last accessed September 21, 2022.

Apoorvanand. 15 January 2021. "India's 'Love Jihad' Laws: Another Attempt to Subjugate Muslims". Al Jazeera. https://www.aljazeera.com/opinions/2021/1/15/indias-love-jihad-laws-another-attempt-to-subjugate-muslims. Last accessed September 21, 2022.

Asrar, Nadim. 17 July 2018. "In India, WhatsApp Stirs Up Deadly Rumours". Al Jazeera. https://www.aljazeera.com/features/2018/7/17/in-india-whatsapp-stirs-up-deadly-rumours. Last accessed September 21, 2022.

Asthana, C. N. 17 July 2021. "For India's Sake, Stop Destroying Communal Harmony with the Bogey of Love Jihad". The Wire. https://thewire.in/communalism/for-indias-sake-stop-destroying-communal-harmony-with-the-bogey-of-love-jihad. Last accessed September 21, 2022.

Bansa, Samarth. 12 June 2019. "How the BJP Used Technology to Secure Modi's Second Win". Cigi. https://www.cigionline.org/articles/how-bjp-used-technology-secure-modis-second-win/. Last accessed September 21, 2022.

Bapu, Prabhu. 2013. *Hindu Mahasabha in Colonial North India, 1915–1930: Constructing Nation and History*. New York: Routledge.

BBC. 18 April 2018. "Minister Ridiculed for Saying Ancient India Invented Internet." https://www.bbc.com/news/world-asia-india-43806078. Last accessed September 21, 2022.

Bhatnagar, Stuti. 2022. "Social Media and Hindu Extremism in India". In *Religion, Extremism and Violence in South Asia*, edited by I. Ahmed, Z.S. Ahmed, H. Brasted and S. Akbarzadeh. Politics of South Asia. Singapore: Palgrave Macmillan. https://doi.org/10.1007/978-981-16-6847-0_4.

Bhattacharjee, Puja. 6 December 2017. "Orange: The Color of Warmth and Comfort". *CNN*. https://edition.cnn.com/2017/12/06/health/colorscope-orange/index.html. Last accessed September 21, 2022.

Bhosale, B. G. 2009. "Indian Nationalism: Gandhi Vis-A-Vis Tilak and Savarkar". *The Indian Journal of Political Science* 70 (2): 419–427. www.jstor.org/stable/42743906.

Brubaker, Rogers. 2017. "Between Nationalism and Civilizationism: The European Populist Moment in Comparative Perspective". *Ethnic and Racial Studies* 40 (8): 1191–1226. https://doi.org/10.1080/01419870.2017.1294700.

Carothers, Thomas, and Andrew O'Donohue, eds. 2019. *Democracies Divided: The Global Challenge of Political Polarization*. Brookings Institution Press. www.jstor.org/stable/10.7864/j.ctvbd8j2p.

Chacko, Priya. 2018. "The Right Turn in India: Authoritarianism, Populism and Neoliberalisation". *Journal of Contemporary Asia*. https://doi.org/10.1080/00472336.2018.1446546.

Chakrabarti, Kaustuv, and Kaustuv K. Bandyopadhyay. 2021. "Populism in Contemporary Indian Politics". In *Populism in Asian Democracies: Features,*

Structures, and Impacts, edited by Sook Jong Lee, Chin-en Wu, and Kaustuv Kanti Bandyopadhyay. Brill. https://brill.com/view/title/57370. Last accessed September 21, 2022.

Chakrabortty, Aditya. 7 April 2014. "Narendra Modi, a Man with a Massacre on His Hands, Is Not the Reasonable Choice for India". *The Guardian.* https://www.theguardian.com/commentisfree/2014/apr/07/narendra-modi-massacre-next-prime-minister-india. Last accessed September 21, 2022.

Chandrababu, Divya. 15 March 2021. "Tamil Nadu's Freebie Culture Is Here to Stay, Say Parties, Experts." *Hindustan Times.* https://www.hindustantimes.com/elections/tamil-nadu-assembly-election/tamil-nadu-s-freebie-culture-is-here-to-stay-say-parties-experts-101615543899074.html. Last accessed September 21, 2022.

Chatterji, P. Angana, Thomas Blom Hansen, and Christophe Jaffrelot. 2020. *Majoritarian State: How Hindu Nationalism is Changing India*. Oxford: Oxford University Press.

Crabtree, James. 30 March 2017. "'If They Kill Even One Hindu, We Will Kill 100!'". *Foreign Policy.* https://foreignpolicy.com/2017/03/30/if-they-kill-even-one-hindu-we-will-kill-100-india-muslims-nationalism-modi/. Last accessed September 21, 2022.

Dawn. 13 October 2015. "RSS and BJP: Battling for India's 'Soul', State by State". https://www.dawn.com/news/1212815/rss-and-bjp-battling-for-india s-soul-state-by-state. Last accessed September 21, 2022.

De la Torre, Carlos. 2019. "Is Left Populism the Radical Democratic Answer?" *Irish Journal of Sociology* 27: 64–71. https://doi.org/10.1177/0791603519827225.

Desai, Meghnad. 2021. "Democracy and Development: India 1947–2002." In *Twenty K.R. Narayanan Orations: Essays by Eminent Persons on the Rapidly Transforming Indian Economy*, edited by Raghbendra Jha, 1st ed. Australia: ANU Press. www.jstor.org/stable/j.ctv1prsr3r.16.

Devare, Aparna. 2013. *History and the Making of a Modern Hindu Self*. India: Taylor & Francis.

Dey, Stela. 5 August 2019. "'Article 370 Root of Terrorism in Kashmir': Amit Shah". NDTV. https://www.ndtv.com/india-news/article-370-root-of-terrorism-in-jammu-and-kashmir-amit-shah-in-rajya-sabha-top-quotes-2080731. Last accessed September 21, 2022.

Dhulipala, Venkat. 2014. "Muslim Mass Contacts and the Rise of the Muslim League". In *State Power, Islam, and the Quest for Pakistan in Late Colonial North India*. Cambridge University Press. https://doi.org/10.1017/CBO9781107280380.004.

Doniger, Wendy. 19 July 2018. "Hanuman". *Encyclopedia Britannica.* https://www.britannica.com/topic/Hanuman. Last accessed September 21, 2022.

Filkins, Dexter. 2 December, 2019. "Blood and Soil in Narendra Modi's India". *The New Yorker*. https://www.newyorker.com/magazine/2019/12/09/blood-and-soil-in-narendra-modis-india. Last accessed December 31, 2022.

Flood, Gavin. 1996. *An Introduction to Hinduism*. Cambridge: Cambridge University Press.

Frawley, David. 2018. *What is Hinduism?: A Guide for the Global Mind*. New Delhi: Bloomsbury India.

Freedom House. 2021. "India". https://freedomhouse.org/country/india. Last accessed September 21, 2022.

Frayer, Lauren, and L. Furkan Khan. 3 May 2019. "The Powerful Group Shaping the Rise of Hindu Nationalism in India". *NPR*. https://www.npr.org/2019/05/03/706808616/the-powerful-group-shaping-the-rise-of-hindu-nationalism-in-india. Last accessed September 21, 2022.

Friedrich, Pieter. 12 March 2020. "Cultural Malware: The Rise of India's RSS". *The Polis Project*. https://thepolisproject.com/cultural-malware-the-rise-of-indias-rss/#.YQIF1egzbIU. Last accessed September 21, 2022.

Gandhi, M. K. 2021. "RamRajya." https://www.mkgandhi.org/momgandhi/chap67.htm. Last accessed September 21, 2022.

Ghosh, Deepshikha. 24 July 2013. "Narendra Modi's 'Hindu Nationalist' Posters Should Be Banned, Says Samajwadi Party". NDTV. https://www.ndtv.com/india-news/narendra-modis-hindu-nationalist-posters-should-be-banned-says-samajwadi-party-529359. Last accessed September 21, 2022.

Gianolla, Cristiano. 2020. "Undermining populism through Gandhi's intercultural democratic discourse." *Journal of Multicultural Discourses*. 15 (1): 26–41 https://doi.org/10.1080/17447143.2020.1734011.

Gidron, Noam, and Bart Bonikowski. 2013. "Varieties of Populism: Literature Review and Research Agenda". Weatherhead Working Paper Series. https://scholar.harvard.edu/files/gidron_bonikowski_populismlitreview_2013.pdf. Last accessed September 21, 2022.

Gondhalekar, Nandini, and Bhattacharya, Sanjoy. 1999. "The All India Hindu Mahasabha and the End of British Rule in India, 1939–1947". *Social Scientist* 27 (7/8): 48–74. www.jstor.org/stable/3518013.

Gupta, D. Moushumi. 27 November 2018. "A Shrill, Hardline Yogi Adityanath Is Just What BJP Needs to Promote Hindutva Narrative". *The Print*. https://theprint.in/politics/a-shrill-hardline-yogi-adityanath-is-just-what-bjp-needs-to-promote-hindutva-narrative/155005/. Last accessed September 21, 2022.

Gupta, Dipankar. 1982. *Nativism in a Metropolis: The Siv Sena in Bombay*. Delhi: Manohar.

Gupta, Sanjay. 2010. "Right Wing Radical Parties in India and France: A Comparative Analysis of the Ideology of the Shiv Sena (Ss) And Front

National (Fn) and Their Impact on the Political System." *The Indian Journal of Political Science* 71 (3): 1017–1039. www.jstor.org/stable/42748425.

Habib, S. Irfan. 2016 "Legacy of the Freedom Struggle: Nehru's Scientific and Cultural Vision." *Social Scientist* 44 (3/4): 29–40. www.jstor.org/stable/24890242.

Halder, Buddhadeb. 17 December 2020. "How the BJP Tried to Manipulate Public Opinion on Social Media in Favour of the CAA." The Wire. https://thewire.in/politics/how-bjp-tried-manipulate-public-opinion-social-media-favour-caa. Last accessed September 21, 2022.

Heredia, Rudolf C. 2009. "Gandhi's Hinduism and Savarkar's Hindutva." *Economic and Political Weekly* 44 (29): 62–67. www.jstor.org/stable/40279289.

Hindustan Times. 26 November 2019. "Yogi Adityanath's Pet Dog Kalu Is an Online Sensation". https://www.hindustantimes.com/it-s-viral/yogi-adityanath-s-pet-dog-kalu-is-an-online-sensation/story-ItXlMsWzrIp33Cc66zjL8N.html. Last accessed September 21, 2022.

Hindustan Times. 6 April 2017. "From Love Jihad, Conversion to SRK: 10 Controversial Comments by UP's New CM Yogi Adityanath". https://www.hindustantimes.com/assembly-elections/from-love-jihad-conversion-to-srk-10-controversial-comments-by-up-s-new-cm-yogi-adityanath/story-5JW2ZFGZzAdIZeIcjcZCNM.html. Last accessed September 21, 2022.

Hindustan Times. 6 April 2017. "Yogi Adityanath Says Nothing Wrong with Hindu Rashtra Concept, BJP Defends Him". https://www.hindustantimes.com/india-news/up-cm-yogi-adityanath-says-there-s-nothing-wrong-with-hindu-rashtra-concept-bjp-defends-him/story-aJcX0rQV7bpclddfm80P8I.html. Last accessed September 21, 2022.

Hindustan Times. 16 August 2018. "Atal Bihari Vajpayee's complex relationship with Rashtriya Swayamsevak Sangh". *The Hindustan Times.* https://www.hindustantimes.com/india-news/atal-bihari-vajpayee-s-complex-relationship-with-rashtriya-swayamsevak-sangh/story-i4PWTtQzyWnJpojnPQap7O.html. Last accessed December 31, 2022.

Human Rights Watch. 1991. "Summary". https://www.hrw.org/reports/1999/indiachr/christians8-01.htm. Last accessed September 21, 2022.

Human Rights Watch. 1999. "Summary". https://www.hrw.org/reports/1999/indiachr/christians8-01.htm.

Human Rights Watch. 2003. "background to the Violence". Gujarat Massacre Report https://www.hrw.org/reports/2003/india0703/Gujarat-02.htm. Last accessed September 21, 2022.

Human Rights Watch. 9 April 2020a. "'Shoot the Traitors' Discrimination Against Muslims Under India's New Citizenship Policy". https://www.hrw.org/report/2020a/04/09/shoot-traitors/discrimination-against-muslims-under-indias-newcitizenship-policy. Last accessed September 21, 2022.

Human Rights Watch. 4 September 2020b. "India: Stop Using Pellet-Firing Shotguns in Kashmir". https://www.hrw.org/news/2020b/09/04/india-stop-using-pellet-firing-shotguns-kashmir. Last accessed September 21, 2022.
Human Rights Watch. 14 August 2020c. "India: New Reports of Extrajudicial Killings in Kashmir". https://www.hrw.org/news/2020c/08/14/india-new-reports-extrajudicial-killings-Kashmir. Last accessed September 21, 2022.
Human Rights Watch. 4 August 2020d. "India: Abuses Persist in Jammu and Kashmir". https://www.hrw.org/news/2020d/08/04/india-abuses-persist-jammu-and-kashmir. Last accessed September 21, 2022.
Huntington, S. 1993. "The Clash of Civilizations?" *Foreign Affairs*. 72 (3): 22–49. https://doi.org/10.2307/20045621.
Heuze, Gerard. 2000. "Populism, Religion, and Nation in Contemporary India: The Evolution of the Shiv Sena in Maharashtra." *Comparative Studies of South Asia, Africa and the Middle East* 20 (1): 3–43. muse.jhu.edu/article/191204. Last accessed September 21, 2022.
Indian Express. 29 January 2015. "Shiv Sena Demands Removal of 'Secular' from Constitution". https://indianexpress.com/article/india/politics/shiv-sena-demands-removal-of-secular-from-constitution/. Last accessed September 21, 2022.
Indian Express. 5 March 2020. "Legal Action Should Be Taken Against Anti-CAA Protesters: VHP General Secy". https://indianexpress.com/article/india/legal-action-should-be-taken-against-anti-caa-protesters-vhp-general-secy-6299627/. Last accessed September 21, 2022.
Indian Express. 30 October 2020. "Yogi's Love Jihad Warning: 'Your Ram Naam Satya Journey Will Begin If You Don't Mend Ways'". https://indianexpress.com/article/cities/lucknow/yogi-adityanath-love-jihad-law-uttar-pradesh-6911537/. Last accessed September 21, 2022.
India Today. 29 November 2019. "Congress Created Shiv Sena to Counter Trade Unions in 1960s: Jairam Ramesh". https://www.indiatoday.in/india/story/congress-created-shiv-sena-to-counter-trade-unions-in-1960s-jairam-ramesh-1623812-2019-11-29. Last accessed September 21, 2022.
Jacobs, Stephen. 2010. *Hinduism Today: An Introduction*. New York and London: Continuum International Publishing Group.
Jaffrelot, Christophe. 2007. "Introduction." In *Hindu Nationalism A Reader*, edited by Christophe Jaffrelot. Princeton: Princeton University Press.
Jaffrelot, Christophe. 2016. "Narendra Modi between Hindutva and subnationalism: The Gujarati asmita of a Hindu Hriday Samrat". *India Review* 15 (2): 196–217. https://doi.org/10.1080/14736489.2016.1165557.
Jaffrelot, Christophe, and Louise Tillin. 2017. "Populism in India." In *The Oxford Handbook of Populism*, edited by Cristobal Kaltwasser, Paul Taggart, Paulina Espeho, and Pierre Ostiguy. Oxford: Oxford University Press.

Jaffrey, Sana, and Dan Slater. 2017. "Violence and Regimes in Asia: Capable States and Durable Settlements". Violence and Regimes in Asia 194 by the Asia Foundation. https://asiafoundation.org/wpcontent/uploads/2017/09/Essays_on_The_State_of_Conflictand_Violence_in_Asia.pdf. Last accessed September 21, 2022.
Jain, Manju Kumari. 2012. "Paradigims Shifts in Thought Process During National Movement: A Study of Savarkar's Ideas". *The Indian Journal of Political Science* 73 (2): 267–272. www.jstor.org/stable/41856589.
Jain, Rupam, and Tom Lasseter. 6 March 2018. "By Rewriting History, Hindu Nationalists Aim to Assert Their Dominance over India". *Reuters*. https://www.reuters.com/investigates/special-report/india-modi-culture/. Last accessed September 21, 2022.
Jaiswal, Anuja. 20 May 2019. "'Commando Training' for Bajrang Dal". *Times of India*. http://timesofindia.indiatimes.com/articleshow/69403130.cms?utm_source=contentofinterest&utm_medium=text&utm_campaign=cppst. Last accessed September 21, 2022.
Jha, K. Dhirendra. 12 November 2016. "Eighty Years on, the RSS Women's Wing Has Not Moved Beyond Seeing the Woman as Mother". *Scroll India*. https://scroll.in/article/821360/eighty-years-on-the-rss-womens-wing-has-not-moved-beyond-seeing-the-woman-as-mother. Last accessed September 21, 2022.
Jha, K. Dhirendra. 8 March 2019. "RSS and the Akharas". *Fountain Ink*. https://fountainink.in/reportage/rss-and-the-akharas. Last accessed September 21, 2022.
Kanungo, Pralaya. 2006. "Myth of the Monolith: The RSS Wrestles to Discipline Its Political Progeny." *Social Scientist* 34 (11/12): 51–69. www.jstor.org/stable/27644183.
Kaura, Uma. 1975. "Provincial Autonomy and the Congress-League Rift, 1937-1939". *International Studies* 14 (4): 587–606. https://doi.org/10.1177/002088177501400403.
Kenny, M. 2017. "Back to the Populist Future?: Understanding Nostalgia in Contemporary Ideological Discourse". *Journal of Political Ideologies* 22 (3): 256–273. https://doi.org/10.1080/13569317.2017.1346773.
Khalid, Saif. 9 October 2017. "Taj Mahal Dropped from Tourism Booklet of Uttar Pradesh". Al Jazeera. https://www.aljazeera.com/news/2017/10/9/taj-mahal-dropped-from-tourism-booklet-of-uttar-pradesh. Last accessed September 21, 2022.
Kinnvall, Catarina. 2014. "The Politics and Ethics of Identity: In Search of Ourselves". *Political Psychology* 35: 303–304. https://doi.org/10.1111/pops.12099.

Kumar, Sajjan. 18 April 2019. "The Limits of Populism." *The Hindu.* https://www.thehindu.com/opinion/lead/the-limits-of-populism/article26867609.ece. Last accessed September 21, 2022.

Lahiry, Sutapa. 2005. "Jana Sangh and Bharatiya Janata Party: A Comparative Assessment of Their Philosophy and Strategy and Their Proximity with the Other Members of the Sangh Parivar". *The Indian Journal of Political Science* 66 (4): 831–850. www.jstor.org/stable/41856171.

Lakshmi, A. 2020." Choreographing Tolerance: Narendra Modi, Hindu Nationalism, and International Yoga Day". *Race and Yoga* 5 (1). http://dx.doi.org/10.5070/R351046987. Retrieved from https://escholarship.org/uc/item/4vz5j2cq. Last accessed September 21, 2022.

Lama-Rewal, T. Stéphanie. 2019. "Political Representation in the Discourse and Practices of the "Party of the Common Man" in India". *Politics and Governance* 7 (3): 179–188. https://doi.org/10.17645/pag.v7i3.2122.

Lammers, J., and M. Baldwin. 2020. "Make America Gracious Again: Collective Nostalgia Can Increase and Decrease Support for Right-Wing Populist Rhetoric". *European Journal of Social Psychology* 50 (5): 943–954. https://doi.org/10.1002/ejsp.2673.

Lefèvre, Corinne. 2020. "Heritage Politics and Policies in Hindu Rashtra". In *The Hindutva Turn: Authoritarianism and Resistance in India*, edited by Aminah Mohammad-Arif, Jules Naudet, and Nicolas Jaoul. *SAMAJ*. https://doi.org/10.4000/samaj.6728.

Leidig, Eviane. 1 June 2016. "Rewriting History: The Ongoing Controversy Over Textbooks in India". LSE Blogs. https://blogs.lse.ac.uk/southasia/2016/06/01/rewriting-history-the-ongoing-controversy-over-textbooks-in-india/. Last accessed September 21, 2022.

Leidig, Eviane. 2020. "Hindutva as a Variant of Right-Wing Extremism". *Patterns of Prejudice.* https://doi.org/10.1080/0031322X.2020.1759861.

Lesch, W. 2020. "Visible Religion and Populism: An Explosive Cocktail". *Religions* 11 (8): 401. https://doi.org/10.3390/rel11080401.

Lochtefeld, G. James. 1994. "The Vishva Hindu Parishad and the Roots of Hindu Militancy". *Journal of the American Academy of Religion* 62: 587–602. http://www.jstor.org/stable/1465279.

Mahmood, Naazir. 1 March 2020. "The Gujarat Massacre and After". *The News on Sunday.* https://www.thenews.com.pk/tns/detail/621744-the-gujarat-massacre-and-after. Last accessed September 21, 2022.

Marzouki, N., D. McDonnell, and O. Roy. 2016. *Saving the People: How Populists Hijack Religion.* Oxford University Press.

McDonnell, Duncan, and Luis Cabrera. 2019. "The Right-Wing Populism of India's Bharatiya Janata Party (and Why Comparativists Should Care)". *Democratization* 26: 484–501. https://doi.org/10.1080/13510347.2018.1551885.

Mirchandani, Maya. 2018. "Digital Hatred, Real Violence: Majoritarian Radicalisation and Social Media in India". ORF. https://www.orfonline.org/research/43665-digital-hatred-real-violence-majoritarian-radicalisation-and-social-media-in-india/. Last accessed September 21, 2022.

Mishra, Ishita, and Prashant Jha. 16 February 2019. "Kashmiri Students in Dehradun Allege Attacks by Bajrang Dal, VHP Activists". *Times of India*. https://timesofindia.indiatimes.com/city/dehradun/kashmiri-students-in-doon-allege-attacks-by-bajrang-dal-vhp-activists/articleshow/68015668.cms. Last accessed September 21, 2022.

Nag, Kingshuk. 2014. *The Saffron Tide*. New Delhi: Rupa Publications.

Nag, Kingshuk. 25 December 2015. "How Atal Bihari Vajpayee Fought and Lost Against the RSS". Scroll India. https://scroll.in/article/777921/how-atal-bihari-vajpayee-fought-and-lost-against-the-rss. Last accessed September 21, 2022.

Nair, Padmaja. 2009. "Religious Political Parties and their Welfare Works: Relations between the RSS, the BJP and the VB Schools in India". Religions and Development Working Program Working paper 37. At University of Birmingham. https://www.birmingham.ac.uk/Documents/college-social-sciences/government-society/research/rad/working-papers/wp-37.pdf. Last accessed September 21, 2022.

News18. Last updated 2018. "Vishva Hindu Parishad Writes to Netflix, Warns of Street Agitations". https://www.news18.com/news/movies/vishva-hindu-parishad-writes-to-netflix-warns-of-street-agitations-2702971.html. Last accessed September 21, 2022.

News18. 2020. "Vishva Hindu Parishad Writes to Netflix, Warns of Street Agitations". *News18*. Last updated July 6, 2020. https://www.news18.com/news/movies/vishva-hindu-parishad-writes-to-netflix-warns-of-street-agitations-2702971.html. Last accessed December 31, 2022.

Nikore, Mitali. 15 January 2014. "The Populist Politics of the Aam Aadmi Party". LSE Blogs. https://blogs.lse.ac.uk/southasia/2014/01/15/the-populist-politics-of-the-aam-aadmi-party/. Last accessed September 21, 2022.

Nizaruddin, Fathima. 2022. "Institutionalized Riot Networks in India and Mobile Instant Messaging Platforms". *Asiascape: Digital Asia* 9 (1–2): 71–94. https://doi.org/10.1163/22142312-bja10028.

Oesterheld, von Joachim. Last updated 2016. "Muslim Response to the Educational Policy of the Central Provinces and Berar Government (1937–1939)". *Suedasien*. http://www.suedasien.info/analysen/1460.html. Last accessed September 21, 2022.

Palshikar, Suhas. 2004. "Shiv Sena: A Tiger with Many Faces?" *Economic and Political Weekly* 39 (14/15): 1497–1507. www.jstor.org/stable/4414867.

Pandey, Ashutosh. 27 February 2019. "India and Pakistan's Troubled History". DW. https://www.dw.com/en/india-and-pakistans-troubled-history/a-47710698. Last accessed September 21, 2022.

Pandey, Neelam, and Krishna, Tarun. 2020. "Kejriwal Promises Freebies for Delhi Ahead of Elections, but Many Voters Don't Want It". *The Print*. February 7. Available online: https://theprint.in/india/arvind-kejriwals-freebies-a-hit-in-slums-but-there-are-many-sceptics-outside/361248/. Last accessed 31 December, 2022.

Patwardhan, Anand. 15 November 2014. "How the Sangh Parivar Systematically Attacks the Very Idea of India". Scroll India. https://scroll.in/article/689584/how-the-sangh-parivar-systematically-attacks-the-very-idea-of-india. Last accessed September 21, 2022.

Peker, Efe. 2019. Religious Populism, Memory, and Violence in India. *New Diversities*. 17: 23

Pradhan, Sharat. 14 September 2020. "For Hindutva Gang, and Now UP Police, Each Hindu-Muslim Marriage Must Be Probed for 'Love Jihad'". *The Print*. https://thewire.in/communalism/uttar-pradesh-love-jihad-police-yogi-adityanath-hindutva-vigilantes. Last accessed September 21, 2022.

PTI. 16 February 2016 "VHP, Bajrang Dal Protest Outside JNU Campus". *Mint*. https://www.livemint.com/Politics/uzbOrozPC1JMloZ7Ma14cO/VHP-Bajrang-Dal-protest-outside-JNU-campus.html. Last accessed September 21, 2022.

PTI. 4 July 2017. "Shiv Sena: Lynching in the Name of Cow Protection Against HINDUTVA". *Mint*. https://www.livemint.com/Politics/FVpc62U3T3un7C1K696wZP/Shiv-Sena-Lynching-in-the-name-of-cow-protection-against-Hi.html. Last accessed September 21, 2022.

PTI. 17 September 2019. "J&K Special Status Removal Significant Step Towards Akhand Bharat: Amit Shah". *The Hindu*. https://www.thehindu.com/news/national/jk-special-status-removal-significant-step-towards-akhand-bharat-amit-shah/article29441410.ece. Last accessed September 21, 2022.

PTI. 23 November 2020. "PM Modi Led 'Trends' Across Social Media, BJP Topped Engagement in Aug-Oct: Report". *Economic Times*. https://economictimes.indiatimes.com/news/politics-and-nation/pm-modi-led-trends-across-social-media-bjp-topped-engagement-in-aug-oct-report/articleshow/79373605.cms?from=mdr. Last accessed September 21, 2022.

Qureshi, S. Y. 14 July 2021. "CM Yogi's UP Population Control Bill is Designed to Serve Only One purpose—2022 Election". *The Print*. https://theprint.in/opinion/cm-yogis-up-population-control-bill-is-designed-to-serve-only-one-purpose-2022-election/695550/. Last accessed September 21, 2022.

Rahman, Maseeh. 28 October 2014. "Indian Prime Minister Claims Genetic Science Existed in Ancient Times". *The Guardian*. https://www.theguardian.com/world/2014/oct/28/indian-prime-minister-genetic-science-existed-ancient-times. Last accessed September 21, 2022.

Raja Ali Saleem, I. Yilmaz, and P. Chacko. 2022. "Civilizationist Populism in South Asia: Turning India Saffron." *Populism & Politics*. European Center for Populism Studies (ECPS). February 24, 2022. https://doi.org/10.55271/pp0009

Ramachandran, Sudha. 2020. "Hindutva Violence in India: Trends and Implications". *Counter Terrorist Trends and Analyses* 12 (4): 15–20. JSTOR, https://www.jstor.org/stable/26918077.

Rashid, Qaisar. 3 November 2020. "Narendra Modi, Akhand Bharat and 'Greater India'". *Future Directions*. https://www.futuredirections.org.au/publication/narendra-modi-akhand-bharat-and-greater-india/. Last accessed September 21, 2022.

Rawal, Swapnil. 18 June 2021. "Sena-BJP Trade Charges Over Hindutva and Marathi Manoos". *Hindustan Times*. https://www.hindustantimes.com/cities/mumbai-news/senabjp-trade-charges-over-hindutva-and-marathi-manoos-101623956659485.html. Last accessed September 21, 2022.

Rogenhofer, J. M., and A. Panievsky. 2020. "Antidemocratic Populism in Power: Comparing Erdoğan's Turkey with Modi's India and Netanyahu's Israel". *Democratization* 27 (8): 1394–1412. https://doi.org/10.1080/13510347.2020.1795135.

Roychowdhury, Adrija. 19 June 2018. "Shiv Sena's Evolution: From Marathi Manoos to Hindutva, from with the BJP to Without the BJP". *The Indian Express*. https://indianexpress.com/article/research/shiv-sena-anniversary-52-bjp-hindutva-maharashtra-5224004/. Last accessed September 21, 2022.

Saaliq, Sheikh, and Krutika Pathi. 17 July 2021. "India's New Law Would Restrain Social Media. Are Rights at Risk?". *The Christian Science Monitor*.https://www.csmonitor.com/World/Asia-South-Central/2021/0715/India-s-new-law-would-restrain-social-media.-Are-rights-at-risk. Last accessed September 21, 2022.

Sahgal, Nayantara. 2013. *Indira Gandhi: Tryst with Power*. New Delhi: Penguin India.

Samanta, Sidhartha. 2011. "The Final Transfer of Power in India, 1937–1947: A Closer Look". Theses and Dissertations at University of Arkansas, Fayetteville. http://scholarworks.uark.edu/etd/258. Last accessed September 21, 2022.

Sarkar, Sumit. 1993. "The Fascism of the Sangh Parivar". *Economic and Political Weekly* 28 (5): 163–167. www.jstor.org/stable/4399339.

Savarkar, Vinayak Damodar. 2009. *Hindu Nationalism: A Reader*, edited by Christophe Jaffrelot. Ukraine: Princeton University Press.

Sawant, B. P. 16 November 2020. "The Manusmriti and a Divided Nation". *The Print.* https://thewire.in/caste/manusmriti-history-discrimination-consti tution. Last accessed September 21, 2022.

Shaikh, Juned. 2005. "Worker Politics, Trade Unions and the Shiv Sena's Rise in Central Bombay." *Economic and Political Weekly* 40 (18): 1893–1900. www.jstor.org/stable/4416576.

Shantha, Sukanya. 14 June 2020. "As Symbols of Discrimination Fall Worldwide, Meet the Women Who Blackened Manu's Statue". *The Print.* https://thewire.in/rights/kantabai-ahire-sheela-pawar-manu-statue-blackened-protest. Last accessed September 21, 2022.

Sharma, Betwa. 12 April 2018. "There Is No Evidence of a Temple Under the Babri Masjid, Just Older Mosques, Says Archeologist". *The Huffington Post.* https://www.huffpost.com/archive/in/entry/there-is-no-evidence-of-a-temple-under-the-babri-masjid-asi-lied-to-the-country-say-archeologists_a_23604990. Last accessed September 21, 2022.

Sharma, Betwa. 18 December 2020. "One Year After Mass Protests, India's Muslims Still Live in Fear". *Foreign Policy.* https://foreignpolicy.com/2020/12/18/one-year-mass-caa-protests-india-muslims-citizenship-amendment-act-modi/. Last accessed September 21, 2022.

Siddiqui, Zeba. 8 August 2018. "Indian Men Who See New Policy as Chance to Marry Kashmiri Women Accused of Chauvinism". *Reuters.* https://www.reuters.com/article/us-india-kashmir-women-idUSKCN1UY104. Last accessed September 21, 2022.

Sikander, Zainab. 5 October 2020. "Babri Ruling Is BJP's Golden Goose. Mathura, Kashi Signal to Erase India's Islamic History". *The Print.* https://theprint.in/opinion/babri-ruling-is-bjps-golden-goose-mathura-kashi-signal-to-erase-indias-islamic-history/516347/. Last accessed September 21, 2022.

Singh, D. K. 8 September 2020. "RSS to Go by What 'Samaaj' Thinks on Kashi & Mathura Mosques, After Seers' Call to Remove Them". *The Print.* https://theprint.in/india/rss-to-go-by-what-samaaj-thinks-on-kashi-mathura-mosques-after-seers-call-to-remove-them/498515/. Last accessed September 21, 2022.

Singh, Manish. 23 May 2019. "Indian PM Narendra Modi's Reelection Spells More Frustration for US Tech Giants". *Tech Crunch.* https://techcrunch.com/2019/05/23/india-modi-silicon-valley-future-internet/. Last accessed September 21, 2022.

Subramanian, Narendra. 2007. "Populism in India." *SAIS Review of International Affairs* 27 (1): 81–91. https://doi.org/10.1353/sais.2007.0019.

Subrahmaniam, Vidya. 9 December 2009. "Two BJP Men, so Alike and so Different". *The Hindu*. https://www.thehindu.com/opinion/lead/Two-BJP-men-so-alike-and-so-different/article16852263.ece. Last accessed September 21, 2022.

Taggart, Paul. 2004. "Populism and Representative Politics in Contemporary Europe". *Journal of Political Ideologies* 9 (3): 269-288. https://doi.org/10.1080/1356931042000263528.

Taş, Hakkı. 2020. "The Chronopolitics of National Populism". *Identities*, 1–19. https://doi.org/10.1080/1070289X.2020.1735160.

Tewari, Saumya. 4 June 2019. "How Smart, Viral Content Helped BJP Trump Congress on Social Media". *Mint*. https://www.livemint.com/politics/news/how-smart-viral-content-helped-bjp-trump-congress-on-social-media-1559663323348.html. Last accessed September 21, 2022.

Thapar, Romila. 27 November 2020. "That Muslims Enslaved Hindus for last 1000 yrs is Historically Unacceptable: Romila Thapar". *The Print*. https://theprint.in/pageturner/excerpt/muslims-enslaved-hindus-for-last-1000-yrs-historically-unacceptable-romila-thapar/552564/. Last accessed September 21, 2022.

Tharoor, Shashi. 2018. *Why I am a Hindu?* Brunswick, Australia: Scribe Publications.

The Economist Intelligence Unit. 2021. "Democracy Index 2020: In Sickness and in Health?" https://www.eiu.com/n/campaigns/democracy-index-2020/. Last accessed September 21, 2022.

The Hindustan Times. 16 August 2018. "Atal Bihari Vajpayee's Complex Relationship with Rashtriya Swayamsevak Sangh". https://www.hindustantimes.com/india-news/atal-bihari-vajpayee-s-complex-relationship-with-rashtriya-swayamsevak-sangh/story-i4PWTtQzyWnJpojnPQap7O.html. Last accessed September 21, 2022.

The Indian Express. 12 December 2019. "Explained: The Nehru-Liaquat Agreement of 1950, Referred to in the CAB Debate". https://indianexpress.com/article/explained/explained-what-was-the-nehru-liaquat-agreement-of-1950-referred-to-in-the-cab-debate-6162191/. Last accessed September 21, 2022.

The Print. 31 August 2018. "Modi Says no More 'Dirt' on Social Media: Crackdown on Hate Speech or BJP Political Gimmick?" https://theprint.in/talk-point/modi-says-no-more-dirt-on-social-media-crackdown-on-hate-speech-or-bjp-political-gimmick/109173/. Last accessed September 21, 2022.

The Wire. 8 November 2018. "Archeologist Who Observed Dig Says No Evidence of Temple Under Babri Masjid". https://thewire.in/history/babri-masjid-asi-excavation-ayodhya-ram-temple. Last accessed September 21, 2022.

The Wire. 9 September 2020. "Right-Wing Groups Want to 'Liberate' Kashi and Mathura Temples; RSS Says Won't Push". https://thewire.in/communalism/babri-hindutva-kashi-and-mathura-temples. Last accessed December 31, 2022.

Times of India. 13 July 2013. "Kareena Kapoor Khan and Saif Ali Khan Trolled for Naming Their Second Son 'Jeh'". https://timesofindia.indiatimes.com/videos/entertainment/hindi/kareena-kapoor-khan-and-saif-ali-khan-trolled-for-naming-their-second-son-jeh/videoshow/84372489.cms?from=mdr. Last accessed September 21, 2022.

Times of India. 30 August 2015. "Shiv Sena to Give Rs 2 Lakh to Every Hindu Family with 5 Kids". http://timesofindia.indiatimes.com/articleshow/48728260.cms?utm_source=contentofinterest&utm_medium=text&utm_campaign=cppst. Last accessed September 21, 2022.

United Nations. 1999. "The Lahore Declaration". https://peacemaker.un.org/sites/peacemaker.un.org/files/IN%20PK_990221_The%20Lahore%20Declaration.pdf. Last accessed September 21, 2022.

Varadarajan, Siddharth. 18 August 2018. "Let Us Not Forget the Glimpse We Got of the Real Vajpayee When the Mask Slipped". The Wire. https://thewire.in/politics/let-us-not-forget-the-glimpse-we-got-of-the-real-vajpayee-when-the-mask-slipped. Last accessed September 21, 2022.

Visana, Vikram. 2020. "Savarkar Before Hindutva: Sovereignty, Republicanism, and Populism in India, c.1900–1920". *Modern Intellectual History*.

Wilberg, Acharya Peter. 2009. *What Is Hinduism*. UK: New Yoga Publications.

Yilmaz, Ihsan. 2018. "Islamic Populism and Creating Desirable Citizens in Erdoğan's New Turkey". *Mediterranean Quarterly* 29 (4): 52–76. muse.jhu.edu/article/717683.

Yilmaz, Ihsan. 2021. *Creating the Desired Citizens: State, Islam and Ideology in Turkey*. New York: Cambridge University Press.

Yilmaz, Ihsan, and Nicholas Morieson. 2021. "A Systematic Literature Review of Populism, Religion and Emotions." *Religions* 12: 272. https://doi.org/10.3390/rel12040272.

Yilmaz, Ihsan, Nicholas Morieson, and Mustafa Demir. 2021a. "Exploring Religions in Relation to Populism: A Tour around the World." *Religions* 12: 301. https://doi.org/10.3390/rel12050301.

Yilmaz, Ihsan, and A. M. Raja Saleem. March 2021b. "A Quest for Identity: The Case of Religious Populism in Pakistan". European Center for Populism Studies. https://www.populismstudies.org/a-quest-for-identity-the-case-of-religious-populism-in-pakistan/. Last accessed September 21, 2022.

Yilmaz, Ihsan, and Kainat Shakil. 3 February 2021. "Pakistan Tehreek-e-Insaf: Pakistan's Iconic Populist Movement". European Center for Populism

Studies. https://www.populismstudies.org/pakistan-tehreek-e-insaf-pakistans-iconic-populist-movement/. Last accessed September 21, 2022.

Buddhism and Civilizational Populism

6.1 Introduction

The relationship between Buddhism and populism is rarely studied, and yet there are concrete examples of Buddhism being instrumentalized by populist leaders in a number of majority Buddhist nations. In his brief survey of religion and populism worldwide, Zuquete (2017) suggests that "Buddhist nationalism in Sri Lanka (Berkwitz 2008)…may provide rich avenues for research, owing to the fact that …a tell-tale indicator of a possible presence of religious populism is the politicization of a religious discourse and mindset".

In Myanmar, too, a form of Buddhist populism has flourished. Amidst political turbulence the Ma Ba Tha/Patriotic Association of Myanmar (MBT), a religious-ethnic populist organization, has won greater support and increased its political significance (Thu 2021). Scholarship has acknowledged the presence of Buddhist-inspired populism, yet there remains a need for "greater examination of Buddhist nationalism and nationalist Buddhist creeds, which are politically important in Myanmar and Sri Lanka", in order to "help scholars to comprehend the rise of religious populism not only in Asia, but across the world" (Yilmaz et al. 2021, 10).

This chapter examines two different political environments, Myanmar and Sri Lanka, in order to discuss the contexts in which Buddhism has become an important component of populist ideology. Given the considerably localized demography of Buddhism in the two countries, unlike other chapters, there is no introduction to a global perspective of Buddhism in other countries.

The chapter first discusses Myanmar, and describes how in this multi-ethnic country (where no single ethnic group comprises more than 2% of the population) religious identity has been heavily politicized. Nearly 89% of the population identify as Buddhist, and therefore the state has often used Buddhist identity to create a sense of national belonging and nationhood. This is not a recent development, as the "To be Burmese means to be Buddhist!" slogan of the 1940s movement for independence demonstrates (Artinger and Rowand 2021). However, 11% of Myanmar's citizens are non-Buddhist, and there is a significant Muslim minority. This situation has been exploited, the chapter shows, by populists who identify Buddhism as a core element of Myanmar's identity, and thus the identity of 'the people' of Myanmar, and therefore portray other religion-based or civilization-based identities as threats to Myanmar's authentic identity and culture. The chapter focuses on post-2012 Myanmar, a period in which the nation's transition to democracy was at first lauded, before ethnic cleansing and the establishing of a military dictatorship in 2021. The 2012–2021 period coincided with a period of increasing religious conflict and anti-pluralism, much of which was instigated by nationalist-populist Buddhist groups. This chapter thus examines the Buddhist populist nationalism that has been promoted by several influential groups, especially MaBaTha and the 969 movement.

In Sri Lanka, the chapter contends, Buddhist nationalist populism has also played an important role in both the political sphere, and also in defining Sri Lankan identity. Unlike ethnically diverse Myanmar, 70% of the population of Sri Lanka is Sinhalese Buddhist, making them a powerful majority ethnic group. Tamils are the largest minority, and constitute around 15% of the population, while Muslims, Hindus, and Christians together make up less than 13% of population (Department of Census and Statistics 2012). In Sri Lanka, then, ethnicity and religion have been somewhat bound together. This puts Sinhalese Buddhists in a powerful position and has allowed them to largely determine Sri Lanka's political agenda and identity. The chapter examines Sinhalese Buddhist Nationalism (SBN) and the BoduBalaSēna/Buddhist Power Army (BBS) organization. The conclusion provides a comparative analysis of the presence of Buddhist populism in Sri Lanka and Myanmar, and discusses the manner in which Buddhism is instrumentalized in the service of civilizational populism.

6.2 Case Studies

The chapter examines the political discourse of Buddhist populists in Myanmar and Sri Lanka, and asks four key questions of the data produced by discourse analysis. First, it explores how the MBT and the 969 movement in Myanmar, and the BBS and Prime Minister Rajapaksa in Sri Lanka incorporate civilizationalism and religion as part of their political discourse. Our case studies demonstrate civilizationalist populism in a Buddhist-dominated environment.

6.2.1 Myanmar: Religion in the Political Landscape

Myanmar is a highly diverse country, and national identity is therefore constructed on the premise of a shared religious identity rather than ethnicity. A British-administered territory, the country was affected by the events of World War II, after which the people of Myanmar increasingly demanded self-rule.

The region officially gained its independence in 1948 but in less than two decades, in 1962, the country became deeply divided on ethnic lines, and separatist movements opposing the government sought self-rule of various territories. A military coup in 1962 left the country ruled by the armed forces until 2011. A brief period of democracy followed, but in 2021—after a period ethnic and religious violence—the military took back power (Maizland 2021). The military's ideology, known as the 'Burmese Way to Socialism', dominated Myanmar's politics from 1962 until the 1980s. Its domination meant not only a communist-inspired centralized control of the military and society, the ideology also attempted to construct a solid identity in order to bind together a highly diverse nation of people (Egreteau and Robinnem 2016; Nakanishi 2013). While the ethnic Burmese have dominated military and civil government politics, Myanmar's national identity has been built predominantly on Buddhism, the shared religion of the majority of the populism (Rosenthal 2018; Wills 2017). From 1962 to the 1980s there was a mainstreaming of the egalitarian ideas of Marxism blended with Buddhist values (Aung-Thwin et al. 1992). Consequently, Buddhist philosophy was embedded in the national identity construction project throughout this period. It is interesting to note that while Buddhism has always been a central force used by Myanmar's political elite, it was also present in opposition movements including in Myanmar's pro-democracy movements. Thus the "use of Buddhism in both supporting and opposing political authority" is common in Myanmar (Walton 2015). As early as the 1940s, when the region was demanding self-rule, the slogan "To be Burmese means to be Buddhist!" was often heard in the independence struggle (Artinger and Rowand 2021). Moreover, the 8888 Uprising in 1988, the 2007 "Saffron Revolution", and support for and opposition to the 2021 military takeover have all involved Buddhist monks and Buddhist movements (Artinger and Rowand 2021; Walton 2015).

Since the 1990s, the combining of Buddhism and nationalism has taken a more exclusive and violent form, in which the defense of the nation and faith is paramount. Willis (2017) notes that "Buddhist religious fanaticism with intense Burmese nationalism and more than a tinge of ethnic chauvinism" has been mainstreamed in Myanmar, where it often incorporates anti-Muslim rhetoric. In a way, it is unusual for a religion like Buddhism to fall prey to violent political narratives. As Walton (2015) observes, in a Buddhist society "the moral standing of monks comes from their detachment from worldly concerns (including politics) and a presumed lack of self-interested motivations", thus by associating themselves with not only politics but the aggressive persecution of perceived "threats" to the nation and dharma, they diminish their religious credibility. Despite this inherent contradiction, the "Burmese *sangha* (monkhood)" has long been involved in politics, "with monks justifying their actions either with reference to their vocational role as defenders and propagators of Buddhism or their obligation to reduce suffering in the world" (Walton 2015).

Within the philosophical ideology of Buddhism violence is neither explicitly nor implicitly encouraged. The sacred text *Dhammapada* quotes Gautama Buddha's forbidding of malicious actions, such as "you should neither harm nor kill" (Buddharakkhita 1996). Buddhist discourse also guides the followers on a path of love. The *Suttanipāta* (Section of the Suttas) text, for example, states "Toward the whole world one should develop loving-kindness, a state of mind without boundaries—above, below, and across—unconfined, without enmity, without adversaries" (Bodhi 2017, 180). In 2012, when the first wave of attacks against the mostly Muslim Rohingya people in Myanmar occurred, the Dalai Lama, the highest spiritual authority of Buddhism, condemned the attacks and urged the Buddhist followers to abide by the Buddhist tradition of non-violence, saying "Buddha always teaches us about forgiveness, tolerance, compassion. If from one corner of your mind, some emotion makes you want to hit, or want to kill, then please remember Buddha's faith. We are followers of Buddha" (Lila 2013). It is not the core teachings of the religion then, but rather prolonged differences between ethnic groups, that have pushed a segment of Burmese Buddhists toward a right-wing discourse in nativism, Buddhism, and ethnic divides (Thu 2021; Rosenthal 2018; Kreibich, Goetz and Murage 2017). While 2012 saw liberalization and attempts to democratize the country, it also witnessed the rapid growth of Buddhist civilizationalism rooted in right-wing populism. In a way, 2012 was a year where "Myanmar's liberalisation after five decades of military dictatorship presented an opportunity to craft a more inclusive national identity and move the country away from its toxic legacy of ethnicity-based conflict" however the deep seated ethnic divides that trace back to two hundred years of resentment and discord proved impossible to heal (Thu 2021; Yilmaz et al. 2021; Crisis Group 2020).

Myanmar's ethnic conflicts are rooted in the colonial period. After annexing Burma into the British Empire, the British wrote a crude list of ethnicities, made with very little understanding of the plurality of the region, and which recognized 135 ethnic groups classified primarily by linguistic uniqueness (Thu 2021; Crisis Group 2020). Fundamentally flawed in its construct, this list remains important in Myanmar, where it is used to deny certain groups citizenship, including the "Chittagong Muslim" or Rohingya who are seen as Bengali rather than Burmese (Thu 2021; Crisis Group 2020; Kreibich et al. 2017). The presence of 'non-native' Burmese in the region is also rooted in the colonial period. The British administration encouraged migrations mainly from India and to an extent from China to Burma to boost manpower on its plantations and in its cultivation activities in the territory (Thu 2021, 200). More recently, these old ethnic tensions have merged with religion, anti-Muslim hate, and populism, and have become a powerful political and social force across the country.

"The Muslim Problem"
Following the democratization process in Myanmar, two quite prominent and interlinked right-wing populist Buddhist collectives emerged. In 2012 the 969 movement, a collective of monks and non-cloistered citizens who claimed themselves to be defenders of Buddhist women, called for the boycotting of Muslim-owned businesses across the country (Bookbinder 2013). In 2014, the Organization for the Protection of Race

and Religion/MaBaTha (MBT), religious organization which shared goals with the 969 movement, emerged and began to gain a significant following. The rise of these radical movements appears to have been precipitated by a desire to 'defend' the Buddhist way of life, which was supposed to be under attack from 'outside' forces, especially Muslims (Walton 2015). Before we discuss these two movements, it is important to first understand their idea of "the Muslim problem", and the reasons behind their fear of Islam and hatred of Myanmar's Muslim population.

Two factors working hand in hand led to the rise of anti-Muslim hatred in Myanmar. Pan-Islamist jihadist activity has been accompanied by a trend toward Islamophobia the world over, and East Asia is no exception. The colonial period in Myanmar witnessed a huge influx of Muslims to the region, and the country's close border with Bangladesh also meant that the Myanmar was often host to ethnically Bengali Muslims, particularly in the Rakhine State (Bakali 2021; Walton 2015; Selth 2010). Historically, Burmese Muslims have, in times of growing ethnic and religious tensions, faced the force of the military. This has, at times, led to armed Muslim groups calling for autonomy. Since 9/11 the "war terror" narrative, in which Muslims are primarily viewed as a security threat, has dominated Myanmar's political discourse on Islam and religious difference (Bakali 2021; Selth 2010). Bakali (2021) notes that since the 2000s Burmese society has accepted acts of violence as 'necessary' to protect the country. Islamophobia has become common in political narratives, and Buddhist extremism has flourished; in a sense violence "has also come to encompass systemic racism and anti-Muslim violence in the global South, with, in Myanmar, the 'war on terror' used to sanitise more recent violence against the Rohingya" (Bakali 2021).

While the Rohingya are not the only Muslim ethnic group in Myanmar, they have been systemically targeted by the state due to their 'alien' status. Since the 1430s, Muslims from South Asia have migrated to the former Arakan State (an independent kingdom in present-day Myanmar until it was made part of the Burmese Empire in 1784) and later the British policy of encouraging Indian and Chinese migration to Burma also increased the Muslim population (Mohajan 2018). The Burmese-Indo conflict of the 1930s and favorable Anglo-Rohingya[1] relations in

---

[1] The occupying British administration in Burma had promised the Rohingya of a separate state once the forced with drew from Burma. In exchange many Burmese Muslims

post-independence Burma left the unwanted Rohingya stateless. Things became more concrete in 1982 when a new citizenship law explicitly denied Rohingya people Burmese citizenship (Blakemore 2019). International bodies have recorded that not only did thousands of Rohingya flee Myanmar in 2017, but those left behind following military "operations" are forced to live in an apartheid system, and suffer under laws limiting the number of children Rohingya couples may have, and bans on inter-faith marriages (Mohajan 2018; Fortifying Rights 2014). Violence targeting the Rohingya is, of course, not new. In 1962 "Operation King Dragon" targeted the Rohingya people using tactics of burning homes, business, mass arrests and rape of women, and Burmese authorities were accused of human rights abuses including rape, destruction of houses and villages, and mass arrests (Blakemore 2019; Mohajan 2018). This cycle was repeated in 1991 under "Operation Clean and Beautiful Nation", which sent 200,000 Rohingya to seek refuge in Bangladesh (Blakemore 2019). However, the recent wave of anti-Rohingya and anti-Muslim violence, which emerged under a democratic government rather than the autocratic rule of the military, has its roots in the Buddhist populism of groups such as the MBT.

Denied citizenship, marginalized by the legal system and subject to military attacks, the Rohingya in Myanmar live in precarious conditions. As a result, many young men from the community have been attracted to international jihadist networks that promise "freedom" from "non-Muslim oppressors" (Selth 2010). The security-driven apparatus of the Myanmar state saw growing resistance within the community as well the exportation of *jihadists* from the country (Selth 2010). Thus since the 2000s the "war on terror" to counter "the Muslim problem" has gained momentum, leading to the 2017 genocide (Frydenlund 2018).

The Civilizationalism of the MBT and 969 Movement

The 969 movement appears to have been initiated by a government official and ex-monk named Kyaw Lwin, who in 1991 was leader of the military government's Department for the Promotion and Propagation of the Sasana ('Sasana' is the Pali language word for religion but usually refers to Buddhism), a body within the Religion Ministry. In 1992, the government body produced a booklet said to be written by Lwin titled

and particularly the Rohingya had taken part in World War II but in 1948 when Burma war granted independence the promised Rohingya state was never granted.

"How to live as a good Buddhist", republished in 2000 with the new title "The Best Buddhist", and which featured the 969 logo on the cover, numbers with a special meaning to Buddhists[2] (Marshall 2013). The 40-page booklet "urged Buddhists to openly display the numbers 969 on their homes, businesses and vehicles" (Moe 2017). The book did not openly call for violence or discrimination against any particular group, but the displaying of 969 was intended to be a way for Buddhist business owners and consumers to distinguish themselves from Muslims, who often displayed the number 786, signifying an Islamic prayer: "the Name of Allah, the Compassionate and Merciful" (Bookbinder 2013). The booklet insinuated that Muslims were trying to demographically and economically "conquer" the Buddhist population, and that Buddhists must fight back (Frydenlund 2018; Moe 2017; Bookbinder 2013). These notions spread throughout Myanmar, partly through its adoption by Buddhist education facilities, such as "Buddhist Sunday Schools, volunteer groups, legal clinics, relief campaigns, donation drives, and other community oriented activities" (Thu 2021, 205).

Fear of Muslims' conquering the Buddhist 'heartland' was combined with the 'war on terror' narrative, and spread throughout Myanmar by Buddhist monks and Buddhist-run education facilities. The Buddhist majority were urged by the anti-Muslim activists to apply "three cuts"—to boycott Muslims in the 2000s. Moe (2017) sums up this strategy as involving the "cutting off all business ties; not allowing Buddhists to marry Muslims; and severing of all social relations with Muslims, including even casual conversations. It stopped short, however, of advocating violence". Thus Buddhist people are urged to support fellow Buddhists in all areas of life and boycott Muslims. This guidance did not emanate primarily from Myanmar's politicians, but rather from Buddhist monks (Frydenlund 2018; Moe 2017; Bookbinder 2013). Trickling down from temples into the political discourse, 969 soon became not only about protecting the business interests of Buddhists, but a movement designed to protect Buddhist women and children who were allegedly being Islamized through inter-faith marriages (Moe 2017).

---

[2] 969 is considered the cosmological opposite of 786, a number associated with Islam, a which has often appeared on Muslim-owned businesses in Myanmar. See Bookbinder, 2013.

Ashin Wirathu, a monk, became the face of the 969 movement. Wirathu was imprisoned by the military junta for hate speech[3] in 2003, and was released as part of a large group of political prisoners set free in 2012 (Hodal 2013). Following his release, he campaigned relentlessly on behalf of the 969 movement, and after it was banned, inspired the formation of MBT, and later became a party leader. Wirathu's activities helped create a wave of Islamophobia in the country, mixing "Buddhist conspiracy theories envisioning an Islamic take-over" and fear of Muslim "terrorist" (Artinger & Rowand 2021; Frydenlund 2018; Bookbinder 2013). This has led MBT and the 969 movement to become identified by many Buddhists in Myanmar as "protectors" of "the Buddhist identity of the country" (Fuller 2018).

In MBT discourse, the Buddhist majority are portrayed as victims of violence instigated by 'others', most often Muslims. MBT has used events such as the destruction of the Bamiyan Buddhas in Afghanistan by the Taliban to create their narrative of a Muslim threat and Buddhist victimhood (Thu 2021, 208). Myanmar's Muslim minority is therefore portrayed as enemies and a danger to inherently peaceful Buddhist society. Yilmaz et al. (2021) note that MBT "claim that Muslims are an existential threat to the nation's Buddhist identity and call for the elimination of threats to this Buddhist national core". MBT enjoys support of various politicians in Myanmar, including some pro-democracy politicians, and such is their power that any political party or critical voice contradicting their populist rhetoric is 'othered' by MBT's leadership, and accused of being "Muslim sympathisers" (Oppenheim 2017; Ellis-Petersen 2019; BBC 2015). For instance, Nobel Peace Prize winner Aung San Suu Kyi and her party National League for Democracy (NLD), perhaps fearful of incurring MBT's wrath, did not nominate Muslim candidates during the 2015 elections, which led to a "Muslim Free Parliament" (Thu 2021, 206). It was also Suu Kyi's government (2016–21) which tolerated MBT-led violent rhetoric against Muslims, rhetoric which helped lead to the 2017 genocide of the Rohingya people (BBC 2018).

Even before the NLD came to power in 2012, MBT used sermons to preach its narrative of a Muslim threat and Buddhist victimhood. Fear of losing votes to nationalist monks has led Myanmar's mainstream parties pass MBT approved "Race and Religion Protection Laws", which

---

[3] The jail sentence came for the monk when this anti-Muslim rhetoric initiated the killing of 10 Muslims in Kyaukse. He was originally sentenced to 25 years in prison.

banned interfaith marriage and religious conversion (Carroll 2015). The MBT monks increasingly involved themselves in mainstream politics in the 2010s, supporting the pro-military Union Solidarity and Development Party (USDP) because they believed "it is the only party that can protect the race and religion of the country" (Thu 2021, 207). MBT also involves itself in transnational civilizational populism. The ideas of the extremist populism monks have been shared with the Sri Lankan radical Buddhism organization the Bodu Bala Sena (discussed further in the chapter), and the two groups have held joint meetings and conventions (Sirilal, 2014). For example, in 2014, Wirathu and Bodu Bala Sena General Secretary Galagoda Atte Gnanasara wrote and signed an agreement to work together to "make the entire south and Southeast Asian region a peaceful region devoid of all forms of fundamentalist movements, extremisms and civil or international wars" (Columbo Telegraph 2014). "In order to achieve the said vision", the agreement says, "Both parties aim to work in collaboration and partnership for the protection, development, and betterment of Buddhists, Buddhist countries, Buddhist heritages and Buddhist civilization" (Columbo Telegraph 2014). The two Buddhist groups further agreed to work toward constructing a "Buddhist International" which would enhance networking between Buddhist groups throughout the region, help protect Buddhist archeological sites, develop Buddhist "organizational and institutional capacities", and to "carry out researches on Buddhist philosophy and subsectors such as economic, social, educational, political derivatives of Buddhist civilization and culture" (Columbo Telegraph 2014). Ashin Wirathu led this union and presented it as an act required to "defend" Buddhism around the world, saying "today, Buddhism is in danger. We need hands to be firmly held together if we hear alarm bells ringing" (Sirilal 2014). On a separate occasion Wirathu also said that "once we [have] won this battle, we will move on to other Muslim targets" indicating that there are no geographical limits to his civilizational populism (Hodal 2013).

Violence Embedded in the Narrative
Time Magazine in 2013 named Wirathu "The Face of Buddhist Terror", and referred to him as the "Buddhist bin Laden" due to the sheer amount of violence that his speeches have inspired (Ellis-Petersen 2019; Safi 2018; Hodal 2013Marshall 2013). Wirathu's emotive speeches call for the "promotion of the Buddhist cosmology and code of values, the maintenance of its purity and the preservation of the Buddhist Burmese state" (Biver

2014). Moreover "The Burmese monks" in MBT "make use of a certain politicized religion that utilizes faith as the basis for the national identity, as well as the source for ultimate values and authority" (Biver 2014). This civilizational populism uses fear of Muslims and poses as a national-religious movement to 'protect the people' in order to legitimize violence against Muslims.

Similar to the so-called 'love jihad' issue in India, the inter-faith marriage debate became a national priority in Myanmar in 2012 when a Buddhist woman was gang raped by Muslims. The 969 monks portrayed the brutal rape as an example of the dangers posed by Islam and Muslims, and portrayed Buddhists as innocent victims of Muslim violence. Since then, Wirathu has implied that all Muslims in Burma "target innocent young Burmese girls and rape them" to which he further claims that "in every town, there is a crude and savage Muslim majority" (Hodal 2013). It is not surprising that in 2012 such words encouraged 'victimized' Buddhists to take up arms and riot, targeting the Rohingya Muslims in Rakhine State. Apparently unsatisfied with the results of the Rakhine State riots of 2012, which displaced 125,000 Rohingya, the firebrand monk in 2013 incited ethnic cleansing by suggesting, "We [Buddhists] are being raped in every town, being sexually harassed in every town, being ganged up on and bullied in every town" (Hodal 2013; Human Rights Watch 2013). Soon after his release from prison in 2012, Wirathu used Facebook and YouTube to share his sermons online. In 2015 he had nearly 37,000 followers on the platform (BBC 2015; Hodal 2013).

This momentum was further solidified when MBT pushed for legal changes to ban conversions and interfaith marriages. To legitimize this popular cause, Muslim culture was stereotyped as highly harmful for women, especially women who converted to Islam following their marriage to Muslim men. Wirathu has strongly suggested that Burmese women who convert to the Islam are killed by their partners if they do not follow Islam correctly, and this he terms a danger to not only Buddhists but to "world peace" (Hodal 2013). MBT monks have also popularized the idea that Muslims converting and marrying Burmese women, and giving birth to children who are raised as Muslims, will lead to a "population explosion" of Muslims, which is part of a conspiracy to take over Myanmar (Hodal 2013). Adding to the ontological insecurity, Muslim businesspeople have been accused of indulging in cronyism, which was the initial argument of 969 movement. These fears and conspiracies have legitimized the call for the elimination of bearded people and the destruction of mosques. The 969 movement even created a pop song called "Song to Whip Up Religious Blood" which became well known in Myanmar (Marshall 2013).

In Wirathu and MBT discourse 'the people' of Myanmar are presented as vulnerable, and in need of the protection offered by MBT, who are presented as peaceful Buddhists acting merely to 'save' their dharma. The monk has reassured his followers that he has read the Qur'an and seeks friendly relations with Muslims, but that Muslims do not wish to improve interfaith relations with Buddhists. He dehumanizes Muslims by comparing them to rabid animals, claiming "You can be full of kindness and love, but you cannot sleep next to a mad dog" (Ellis-Petersen 2019).

At an earlier occasion he describes the Muslim minority as barbarians puppets with support from international militant jihadi wings, "The local Muslims are crude and savage because the extremists are pulling the strings, providing them with financial, military and technical power" (Hodal 2013). The idea of safety and "the other" being barbaric removes space for dialogue and promise actions to ensure ethnic cleansing. In 2017 when the military carried out the Rohingya genocide Wirathu explained why force was necessary, "It only takes one terrorist to be amongst them [...] Look at what has happened in the west. I do not want that to happen in my country. All I am doing is warning people to beware" (Oppenheim 2017).

Thus violence against Muslims is necessary to ensure Buddhist Burmese do not become "weak" victims of Muslim aggression, and do give up their land to Muslims (Ellis-Petersen 2019). When confronted with evidence that their words have inspired genocide or war crimes, MBT brushes the allegations away with humor or simple denial. Following the horrific reports of rape being used as a tool of violence against Rohingya women, Wirathu laughed and dismissed the idea by saying, "Impossible. Their bodies are too disgusting" (Oppenheim 2017). He also constantly denies the Rohingya people's sufferings, such as their precarious condition in Cox's Bazar in Bangladesh and within Rakhine state. He argues that he has visited the camps himself and there is nothing wrong with them: "Bangladeshis are posing for the media. They are not starving. They have so much food that they are selling it on in their shops—stealing even from their own" (Oppenheim 2017).

MBT's populist-civilizational rhetoric has the power to 'other' those who question the group's ideology and methods. MBT monks have supported the military over pro-democratic voices, accusing the latter of favoring 'alien' Muslims over 'the people' of Myanmar. Wirathu has personally called out "Aung San Suu Kyi" for "help[ing] the Bengali", and he claims to have done the nation a service by "blocking" her from continuing in a position of power (Oppenheim 2017). Wirathu's demonization of his ideological enemies allows him to portray himself as a protective hero, and the opposition as villains and supporters of Muslim oppressors. Wirathu gained international attention when he verbally attacked the country's special envoy to the United Nations for addressing the plight of Muslims in Myanmar. Wirathu's derogatory remarks were highly insulting, "We have already made [our] Race Protection Law public. But this bitch, without studying [the legislation], kept on complaining how it is against human rights [...] If you are so willing, you should offer your arse to the kalar [racist slur meaning dark]. But you will never sell off our Arakan State [former name of Rakhine]!" and the abuse continued, "Just because you hold a position at the United Nations doesn't make you an honourable woman. In our country, you are just a whore" (France24 2015).

A year before the massacres in 2017, MBT ran a campaign that targeted Muslims on Facebook (Safi 2018). A survey of 15,000 Facebook posts of users who favored the MBT group showed they viewed the organization and military operations against Muslims in a positive light (Safi 2018). At the same time, rumors such as "mosques in Yangon are stockpiling weapons in an attempt to blow up various Buddhist pagodas and Shwedagon pagoda", were spread throughout social media, and aided the call for a "Muslim-free" Myanmar, and saw the Rohingya racially and religiously abused by terms as "kalars[4]" and "Bengali terrorists" on social media (Hogan and Safi 2018; Institute for War and Peace Reporting 2017). In 2018, Wirathu's Facebook page was banned when evidence surfaced that the platform had a key role to play in the 2017 genocide, chiefly by allowing MBT supporters to spread malicious rumors about Muslim people planning attacks on Buddhists. Wirathu never commented on this ban, but met a previous block of 30 days with the phrase "Facebook is occupied by the Muslims" (Straits Times 2018). The company has also used an automated censorship system to ban racial slurs such as kalar (Sin 2017). While the page of the monk has been banned, social media outlets are always free to share Wirathu's and MBT's videos and

---

[4] An anti-Muslim slur used to refer to Muslim in Myanmar. It also denotes someone from an Indian background in the country. It is a derogatory racial-religious slur.

materials. The automated ban of words has also been met with mixed success (Sin 2017).

Wirathu's emotional provocation is central to his popularity and the growth of Buddhist populism in Myanmar. His civilizational rhetoric is more identitarian in nature than religious, for it draws little from Buddhist texts and spirituality, yet it remains effective at galvanizing support from the country's Buddhist masses. In this spiteful narrative, in which the monks are 'saving' the nation from 'evil' Muslims, Wirathu somehow emerges as a symbol of love and salvation of Burmese Buddhists: "I am defending my loved one […] like you would defend your loved one. I am only warning people about Muslims. Consider it like if you had a dog, that would bark at strangers coming to your house—it is to warn you. I am like that dog. I bark" (Oppenheim 2017).

6.2.2 Sri Lanka: Religion in the Political Landscape

Sri Lankan population is religiously and ethnically diverse. 74.9% of the population are ethnic Sinhalese, while Tamils and Moors make up 15.3 and 9.3%, respectively. A large majority, around 70% of the population, is Buddhist, but there are significant Hindu (12.6%), Muslim (9.7%), and Christian (7.4%) minorities (Jayasinghe 2021, 179). Sinhalese Buddhists, then, are the dominant group in Sri Lankan politics and society.

Much like in Myanmar, the colonial era classification of race in British Ceylon continues to have a profound impact on identity in contemporary Sri Lanka, where it helps to define, legally, the racial and ethnic groups that live within the country (Sivasundaram 2010). However, the racial-religious divide in Sri Lanka predates British colonization. The *Mahāvamsa* (Great Chronicle), an ancient sacred text composed in the 6th C.E., is a "part-mythological narrative 'written to legitimize, cement and propagate the Buddhist association with Sri Lanka'" and which continues to shape Sri Lankan's perceptions of their own national identity (Jayasinghe 2021, 180). By combining the narrative tradition rooted in the *Mahāvamsa* with the colonial classification of races, many contemporary Sri Lankans have come to conceive of Sinhalese Buddhists as the 'original' or 'real' inhabitants of the land, and to perceive Arab Moors and Tamil Indians as 'outsiders' (Jayasinghe 2021; Shakil 2021; Mihlar 2020).

After the Second World War European colonial powers found themselves in retreat. In Sri Lanka, the burgeoning independence movement fought a long struggle against British colonialism which led, in 1948, to the creation of an independent Dominion of Ceylon. It was during this period that "electoral politics in the island state quickly became a fierce contest of appeals to ethnicity", leading to the rise of Sinhalese Buddhist Nationalism (SBN) and the domination of the Sinhalese over other ethnic groups (Jayasinghe 2021, 180). Early post-Independence political discourse thus presented a national vision which enabled the otherizing of non-Sinhalese and non-Buddhists.

The power of Sinhalese Buddhist Nationalism led to the state-led systematic discrimination of the Tamil minorities, who reacted by forming the resistance group the Tamil Tigers (LTTE) (Jayasinghe 2021; Shakil 2021; Yilmaz et al. 2021; Uyangoda 2007). Tamils were considered "aliens" with no claims in the newly independent Sri Lanka, and were frequently denied citizenship, deported to India, became victims of ethnically motivated killings, and were at times prevented from entering higher education—events that led to a civil war (Carothers & O'Donohue 2020). In this context the militant Tamil Tigers, "became active in seeking an independent homeland for the Tamils. The conflict, which ended in 2009, also had a religious dimension as the Tamil population is predominately Hindu, and the government is mainly Buddhist. Over two decades of fighting, a number of failed efforts were made to bring peace. This led to thousands of casualties on both sides … and hindered economic development" (Shakil 2021). While the end of a civil war opened a peace process, populist Prime Minister Mahinda Rajapaksa in 2009 portrayed the war as a victory for SBN (Jayasinghe 2021, 183). Sri Lankan Prime Minister until 2015, Rajapaksa capitalized on ethnic and religious divisions between Tamils and Sinhalese in his rhetoric, but following the end of the civil war shifted to process of otherizing the country's Muslim minority community (Jayasinghe 2021; Shakil 2021; Yilmaz et al. 2021; Mihlar 2020; Devotta 2018).

During his 2009–2015 tenure as Prime Minister, Rajapaksa portrayed himself as fighting for 'the people' against Sri Lanka's elites, who he claimed were corrupt, and promised to improve the country's economy (Shakil 2021). At the same time there was second dimension to his populism, which was rooted in SBN: "During Rajapaksa's rule, critics of his political style and agenda were portrayed as enemies of the nation (SBN) or collaborators with the enemy. Sri Lankan society was divided between the "patriot" (dēshapremi) and the "traitor" (dēshadrōhi)" (Jayasinghe 2021, p. 183), with opponents of Rajapaksa portrayed as treasonous enemies. Against this backdrop, "Rajapaksa shied away from criticizing the unlawful activities of SBN groups, including violence against Muslims and other minorities, due to the power and influence of SBN in Sri Lankan politics and society" (Yilmaz et al. 2021). While the war against the Tamil Tigers is over, and even though Tamil people largely do not yet feel entirely welcome in Sri Lanka, SBN discourse has moved from othering Tamils to incite fear of Muslims and other minorities (Mihlar 2020). SBN has, since the end of the civil war, become increasingly powerful due to a wave of anti-Muslim feeling growing since the 9/11 attacks and rise of international jihadism. Muslims are, in the post-9/11, post-civil war environment, perceived as "a security threat" and accused of "extremism" and "intolerance" by the Sri Lankan state (Haniffa 2021; Mihlar 2020). Other minority groups have also sought to demonize Muslims, though in different ways. For example, "Tamil anti-Muslim hatred, attacks and violence focus on the group whilst Sinhala/Buddhists target the group and the religion" (Mihlar 2020).

Rajapaksa, having lost his position as Prime Minister in 2015, returned to political prominence when Gotabaya Rajapaksa, his brother and a former army leader during the civil war, came to power in 2019 (Jayasuriya 2019). While G. Rajapaksa used populist anti-elitist rhetoric, his main appeal to voters was that he was a former war "hero" and "a strongman" who led Sri Lanka to "victory" against the Tamil "insurgents". But with the civil war receding into memory, the "strongman" instead portrays himself as protecting the nation from Muslim radicals, such as the Muslims responsible for the Easter Bombing (Shakil 2021). The Easter Sunday Bombings in Sri Lanka brought anti-Muslim rhetoric to the forefront of society, and legitimized the Islamophobia inherent in SBN. Multiple bombings killed 340 people, including 40 foreigners, at various resorts and churches in Colombo, leaving the country devastated and in search for answers (DeVotta 2019). The bombings brought attention to the presence of Salafi movements and madrasas in the country, and national attention was focused on National Thowheed Jamath (NTJ), a local right-wing Islamist group, and Islamic State (IS), who were thought to be behind the attacks (BBC 2020). The bombings confirmed fears that Muslims were becoming radicalized in Sri Lanka. Even before bombings there were reports of Sri Lankan Muslims from various backgrounds joining IS in order to perform "jihad" in Syria and other Middle Eastern regions (Aneez 2016). Since 2019, these fears have become part of Sri

Lankan domestic political discourse, and led to a series of anti-Muslim legislation.

As Prime Minister, G. Rajapaksa has punished Muslims, banning face veils, conducting arbitrary arrests of alleged radical Muslims, and closed down seminaries. Formally, under the "Deradicalisation from holding violent extremist religious ideology" section of the Prevention of Terrorism Act, the country has banned the wearing of burqas and closed some 1,000 Islamic organizations to prevent extremism (Haniffa 2021; Imtiyaz 2021). This fear is the legal and political manifestation of a belief that Muslims, funded by foreign powers such as the gulf countries, are attempting to Islamize Sri Lanka (Mihlar 2020; Barakat 2019). In addition to state-led arbitrary arrests of Muslim lawyers and poets, COVID-19 brought forth institutional discrimination toward the Moors based on scapegoating. During the pandemic some of the first cases of the disease were found in travelers returning from India's Tablighi Jama forum in 2020, making Muslims the first to be detected with the virus. The forcible cremation policy for COVID-19 patients affected the Muslim community further, because Muslims traditionally bury their diseased. There is also a disproportionate number of Muslims who have been badly affected by the pandemic compared to the rest of the population, owing to poor access to health care and other provisions (Mihlar 2020). In a sense, Muslims have been blamed for the pandemic and at the same time have been forcibly subjected to cremations while facing the brunt of the pandemic. This Islamophobia has trickled down from SBN to Tamils and Christians in Sri Lanka, who have themselves adopted this framing of Muslims as a security threat (Mihlar 2020).

Sri Lanka's economic collapse in 2022, which was the result of a loss of tourist income following the COVID-19 Pandemic, and fiscal irresponsibility, excessive government borrowing, and corruption, led to Gotabaya Rajapaksa fleeing the country and resigning from exile in Singapore. However, this does not mean that there has been wholesale political change in Sri Lanka. Instead, and despite mass demonstrations against the government, the Sri Lankan establishment remains largely in power in the country. For example, before fleeing the country Rajapaksa made Prime Minister Ranil Wickremesinghe acting president. Although Wickremesinghe was not a member of Rajapaksa's Podujana Peramuna or People's Front Party, his United National Party has been a member of coalition government's alongside Podujana Peramuna, and he himself has been an establishment political figure for decades, having served in a number of ministries and as Prime Minister. Moreover, Gotabaya Rajapaksa has returned from exile to Sri Lanka in September, 2022, suggesting that he may intend to continue to play a role in Sri Lankan politics.

"The Muslim Problem": Bodu Bala Sēna
The BoduBalaSēna/Buddhist Power Army (BBS) is a right-wing Buddhist organization which cooperated with the state in order to reproduce anti-Muslims discourse, and which supports and often spearheads legislative measures that target Muslims. BBS "is unique for being almost exclusively an anti-Muslim front" and does not target Hindus and Tamils with violence, unlike the SBN (Jayasinghe 2021, 186). Much like the MBT in Myanmar, it incites violence toward Muslims, and has done so since its formation in 2012. Yilmaz et al. (2021) note, "Such is the power of these nationalist and anti-Muslim groups that the government of Sri Lanka frequently ignores their violent actions, much as the governments of Myanmar have ignored Buddhist violence against minorities". While BBS and BMT not only share similar populist ideologies, they also enjoy the same level of support from their respective states. While BBS is primarily anti-Muslim, it is also known to attack and criticize Christians in Sri Lanka (UNHRC 2014).

The BBS was formed by a group of hard-line Buddhist monks who unlike the identarian populist SBN are a primarily religious populist organization. Silva (2016) notes that most of the "credibility" of the BBS is the result of their ability to spread rumors and capitalize on scandals involving Muslims in the country. BBS accuse Muslims of trying to Islamize Sir Lanka, and they have used political ill will and merged it with rumors and conspiracies to draw support from Buddhists. Silva (2016) notes that the BBS not only frames Muslims as an "ethnic other", but creates a "moral panic" around Muslims. This panic is key in creating demand in Sri Lanka's Buddhists for a civilizational populism, where the right-wing monks are given power to protect Buddhism from the threat of Islam. Since 2012, the group has expanded its membership and held its first national convention in 2019 (Reuters 2019).

BBS leader Galagoda Aththe Gnanasara and his fellow monks portray themselves as saving the religion and culture of 'the people', or the Buddhist people of Sri Lanka. They demand protection for Buddhists in the country who are "disadvantaged", they claim, by undue favors allegedly given to Muslims (Reuters 2019; BBC 2013a, b; Minority

Rights Groups International 2013). For example, BBS monks have called out the presence of birth control measures such as vasectomy and tubal ligation in state-funded hospitals (Amarasuriya 2015) in away linked to the sterilization of the "the people" myths. It takes up "causes" such as protesting and at times rioting to address poor treatment of Sri Lankan Buddhists diaspora working in the Gulf and other countries (Hume 2013). Devotta (2018) notes that there are unfounded fears of the Muslims secretly sterilizing "the people" to gain a "demographical advantage" for domination. BBS also takes "direct action" by not only protesting, but by attacking popular tourist bars to gain attention for their "cause" (Hume 2013).

Over time the BBS has developed into a country-wide network that "advocates" for Sinhalese Buddhist "rights" and commits sporadic outbursts of violence (Reed 2021). BBS leader Gnanasara defends his organization's aggressive advocacy, saying "This is a government created by Sinhala-Buddhists and it must remain Sinhala-Buddhist. This is a Sinhala country, Sinhala government. Democratic and pluralistic values are killing the Sinhala race" (Al Maeena 2013). Its activism is enshrined in its "Maharagama Declaration" (Daily FT 2013). This ten-point declaration promotes the use of a Sinhala civilian police force to counter Muslim "extremists", a ban on halal certification, encourages monks to promote Sinhala-Buddhists, calls for the state protection of Sihala-owned businesses, and promotes action to protect the "Sinhala race" (Daily FT 2013).

Communal rioting is part of this 'social justice' movement. Any criminal incident involving Muslims, verified or unverifiable, might cause the BBS collective to gather and take the law into their own hands. The group has accused the state of biased treatment against Sinhala. This belief that the majority population suffers from state discrimination further instigates violence toward the Muslims. One such incident surfaced in 2013 when an argument between Muslim youth and a Sinhalese Buddhist taxi driver became a flashpoint. The organization pressured the local police, using their street power, to arrest the Muslims involved (Hume 2013). BBS justifies its behavior by claiming that the group is merely "demanding justice" for the wronged. Gunaratna (2018) notes that since 2012, Sinhala-Muslim Riots have become a common occurrence and that BBS monks are a key driving force behind the increasing communal violence. He observes that the organization has mainstreamed and legitimized preexisting communal rifts, and that though "its propaganda campaign, BBS falsely showcased to the public that it had tacit governmental support to legitimise its cause" (Gunaratna 2018, 2). Having taken these steps, "BBS then turned to engage the masses by holding a series of public rallies", thus taking advantage of its considerable street power (Gunaratna 2018, 2).

The government of Sri Lanka, which depends on the votes of the majority and support from the monks, has a tendency to not press charges against the BBS rioters. In 2017, Buddhist vigilantes who targeted mosques and Muslim-owned businesses with petrol-bombs have never been arrested or tried by police (Gunaratna 2018). Gnanasara himself, after being convicted in separate cases for inciting violence and hatred, was pardoned by the now former President Maithripala Sirisena (Reuters 2019). This could have been Sirisena's futile attempt to secure victory in upcoming elections by appealing to Sinhalese voter, but it sent a clear message to the minorities that BBS is above the law (Reuters 2019; BBC 2013a, b).

BBS has a tendency to target Muslim-owned businesses and corporations, making it an inhospitable environment for the community to flourish within. At the same time, its actions are indicative of the victimhood narrative it propagates, and in which Sinhalese Buddhists are victims of an unjust economic system due to an alleged Muslim monopoly over commerce. This means that BBS perceives Muslims as both a cultural and economic threat to Sinhalese Buddhists. According to Gnanasara, Muslims vandalize and desecrate Buddhist heritage sites, and thus their business should be boycotted until they cease. Clothing outlets such as Fashion Bug and No Limit, owned by Muslims, have not only been boycotted by Sinhalese Buddhists but they have been attacked by mods let by BBS monks (France24 2013). Riots in 2014 and 2017 thus targeted Muslim neighborhoods and worship places but also Muslim-owned businesses (Gunaratna 2018).

BBS has also pushed for removal of not only Muslims' non-tangible culture, but also tangible Muslim heritage. For example, the group, in an attempt to erase Muslim history on the island state, has called for the destruction of a 10th-century mosque located at the Kuragala Buddhist monastery in the Kandy region (Sri Lanka Mirror 2013). In a similar bid to remove Islam from the country, it ended the existence of a halal certification board, which was framed as the group's key victory (2013b). This was part of a broader campaign to end symbolic displays of Muslimness that "threatened" the Buddhist community. After months of protests and sporadic rioting the BSS was able to abolish the halal certification board, and years in 2021 achieved its goal of imposing a ban of burkas (Haniffa 2021; BBC 2013a,b). While Sinhala Ravaya and Mahasen Balakaya are two other Islamophobic groups in Sri Lanka, the BBS alone has achieved unparalleled success in the propagation of its civilizational discourse. It is also an exporter of civilizational populism, and not only collaborates with MBT in Myanmar, but organizes protests when incidents targeting Buddhists take place overseas (Voice of America 2013). The movement thus constructs a shared Buddhist identity that is under a civilizational threat, particularly from Muslims, and requires protection.

Violence, Religion, and Civilizationalism in BBS and SBN Discourses

Ramachandran (2018) describes the Sinhalese Buddhists of Sri Lanka as possessing "a majority with a minority complex", that makes the majority feel, despite its advantages, that it faces an existential threat from alien 'others'. At the same time it presents the Sinhalese Buddhists as the "sons of the soil", and urges them to protect and safeguard 'the people", and their legacy and culture (Ramachandran 2018). BBS and SBN are in general exploit the Sinhalese Buddhists' 'minority complex', and encourage the majority population to believe that their hardships are caused by minority groups—in particular Muslims—who wish to destroy their way of life. Creating a sense of victimhood among the Sinhalese is thus an important part of the BBS and SBN plan to dominate Sri Lankan politics, because once the majority comes to believe it is being attacked by minorities, the actions of vigilante groups such as BBS are legitimized—sometimes by the state itself. Dilanthe Withanage, the chief-executive officer BBS, rationalizes the group's attacks on minorities by claiming that the "Sinhalese are the race who protected Theravada Buddhism for over 2,000 years without any interruption. So, therefore, Sinhalese have historical link to Buddhism. We don't have ownership of Buddhism, but we have the historical link to Buddhism. Unfortunately, if you look at the present situation there's no foundation. There's no background for the protection of Buddhism in Sri Lanka. And I believe that the threat, or challenge, comes from two sides. One, from us. From Sinhalese Buddhists. That's internal threat, internal challenge. The second is external forces, external challenge" (Walko 2016). This statement not only defines the populist-civilizational parameters on which BBS populism is defined, but it also demonstrates the emotions attached to Buddhism and its protection in Sri Lanka. In the BBS narrative, racial pride and nostalgia for a glorious past in which the Sinhalese protected Theravada Buddhism is mixed with feelings of victimhood, and a belief that minorities are threatening the future of Buddhist civilization in Sri Lanka, and that Buddhists must use violence to protect their culture. Thus BBS activism, masked as protective actions against minorities, has earned BBS a position within the wave of "saffron fascism" spreading throughout parts of Asia (Hume 2014).

Withanage's statement on why he sees Muslims as a threat or 'problem' is reflective of global trends in Islamophobia. Thus Withanage claims that "what's happening in Iraq, what's happening in other European countries, same thing is happening in Sri Lanka in a very secret, very silent manner. And that is the next danger we are facing" (Walko 2016). This narrative uses a narrative in which Muslims are conspiring to Islamize whole continents in order to create a sense of fear in Buddhists, and to justify Withanage's violence against Muslims in Sri Lanka. Furthermore, Withanage claims that Muslims have failed to assimilate into Sri Lankan culture, but instead demand special privileges: "The problem is that we don't want unnecessary privileges for anybody in this country. We're all people. We all have same rights. There's no issue about this. But, because you are Muslim you have a different marriage law. You have different schools. So that is social division. We are against that. That is promoting extremism" (Walko 2016). This narrative equally empowers and frightens his audience, portraying Muslims as a threat, but showing strength by claiming that he and his group are standing up to Muslims, and preventing their takeover of Sri Lanka.

Gnanasara, too, has not merely preached fear of the Muslim "extremists", but has urged his congregation to confront this fear. For example, in a speech he told his audience that "from today onwards, each of you must become an unofficial civilian police force against Muslim extremism. These so-called democrats are destroying the Sinhala race" (Daily FT 2013). This speech was not merely designed to inspire fear of and anger toward Muslims in ordinary Buddhists, but was also contrived to increase Buddhists' distrust of the state. The notion spread by some BBS members that the state itself cannot be trusted to protect Buddhists and Buddhism, and that it may be helping Muslims Islamize the country, is designed to generate feelings of alienation and mistrust of the government and the democratic process among BBS supporters. This feeling is articulated by Withanage, who remarked, "according to our Constitution, Buddhism should be given full-most priority. But we believe that this is not practiced in Sri Lanka at present" (Walko 2016).

It is thus not surprising that in addition to vigilantism, BBS has called for the formation of its own government, with monks as the spiritual and political leaders. At their annual meeting in Colombo in 2019, Gnanasara proposed that "We [BBS monks] will create a parliament that will be accountable for the country, a parliament that will protect Sinhalese" (Reuters 2019). He claimed that his group would be more successful at solving the 'Muslim problem' than the government because "we can talk to them face to face in villages and create the Muslim culture as we want without going for extremism. It's our responsibility because this is a Sinhalese country. We are the historical owners of this country" (Reuters 2019). He also announced with confidence that "we have already done our calculations. Everybody now talks about parliament democracy. If the need is to have a democratic parliament, then we monks have to own that" (Reuters 2019). He ended his 2019 address on a hopeful note, claiming that "if all the monks get together, we can win with the help of robes" (Reuters 2019). This key address highlights how the BBS and wider SBN narrative are used to portray Buddhist monks as inherently peaceful and thus ideal candidates for national leadership. Moreover, the power of "getting together" to solve all issues adds to an extreme sense of internal locus of control, which only emboldens the BBS.

For nearly fifteen years the Rajapaksa brothers have embraced SBN, a discourse that supports their electoral politics. Similar to the BBS monks, the rhetoric of the Rajapaksa brothers uses conspiracy theories and stereotypes to 'other'—on civilizational lines—minority groups, portraying them as threats to the majority Sinhalese Buddhist population. SBN was historically constructed to portray all non-Buddhists as a threat, but in line with global post-9/11 trends, the fear of Muslim 'extremism" has become central to its discourse, and this is reflected in the Rajapaksa brothers' penal populism in which they punish Muslims and wider securitizing rhetoric. The elder Rajapaksa attempted to instill in the electorate feelings of suspicion toward Muslims, many of them rooted in conspiracies. When asked about the increasing attacks on Muslims and rioting, he justified the violence by questioning the reports, saying "What was in the background? Why were they attacked? ... [A Sinhala-Buddhist] girl was raped. Seven years old girl was raped [by a Muslim coworker]. Then naturally they [the girl's community] will go and attack them whether they belong to any community or any religion... There were incidents like that. All incidents have some background [like] that" (Gunasekara 2017). On another occasion he again gave support to conspiracies that IS was injecting HIV/AIDS into the fruit being sent to Sri Lanka to destroy the Buddhist country (Goonewardena 2020). These statements, combined with his failure to condemn BBS-led violence against non-Buddhists, have strengthened public fear of 'extremist' Muslims while encouraging vandalism and acts of vengeance against innocent Muslims (Goonewardena 2020).

Both brothers have stressed the importance of cracking down on extremists, which feeds on the existential crisis and minority complex embedded in SBN philosophy. Gotabaya Rajapaksa, during his 2019 electoral run and following the Easter bombings, assured the traumatized masses that his "main task would be to ensure that our motherland which is once again under threat from terrorist and extremist elements is safe and protected" (Haniffa 2021).

His statement is designed to incite fear in his audience, and to normalize the state's growing authoritarianism and actions against Muslims and other minority groups. The younger Rajapaksa brother has also encouraged this narrative of fear, and has come to embrace BBS and their anti-Muslim narrative. Even before he ran for president, he justified the actions of radical monks and their demands by arguing that "it is the monks who protect our country, religion and race. [...] No one should doubt these clergy. We're here to give you encouragement" (BBC 2013a, b).

In this environment in which Prime Ministers and monks spread outrageous conspiracy theories about Muslims, it is hardly surprising that 'fake news' spread to support the right-wing populist narrative has contributed to communal rioting. Mostly these are video clips shared by non-verified news sources that are spread across Sir Lanka and beyond. The most prominent example shows a Muslim man who ran a restaurant and knows little Sinhalese being forced to say "yes" when the aggressive interviewer asked him if he mixed "sterilization pills" into the food he served at the restaurant. Obviously, there are no "sterilization pills", but BBS has promoted this conspiracy theory, and thus the video was an attempt to 'prove' the validity of this absurd conspiracy (Sunday Observer 2018). However, facts mattered little and the video led to rioting in Ampara town, where dozens were injured and the young man's business was destroyed by a Sinhalese-Buddhist mob (Sunday Observer 2018). In

2019, after the Eastern bombings a video showing Muslim protestors allegedly protesting against the Sri Lankan government's crackdown and supporting *jihadist* terrorism surfaced and went viral in Sri Lanka and India. It was later found that it was a doctored video (Kundu 2019). In a bizarre incident, when a 38-year-old Muslim man posted on Facebook "1 day u will cry", his post led to vandalism of a mosque in his region, where a copy of the Qur'an was also desecrated and two motorbikes parked at the mosque vandalized. There were also reports of people throwing stones at mosques and Muslim-led businesses (Ulmer & Rajarathnam 2019). This incident took place in the wake of the 2019 Easter Bombing and subsequently the government decided to temporarily close down social media to maintain law and order. Following the economic collapse of the nation, in which the Rajapaksa government's incompetence and the COVID-19 pandemic led the country to default on its debt, the Prime Minister was forced to flee the country. Whether Sri Lanka will move away from Sinhalese Buddhist Nationalism and populist rhetoric claiming that Muslims are attempting to destroy the good and pious Buddhist 'people' of the country, and toward pluralism and a more tolerant society, remains unknown.

6.3 Discussion of Case Studies

The chapter finds that, in the cases of Sri Lanka and Myanmar, Buddhist nationalists have turned to civilizational populism in order to enhance their power and construct a more homogenous society. They have done this by portraying non-Buddhists, and in particular Muslims, as a foreign and civilizational enemy which must be excluded from power in order to 'save' the people from foreign domination. These efforts have been pushed by a discourse which 'others' non-Buddhists, but especially Muslims in the post-9/11 and post-civil war environment, demonizing them as a foreign threat, and which simultaneously presents a positive view of Buddhism as the authentic religion of the nation and its people, while also portraying Buddhism and Buddhists as living under the grave threat coming from non-Buddhists. At times, anger toward elites for 'helping' or 'supporting' Muslims has been encouraged by Buddhist populists, along with claims that Muslims should not be allowed to prosper within a Buddhist nation and threaten Buddhist hegemony. This discourse has proven electorally and politically successful for Buddhist populists in Myanmar and Sri Lanka, who have used it to frame their respective nations as part of a larger Buddhist civilization threatened by Islam and other forces. In framing their societies in this manner, they are able to justify both state violence and oppression against minorities, as well as vigilante activities such as the anti-Muslim rioting and the desecrations of Mosques (see Tables 6.1 and 6.2).

We have also identified several key similarities and differences between MBT and BBS. The ideologies of both movements have found their own definitions rooted in faith or a mixture religion and ethnicity to create their typologies of 'the people' and 'others'. These groups, and their strategies of cooperation with political parties, are a shared survival strategy, and not a genuine form of religion-inspired activity. However, while MBT has not shown a clear indication of entering politics in its own right, its Sri Lankan counterpart, at least since its 2019 convention, appears eager to go beyond the seminaries and into political life.

Both groups present non-Buddhists as threats to Buddhist civilization, but in the post-9/11 world Muslims have become the prime antagonists in the crisis each group performs in order to generate public demand for civilizational Buddhist populism. MBT and BBS anti-Muslim discourses are therefore part of a global wave of Islamophobia that is shaping identitarian and religious populism around the world. A host of conspiracy theories such as the notion that Muslims are attempting to stage a "demographic takeover", of Buddhist nations, or claims that Muslims are raping or oppressing Buddhist women, have fueled a narrative of fear and Buddhist victimhood. These feelings of fear help to encourage a sense of victimhood within Buddhists in Myanmar and Sri Lanka, and produce a desire for self-protection and to take control over a dangerous situation.

Both MBT and BBS are unforgiving of 'elites' who, they claim, support, or voice their concerns for Muslims and other despised minorities. The sheer power and appeal of populist-civilizational rhetoric has transformed politics in Myanmar and Sri Lanka, and is partly responsible for the genocide of Rohingya Muslims in Myanmar's Rakhine province. Both groups also seem to share a concern from Buddhism beyond their respective countries. It is possible that MBT and BBS, or other Buddhist nationalists, could in time increase cooperation and become a transnational movement promoting Buddhist interests across a variety of majority Buddhist regions.

SBN, however, is somewhat different to BBS and MBT insofar as it is less religious and more identitarian in its discourse and ideology. SBN politicians seek the support of groups such as BBS, but remain oriented

Table 6.1 Narratives of Buddhist populist parties

	Pro-Violent Narratives	Links or Overlaps with the Far Right	Transnational Dimension, Diasporas
MBT	-Formed from the 969 vigilante movement -Claims that Muslims and "others" are trying to dominate the culture and economy as well as demographically "take over" the sacred homeland -The "outsiders" need to be eliminated and the rightful inhabitants and their faith need to be protected -"The others" are a security threat and can only be dealt with through violence	-Has shown support for BBS and seeks to foster ties with a global network of right-wing Buddhist ideologues in a pan-Buddhist fashion	-Not evident
BBS	Claims Muslims are trying to dominate the nation and its economy and demographically "takeover" the sacred homeland -"Outsiders" must be eliminated and the rightful inhabitants and their faith protected -The state and its elite are co-conspirators with Muslims -Muslims and "others" are a security threat	-Carries out protests when incidents of violence target Buddhist minorities in other regions of the world e.g., Bangladesh -Supports MBT and seeks to foster ties with a global network of right-wing Buddhist ideologues in a pan-Buddhist fashion -Supports politicians who embrace SBN	-Holds support rallies for diaspora in the Gulf when they are treated poorly by employers -Seeks ties with a global network of right-wing Buddhist ideologues
SBN	-Sinhala-Buddhist people are the rightful people and protectors of the land -"Others" (particularly Muslims) are terrorists, insurgents, and extremists -Advocates use of "strongman" measures to "go hard" on "the others"	-Supports BBS and right-wing Sinhala-Buddhist actors	-Not evident

Table 6.2 Comparison of Buddhist case studies

	Populist divide/Identity	Crises	Civilizationalism	Victimhood
MBT	"The people": The Buddhist majority "The others": All minorities who are non-Buddhist, especially Muslims. From within the Buddhist spectrum those who support "the others" or object to ideas and actions of the MBT" are classified as "the others"	-The chastity of Burmese women; losing Buddhist family and members to Islam - Non-Buddhists are an economic threat and must be boycotted -The presence of non-Buddhists leads to issues of security due to their "criminal nature"	-Buddhists are guardians of the faith and the land - Buddhist Sinhalese are the original inhabitants of the land; others are 'foreign' -Muslim "others" are a source of ontological insecurity due to their economic and socio-religious practices -Incompatibly with the "extreme" and "orthodox" nature of the Muslim "other's" faith -Buddhist women and families are in danger -Rohingya never seen as Burmese despite living within the country's borders	-Burmese women in marriages with Muslim men are oppressed -Muslims are raping Burmese Buddhist women -Subjected to a demographical conspiracy where Muslims are breeding quickly in order to take possession of Myanmar -Muslims use their business networks to keep Buddhists in poverty - "The people" are victims of Muslim terrorism and discrimination
BBS	"The people": Sinhala-Buddhist "The others": All other identities that are non-Sinhala-Buddhist. It also categorizes Sinhala-Buddhists who object to its populism and vigilante actions as "the others" -Muslims are the primary 'other'	-Buddhism in Sri Lanka and around the word perceived to be threatened by "others" belonging to foreign civilizations -Uses conspiracies and stereotypes to legitimize fear of "others" and the need to pick up arms and defend Buddhism	-Sinhala-Buddhist are guardians of the faith and land -Sinhala-Buddhists are authentic inhabitants of the land -The others try to be "treated differently" and have different conservative beliefs that are threatening "the people" civilisation	- "The people" are victims of the violence instigated by Muslims -Sinhala-Buddhists are left behind economically due to Muslims controlling economy -Governing elites are biased in favor of "the others"

	Populist divide/Identity	Crises	Civilizationalism	Victimhood
SBN	"The people": Sinhala-Buddhist "The others": All other identities that are non-Sinhala-Buddhist. It also categorizes Sinhala-Buddhists who object to its populism and vigilante actions as "the others"	-Sinhala-Buddhists are being subjected to extremist terrorism partially by Tamils and post-2009 Muslims -Buddhism is endangered by the presence of Muslims	-Sinhala-Buddhists have a divine right to the land and all others are "outsiders" -Seeks to protect the rights and culture of "the people" at all costs	-Buddhists are victims of Muslims and others -Muslims are "taking over" the nation and attacking Buddhists everywhere

toward a penal populism that is less rooted in notions of saving or advancing Buddhist civilization and more focused on countering Islamic 'extremism'. SBN has also shown a clear ability to adapt to changing political times. Its transitioning from othering Tamils to Muslims in Sri Lanka is testimony to its adaptability. Like BBS, SBN holds fast to the identity based on ethnoreligious parameters it uses to create populist divisions within Sri Lankan society, and uses rhetoric which evokes fear in order to create a desire within the Buddhist public for a "strongman" to lead the country out of an exaggerated security crisis.

The rise of MBT, BBS, and SBN is not sporadic or spontaneous. These organizations and parties are the culmination of decades or even centuries of built-up resentment felt by the majority toward ethnic and religious 'outsiders'. The advent of the internet and global disenchantment with the democratic system has empowered these voices, and allowed them to manifest in a more organized and mainstream fashion. Buddhism in principle denounces all violence, but these far-right populist voices in Asia's South and East demonstrate how populism, when mixed with civilizationalism, can lead adherents to one of the world's most peaceful religions to perpetrate acts of aggression and violence against innocent people.

References

Al Maeena, A. Tariq. 23 February 2013. "Neo-fascism on the Rise in Sri Lanka". *Gulf News*. https://gulfnews.com/opinion/op-eds/neo-fascism-on-the-rise-in-sri-lanka-1.1150052. Last accessed September 21, 2022.

Amarasuriya, Harini. 2015 "Protests and Counter Protests: Competing Civil Society Spaces in Post-War Sri Lanka". *Economic and Political Weekly* 50, no. 9, 49–55. www.jstor.org/stable/24481515.

Aneez, Shihar. 18 November 2016. "Sri Lanka says 32 'Elite' Muslims have joined Islamic State in Syria". *Reuters*. https://www.reuters.com/article/us-mideast-crisis-syria-sri-lanka-idUSKBN13D1EE. Last accessed September 21, 2022.

Artinger, Brenna and Rowand, Michael. 16 February 2021. "When Buddhists Back the Army". *Foreign Policy*. https://foreignpolicy.com/2021/02/16/myanmar-rohingya-coup-buddhists-protest/. Last accessed September 21, 2022.

Aung-Thwin, Maureen, et al. 1992. "The Burmese Ways to Socialism." *Third World Quarterly*, 13 (1): 67–75. www.jstor.org/stable/3992410.

Bakali, Naved. 2021. Islamophobia in Myanmar: The Rohingya Genocide and the 'War on Terror.' *Race & Class* 62 (4): 53–71. https://doi.org/10.1177/0306396820977753.
Barakat, Sultan. 21 November 2019. "Sri Lanka's Muslims have Reason to Fear the New Rajapaksa era". *Al Jazeera*. https://www.aljazeera.com/opinions/2019/11/21/sri-lankas-muslims-have-reason-to-fear-the-new-rajapaksa-era. Last accessed September 21, 2022.
BBC. 20 April 2020. "Sri Lanka attacks: Easter Sunday bombings marked one year on." https://www.bbc.com/news/world-asia-52357200. Last accessed September 21, 2022.
BBC. 25 January 2018. "How Aung San Suu Kyi Sees the Rohingya Crisis". https://www.bbc.co.uk/news/world-asia-42824778. Last accessed September 21, 2022.
BBC. 25 January 2015. "Ashin Wirathu: Myanmar and its vitriolic monk". https://www.bbc.com/news/world-asia-30930997. Last accessed September 21, 2022.
BBC. 17 February 2013a. "Sri Lanka Hardline Group Calls for Halal Boycott".https://www.bbc.com/news/world-asia-21494959. Last accessed September 21, 2022.
BBC. 25 March 2013b. "The hardline Buddhists targeting Sri Lanka's Muslims". https://www.bbc.com/news/world-asia-21840600. Last accessed September 21, 2022.
Berkwitz, Stephen C. 2008. "Resisting the global in Buddhist nationalism: Venerable Soma's discourse of decline and reform". *The Journal of Asian Studies* 67 (1): 73–10. (1) (PDF) Populism and Religion. Available from: https://www.researchgate.net/publication/321805689_Populism_and_Religion. Last accessed January 1, 2023.
Biver, Emilie. 2014. "Religious Nationalism: Myanmar and the Role of Buddhism in Anti- Muslim Narratives". https://www.researchgate.net/publication/268153592_Religious_nationalism_Myanmar_and_the_role_of_Buddhism_in_anti-Muslim_narratives. Last accessed September 21, 2022.
Bodhi. 2017. *The Suttanipata: An Ancient Collection of the Buddha's Discourses Together with Its Commentaries*. United States: Wisdom Publications.
Bookbinder, Alex. 9 April 2013. "969: The Strange Numerological Basis for Burma's Religious Violence". *The Atlantic*. https://www.theatlantic.com/international/archive/2013/04/969-the-strange-numerological-basis-for-burmas-religious-violence/274816/. Last accessed September 21, 2022.
Buddharakkhita, Acharya. 1996. The *Dhammapada: The Buddha's Path of Wisdom*. https://www.accesstoinsight.org/tipitaka/kn/dhp/dhp.intro.budd.html. Last accessed September 21, 2022.
Carothers, Thomas, and Andrew O'Donohue. 2020. Political Polarization in South and Southeast Asia: Old Divisions, New Dangers. *Research Report by*

Carnegie Endowment for International Peace. https://doi.org/10.2307/res rep26920.

Carroll, Joshua. 23 September 2015. "Buddhist Monks in Myanmar Celebrate Repressive Laws". *Al-Jazeera*. https://www.aljazeera.com/indepth/features/2015/09/buddhist-monks-myanmar-celebrate-repressive-laws-150922111750765.html. Last accessed September 21, 2022.

Columbo Telegraph. 1 October 2014. "Full Text: Wirathu And Gnanasara Sign Agreement". *Columbo Telegraph*. https://www.colombotelegraph.com/index.php/full-text-wirathu-and-gnanasara-sign-agreement/. Last accessed January 1, 2023.

Daily FT. 18 February 2013. ""This is a Sinhala country, Sinhala Government": Bodu Bala Sena". https://web.archive.org/web/20150924040221/http://www.ft.lk/2013/02/18/this-is-a-sinhala-country-sinhala-government-bodu-bala-sena/. Last accessed September 21, 2022.

Daily News. 19 April 2021. "Laws to control fake social media platforms". https://www.dailynews.lk/2021/04/19/local/246966/laws-control-fake-social-media-platforms. Last accessed September 21, 2022.

Department of Census and Statistics. 2012. "Census of Population and Housing of Sri Lanka". Colombo: Department of Census and Statistics. http://www.statistics.gov.lk/pophousat/cph2011/Pages/Activities/Reports/FinalReport/Population/Table%20A3.pdf. Last accessed September 21, 2022.

DeVotta, Neil. 25 April 2019. "Sri Lanka's Christians and Muslims Weren't Enemies". *Foreign Policy*. https://foreignpolicy.com/2019/04/25/sri-lankas-christians-and-muslims-werent-enemies/. Last accessed September 21, 2022.

Devotta, Neil. 2018. Religious Intolerance in Post-Civil War Sri Lanka. *Asian Affairs* 49: 278–300. https://doi.org/10.1080/03068374.2018.1467660.

Egreteau, Renaud, and François Robinne, editors. 2016. *Metamorphosis: Studies in Social and Political Change in Myanmar*. NUS Press.

Ellis-Petersen, Hannah. 29 May 2019. "Myanmar Police Hunt 'Buddhist Bin Laden' over Suu Kyi comments". *The Guardian*. https://www.theguardian.com/world/2019/may/29/myanmar-police-hunt-buddhist-bin-laden-over-suu-kyi-comments. Last accessed September 21, 2022.

Fortifying Rights. 2014. "Policies of Persecution: Ending Abusive State Policies Against Rohingya Muslims in Myanmar". https://www.fortifyrights.org/downloads/Policies_of_Persecution_Feb_25_Fortify_Rights.pdf. Last accessed September 21, 2022.

France24. 21 January 2021. "Buddhist monk calls UN expert 'whore' over Muslim support". https://www.france24.com/en/20150121-burma-buddhist-monk-un-expert-whore-anti-muslim-wirathu. Last accessed September 21, 2022.

France24. 29 May 2013. "Sri Lanka police stand by as Buddhist monks attack Muslim-owned store". https://observers.france24.com/en/20130329-sri-lanka-police-buddhist-muslim-store. Last accessed September 21, 2022.

Frydenlund, Iselin. 2018. "Buddhist Islamophobia: Actors, Tropes, Contexts". In: *Handbook of Conspiracy Theory and Contemporary Religion*. Brill. DOI: https://doi.org/10.1163/9789004382022014.

Fuller, Paul. 2018. "The Narratives of Ethnocentric Buddhist Identity". http://jbasr.com/ojs/index.php/jbasr/article/view/25. Last accessed September 21, 2022.

Goonewardena, Kanishka. 2020. Populism, Nationalism and Marxism in Sri Lanka: From Anti-Colonial Struggle to Authoritarian Neoliberalism. *Geografiska Annaler: Series b, Human Geography* 102 (3): 289–304. https://doi.org/10.1080/04353684.2020.1780146.

Gunaratna, Rohan. 2018 "Sinhala-Muslim Riots in Sri Lanka: The Need for Restoring Communal History". *Counter Terrorist Trends and Analyses* 10 (4): 1–4. www.jstor.org/stable/26402133.

Gunasekara, Tisaranee. 21 May 2017. "Blood-and-Faith Populism and Sri Lanka's Future." *Ground Views*. May 21, 2017. https://groundviews.org/2017/05/21/blood-and-faith-populism-and-sri-lankas-future/. Last accessed September 21, 2022.

Hodal, Kate. 18 April 2013. "Buddhist Monk uses Racism and Rumours to Spread Hatred in Burma". *The Guardian*. https://www.theguardian.com/world/2013/apr/18/buddhist-monk-spreads-hatred-burma. Last accessed September 21, 2022.

Haniffa, Farzana. 12 April 2021. "What is Behind the Anti-Muslim Measures in Sri Lanka?". *Al Jazeera*. https://www.aljazeera.com/opinions/2021/4/12/what-is-behind-the-anti-muslim-measures-in-sri-lanka. Last accessed September 21, 2022.

Hogan, Libby, and Safi, Michael. 3 April 2018. "Revealed: Facebook hate speech exploded in Myanmar during Rohingya crisis". *The Guardian*. https://www.theguardian.com/world/2018/apr/03/revealed-facebook-hate-speech-exploded-in-myanmar-during-rohingya-crisis. Last accessed January 1, 2023.

Human Rights Watch. 22 April 2013. "Burma: End 'Ethnic Cleansing' of Rohingya Muslims". https://www.hrw.org/news/2013/04/22/burma-end-ethnic-cleansing-rohingya-muslims. Last accessed September 21, 2022.

Hume, Tim. 18 July 2014. "'Fascists' in Saffron Robes? The Rise of Sri Lanka's Buddhist Ultra-Nationalists". *CNN*. https://edition.cnn.com/2014/07/17/world/asia/sri-lanka-bodu-bala-sena-profile/index.html. Last accessed September 21, 2022.

Imtiyaz, M. R. A. 22 May 2021. "Rajapaksa Steps up Sri Lanka's anti-Muslim measures". *East Asia Forum.* https://www.eastasiaforum.org/2021/05/22/rajapaksa-steps-up-sri-lankas-anti-muslim-measures/. Last accessed September 21, 2022.

Institute for War and Peace Reporting. 12 September 2017. *How Social Media Spurred Myanmar's Latest Violence.* Available at: https://www.refworld.org/docid/59b7f2c94.html. Last accessed 1 January 2023.

International Crises Group. 28 August 2020. "Identity Crisis: Ethnicity and Conflict in Myanmar". https://www.crisisgroup.org/asia/south-east-asia/myanmar/312-identity-crisis-ethnicity-and-conflict-myanmar. Last accessed September 21, 2022.

Lila, Muhammad. 22 April 2013. "Dalai Lama Pleads for Myanmar Monks to End Violence Amid Damning Rights Report". *ABC News.* https://abcnews.go.com/International/dalai-lama-pleads-myanmar-monks-end-violence-amid/story?id=19013148. Last accessed September 21, 2022.

Jayasinghe, Pasan. 2021. "Hegemonic Populism: Sinhalese Buddhist Nationalist Populism in Contemporary Sri Lanka". In *Populism in Asian Democracies: Features, Structures, and Impact.* Edited by Sook Jong Lee, Chin-enWu and Kaustuv Kanti Bandyopadhyay. Leiden and Boston: Brill

Jayasuriya, Kanishka. 27 November 2019. "The Sri Lankan Election and Authoritarian Populism." *The East Asia Forum.* https://www.eastasiaforum.org/2019/11/27/the-sri-lankan-election-and-authoritarian-populism/. Last accessed September 21, 2022.

Kreibich, Mirco, Goetz, Johanna and Murage, M. Alice. 24 May 2017. "Myanmar's Religious and Ethnic Conflicts: no end in sight". *Henrich Boll Stiftung.* https://www.boell.de/en/2017/05/24/myanmars-religious-and-ethnic-conflicts-no-end-sight. Last accessed September 21, 2022.

Kundu, Chayan. 30 April 2019. "Viral video showing Muslims protesting crackdown by Sri Lanka after blasts is false". *India Today.* https://www.indiatoday.in/fact-check/story/viral-video-showing-muslims-protesting-crackdown-by-sri-lanka-after-blasts-is-false-1514064-2019-04-30. Last accessed September 21, 2022.

Maizland, Lindsay. 10 February 2021. "Myanmar's Troubled History: Coups, Military Rule, and Ethnic Conflict". *Council of Foreign Relations.* https://www.cfr.org/backgrounder/myanmar-history-coup-military-rule-ethnic-conflict-rohingya. Last accessed September 21, 2022.

Marshall, R. C. Andrew. 27 June 2013. "Special Report: Myanmar Gives Official Blessing to Anti-Muslim Monks". *Reuters.* https://www.reuters.com/article/us-myanmar-969-specialreport-idUSBRE95Q04720130627

Mihlar, Farah. 2020. "Islamophobia AntiMuslim Civil Society or Individuals". *OHCHR*. https://www.ohchr.org/sites/default/files/Documents/Issues/Religion/Islamophobia-AntiMuslim/Civil%20Society%20or%20Individuals/FarahMihlar.pdf. Last accessed September 21, 2022.

Minorities Rights Group International. 18 March 2013. "Islamophobia and Attacks on Muslims in Sri Lanka." https://minorityrights.org/publications/islamophobia-and-attacks-on-muslims-in-sri-lanka-march-2013/. Last accessed September 21, 2022.

Moe, Z. Kyaw. 9 March 2017. "A Radically Different Dhamma". *The Irrawaddy*. https://www.irrawaddy.com/from-the-archive/radically-different-dhamma-2.html. Last accessed September 21, 2022.

Mohajan, Haradhan. 2018. "History of Rakhine State and the Origin of the Rohingya Muslims". *IKAT: The Indonesian Journal of Southeast Asian Studies* 2, no. 1, 19–46. https://mpra.ub.uni-muenchen.de/88186/. Last accessed September 21, 2022.

Nakanishi, Yoshihiro. 2013. *Strong Soldiers, Failed Revolution: The State and Military in Burma, 1962–88*. NUS Press. www.jstor.org/stable/j.ctv1qv1qg. Last accessed September 21, 2022.

Oppenheim, Marella. 12 May 2017. "'It Only Takes One Terrorist': The Buddhist Monk Who Reviles Myanmar's Muslims". *The Guardian*. https://www.theguardian.com/global-development/2017/may/12/only-takes-one-terrorist-buddhist-monk-reviles-myanmar-muslims-rohingya-refugees-ashin-wirathu. Last accessed September 21, 2022.

Reed, Susan A. 2021. "Bathed in Blood: Ritual Performance as Political Critique". *Asian Ethnology* 80 (1): 165–198. www.jstor.org/stable/27032443.

Reuters. 22 May 2019. "Sri Lanka President Pardons Hardline Buddhist Monk". https://web.archive.org/web/20190531103355/https://af.reuters.com/article/worldNews/idAFKCN1SS23V. Last accessed September 21, 2022.

Reuters. 7 July 2019. "Hardline Sri Lanka Monk Calls for Buddhist Sinhalese Government". https://www.reuters.com/article/uk-sri-lanka-buddhist-idUKKCN1U2076

Rosenthal, Randy. 13 November 2018. "What's the Connection between Buddhism and Ethnic Cleansing in Myanmar?". *Lion's Roar*. https://www.lionsroar.com/what-does-buddhism-have-to-do-with-the-ethnic-cleansing-in-myanmar/. Last accessed September 21, 2022.

Safi, Michel. 3 April 2018. "Revealed: Facebook Hate Speech Exploded in Myanmar during Rohingya crisis". *The Guardian*. https://www.theguardian.com/world/2018/apr/03/revealed-facebook-hate-speech-exploded-in-myanmar-during-rohingya-crisis. Last accessed September 21, 2022.

Selth, Andrew 2004. "Burma's Muslims and the War on Terror". *Studies in Conflict & Terrorism* 27(2): 107–126, https://doi.org/10.1080/10576100490275094.

Selth, Andrew. 2010. "Myanmar's Nuclear Ambitions". *Survival* 52 (5): 5–12. https://doi.org/10.1080/00396338.2010.522091.

Shakil, Kainat. 23 February 2021. "Sri Lanka". European Centre for Populism Studies. https://www.populismstudies.org/tag/sri-lanka/. Last accessed September 21, 2022.

Silva, T. Kalinga. 2016. "Gossip, Rumor, and Propaganda in Anti-muslim Campaigns of the Bodu Bala Sena". In *Buddhist Extremists and Muslim Minorities: Religious Conflict in Contemporary Sri Lanka*. Ed., John Clifford Holt. Oxford University Press. https://doi.org/10.1093/acprof:oso/9780190624378.001.0001.

Sin, Thant. 3 June 2017. "Facebook Bans Racist Word 'Kalar' in Myanmar, Triggers Censorship". *The Business Standard*. https://www.business-standard.com/article/international/facebook-bans-racist-word-kalar-in-myanmar-triggers-censorship-117060300423_1.html. Last accessed September 21, 2022.

Sirilal, Ranga. 29 September 2014. "Radical Myanmar monk joins hands with Sri Lankan Buddhists". *Reuters*. https://www.reuters.com/article/us-sri-lanka-buddhism-myanmar-idUSKCN0HO0GD20140929. Last accessed September 21, 2022.

Sivasundaram, Sujit. April 2010. "Ethnicity, Indigeneity, and Migration in the Advent of British Rule to Sri Lanka". *The American Historical Review* 115 (2): 428–452. https://doi.org/10.1086/ahr.115.2.428.

Ramachandran, Sudha. 13 March 2018. "Sri Lanka's Anti-Muslim Violence". *The Diplomat*. https://thediplomat.com/2018/03/sri-lankas-anti-muslim-violence/. Last accessed September 21, 2022.

Rule to Sri Lanka". *The American Historical Review*, 115 (2): 428–452. www.jstor.org/stable/23302578.

Sri Lanka Mirror. 18 March 2013. "Eviction notice for Muslims in Kuragala". https://web.archive.org/web/20130322001805/http://www.mirror.lk/news/5974-eviction-notice-for-muslims. Last accessed September 21, 2022.

Sunday Observer. 4 March 2018. "Tension in Ampara after Fake 'Sterilization Pills' Controversy". http://www.sundayobserver.lk/2018/03/04/news/tension-ampara-after-fake-%E2%80%98sterilization-pills%E2%80%99-controversy. Last accessed September 21, 2022.

Thu, Myat. 2021. "Populism in Mynmar". In *Populism in Asian Democracies: Features, Structures, and Impact*. Ed., Sook Jong Lee, Chin-en Wu and Kaustuv Kanti Bandyopadhyay. Leiden and Boston: Brill.

Ulmer, Alexandra and Rajarathnam, Omar. 13 May 2019. "Sri Lanka Clashes Kill One; Imposes Nationwide Curfew after Mosques Attacked". *Al Jazeera*.

https://www.reuters.com/article/us-sri-lanka-blasts-socialmedia/sri-lanka-blocks-social-media-after-worst-anti-muslim-unrest-since-easter-bombings-idUSKCN1SJ02I. Last accessed September 21, 2022.
UNHRC. 2 July 2014. "Sri Lanka Must do More to Rein in Hate Speech, Faith-Based Violence—UN Rights Experts". https://www.refworld.org/docid/53ba55df4.html. Last accessed September 21, 2022.
Uyangoda, Jayadeva. 2007. "Ethnic Conflict in Sri Lanka: Changing Dynamics". *Policy Studies* 32. Washington, DC: East-West Centre. https://www.files.ethz.ch/isn/35338/PS032.pdf. Last accessed January 1, 2023.
Walko, Zachary. 29 June 2016. "Interview: Dilanthe Withanage on Sinhala-Buddhist Nationalism". *The Diplomat*. https://thediplomat.com/2016/06/interview-dilanthe-withanage-on-sinhala-buddhist-nationalism/. Last accessed January 1, 2023.
Walton, J. Matthew. 2015. *Burmese Buddhist Politics* ". https://doi.org/10.1093/oxfordhb/9780199935420.013.21.
Voice of America. 4 October 2012. "Sri Lanka's Buddhist Monks Protest Bangladesh Violence". https://www.voanews.com/east-asia/sri-lankas-buddhist-monks-protest-bangladesh-violence. Last accessed September 21, 2022.
Wills, Matthew. 29 September 2017. "How Buddhism Is Being Used to Justify Violence in Myanmar". *JStor Daily*. https://daily.jstor.org/how-is-buddhism-being-used-to-justify-violence-in-myanmar/. Last accessed September 21, 2022.
Yilmaz, Ihsan, Nicholas Morieson, and Mustafa Demir. 2021. Exploring Religions in Relation to Populism: A Tour around the World. *Religions* 12: 301. https://doi.org/10.3390/rel12050301.
Zúquete, P. Jose. 2017. "Populism and Religion". In *Oxford Handbooks Online*. Ed., Cristóbal Rovira Kaltwasser, Paul Taggart, Paulina Ochoa Espejo, and Pierre Ostiguy. Oxford University Press. https://doi.org/10.1093/oxfordhb/9780198803560.013.22

CHAPTER 7

Judaism and Civilizational Populism

7.1 Introduction

This chapter examines civilizational populism in Israel, and focuses on the largest and most powerful party in Israel since the 1980s, Likud, and its most significant leader of the past twenty years, Benjamin Netanyahu. Netanyahu is widely regarded as a populist, and to have moved Likud toward right-wing populism since becoming party chairman in 1993. This move toward right-wing populism has proven electorally successful for Likud, although it has had serious consequences for Israeli society and for the Palestinians. The civilizational narratives within Netanyahu's populist discourses have not been explicitly examined previously. However, this chapter shows how Netanyahu incorporates civilizationalism into his populist discourses by, first, using the notion that Jewish civilization predates all others in the region to establish the legitimacy of the state of Israel, the hegemony of Jewish culture within Israel, and at times his own political decisions. Second, through his portrayal of the Arab-Muslim world as an antisemitic and barbaric bloc that, far from being a civilization, threatens Western civilization through its barbarism. Equally, this chapter shows how Netanyahu argues that Israel is akin to protective wall that protects Western civilization from the Islamist barbarians who wish to destroy it, and therefore on this basis calls for Europeans and North Americans to support Israel in its battle for civilization and against the forces of barbarism. Combined, these narratives serve to assist Netanyahu in his populist division of Israeli society into three antagonistic groups: 'the people', the 'elite', and 'others'. In Netanyahu's discourse, the chapter shows, 'others' are non-civilized Arab-Muslims who desire the destruction of both the Jewish people and Western civilization; "elites" are left-wing parties and liberal Jews who Netanyahu portrays as abandoning Jewish culture and helping Arabs destroy civilization; "the People" are all the Jewish people, who are authentic and morally good: authentic because their ancestors were the first people of the land, and morally good because they are civilized Jews. This chapter begins with an overview of Israel's history, which is followed by a discussion on civilizational in Israel, and following this an examination of the use of civilizationalism within the populist rhetoric of Likud Party leader Benjamin Netanyahu.

Israel is the only country in which a majority of citizens identify with Judaism; Jewish believers are otherwise dispersed around the world and nowhere make up a majority. The oldest of the Abrahamic religions, it has an estimated 17.4 million followers around the world which is vastly smaller than the number of Christians and Muslims (DellaPergola 2019). Within Israel, national identity is often intertwined with 'Jewishness', a notion which played an important role in the country's creation and subsequent development. Israel is a product of the nineteenth-century Zionist movement, which removed itself somewhat from Orthodox Judaism and, influenced by European nationalism, sought to create a nation for the Jewish people. Thus Zionism, and by extension Israel, has always possessed a "Romantic nationalist culture with a strong expressivist dimension; that is, a strong emphasis on self-expression and notions such as authenticity", at least compared to Orthodox Judaism where "the Torah and God's commandments are imposed externally on the Jew" (Fischern 2014).

By the end of the nineteenth century religion and a sense of Jewish spirituality played an important role in the Zionist movement, but the movement was always strongly and predominately nationalist (Hassan 1988). The rise of Zionism was largely a response to growing anti-Semitism in Europe, which would eventually explode and lead to the catastrophic events of the Holocaust. Theodor Herzl, an Austrian Jewish journalist, responding to the growing darkness in Europe, lobbied for a Jewish homeland in the hills of ancient Jerusalem (Zion), where settlers from Eastern European regions were already settling after feeling unwelcomed in their European homesteads (Berry and Philo 2006; Hassan 1988). Shumsky (2018) notes that Herzl's vision was a homeland with "cultural–national" aspects, or a kind of "non-Jewish" homeland "for Jews" in the ancient heartland. Prota and Filc (2020) admit that, to a degree, Herzl's dream remains alive in Israel in the form of the detachment between Synagogue and state. However the authors point out that "Zionism could not completely detach itself from its religious roots, as religion was indispensable as a marker of boundaries and a mobilizing force" (Prota and Filc 2020). The turbulent events that followed the Ottoman Empire's collapse left a power vacuum in the Arab peninsula that allowed the Zionist movement to take a more aggressive nationalist stance, and begin to create a Jewish state. The early political leadership of the Israeli Labor Party propagated a narrative of self-defense, legitimizing the idea that Zionism meant protecting the Jewish nation from hostile foreign forces (Prota and Filc 2020). The aggressive pursuit of protecting the Jewish nation oriented early Israeli politics toward nationalism; however, Zionism remained attached to Judaism and "continued to be directed by powerful religious structures" (Ben-Porat 2000; Prota and Filc 2020; Raz-Krakotzkin 2000).

Jewish nationalism in its Zionist and neo-Zionist forms has often been a powerful political force in Israel, especially in the shape of right-wing populist discourse (Pinson 2021; Rogenhofer and Ayala Panievsky 2020). For example, the Sephardim Shomrei Torah/ Sephardi Torah Guardians (Shas) formed in 1984, rooted its populism in religious notions of Jewishness rather than in Zionist nationalism. While Shas has never been able to form a majority government, it has over the years secured several seats in Israeli parliament that have allowed it to form coalitions with larger parties. Since 1984 Shas has used a populist religious discourse, yet other parties, including the powerful National Liberation Movement (Likud), have also increasingly oriented themselves toward populism, although in the case of Likud their populism is combined with Zionism.

7.2 Civilizationalism in Israel

To what civilization does the state of Israel belong? It is perhaps instructive to observe that Samuel P. Huntington was curiously silent about Israel, and did not identify a specific Jewish civilization among the world civilizations he described in *The Clash of Civilizations and the Remaking of World Order* (1996). In his critique of Huntington's book, realist International Relations scholar Stephen Walt remarked that it is difficult to place, from Huntington's civilizational approach, Israel within 'Western civilization'. According to Walt (1997, 186), "Israel is not a member of the West (at least not by Huntington's criteria) and is probably becoming less 'Western' as religious fundamentalism becomes more salient and as the Sephardic population becomes more influential. A 'civilizational' approach to U.S. foreign policy can justify close ties with Europeans (as the common descendants of Western Christendom) but not Israelis".

It is not automatically, therefore, obvious that Israel or the Jewish people or the state of Israel belong to Western civilization. At the same time, this has not stopped various political actors from classifying Israel and the Jewish people as Western. As we have shown in previous chapters, many European and North American civilizational populist parties appear to claim if not the Jewish people, than at least the Jewish scriptures, to be part of 'Judeo-Christian civilization'. The Trump Administration, for example, emphasized America's closeness to Israel, and appeared to regard the country as part of a broader Judeo-Christian civilization which required defending from Islam (Haynes 2020). The notion that Western civilization encompasses Israel is at times, reflected in the words of Israel's leaders. For example, following the 2015 murder of four Jews in a Paris kosher supermarket, and the mass murder of Charlie Hebdo cartoonists by an Islamist group, Netanyahu called upon Europeans to "wake up" and act to defend "our common civilization" (The New York Times 2015). Linking the murder of cartoonists in France with the Israeli-Palestinian conflict, Netanyahu said "Israel stands with Europe; Europe must stand with Israel" (The New York Times 2015). However, on another occasion Netanyahu told French Jews return "home" to Israel, and suggested that the murder of Jews in a kosher supermarket proved that France was no longer safe for Jews (The New York Times 2015).

Thus at times Netanyahu has claimed that Israel is part of the West, which makes sense insofar as Israel was a creation of Western powers and populated, especially at first, largely by European Jews. However, at other times he emphasizes the *sui generis* nature of Israel and the Jewish people. Of course, one cannot be conclusive about where a civilization begins and ends. In the case of Israel, the nation is at once a product of Western civilization but also the product of a genocide perpetrated by Europeans who believed the Jews were non-Western people who did not belong in Europe. Some ambiguity about Israel's civilizational classification is thus unavoidable for all those who wish to definitively place Israel within a civilization, an act which is perhaps ultimately foolish and dangerous.

There is a close link between the state of Israel and conceptions of Jewish civilization, both ancient and modern. According to Israeli politician and academic Yossi Shain (2019; Ferziger 2020) "Since its establishment in 1948, the State of Israel has gradually situated itself as the most important factor in all areas of worldwide Jewish life....The nation of Israel and Jewish civilization are defined today more than ever through the political, military, and cultural power of the sovereign Jewish state". At the same time, Israel's legitimacy lies, in part, on its claim to be the modern manifestation of the ancient Jewish civilization that existed—and indeed predates—the coming of the Arabs and Islam to the Land of Israel. While Israel was founded as a modern European style secular nationalist nation-state, its leaders also sought to connect Jewish people—who spoke many different languages—with their ancient past by making Modern Hebrew the official language of Israel, and teaching it to all schoolchildren. Indeed, the decision to make Hebrew—a Semitic language—the national language perhaps further removed Israel from European culture. This decision was made to bind the people together as one, but also to create a distinctly Jewish state, with its own language and culture (Nevo and Verbov 2011). William Safran (2005, 43), in his study of the rise of Hebrew and its impact on Israeli nationalism, observes that "in the early years of Jewish resettlement in Palestine, Hebrew slowly emerged as the popular language, a compromise between the Yiddish spoken by Eastern European immigrants and the Arabic or Ladino current among many Middle Eastern Jews". However, following the "establishment of the state and the massive influx of Jewish displaced persons, mostly speakers of Yiddish, that language, regarded as a potential threat to the primacy of Hebrew, was systematically fought by the country's political and cultural elite. Today, the position of Hebrew as the national language of Israel is secure" (Safran 2005, 43).

In the Europe of the nineteenth century, the "quest for political independence was based, more than anything else, on the 'prepolitical' existence of a common language" (Safran 2005, 43). In a similar way, for most of the leaders of nineteenth-century Zionism, "the revival of Hebrew was a precondition for Jewish nation-building" (Safran 2005, 44). This was due to a number of factors, including the secularizing of the Jewish people in Europe, and the multitude of different languages spoken by Jews. However, it was also due to the Jewish people not possessing their own land, but rather having only a distant "memory of territory" (Safran 2005, 44). Thus, Zionism is different in important ways from other European nationalisms, insofar as it was connected not to an existing territory, but to the memory of one that ceased to exist almost two millennia in the past, and before the existence of nation-states.

This is perhaps the reason that Israeli archaeologists are increasingly encouraged to 'discover' ancient cities of Jewish civilization in Israel, and to 'disprove' the link between the Palestinians and the Philistines described in the Bible, and who evidently also lived alongside the Jewish people. Indeed, the legitimacy of the state of Israel rests, in part, on the history of Jewish civilization in the region. This being so, political groups have instrumentalized archaeology to 'prove' that Jewish civilization in the region predates all others. Israeli archaeologist Raphael Greenberg claims that "in order to answer the continuing demands of mainly politics actors" Israeli "archaeologists have given up many of their best practices" (Solomon 2010). Greenberg claims that the Ir David Foundation, which encourages Jewish settlement in Palestinian territories, is funding archaeological digs intended to find 'evidence' of prior Jewish settlement and thus to define those areas as belonging to the state of Israel (Solomon 2010). The desire to 'prove' that Jewish civilization predates Arab civilization in Israel, and thus legitimize the Jewish state via a connection between modern Israel and ancient Jewish civilization, is so important to Netanyahu that he has gleefully tweeted to his followers the results of DNA tests which he claims prove that the Palestinians are relative newcomers to the region (Jerusalem Post 2019). Indeed, Netanyahu claims that the Philistines were Southern Europeans, but that the modern Palestinians are from the Arabian Peninsula (Jerusalem Post 2019). This notion that the Palestinians are inauthentic to the Land of Israel, a land which properly belongs to the Jewish people, and that this can be proven by archaeology and DNA testing, is thus used by Netanyahu to justify the Jewish character of Israel, and the oppression of the Palestinians is their increasing marginalization in Israel.

7.3 Case Study: Civilizational Populism of the National Liberal Movement (Likud)

Populism has long been present in Israel, but has been part of mainstream politics since the 1990s (Ben-Porat et al. 2021, 6). The mainstreaming of populism is perhaps largely the product of the rise to power of the right-wing populist Likud party, and in particular its leader and former Israeli

Prime Minister Benjamin Netanyahu. Yet Likud is not the only populist party in Israel. It's frequent coalition partner, Shas, is also a populist party, although of a strikingly different kind. Indeed, Shas and Likud represent different ethnic and religious groups, and therefore their discourses identify 'the people', 'others', and 'elites' in different ways. Shas represents the Haredi and Sephardic people of Israel, who are often marginalized, and who at times resent the economically dominant Ashkenazi Jews (Filc 2016). Likud, however, established a far broader base and has, since 1977, been the most powerful single political party in Israel.

Likud was formed in 1973 by Menachem Begin and Ariel Sharon. The party drew support from several other right-wing parties and eventually formed a coalition which pushed the once dominant Labor Party from government and into opposition in 1977 (Porat and Filc 2022). According to Porat and Filc (2022) Likud was initially a nationalist though not illiberal party that sought greater inclusion of the Mizrahim within Israeli society, a group marginalized by Labor. The support of Mizrahi Jews enabled Likud to defeat the once hegemonic Labor party and to establish themselves as the new ruling party of Israel (Porat and Filc 2022).

First leader Menachem Begin was arguably a populist, and attacked Labor party elites for marginalizing Mizrahi Jews and other groups, and giving special privileges to secular Ashkenazi Jews (Porat and Filc 2022). Begin also incorporated religious language into Likud discourse, and claimed, upon winning the 1977 national elections, that "We shall follow the name of our Lord forever...I announce that the government of Israel will not ask any nation...to acknowledge our right to exist...we have received that right from God" (Porat and Filc 2022). Begin's religious language and his use of Jewish symbols demonstrated the close relationship between "Likud and the religious-nationalist parties but also echoed the traditionalist elements with the Likud and the rejection of Labor's alleged secularism" (Porat and Filc 2022). Begin believed that there could never be a separating of nation and people in Judaism, yet he was also a liberal who demanded equal rights for Arab Israelis, saying "we believe that in the Jewish state all citizens must have equal rights, without no differences of religion, nationality or origin" (Porat and Filc 2022).

Over time, Likud transformed into a right-wing populist party which, far from calling for equal rights for Arabs and non-Jews, sought to demonize and exclude them from society. This change was crystalized by the election of Benjamin Netanyahu as party chairman in 1993. Under

Netanyahu's leadership, the Likud-led right-wing coalition gained traction with voters through its conservative nationalist rhetoric and policies, and through its promotion of economic neo-liberalism supported by a 'strong man image' perpetuated through political authoritarianism (ECPS 2020; Filc 2009). In 1996 Netanyahu became prime minister of Israel, governing in an authoritarianism style and using populist right-wing "rhetoric dominated by ethnic nationalism, xenophobia, and anti-elite sentiment against the academia, the media, and the country's left-wing parties" (ECPS 2020; also see (Rogenhofer and Panievsky 2020; Bagaini 2019, 6). Netanyahu's nationalism, particularly in the 2000s, marked a break from the secularism of the Labor.

Party-dominated period in Israeli politics. Netanyahu's discourse and policies were frequently ultra-nationalist and discriminatory toward the non-Jewish minorities, leading to increased militarization and the persecution of Muslims and Christians in settlement zones (ECPS 2020; Prota and Filc 2020).

During its terms in power in the 2000s and 2010s Likud has often relied on populist nationalism, and attempted to divide society between 'the people'—Jews who were historically persecuted and who must now defend their homeland—and 'others'—intruders in the land of the Jews, and who were often responsible for terrorist attacks and other forms of anti-Jewish violence (ECPS 2020; Prota and Filc 2020). By 2015, the idea that "Netanyahu is good for the Jews" had become a powerful re-election tool for Likud, and the idea that the Muslim Arabs, who were portrayed by Likud as "infiltrators" and a "Trojan Horse", might be expelled became mainstream (Ghanem and Khatib 2017). Likud's discourse encouraged the growth of nativism in Israeli society, and correspondingly their own populist discourse became more nativist.

Seizing on the Israeli people's ontological fears, Likud's leaders sought to demonize Israel's perceived enemies, especially Muslim Palestinians. In this way, nativism became deeply embedded in Likud discourse, in an attempt to generate feelings of fear and anger in Israeli society, and to solidify Israeli identity in a form advantageous to Likud. At the same time, Likud increasingly, throughout the late 1990s and beyond, sought to position themselves as the voice of the Israeli people, and portrayed the secular left as an 'elite' which would not or could not protect the Israeli people from their enemies. Post-1997, and thus in the period in which Likud increasingly oriented itself toward populism and began to dominate Israeli politics, the party portrayed itself as fighting against a corrupt and ineffectual elite, and preying on the deepest fears of the Jewish people sought to identify itself as the chief defender of the Jewish people.

Likud's otherizing of non-Jews, and especially Arabs and their secular/liberal supporters within Israel, has led Prota and Filc (2020) to note three key aspects of religion's populist instrumentalization by the party under the leadership of Netanyahu: "First, religiosity or attachment to religion becomes a litmus test for loyalty, separating authentic members of the nation from cosmopolitan and disloyal elites. Second, religious language and symbols accentuate fears and shape demands for action, to protect the nation and its borders. Third, consequently, more and more leaders, not only in the Likud, adopt religious tropes and symbols to demonstrate loyalty and garner support". Rogenhofer and Panievsky (2020) carried out a comparative analysis of Netanyahu, Modi, and Erdoğan in their respective countries to explore each leader's authoritarian populism. They note that, "Netanyahu's emphasis on Israel's Jewishness all point to a conflation of religion with the national vision" (Rogenhofer and Panievsky 2020, 1395).

Likud's "Exclusionary populism", according to Porat and Filc (2022), was based upon "Netanyahu's nativist definition of the people" and "advocated a closed ethno-national unity, threatened by foreign enemies, non-Jewish citizens, and by Jewish-Israeli opposition advocating equal citizenship". Opposition parties and critics of Likud and Netanyahu were portrayed by Likud "as detached elites not committed to Jewish nationality and to the Jewish State" (Porat and Filc 2022). Porat and Filc (2022) describe Netanyahu's populist discourse as defining the identity of the people of Israel as "the Jewish people, defined by descent" and their enemies as "the anti-people marked by antisemistism". They argue that Netanyahu "builds a chain of equivalences in which the Islamic State of Iraq and Syria/Levant (ISIS) is like Iran, Iran is like Hezbollah, Hezbollah is like Hamas, Hamas is like Abu Mazen and the Palestinian Authority and all the Palestinians in the OT, the Palestinians in the OT are like the Israeli Arab citizens, and the Israeli Arab citizens are like the Israeli left, their loyalty to state and nation suspected". For example, Porat and Filc (2022) observe, when campaigning in 2015 Netanyahu claimed that

> …Hamas already declared that they will sue the state of Israel. I won't be surprised if we will hear similar things from Hezbollah, ISIS and Al Qaeda. A few days after Islamist terror committed a massacre in France,

the prosecutor decided to investigate Israel that defends its citizens from the extremist Islamic terrorist organization Hamas that aims to massacre Jews. It is the same Hamas that has a pact with the Palestinian Authority.

"Netanyahu's ethnoreligious discourses nurture a dichotomy between an exclusively defined 'Jewish people' and their 'enemies', i.e., Israeli Arabs and their Jewish allies", not only created rifts between the non-Jews and Jews, but also created a political deadlock between centrist, left, secular parties in their engagement with the government coalition (Rogenhofer & Panievsky 2020, 1403–4). The ethnoreligious divides exploited and to a degree engendered by Netanyahu were part of an effort to blur "religion and nationalism to define the Jewish claim to Israel in Biblical terms, deny Palestinians' national identity and frame a civilizational struggle between the Judeo-Christian world and 'murderous Islamism'" (Rogenhofer and Panievsky 2020, 9). Levi and Agmon (2020) note that the idea of a Zionist homeland that is Jewish-centric has made Israeli politics highly "security-driven", and a place in which "economics and culture become secondary considerations", and crisis and fear become driving forces—fear leading to a desire among a large section of the electorate for a strongman to protect the Jewish nation.

In 2018 Netanyahu effectively paved the way for ethnoreligious populism to dominate Israeli politics and political discourse through the Nation-State Law. Under this highly controversial bill the secular state envisioned in early Zionism was eliminated, as the law declares Israel a "Jewish Nation-State of the Jewish people" (Halbfinger and Kershner 2018). Netanyahu boasted that the legislation made certain that "Israel is the nation-state of the Jewish people and respects the rights of all of its *citizens*" (BBC News 2018). It also mandates that Jerusalem be recognized as the "complete and united... capital of Israel" and claims the "development of Jewish settlement" is of great "national value", language that led to escalating violence between Palestinians and Israelis (BBC News 2018). The passage of the bill also contradicted the spirit of the state's foundation, which promised equality for all, by downgrading Arabic from an official language to a language with "special status", and leaving Hebrew as the only official language of Israel (Halbfinger and Kershner 2018). These measures combined emphasize how a Likud has often relied on religion to define Israeli identity, and the identity of Israel's enemies.

Netanyahu and Likud lost government following the 2021 legislative election, and the new government was a coalition between right-wing and centrist parties (including the secularist Yesh Atid party and conservative nationalist Yamina) and which established a rotation government. Thus while Netanyahu was no longer prime minister, Israel remained government by largely right-wing forces which continued Netanyahu's demonization of Arabs and Muslims. For example, Naftali Bennett, leader of the Yamina coalition who served as prime minister between 13 June 2021 and 30 June 2022, is regarded as more right-wing and nationalist than Netanyahu, and has stated the establishing of a Palestinian state would be a "terrible mistake" (Jerusalem Post 2021).

7.3.1 Civilizationalism in Netanyahu's Populist Discourse

Who is Benjamin Netanyahu? Netanyahu is, as his biographer Anshel Pfeffer (2018, 5) put it, both part of the old Israeli elite and a member of the "seething underdogs" who believe they have been failed by the elite. This second group, Pfeffer writes, which comprises religious Jews, right-wing Revisionists, Mizrahim, and petit-bourgeois Israelis, sees in Netanyahu a champion, and it is they who now largely control Israel's destiny (Pfeffer 2018, 4–5). Indeed, with the support of this coalition behind him, and having vanquished much of the old secular left elite, Netanyahu is today the most important and formidable politician in Israel. Yet Netanyahu is also a product of America, a country in which he lived much of his early life and later worked (Pfeffer 2018, 5). Netanyahu was born in Tel Aviv in 1949. His mother, born in Petah Tikva, a Haredi Jewish settlement near Tel Aviv, was an American citizen, and thus so was Netanyahu (Pfeffer 2018, 48). His father, Benzion Netanyahu, was a historian who, having seen the destruction of Jewish life in Europe during the Holocaust impressed upon his son the "vulnerability of the Jewish people to anti-Semitism" (Shahbari 2021, 34). Netanyahu lived from 1956 to 1958, and then again from 1963 to 1967 in Philadelphia, where his father taught at Dropsie College (Moyer 2015). Netanyahu returned to Israel to serve in the military during the 1967–1970 War of Attrition, fought between Israel and the allied forces of the Palestine Liberation Organisation (PLO), Egypt, and Jordan. He returned to the United States to study at the MIT Sloan School of Management and later worked as a business consultant in Boston (Bishku 2019).

In 1987, following a period working in Israel and later at Israel's embassy in Washington D.C, Netanyahu joined Likud (Pfeffer 2018, 45). He rose quickly through the party ranks and became, in 1993, party chairman. He became prime pinister—the first Israeli prime minister to be born in the State of Israel—in 1996, following the tragic assassination of Yitzhak Rabin and the perceived failure of Shimon Peres to stop Palestinian terrorist attacks against Israeli citizens (Netanyahu 1996). Likud lost power following the 1999 elections, but Netanyahu returned as Finance Minister in the Likud-dominated Sharon government, and returned as party leader in 2006 following the government defeat in elections. Likud won elections in 2009, and Netanyahu became prime minister again, a post he held until Likud was defeated in elections in 2021. After 2021 Netanyahu remained leader of Likud and thus leader of the opposition, with Likud retaining its status as the largest party in the Knesset. During the 2009–2021 period Netanyahu dominated Israeli politics, and the nation was altered forever by his right-wing populist policies and rhetoric. A key component of his discourse throughout this period was populist civilizationalism.

Netanyahu's civilizationalism has two major components. First, he uses the notion that Jewish civilization predates all others in the region to establish the legitimacy of the state of Israel, the hegemony of Jewish culture within Israel, and at times his own political decisions. Second, he describes the Arab-Muslim world as an antisemitic and barbaric bloc that, far from being a civilization, threatens Western civilization. Israel, he argues, is a protective wall that Western civilization requires to defend itself from Muslim barbarians who wish to destroy it, and therefore on this basis Netanyahu calls for Europeans and North Americans to support Israel in its battle for civilization and against the forces of barbarism. Combined, these narratives serve to assist Netanyahu in his populist division of Israeli society into three antagonistic groups: 'the people', the 'elite', and 'others'. In Netanyahu's discourse 'others' are non-civilized Arab-Muslims who wish to destroy the Jewish people and Western civilization; "elites" are left-wing parties and liberal Jews who Netanyahu portrays as abandoning Jewish culture and helping Arabs destroy civilization; "the People" are all the Jewish people, who are authentic and morally good: authentic because their ancestors were the first people of the land, and morally good because they are civilized Jews.

Archaeology has long been an instrument through which the Israeli political actors have sought to legitimize the nation and, in some cases,

Jewish settlement in Palestinian territories (Desjarlais 2013; Greenberg 2007, 2009, 2021). Desjarlais, for example, argues that "archaeological practice in Palestine/Israel is part of a spatial and temporal project that serves to produce a continuous link between the ancient Israelite past and the modern Israeli nation-state, justifying the creation of the Israeli state by reference to the past and through familiar frontier myths". Archaeological practice in Israel, then, brings together two key civilizational narratives: first, that the Jewish people uniquely and solely belong to the Land of Israel due to an ancestral and cultural connection to ancient Jewish civilization; and second, the frontier narrative that asserts that the Jewish people brought civilization to Israel, which was in a state of barbarism before their arrival.

Chief among the political groups who use archaeology to legitimize Jewish hegemony is the Ir David Foundation, known as Elad in Hebrew, which finances digs across the Old City of Jerusalem. Elad wishes to uncover proof of ancient Jewish civilization in Jerusalem through various projects including the controversial 'City of David' archaeological park, and the Temple Mount Sifting Project, a project funded by the (The Times of Israel 2017; The Palestinian Chronicle 2016). The purpose of this project is to establish the Temple Mount area as a historically Jewish area and to deny any connection between Palestinians and the Old City of Jerusalem. The 'City of David' is an archaeological site located on a spur south of the Temple Mount and just outside the walls of the Old City (Greenberg 2009). The term 'City of David' is derived from "a biblical epithet, 'ir david' (II Samuel 5:9), that appears to indicate David's citadel rather than the city as such" and "can be attributed to French archaeologist, Raymond Weill, who mounted the first open-area excavations on the south-east spur in 1913–1914, on land acquired for the purpose by Baron Edmond de Rothschild (Weill 1920, 1947)" (Greenberg 2009, 38). The identification of the site as the City of David appears to be, in part, politically motivated. Greenberg (2009, 37), for example, observes that 'City of David' was "rarely employed in the literature; excavators generally preferred 'Ophel', another biblical term that appears to refer to the northernmost part of the spur". Rather, there has been, according to Greenberg (2009, 38), a deliberate sanctification of the site, a "secular and political sanctification, and as such its character and content are open to reinterpretation to a far greater extent than is the case with holy places proper, where the authority for the validation of historical claims is embedded in a chain of command that resists academic scrutiny".

The most important of the Ir David Foundation's activities is the running of a large archaeological park in Jerusalem which encompassed the 'City of David' site, a task which is part of their overall strategy of connecting contemporary Jews with their ancient Biblical roots, and encouraging Jewish settlement in Palestinian areas so as to Judaize the area. While the Ir David Foundation did not originally run the archaeological park, the group took on the role shortly after the beginning of the intifada. It is perhaps curious that the Israeli government of the day should have given a Jewish NGO run by a militant settler group the task of running what is essentially a national park. Since taking control of the park, the Ir David Foundation has used its power to promote "a new, powerful narrative exploiting to the hilt the biblical and Jewish connotations of the site (and excluding almost every other viewpoint)" and has since 1994 "underwritten several excavations—including, most recently, that of the purported palace of King David (Mazar 2006)—the results of which have been recruited to enhance the presentation of Jewish continuity" (Greenberg 2009, 41). The foundation does not merely engage in archaeological digging and preservation in the City of David park, but "purchases homes in the surrounding Arab village of Silwan—sometimes via Muslim middle men—and rents them to Jews, a move that has led to charges that he is fueling tensions in the city" (The Times of Israel 2017). Today, the Ir David Foundation's website describes the City of David site in a manner that gives the reader the impression that only Jewish people ever inhabited the area. For example, the website's 'about us' page reads:

> The story of the City of David began over 3,000 years ago, when King David left the city of Hebron for a small hilltop city known as Jerusalem, establishing it as the unified capital of the tribes of Israel. Years later, David's son, King Solomon, built the First Temple next to the City of David on top of Mount Moriah, the site of the binding of Isaac, and with it, this hilltop became one of the most important sites in the world.
> Today, the story of the City of David continues. Deep underground, the City of David is revealing some of the most exciting archeological finds of the ancient world. While above ground, the city is a vibrant center of activity with a visitor's center that welcomes visitors for an exciting tour to the site where much of the Bible was written. (City of David 2022)

The Ir David Foundation's founder, David Be 'eri, was awarded in 2017 the "Israel Prize for lifetime achievement". Then education Minister in the fourth Netanyahu government Naftali Bennett announced the award, and called Be'eri "one of the greatest builders of Jerusalem during the modern era" (The Times of Israel 2017). This was despite—or perhaps because of—the Ir Foundation's role in supporting Jewish settlements in Arab areas and if not falsifying than perhaps misinterpreting for political reasons the archaeological record (Greenberg 2009).

One of the Ir David Foundation's projects involves sifting soil on the sensitive Temple Mount area sacred to all three Abrahamic faiths. According to the Temple Mount Sifting Project website, the project "is under the auspices of Bar-Ilan University, and is funded by private donors through the Israel Archaeology Foundation. The sifting activity operated during the years 2005–2017 at the Emek Tzurim national park with the cooperation and funding of the Ir-David foundation. On June 2019 the sifting facility moved to the Masu'ot Lookout with generous support from American Friends of Beit Orot" (Temple Mount Sifting Project 2022). While the project may do good work in uncovering the ancient and medieval history of the area, the involvement of the Ir David Foundation is a sign that the project may be used to create an impression of continuous Jewish presence in the area and portray Palestinians as inauthentic.

In 2016, when funds for the project began to run out, then Prime Minister Netanyahu intervened and used taxpayers' money to continue the project (Haaretz 2016). When UNESCO was critical of the project for politicizing the historical record and essentially Judaizing the Temple Mount, Netanyahu used the occasion to defend the project and, in what he called a "crushing response" to the United Nations body's denial of Jewish history, announced that his government would fund the project to ensure that its work continued (Haaretz 2016). In this way, Netanyahu and his government were using the Ir David Foundation and perhaps politicized archaeologists to promote the narrative that the Temple Mount belongs to the Jewish people, and that Arabs and others are mere newcomers who have no rights to the area. An example of the manner in which Netanyahu has used archaeological discoveries for political propaganda purposes is well described by Shimon Amit, who notes how

> even a simple discovery can trigger the national propaganda machine. For instance, in September, 2013, [Israeli archaeologist Eilat] Mazar announced that her expedition at the Ophel, a site located between the Temple Mount and the City of David, had found gold treasure from the

late Byzantine period (around the 7th century CE). The treasure includes a gold medallion with images of a menorah (the national symbol of the state of Israel), a shofar, and a Torah scroll, and it immediately became a major topic in the news (Reinstein 2013; Hasson 2013b). The news reports on the discovery were followed by the usual talkbacks about the Jewish right to the land and the Palestinian fiction. Right wing Prime Minister Benjamin Netanyahu called Mazar and congratulated her. The Israel Ministry of Foreign Affairs published the discovery, as it usually does in cases of archaeological finds that relate to Jewish history in Israel. According to the publication, Netanyahu said to Mazar: This is a magnificent discovery. Nationally, it attests to the ancient Jewish presence and to the sanctity of the place; this is as clear as the sun and it is tremendous… This is historic testimony, of the highest order, to the Jewish people's link to Jerusalem, to its land and to its heritage. (Amit 2022, 43)

Amit (2022, 44) also observes how "on November 17, 2013, Naftali Bennett, Economy Minister and leader of The Jewish Home party that represents the religious right wing and the settlers, gave an interview to the CNN". When asked about the settlements in the occupied territories, he waved an ancient coin and told Christiane Amanpour: "this coin, which says 'Freedom of Zion' in Hebrew, was used by Jews 2,000 years ago in the state of Israel, in what you call occupied. One cannot occupy his own home". These examples serve to show how Israeli right-wing politicians, and especially Netanyahu, use archaeological finds to buttress and promote their narrative that the Land of Israel belongs solely to the Jewish people.

Second, civilizationalism is used to legitimize his rule and policies by portraying Islam as a non-civilization bent on destroying the Jewish people and Europeans—civilization. Jewish settlers bring civilization to an empty or barbaric land. This takes two different forms. The first is the 'frontier' narrative, in which Israel is described as a barbarous land which the Jewish people, upon their establishing of the State of Israel, tamed and turned into a paradise. One cannot deny the achievements of the Israeli people since 1948, who defended their new state from a large-scale Arab invasion, and created a modern economy in a relatively short period. However, the frontier myth denies the existence of Palestinian history in the region, and portrays them as non-civilized and unimportant people who were essentially squatting on Jewish land (Desjarlais 2013). According to Desjarlais (2013), "Like other nationalist movements, the Israeli national narrative seeks to construct a shared history (although only for its Jewish population), develop a myth of origin that traces the roots of the modern nation to noble forbearers, and describe the development of the nation's history in terms of a 'golden age' and a 'dark age' when the nation was ruled by foreigners". This myth incorporates, she argues (citing the work of John Coakley on this subject) (2004), "the idea that the nation is entitled to reestablish the greatness of the golden age by re-conquering territory it once held" (Desjarlais 2013). For example, as Desjarlais notes (2013), the partially government funded Jewish National Fund's website describes British mandate era Palestine as "fallen", "empty", "godforsaken land", and moreover a "desolate place" consisting of "barren hills and abandoned rocks", while the early Zionist settlers are described as "pioneers of the State" responsible for "agricultural and botanical miracles" and "triumph" over the "neglect" of the previous 2000 years. Put simply, the myth of Israel involves claims that the establishing of the State of Israel made the desert bloom (George 1979).

The discourse of Netanyahu reflects this notion that before Jewish settlement the Land of Israel was in a barbaric state. Netanyahu has stated that the Jewish people "have literally made the desert bloom, building a vibrant and dynamic hi-tech economy. We have built a robust and healthy democracy, where freedom is sacrosanct and human rights enshrined in our laws for all" (Netanyahu 2015). Equally, Netanyahu contrasts Jewish success and civilization with Arab failure and barbarism. Repeating 'clash of civilizations' rhetoric is important to Netanyahu, and is used to both garner sympathy for Israel and support from Western countries affected by Islamist terrorism. Yet Netanyahu explicitly rejects the notion of a clash of civilizations, but instead claims that there is a clash between Western civilization and the uncivilized barbarism of "radical Islam". For example, in a speech to the UN General Assembly condemning Iran Netanyahu (2009) claimed that.

> History has shown us time and again that what starts with attacks on the Jews eventually ends up engulfing many others. This Iranian regime is fueled by an extreme fundamentalism that burst onto the world scene three decades ago after lying dormant for centuries. In the past thirty years, this fanaticism has swept the globe with a murderous violence and cold-blooded impartiality in its choice of victims. It has callously slaughtered Moslems and Christians, Jews and Hindus, and many others. Though it is comprised of different offshoots, the adherents of this unforgiving creed

seek to return humanity to medieval times. Wherever they can, they impose a backward regimented society where women, minorities, gays, or anyone not deemed to be a true believer is brutally subjugated. The struggle against this fanaticism does not pit faith against faith nor civilization against civilization. It pits civilization against barbarism, the 21st century against the 9th century, those who sanctify life against those who glorify death. The primitivism of the 9th century ought to be no match for the progress of the 21st century.

In a 2016 press conference in Berlin with then German Chancellor Angela Merkel, Netanyahu called Israel "the protective wall of western civilization" (EFE, 2016). Israel, Netanyahu appears to suggest, protects the West from Jihadist violence, which is instead focused on Israel. By defending itself from Islamic radicals, Netanyahu suggests, Israel is also defending Western values in a region in which they are threatened by barbarism and primitivism. Indeed, Netanyahu's responses to Islamist terror incidents in Europe serve as an example of his civilizationalism, and indeed of the civilizationalism unique to Israel. The murder of four French Jews in a Hypercacher Kosher supermarket in Paris prompted Netanyahu to first demand that the French and moreover the European Union "wake up" to the threat of Islamist terrorism and act to protect "our common civilization" (The New York Times 2015). However, at the same time he also, as political economist and commentator Bernard Avishai points out, called on Jews to "self-segregate: affirm, in principle, the liberal values of the West, but deny that they ever worked well enough for diaspora Jews; insist that we fight for our freedoms from our own ground" (The New York Times 2015). Thus for Netanyahu the Jewish people are perhaps half in and half out of Western civilization. One the one hand, Israel is a modern European-style democratic nation-state which protects individual rights, and therefore part of Western civilization. But on the other hand the Jewish people cannot trust anyone but themselves to protect Jewish lives, and therefore they must self-segregate in the land of their ancestors and reject core elements of Western-style liberal democracy such as religious pluralism and equal rights for all.

In a 2022 interview, Netanyahu claimed "there is a constant battle between the forces of modernity and the forces of medievalism. That's what we face today in the Middle East facing militant Islam. Facing militant Islam is only not only Israel, but many of our Arab neighbors will understand that their future also could be compromised and endangered and crushed by these forces that hark back to a very dark past. So I would say that you can continue to move the arc forward… the arch forward, if you have the necessary will and power to protect civilization and to nurture it, but it could easily be wiped away by larger forces" (Netanyahu 2022). In the same interview, he praised Winston Churchill, saying "Churchill's worldview as I see it, was not simply that he was belonging to the British empire, was a nineteenth-century example of a patriot of the British empire. I think it was more than that. I think his was a civilizational… he had a civilizational view" (Netanyahu 2022).

Here again Netanyahu describes his enemies as non-civilized Islamist radicals, and frames Israel's self-defense as a defense of civilization. Moreover, he appears to also claim that he, like Churchill, sees the world through a civilizational lens, and is defending civilization from its enemies. The notion that Israel represents civilization in a battle against barbarism is a hallmark, according to Tuastad (2003) and Linklater (2020), of the neo-Orientalism and neo-barbarism discourses which became mainstream in the United States after the 9/11 attacks. Yet the "civilizational portrayal" of Israel as an "outpost" of Western civilization is often "embraced by Israel's detractors and supporters alike" (Slabodsky 2014, 147). For example, Zionism as a project sought to give the Jewish people a homeland, but used the European colonial model as the basis of a Jewish state. Thus, nineteenth and early twentieth century style European colonialism in the form of Zionism "was applied in its extreme in the 1940s and since at least the 1970s has reinforced systemic patterns of domination and ultimately naturalized the Jewish state as a Western outpost against barbarism" (Slabodsky 2014, 146). In constructing their own European-style state, Slabodsky (2014, 157) argues, the Zionists were seeking to overcome their status as barbarians within Western civilization by becoming members of a "civilized nation among civilized nations" like "any other Western people". In doing so, Slabodsky (2014) suggests, they inadvertently replicated the barbaric-civilized dichotomy within Israel, turning the Palestinians into barbarians and themselves into civilized Westerners. And this may account for the readiness, all geopolitical considerations aside, for Netanyahu's readiness to affirm Israel's place within Western civilization and as a civilized outpost in a barbaric region, but also the unique nature of Israel as a homeland for the persecuted Jewish people.

Israeli Jews sympathetic to the Palestinian cause are portrayed by Netanyahu as traitors and part "of the allegedly "anti-patriotic" left, which favors Israel's enemies over the "people" (Rogenhofer and Panievsky 2020). For example, according to Rogenhofer and Ayala Panievsky (2020) "during the 2015 elections the Likud aired television ads showcasing a fictional support group meeting where unionists, public broadcasters and *Hamas* terrorists comfort one another against Netanyahu. When Netanyahu enters the frame, the slogan 'It is Us or Them'—the prime motto of divisive populism—appears, underscoring Netanyahu's willingness to take on these 'enemies of the people' directly". Thus if Hamas is part of the enemies of civilization, then so too are the Israeli left and other Jewish people who oppose Netanyahu's support for Jewish settlements and other forms of oppression and dispossession of the Palestinians.

7.4 Discussion of Case Study

Based on this chapter, we find that Netanyahu's populist civilizationalism contains two key elements. First, he claims that Jewish civilization predates all others in the region, a claim used to establish the legitimacy of the state of Israel, the hegemony of Jewish culture within Israel, and at times his own political decisions. Second, he portrays the Arab-Muslim world as an anti-Semitic and barbaric group of peoples who wish to destroy not only Israel but broader Western civilization. Israel, according to Netanyahu, is protecting the West from Arab-Muslim barbarism by acting as a shield, or first defense against those who wish to end Western civilization including Israel. Thus, according to Netanyahu Israel's 'old elite'—the Ashkenazi secular leftists who oppose Netanyahu and Likud, and often seek peace with the Palestinians and a Palestinian state—are on the side of the barbarians who wish to destroy Israel and civilization. Combining these elements into a single narrative, Netanyahu divides Israeli society into three antagonistic groups: 'the people', the 'elite', and 'others'. Inside this narrative the 'others' are non-civilized Arab-Muslims who wish to destroy the Jewish people and Western civilization; "elites" are left-wing parties and liberal Jews who Netanyahu portrays as abandoning Jewish culture and helping Arabs destroy civilization; "the People" are all the Jewish people, who are authentic and morally good.

The authenticity of the Jewish people is proven by archaeological digs and DNA testing, techniques which also, according to Netanyahu, prove the Palestinians to be inauthentic and essentially invaders in a genuinely Jewish land. Furthermore, the Jewish people are encouraged to perceive themselves as victims of Palestinian, Arab, and Muslim aggression. In Netanyahu's discourse, the Jewish people have the sole right to live in the Land of Israel, and all others must accept their hegemony. When Palestinians resist, sometimes violently, Netanyahu and Likud characterize their actions as unfair attacks on the Jewish people and a product not of a conflict over land, but of anti-Semitism and barbarism.

Netanyahu's civilizationalism is somewhat different to the other civilizationalisms we have described in this book. For example, Netanyahu is not always precise about the civilization to which Israel belongs. He places Israel within, at times, Western civilization. Yet this is most often done when before a European audience, and perhaps designed to encourage them to increase support for Israel. Or, at other times, to portray the Israeli-Palestinian conflict as both a continuation of age-old anti-Semitism and as a part of the broader problem of Islamist terrorism in Europe. Yet he also calls for Jews to move to Israel, and relies on archaeological digs to prove that Jewish civilization pre-dated Arab civilization, and uses this information to justify the dispossession of the Palestinians which he portrays as the rightful returning of Jews to their homeland. Equally, unlike some of the other civilizational populist parties we have examined, there is not a strong transnational element to Likud and Netanyahu's civilizationalism, for the obvious reasons that Israel is the only majority Jewish nation, and the overall global Jewish population is vastly lower than any of the other major ancient faiths. However, Netanyahu has sought to center Israel at the core of Jewish life and culture insofar as he calls for Jews everywhere to return to Israel on the grounds that they are unsafe outside the nation. Equally, he has attempted to incorporate Israel into broader Judeo-Christian civilization, and in this way encourage Europeans and Americans, and in particular Christian Zionists, to support Israel in its conflict with the Palestinians and Iran.

By situating Israel within Judeo-Christian civilization, Netanyahu is able to 'other' Palestinians who resist Israeli oppression and portray them as barbaric and uncivilized enemies of Judeo-Christian civilization, and morally equivalent to Islamist terrorists who murder Jews and others in Europe. This creates a sense of crisis in Israel, in which Israel is perceived to be surrounded on all sides by anti-Semites who wish to destroy the country. At the same time, Netanyahu tells Jews in Europe that they are not safe on the continent, and that they ought to return to their ancestral homeland, rhetoric designed to further increase the sense of fear and crisis among Jewish people. Of course, one cannot dismiss claims of anti-Semitism, a genuine evil which refuses to disappear. However, Netanyahu's claims are sometimes hyperbolic and motivated by a desire to increase the Jewish population of Israel. Equally, they are part of an attempt to construct a sense of crisis from which he and his party profits, and through which he attempts to find greater support from North American and European nations such as France and the United States that have suffered Islamist terror attacks.

The rise of Likud since the late 1970s and emergence of Netanyahu as the most powerful and influential politician of his generation has had a lasting and powerful effect on Israel and on the Palestinians. Likud has successfully ended the hegemony of the Israeli left and Labor Party, and paved the way for an Israel that is increasingly religious and right-wing, and which increasingly perceives Arabs and Muslims as dangerous enemies of civilization. (See Table 7.1 and Table 7.2.)

Table 7.1 Likud/Netanyahu Judaist populist case study

	Pro-Violent Narratives	*Links or Overlaps with the Far Right*	*Transnational Dimension, Diasporas*
Likud/Netanyahu	- Dispossession of Palestinians is justified by Jewish ownership of the Land of Israel - Police-military violence against Palestinians is necessary to protect Israel and civilization from barbaric Islamic radicals	- Support for Jewish settler groups, Ir David Foundation - Receives support from right-wing Christian Zionist groups in the United States	- Calls for Jewish diaspora to return home to Israel, and to encourage them to support Israel and to feel fearful when living outside of Israel

Table 7.2 Populism in Likud/Netanyahu Politics

	Populist division/Identity	Crisis	Civilizationalism	Victimhood
Likud/Netanyahu	- "The people": All the Jewish people - "The others": secular Ashkenazi Jews of the old leftist elite who are Blamed for economic inequality and castigated for their sympathy toward Palestinians -Arabs and Muslims, who are non-civilized and barbaric anti-Semites who wish to destroy Israel	-Arab-Muslim world and Iran wish to destroy Israel	-Israel is both the heir to ancient Jewish civilization and a part of contemporary Judeo-Christian civilization. The Land of Israel belongs solely to the Jewish people, and this is proven by archaeological digs and DNA testing -Israel is a "protective wall" which defends Judeo-Christian civilization from barbaric Islamic radicals	Three dimensions are as follows - "The elite": the powerful secular people in Israel who have created an economic system that does not allow for equal opportunity -Liberal and secular left-wing Jews of the 'old elite' who refuse to defend Israel against the Palestinians and Iranians -Palestinians are terrorists and anti-Semites who attack Jews despite and refuse to acknowledge the Jewish people as the true owners of the Land of Israel

References

Amit, Shimon. 2022. "Israel vs. Judah, 2022: The Socio-Political Aspects of Biblical Archaeology in Contemporary Israel". DAMQATUM—THE CEHAO NEWSLETTER N. 17 2021. pp. 30–74. https://www.academia.edu/72009173/Israel_vs_Judah_2022_The_Socio_Political_Aspects_of_Biblical_Archaeology_in_Contemporary_Israel. Last accessed September 21, 2022.

Bagaini, Anna. 2019. "The Origins of Right-Wing Populism in Israel: Peace Process and Collective Identities' Struggle." *Panel Paper presented at The Populism-Identity* https://ecpr.eu/Events/Event/PaperDetails/47201. Last accessed September 21, 2022.

BBC News. 19 July 2018. "Jewish Nation State: Israel Approves Controversial Bill." https://www.bbc.com/news/world-middle-east-44881554. Last accessed September 21, 2022.

Ben-Porat, Guy. 2000. In a State of Holiness. *Alternatives* 25: 223–246. https://doi.org/10.1177/030437540002500203.

Ben-Porat, Guy, Dani Filc, Ahmet Erdi Ozturk, and Luca Ozzano. 2021. Populism, Religion and Family Values Policies in Israel, Italy and Turkey, *Mediterranean Politics*. doi: https://doi.org/10.1080/13629395.2021.1901484.

Berry, Mike, and Greg Philo. 2006. *Israel and Palestine: Competing Histories*. Pluto Press.www.jstor.org/stable/j.ctt18fsc8f.

Bishku, M.B. 2019. Are Turkey's Recep Tayyip Erdoğan and Israel's Benjamin Netanyahu "Two Sides of the Same Coin"? *Journal of South Asian and Middle Eastern Studies* 43(1): 57–87. https://doi.org/10.1353/jsa.2019.0000.

C1. Pm Benjamin Netanyahu, Speech to the Un General Assembly, New York, 24 September 2009 (Excerpts). (2010). *Journal of Palestine Studies, 39*(2): 208–210. https://doi.org/10.1525/jps.2010.xxxix.2.208.

City of David. 2022. https://www.cityofdavid.org.il/en/The-Ir-David-Foundation. Last accessed September 21, 2022.

Coakley, John. 2004. Mobilizing the Past: Nationalist Images of History. *Nationalism and Ethnic Politics* 10 (1): 531–560. https://doi.org/10.1080/13537110490900340.

Desjarlais, Peige (2013) "Excavating Zion: Archaeology and Nation-making in Palestine/Israel," *Totem: The University of Western Ontario Journal of Anthropology*, 21 (2). https://ir.lib.uwo.ca/totem/vol21/iss1/2.

DellaPergola, Sergio. 2019. "World Jewish Population, 2019". In *The American Jewish Year Book*, 2019. Ed. Arnold Dashefsky and Ira M. Sheskin, Volume 119. Cham, Switzerland: Springer. https://www.jewishdatabank.org/content/upload/bjdb/2019_World_Jewish_Population_(AJYB,_DellaPergola)_DataBank_Final.pdf. Last accessed September 21, 2022.

ECPS. Last updated 2020. "Israel". https://www.populismstudies.org/tag/isr ael/. Last accessed September 21, 2022.
EFE. 2016. "Netanyahu says Israel Protective Wall of Western Civilization in Middle East". 16 February 2016. https://www.efe.com/efe/english/world/netanyahu-says-israel-protective-wall-of-western-civilization-in-middle-east/50000262-2841545. Last accessed September 21, 2022.
Ferziger AS. 2020. Israelization and Lived Religion: Conflicting Accounts of Contemporary Judaism. 40 (3): 403–430. https://doi.org/10.1007/s12397-020-09324-4. Epub 2020 Jun 2. PMID: 32836551; PMCID: PMC7265156.
Filc, Dani. 2016. 'We are the (Chosen) People, you are not' The Case of Shas Populism. In *Saving the People: How Populists Hijack Religion*. Eds. by Nadia Marzouki, Duncan McDonnell and Olivier Roy. London: C. Hurst & Co.
Filc, Dani. 2009. "Radicalization of Inclusion, Radicalization of Exclusion: The Shas Party". In *The Political Right in Israel*. London: Routledge.
Fischer, Sholom. 2014. "Two Orthodox Cultures: "Centrist" Orthodoxy and Religious Zionism". In *Reconsidering Israel-Diaspora Relations*. Leiden, The Netherlands: Brill. https://doi.org/10.1163/9789004277076_00.
George, A. 1979. "Making the Desert Bloom" A Myth Examined. *Journal of Palestine Studies* 8 (2): 88–100. https://doi.org/10.2307/2536511.
Ghanem, As' ad, and Khatib, Ibrahim. 2017. "The Nationalisation of the Israeli Ethnocratic Regime and the Palestinian Minority's Shrinking Citizenship".*Citizenship Studies* 21 (8): 89–902. https://doi.org/10.1080/13621025.2017.1380651.
Greenberg, Raphael. 2007. CONTESTED SITES: ARCHAEOLOGY AND THE BATTLE FOR JERUSALEM. *Jewish Quarterly* 54 (4): 20–26. doi: https://doi.org/10.1080/0449010X.2007.10706295.
Greenburg, Raphael. 2009. Towards an Inclusive Archaeology in Jerusalem: The Case of Silwan/The City of David. *Public Archaeology* 8 (1): 35–50. https://doi.org/10.1179/175355309X402745.
Greenberg, Raphael. 2021. Pompeo in Silwan: Judeo-Christian Nationalism, Kitsch, and Empire in Ancient Jerusalem. Forum Kritische Archäologie 10: 55–66. URL http://www.kritischearchaeologie.de DOI ISSN 2194–346X. https://doi.org/10.17169/refubium-3095.
Haaretz. 2016. ""Amid UNESCO Flap, Israel Will Sponsor Rightist NGO's Temple Mount Project". October 21, 2016. https://www.haaretz.com/israel-news/2016-10-21/ty-article/.premium/after-unesco-flap-israel-to-fund-ngos-temple-mount-project/0000017f-e0a4-d804-ad7f-f1fe75220000. Last accessed September 21, 2022.
Halbfinger, M. David and Kershner, Isabel. 19 July 2018. "Israeli Law Declares the Country the 'Nation-State of the Jewish People'". *The New York Times*. https://www.nytimes.com/2018/07/19/world/middleeast/israel-law-jews-arabic.html. Last accessed September 21, 2022.

Hasson, Nir. 9 September 2013b. "Ancient Golden Treasure Trove Found at Foot of Jerusalem's Temple Mount." *Haaretz.co.il*.. English version available at http://www.haaretz.com/archaeology/.premium-1.545965. Last accessed January 1, 2023.

Hassan, S. Shamir. 1998. "DEVELOPMENT OF ZIONIST IDEOLOGY." *Proceedings of The Indian History Congress* 59: 924–933. www.jstor.org/stable/44147065.

Haynes, Jeffrey. 2020. "Trump and the Politics of International Religious Freedom." *Religions* 11 (8): 385. https://doi.org/10.3390/rel11080385.

Jerusalem Post. 2019a. "Netanyahu: Archaeology, DNA Prove Palestinians not Native to Land of Israel". July 7, 2019. https://www.jpost.com/arab-israeli-conflict/netanyahu-archaeology-dna-prove-palestinians-not-native-to-land-of-israel-594872. Last accessed September 21, 2022.

Jerusalem Post. 2021. "Palestinian Statehood would be a 'Terrible Mistake'—Bennett". 15 September, 2021. https://www.jpost.com/israel-news/bennett-palestinian-statehood-would-be-a-terrible-mistake-679518. Last accessed September 21, 2022.

Julius Maximilian Rogenhofer & Ayala Panievsky. 2020. Antidemocratic Populism in Power: Comparing Erdoğan's Turkey with Modi's India and Netanyahu's Israel. *Democratization* 27 (8): 1394–1412. https://doi.org/10.1080/13510347.2020.1795135.

Juliusand, Rogenhofer M., and Ayala Panievsky. 2020. Antidemocraticpopulism in Power: Comparing Erdoğan's Turkey with Modi's India and Netanyahu's Israel. *Democratization*. https://doi.org/10.1080/13510347.2020.1795135.

Linklater, Andrew. 2020. 'The Return of Discourses of Civilization and Barbarism' , *The Idea of Civilization and the Making of the Global Order* (Bristol, 2020; online edn, Policy Press Scholarship Online , 20 May 2021), https://doi.org/10.1332/policypress/9781529213874.003.0002, Last accessed September 7, 2022.

Levi, Yonatan, and Shai Agmon. 2020. "Beyond Culture and Economy: Israel's Security-Driven Populism". *Contemporary Politics* 26.

Mazar, Eilat. 2006. Did I find King David's palace? *The Biblical archaeology review* 32 (1). https://www.biblicalarchaeology.org/daily/biblical-topics/hebrew-bible/did-i-find-king-davids-palace/. Last accessed January 1, 2023.

Moyer, Justin. 2015. "Why Benjamin Netanyahu is so tough: He's from Philadelphia". *The Washington Post*. https://www.washingtonpost.com/news/morning-mix/wp/2015/03/03/why-benjamin-netanyahu-is-so-tough-hes-from-philadelphia/. Last accessed September 21, 2022.

Nathan, Emmanueland Topolski, Anya Eds. 2016. *Is There a Judeo-Christian Tradition? A European Perspective*. Berlin and Boston: DeGruyter.

Netanyahu, Benjamin. 2015. "PM Netanyahu's Greeting for Independence Day 2015". Consulate General of Israel to the Mid-Atlantic. https://embassies.gov.il/philadelphia/NewsAndEvents/Pages/PM-Netanyahu's-Greeting-for-Independence-Day-2015-.aspx. Last accessed September 21, 2022.

Netanyahu, Benjamin. 1996. The Presentation of the Israeli Government to the Knesset. *Vital Speeches of the Day* 62 (19): 578.

Netanyahu, Benjamin. 2022. "Secrets Of Statecraft: The Historical Heritage Of Bibi Netanyahu". Hoover Institution.https://www.hoover.org/research/secrets-statecraft-historical-heritage-bibi-netanyahu. Last accessed September 21, 2022.

Nevo, N., Verbov, D. (2011). Hebrew Language in Israel and the Diaspora. In International Handbook of Jewish Education. *International Handbooks of Religion and Education*, Eds. Miller, H., Grant, L., Pomson, A. 5. Springer, Dordrecht. https://doi.org/10.1007/978-94-007-0354-4_25.

Pfeffer, A., 2018. *Bibi: The Turbulent Life and Times of Benjamin Netanyahu*. Oxford University Press.

Pinson, Halleli. 2021. Neo Zionist Right-Wing Populist Discourse and Activism in the Israel Education System. *Globalisation, Societies and Education*. https://doi.org/10.1080/14767724.2021.1872372.

Porat, B. Guy., and Dani Filc. 2020. Remember to be Jewish: Religious Populism in Israel. *Politics and Religion* 1–24. https://doi.org/10.1017/S175504832 0000681.

Raz-Krakotzkin, Amnon. 2000. "Rabin's Legacy: On Secularism, Nationalism and Orientalism." In *Contested Memory: Myth, Nationalism and Democracy*. Eds. Grinberg, L. Beersheba. Humphrey Institute: Ben-Gurion University.

Reinstein, Ziv. 9 September 2013. "Gold Treasure Including a Model of Menorah was Discovered Near Temple Mount." *Ynet.co.il.*. Available at http://www.ynet.co.il/articles/0,7340,L-4427447,00.html. Last accessed January 1, 2023.

Safran, William. 2005. Language and Nation-building in Israel: Hebrew and its Rivals. *Nations and Nationalism* 11 (1): 43–63. https://doi.org/10.1111/j.1354-5078.2005.00191.x.

Shahbari, Ilham. Sept. 2021. Israel Takes Stock: The Legacy of Benjamin Netanyahu. *Political Insight* 12 (3): 34–36. https://doi.org/10.1177/20419058211045146.

Shumsky, Dmitry. 2018. "Theodor Herzl: A Non-Jewish State of Jews". In *Beyond the Nation-State*. New Haven: Yale University Press. https://doi.org/10.12987/9780300241099-004.

Shain, Yossi. *Ha-me'ah ha-Yisraelit: Ha-Yisraelizaziyah shel ha-Yahadut*. Tel Aviv: Yedioth Ahronoth; 2019.

Slabodsky, Santiago. 2014. *Decolonial Judaism Triumphal Failures of Barbaric Thinking*. New York: Palgrave Macmillan.

Solomon, Erika. 25 March 2010. "FEATURE - Researchers dig up controversy in Jerusalem." *Reuters*. https://www.reuters.com/article/idINIndia-471825 20100324. Last accessed January 1, 2023.

Temple Mount Sifting Project. 2022. https://tmsifting.org/en/brief-introduct ion-to-the-project/. Last accessed September 21, 2022.

The New York Times. 2015. "Netanyahu Sells French Jews Short". 16 January, 2015. https://www.nytimes.com/2015/01/16/opinion/netanyahu-sells-fre nch-jews-short.html. Last accessed September 21, 2022.

The Times of Israel. 2017. "Controversial 'builder' of Jewish East Jerusalem awarded Israel Prize". Sue Surkes. 16 March 2017. https://www.timesofis rael.com/builder-of-jewish-east-jerusalem-awarded-israel-prize/. Last accessed September 21, 2022.

Tuastad, Dag. (2003). Neo-Orientalism and the New Barbarism Thesis: Aspects of Symbolic Violence in the Middle East Conflict(s). *Third World Quarterly*, 24 (4): 591–599. http://www.jstor.org/stable/3993426.

Yilmaz, Ihsan, Nicholas Morieson, and Mustafa Demir. 2021. Exploring Religions in Relation to Populism: A Tour Around the World. *Religions* 12: 301. https://doi.org/10.3390/rel12050301/.

Yilmaz, Ihsan and Morieson, Nicholas. 2021. "A Systematic Literature Review of Populism, Religion and Emotions". *Religions* 12 (4): 272. https://doi.org/10.3390/rel12040272

Yilmaz, Ihsan and Morieson, Nicholas. 2022. *Religious populism in Israel: The case of Shas*. European Center for Populism Studies (ECPS). Brussels, Belgium. doi: https://doi.org/10.55271/pp0011.

Zúquete, P. Jose. 2017. "Populism and Religion". In *The Oxford Handbook of Populism*. Eds. Cristóbal Rovira Kaltwasser, Paul Taggart, Paulina Ochoa Espejo, and Pierre Ostiguy. Oxford University Press. doi: https://doi.org/10.1093/oxfordhb/9780198803560.013.22.

CHAPTER 8

Predicament of Civilizational Populism

8.1 Conclusions

Based on our case studies, we believe that it is possible to define civilizational populism as a group of ideas that together considers that politics should be an expression of the volonté générale (general will) of the people, and society to be ultimately separated into two homogenous and antagonistic groups, 'the pure people' versus 'the corrupt elite' who collaborate with the dangerous others belonging to other civilizations that are hostile and present a clear and present danger to the civilization and way of life of the pure people. Our definition of civilizational populism takes into account the fact that the idea of civilizationalism is the essential core in this type of populism, and is used to define populism's key signifiers in primarily civilizational terms. Civilizational populism is not, the preceding chapters show, a European and North American Christianity-based phenomenon, but evident in a variety of societies and religious contexts, including in the world's most followed religious traditions (Yilmaz and Morieson 2022a).[1]

---

[1] This chapter contains material adapted from Yilmaz, Ihsan, and Nicholas Morieson. 2022b. Religious Populisms in the Asia Pacific. Religions 13: 802. https://doi.org/10.3390/rel13090802.

© The Author(s), under exclusive license to Springer Nature Singapore Pte Ltd. 2023
I. Yilmaz and N. Morieson, *Religions and the Global Rise of Civilizational Populism*, Palgrave Studies in Populisms,
https://doi.org/10.1007/978-981-19-9052-6_8

How, then, do populists across the world, and in a variety of different religious, geographic, and political contexts, incorporate ideas of 'civilization' into their discourses? Civilizationalism, when incorporated into populism, helps define populism's key signifiers: 'the pure people', 'the corrupt elite', and 'dangerous 'others'. In each case study examined in this book, populists have been shown to use a civilization-based classification of peoples to draw boundaries around 'the people', 'elites', and 'others'. In civilizational populism 'the people' are pure, good, and authentic because they belong to a civilization which is itself superior to and more moral than all others, and which created the nation and culture which populists 'defend'. Conversely, in civilizational populism elites are described in narrative as having betrayed 'the people' insofar as they rejected the religion, culture, values, and identity that shaped and were shaped by their civilization. Equally, in each case we studied, civilizational populists described religious minorities as 'dangerous' others who are morally bad insofar as they belonged to an inferior religion and thus to an inferior civilization. The precise nature of these civilizational, victimhood, and crisis narratives differs in each form of civilizational populism. However, in each case the people are described as victims, and also as moral and good, while 'elites' and their internal collaborators such as undesired minorities are conversely described in the same narrative as immoral traitors who have driven society into a crisis.

Religions play a key role in populism in both relatively secular societies and deeply religious ones, and leaders and parties have employed it in varying contexts to different degrees. The civilizational populist movements we studied all incorporate religion, if in somewhat different ways, into their discourses. Religion, first, may provide the core identity of the civilizations which civilizational populist movements claim to defend. Indeed, this is the case in all the examples of civilizational populism examined in the book, even when there is no other religious content to the movement's political discourse or ideology. At times, civilizational populists patronize religious organizations and rely of them for support, as has occurred in Hungary, India, and Turkey. In other cases, organized religious groups themselves engage in populist politics, such as in Myanmar and Sri Lanka. However, it is important to acknowledge that religious faith is not always the most important element in civilizational populism. Rather, religious faith is most often understood by civilizational populists to be one element of 'civilization'. For example, in Hindutva, Hinduism as a religion is only one element of Hindu culture and civilization. In the Trump movement, Christianity is merely one part of the

American culture and identity Trump defends. In Western European civilizational populism, Christianity is less a religion and more of an identity, and is part of a sacred matrix which also contains secularism and 'ethnic European people.' It is also important to note that BBS and MaBaTha seek to defend not so much Buddhist 'faith', but Buddhist civilization, throughout Asia, and to deepen ties between Buddhist groups not to increase religiosity, but to increase Buddhist cultural and political power.

Indeed, in each case we have examined in this book religion, people, and land are merged into a single concept ('civilization') which is used to define the key signifiers of populism: 'the pure people', 'corrupt elites', and dangerous 'others' who collaborate with foreign enemy civilizations. Religion is a key component of civilizational populism throughout all our case studies. However, religion's role differs within each form of civilizational populism. It may be useful to acknowledge that there remains an important difference between primarily secular civilizational populists, for whom religion is merely the progenitor of the civilization and culture they wish to defend, and religious populists who act in part based on religious conviction. However, we must also admit that the boundary between the two is often blurred. For example, religious populist figures such as Narendra Modi, Imran Khan, and many others, borrow from their respective religions a sense of identity which they use to define the ingroup they attempt to construct, but also base their political agenda in part on religious beliefs and practices, and have close ties to religious organizations and figures. Secularists such as Marine Le Pen and Geert Wilders—among many others—seek to portray secularism and humanism as a direct descendent of Christianity, if one is influenced by Greek, Roman, and Enlightenment era ideas and values. Yet there are many populists movements, parties, and leaders who fall somewhere between the two poles, and who—like the groups associated with SBN in Sri Lanka or Hungary's Fidesz—seek support from organized religion, and may at times attempt to integrate organized religion into the state apparatus.

At the same time, civilizational populism may be entirely devoid of religious faith, values, and spirituality, especially in Western Europe where Christianity is reduced to an identity and partial source of national culture. In the discourse of Western European populist figures such as Geert Wilders and Marine Le Pen, Christianity is a civilization first, and not merely a religion, and therefore European secularism and even atheism can be categorized as products of Christianity.

We have found a pattern in which civilizational populists claim that elites have plunged the nation into crisis across many of our case studies. Typically, the crisis is framed as the result of elite immorality and betrayal, and of religious minorities refusing to adopt the culture and religion of the majority population. In India, Myanmar, Sri Lanka, and most Western nations this process takes the form of an "Islamization" narrative, in which Muslims are framed by populists as an invading force attempting to 'take over' their host society. At times rhetoric claiming that the West and Islam are involved in a clash of civilizations is evident. Yet in the Islamic world a different narrative is used by populists, one in which secular elites, internal minority groups, and 'the West' and Israel are working together to undermine Islam and spread Western immoralities. Civilizational populism may therefore work best when it can harness the deepest fears of the majority population, particularly the fear of being 'replaced' in some way, and thus when it can either exploit or produce a 'minority-majority complex'.

There are important differences in how religion is instrumentalized by secular and religious civilizational populists. Religious populists can mobilize the public by provoking religious rage, which can be turned against religious 'others' and elites. For example, Indian populists have encouraged religious rage in Hindu Indians by demonizing non-Hindus—especially Muslims—who eat beef. Hindu mobs have been mobilized by BJP populists on the mere accusation of members of a religious minority eating beef, resulting in several murders of people suspected of killing cows or eating beef. Secular populists cannot produce religious fury or indignation. Instead, they often frame religious minorities—almost always Muslims—as existential threats to secular society. European Christian identitarian populists provoke fear among the public by portraying Islam as a backward religion, or a totalitarian political faith, which is antithetical to the Judeo-Christian and secular values of the West. Curiously, religious and identitarian populists can draw on both civilizational and nationalist feeling, sometimes simultaneously. By identifying 'the people' with a religion-defined national culture and civilization, both have at times portrayed elites and religious minorities as threats to their respective national cultures, as well as the larger civilization to which their nation belongs. Populists may also exploit feelings of nostalgia for a partly imagined past, in which the 'Judeo-Christian' West was untroubled by the threat of Islam and progressive politics.

What are the consequences of civilizational populism entering the political mainstream? Our case studies indicate that civilizational populism is a growing phenomenon, and a threat to democracy and pluralism throughout the world. Civilizational populism, we find, is an inherently anti-plural ideology, and posits that religious minorities pose a threat to 'the people'—most often understood as the majority group, but sometimes as the authentic inhabitants of the land whether they be a majority or a minority. As a result, wherever they gain power and influence, civilizational populists attempt to exclude religious minorities or 'othered' groups from public life, and at times launch violent attacks against them. In the worst cases, civilizational populist discourse has played a role in supporting ethnoreligious cleansing and genocide. The anti-plural ideology of civilizational populism perceives religious difference as a threat to the identity and culture of the majority group, and maintains that democracy ought to represent only the will of the majority. Indeed, without the separation of powers and equality under the law, democracy can lose its emancipatory potential and devolve into mob rule and blind violence against minorities. We have found that civilizational populists consistently use emotion-driven pro-violence rhetoric, that there are often links or overlaps between civilizational populism and far-right movements, and that civilizational populists at times attempt to cooperate with similar groups beyond their national borders.

Civilizational populism has had a significant impact on a variety of societies. Like other populists, civilizational populists will often, when in government, attack some of the principles of liberal democracy including the separation of power and the rule of law. Populists act in this way because they believe democracy ought to represent the will of the people. As a result, populists are often skeptical of checks and balances on executive power, and perceive judicial independence as a form of unwanted 'elite' interference in government. For example, then Turkish Prime Minister Erdoğan held a successful referendum in 2017, and which made significant changes to the constitution that eroded the separation of powers, and gave the president—previously a mostly ceremonial role—unprecedented power. In Poland, the PiS government has attacked judicial independence, breaking down the separation of powers (Hoffman, 2021; Duncan and Macy, 2020–21). Buddhist nationalist populists in Myanmar have taken this attack a step further by supporting military coups on the basis that the military serves the interests of 'the people' better than a democratically elected government of 'elites'.

Equally, civilizational populists attack pluralism because they perceive minorities as inauthentic and immoral, and believe their presence threatens the rightful hegemony of the majority. Thus we find civilizational populist parties such as Poland's governing PiS eroding the principle of tolerance of minorities by demonizing Muslims. Muslim immigrants, according to PiS, are a "ticking time bomb" which will in time explode and destroy forever Poland's homogenous Christian identity. Moreover, on this basis the party refused to permit any Muslim asylum in Poland (Cienski 2017; Stanley 2016, 63). Equally, in Israel we find the Netanyahu-led Likud government claiming that archaeological finds prove the Land of Israel was part of Jewish civilization before the coming of the Arabs, and this means the Jews are the authentic people of Israel, and the Arabs are inauthentic invaders. Equally, Netanyahu has at times claimed Israel is protecting the common civilization that binds Israel, Europe, and North America together as one from the uncivilized barbarism of Islamic radicalism. Indeed, the chapters of this book are filled with examples of civilizational populists attacking pluralism, indicating that anti-pluralism is a key element of civilizational populism.

In almost all cases we have studied, populists accuse elites of permitting minorities to cause a 'crisis' of civilizational proportions, and which requires immediate action to correct. This immediate action may include voting for a populist party, but it may also involve violence. Civilizational populist leaders are also responsible in part or whole for a significant amount of violence the world over. The potential for violence is inherent in civilizational populism itself, insofar as it divides society into antagonistic groups, encourages 'the people' to believe they are victims of a corrupt elite and threatens others—who together represent an existential threat—and encourages them to feel angry and 'defend' themselves. This emotional narrative legitimizes violence against 'others', although it does not always lead to overt violence. At times, this narrative may lead to the suppression of religious 'others', including the bans on Islamic dress instituted in France and Sri Lanka. Civilizational populist narratives have contributed to communal rioting in India, particularly under the leadership of Narendra Modi, and in Sri Lanka under the rule of the Rajapaksas. When civilizational populists become national rulers they often use the power of the state to destroy their enemies. For example, in Turkey Erdoğan has used his authority and influence to compel the state to demonize the Gülen movement due to the group's involvement in a failed coup, and jail and intimidate journalists, academics, and activists who oppose his neo-Ottoman and Islamist ideology. In the worst case we have studied, MBT civilizational populists in Myanmar played a role in provoking and justifying genocidal violence against Muslims in Rakhine state. By framing groups of people as inherently dangerous and the cause of all social and economic problems in the nation, populists are creating an environment in which violence against these groups may appear justified.

It is also possible to surmise that non-Western civilizational populists are arguably more effective and politically successful and more violent and dangerous than European and American civilizational populists. Yet they receive far less scholarly attention than their European and American counterparts due to Eurocentric bias in the extent of scholarship but also because non-Western populists rarely "oppose trade or immigration, or regional organisation" or do anything likely to upset major powers or political elites beyond their own nations (Swain 2022). This is unfortunate, because like European civilizational populists, Asia–Pacific populists portray themselves as political outsiders who come from the people and represent their interests, while also claiming that "elites" in government, bureaucracy, academia, and the media, are corrupt and despise the people. Equally, like European civilizational populists, non-Western populists use religion-based civilizationalism as a tool to define ingroups and outgroups, to legitimize their rule, and to justify attacks on minority religious groups. And like European and American right-wing populists, non-Western civilizational populists have had a deleterious impact on democracy, pluralism, and, at times, the rule of law. North American and European populists run on explicit anti-immigrant platforms and claim that non-Christian immigrants present the gravest threat to the people and their Christian or Judeo-Christian culture and identity. Beyond the wealthy West, where controlled mass immigration is rare, anti-immigrant language plays a vastly less important role in religious populism. Instead, non-Western civilizational populists target religious minority populations and sometimes ethnic minorities, and portray them as dangerous internal enemies who threaten the rightful hegemony of "the people" or of the majority ethnoreligious group. Indeed, civilizational populists beyond the Western world frequently portray minority groups as obstacles to national redemption or flourishing, and they are sometimes working with foreign nations to prevent their nation from becoming "great".

Is there a transnational dimension to civilizational populism? Intriguingly, civilizational populism does not yet possess a strong transnational element. At the same time, many civilizational populist movements are attempting to create transnational links and, at times, coordinate with one another. One barrier to the creation of transnational civilizational populism is that the movements' conception of the world is only partially civilizational. This final point is important: the civilizational populists we have studied are all—to varying degrees—nationalists first and foremost. Civilizationalism is—in most of the cases we have studied—merely a concept they invoke in order to find a way to buttress the nation and protect it from its real and imagined enemies. When Trump spoke of protecting Judeo-Christian civilization in Poland, he was not attempting to create a transnational association of Christian nations. However, there are exceptions. We might consider Turkey's AKP as a party which has transnational goals which it pursues by instrumentalizing its diaspora population, and by involving itself in neighboring countries' internal conflicts. Equally, the civilizational populists of Europe often band together in blocs inside European Parliament in order to consolidate power. Geert Wilders himself is something of a transnational figure, who goes on speaking tours of foreign nations in an attempt to boost his profile and gather support from like-minded groups and individuals. And while BBS and MaBaTha/969 cooperation remains weak, the two groups clearly wish to create a more powerful Buddhist political presence in Asia that stretches beyond national borders. Thus while civilizational populism remains almost entirely within the bounds of individual nation-states, and nationalist in orientation, religion provides an ideal bridge across nations upon which may be built a common populist agenda, if not a new transnational 'Christian' or 'Islamic' identity. Benjamin et al. (2020, 146) observe that while transnational populism is rare, it may become more common due to the power of networked media to draw populists together across the world in common projects. In both cases, it is possible to comprehend how by making use of networked media—e.g. Facebook, Twitter, YouTube—civilizational populists may find ways to construct a 'people' beyond the confines of the nation-state. In time, populists may come to believe that 'the people' may share a religion or culture that exists not merely within a single nation, but across several nations.

The power of civilizationalism, and the concomitant belief in the reality of a clash of civilizations, is increasingly evident in global politics, including in the excesses of the so-called War on Terror, and in Russia's justifications for invading Ukraine. There can be no doubt, then, that civilizationalism is a dangerous and potent force in global politics. We should not therefore turn aside and ignore the civilizationalism within populist parties and movements. We end this book, then, with a call for scholars to explore further civilizational populism. There remains little literature on the role Christianity and Islam play in African populism. This is particularly unfortunate, because in Sub-Saharan Africa, millions of believers live in fragile yet democratic states where populism may easily become a significant force in politics.

Equally, we do not know if there is an African civilizational populism in sub-Saharan Africa. There is a possible civilizational aspect to the populist ideology of former Tanzanian President John Magufuli. At the very last, Magufuli serves as an example of how ultra-nationalism and Christian conservatism have been used to construct successful populist movement in an African context (BBC, 2021b). Magufuli, known as the "bulldozer" of Tanzania, became president of the country in 2015 promising to end corrupt and wasteful practices in Tanzania's government and bureaucratic elite. Magufuli argued that the "political elite" has for too long worked with "white people" to exploit Africa of its resources, and that it was time for the country and region to take back control of its natural resources and enjoy its wealth (Shakil 2021). As president of Tanzania, he "often styled himself as an African nationalist and devout Catholic waging war against foreign powers seeking to exploit the East African nation" (BBC 2021). Magufuli's populism extended beyond anti-elitism, and the exploitation of the traumas associated with colonialism, and began to incorporate the instrumentalization of Christianity. As president he claimed birth control and LBGTQ + rights were the product of an insidious Western influence contrary to Christian teachings. He argued that women's rights activists who called for family planning were "lazy" people who did not want to work, and urged Tanzanians to have more children (Shakil 2021). Magufuli cut funding to HIV/AIDS prevention and treatment projects, and instead introduced an "anus exam" to detect homosexual practices, leading to jail time for men found guilty of homosexual practices (Degenstein 2019).

The spread of COVID-19 in Tanzania provided Magufuli with an opportunity to merge religious civilizationalism with populist rhetoric. He refused to acknowledge the danger posed by COVID-19, and instead called Tanzanians to attend church in order to pray for God to cleanse the country of the virus (Shakil 2021). Magufuli urged Tanzanians to use local snake oil and pray, claiming this would cure them of the virus, because "Corona is the devil, and it cannot survive in the body of Jesus"

(Fabricus 2020). Even as COVID-19 infections surged in 2021, Magufuli denounced the use of imported COVID-19 testing kits, telling the people of his country "to take health precautions including the use of steam inhalation". "You inhale while you pray to God", he recommended, "you pray while farming maize, potatoes, so that you can eat well and corona fails to enter your body. They will scare you a lot, my fellow Tanzanians, but you should stand firm" (Reuters 2021). Magufuli claimed that vaccinations were not necessary, but were rather part of a Western conspiracy. "Vaccines are not good. If they were, then the white man would have brought vaccines for HIV/AIDS. […] Tanzanians should be careful with these imported things. You should not think that they love you a lot. This nation is rich, Africa is rich, everyone wants some of it", Magufuli claimed. He also criticized people attempting to obtain vaccinations in an address, stating "I know some Tanzanians who left the country to other countries and got vaccinated. From there, they brought a strange type of corona. Stand firm" (Reuters 2021). Less than three months after this statement, in March 2021, Magufuli died from suspected COVID-19 complications.

Tanzanian populism possesses a strong religious dimension, but also a unique racial dimension due to the emphasis Magufuli placed upon defending Africans from Western colonization. However, Magufuli does not emphasize the importance of defending indigenous African civilization, and therefore it is difficult to classify him as a civilizational populist. More scholarship is therefore required to comprehend whether there is a civilizationalism emerging in Africa and its relationship with populism.

Islam's relationship with populism, too, would benefit from greater scholarly engagement. While much is written on the relationship between religion and politics within Islamist movements, rarely is the role of populist ideation, strategy, or discourse studied within the same contexts. In particular, scholars would benefit from considering how religion and populism interact in the often turbulent democracies of the Muslim majority world, where religion has at times been used to construct ingroups and demonize outgroups. Moreover, there are cases in many young democracies in which religious populism has supported autocratic populism. This nexus between religion(s) and authoritarianism needs to be more closely examined in order to understand how religious narratives can begin a process of de-democratization in countries under populist rule, as appears to have occurred in Turkey under the AKP regime (Yılmaz and Turner 2019).

8 PREDICAMENT OF CIVILIZATIONAL POPULISM

The relationship between Judaism and civilizational populism ought also to be explored more, in terms of Judaism's place within the concept of 'Judeo-Christian' civilization, and also within the context of Israeli politics. Our chapter on Israel focused on Netanyahu and Likud, yet there may be scope to examine the civilizational populism of other Israeli political leaders and parties, including the religious populist Shas party, their relationships with Christian Zionism and the Jewish diaspora, and various other Western nations (Yilmaz and Morieson 2022a, b). Moreover, scholars would benefit from further study of the various major stakeholders in society and their engagement with the phenomena. For example, religious organizations' response to and engagement with populism, which may take the form of participation in religious populism, or indeed countering religious populism, is an area rarely studied but may prove highly useful to scholars interested in combating populism in its various forms. The media's role in transmitting or countering civilizational populism is of key importance, especially in regard to social media and its widespread use. For example, the occurrence of "cow-lynching" in India or, more generally, the role of "fake news" in promoting religious populism are important issues that ought to be explored in the context and beyond Western politics. Given the nature and widespread use of social media across the entire world, it is also important for scholars to begin researching the role of religion in transnational populism. The contemporary literature on transnational populism, while not large, provides ample material to begin examining the manner in which religion—perhaps through the promotion of civilizationalism—may help populist movements move beyond national borders.

Finally, it is worth considering how continued disillusionment with 'elites' and the broader class of people who govern democracies may lead not only to more populism, but to more civilizationalism, authoritarianism, and violence. On the one hand, in this book we have described many examples of successful populist movements. These movements often devolve into authoritarianism due to populism's opposition to checks and balances that appear to obstruct the popular will. Yet one wonders whether, as the elites grow more remote from ordinary people and use their power within state institutions to obstruct right-wing populists, right-wing populists will abandon democracy altogether and instead embrace authoritarianism and (especially vigilante but also anti-government) violence. Indeed, there are already examples of right-wing populists admiring and even supporting authoritarian civilization-states Russia and China. On this pessimistic note we end our book, which is, despite its length and breadth, intended as a starting point for future investigations of civilizational populism, and thus we conclude with call for scholars to engage more with the issues we have discussed.

REFERENCES

BBC. 17 March, 2021. "John Magufuli: Tanzania's 'buldozer' President." https://www.bbc.com/news/world-africa-56293519. Last accessed September 21, 2022.

BBC. 18 March 2021. "John Magufuli: Tanzania's president dies aged 61 after Covid rumours". https://www.bbc.com/news/world-africa-56437852. Last accessed September 21, 2022.

Benjamin, De Cleen, Moffitt Benjamin, Panayotu Panos, and Yannis Stavrakakis. 2020. "The Potentials and Difficulties of Transnational Populism: The Case of the Democracy in Europe Movement 2025 (DiEM25)". *Political Studies* 68, no. 1, 146–166. https://doi.org/10.1177/0032321719847576.

Degenstein, Dane. 2019. "Magufuli moves hearts with humble past – humility, populism and authoritarianism in Tanzania." *African Connections and Disruptions*. https://www.nomadit.co.uk/conference/ecas2019/paper/48829. Last accessed September 21, 2022.

Duncan, Allyson K and Macy, John. 2020–2021. "The Collapse of Judicial Independence in Poland: A Cautionary Tale". 104:3. *Judicature*. https://judicature.duke.edu/articles/the-collapse-of-judicial-independence-in-poland-a-cautionary-tale/. Last accessed September 21, 2022.

Fabricus, Peter. 27 March 2020. "Magufuli Confronts COVID-19 with Prayer and Snake Oil". *Atlantic Council*. https://issafrica.org/iss-today/magufuli-confronts-covid-19-with-prayer-and-snake-oil.

Hoffmann, Michael. 2021. "[PiS]sing off the Courts: the PiSParty's Effect on Judicial Independence in Poland". 51: 1153. https://scholarship.law.vanderbilt.edu/vjtl/vol51/iss4/5.

Reuters. 28 January 2021. "Decrying vaccines, Tanzania leader says 'God will protect' from COVID-19". *Reuters*. https://www.reuters.com/article/us-health-coronavirus-tanzania-idUSKBN29W1Z6.

Shakil, Kainat. 2021. "Tanzania". *European Center for Populism Studies*. https://www.populismstudies.org/tag/tanzania/.

Stanley, Ben. 2016. "Defenders of the Cross: Populist Politics and Religion in Post-Communist Poland". In *Saving the People How Populists Hijack Religion*, edited by Nadia Marzouki, Duncan McDonnell, and Olivier Roy. London: C. Hurst & Co.

Swain, Ashok. 2022. Populism in Asia is more robust than in Europe. *Gulf News*. Available online: https://gulfnews.com/opinion/op-eds/populism-in-asia-is-more-robust-than-in-europe-1.89174536. Last accessed June 17, 2022.

Wilders, Geert. 2016. "Wilders Plan: Time for Liberation". *Geert Wilders Weblog*. https://geertwilders.nl/index.php/94-english/2015-wilders-plan-time-for-liberation. Last accessed September 21, 2022.

Yilmaz, Ihsan and Morieson, Nicholas. 2021. "A Systematic Literature Review of Populism, Religion and Emotions". *Religions* 12 (4): 272. https://doi.org/10.3390/rel12040272

Yilmaz, Ihsan, Nicholas Morieson, and Mustafa Demir. 2021. Exploring Religions in Relation to Populism: A Tour around the World. *Religions* 12: 301. https://doi.org/10.3390/rel12050301.

Yilmaz, Ihsan and Shakil, Kainat. 15 April 2021c. "Transnational Islamist Populism between Pakistan and Turkey: The Case of Dirilis – Ertugrul". *European Center for PopulismStudies*. https://www.populismstudies.org/transnational-islamist-populism-between-pakistan-and-turkey-the-case-of-dirilis-ertugrul/. Last accessed September 21, 2022.

Yilmaz, Ihsan and Morieson, Nicholas. 2022a. *Religious Populism in Israel: The Case of Shas*. European Center for Populism Studies (ECPS). Brussels, Belgium. https://doi.org/10.55271/pp0011.

Yilmaz, Ihsan, and Morieson, Nicholas. 2022b. "Civilizational Populism: Definition, Literature, Theory, and Practice". *Religions*.

Yilmaz, Zafer, and Bryan S. Turner. 2019. Turkey's Deepening Authoritarianism and the Fall of Electoral Democracy. *British Journal of Middle East Studies*. 691–698. https://doi.org/10.1080/13530194.2019.1642662.

Index

A
Ahmadinejad, Mahmoud, 51, 52
Ahok, 15, 74–77, 79, 84, 85, 93–95
Al Qaeda, 25, 49, 146, 265
Ansar al-Sharia (AST), 56
Australia, 15, 112, 117, 118, 137, 142, 164, 165
Ayatollah Khomeini, 50, 51

B
Bharatiya Janata Party (BJP), 9, 16–18, 177–179, 181, 184, 187–204, 286
Bodu Bala Sena (BBS), 221, 228, 236–242, 244–246, 248, 285, 290
Bolsonaro, Jair, 119, 155
Brazil, 119, 154, 155
Britain, 51
Brubaker, Rogers, 5, 7, 13, 27, 36–38, 63, 112, 113, 115, 118, 135, 136, 143, 156, 160

Buddhism, 7, 18, 139, 178, 180, 182, 219–223, 225, 228, 236, 239, 240, 243, 244, 246–248

C
Canovan, Margaret, 3, 4, 32, 34, 35
China, 1, 2, 5, 7, 25, 63, 95, 124, 164, 165, 223, 293
Christianity, 7, 9, 15, 16, 18, 36, 37, 64, 65, 109–118, 121–123, 125–127, 129–133, 136, 138–140, 144, 147, 150, 154–158, 164, 178–180, 284, 285, 291
Christian schools, 139
Civilizational populism, 4, 5, 7–13, 15, 18, 20, 21, 35–40, 45, 46, 58, 59, 65, 71, 73, 80, 112, 113, 118, 128, 131, 138, 141, 150, 154, 161, 164, 192, 194, 198, 199, 203, 220, 228, 236, 239, 243, 257, 262, 283–291, 293, 294

D
Diyanet, 63–65, 89

E
Egypt, 13, 48, 49, 149, 267
Ennahda, 56, 57
Erdoğan, Recep Tayyip, 14, 45–47, 49, 59–70, 88–93, 96, 265, 287, 288

F
Fascism, 1
Fidesz (Fiatal Demokratak Szovetsege), 119–125, 130, 154–156, 161, 162, 165, 285
Fortuyn, Pim, 132, 133, 142
France, 9, 37, 55, 78, 111, 113–115, 138, 260, 265, 278, 288

G
Genocide, 54, 60, 225, 227, 230, 231, 244, 260, 287
Germany, 37, 115, 185
Gnanasara, Galagoda Aththe, 228, 236–238, 240, 241
Greece, 37, 116
Gülen, Fethullah, 67

H
Hanson, Pauline, 117, 118
Hinduism, 7, 16, 18, 178–187, 193, 200, 203, 284
Hindutva, 16–18, 177, 178, 180–191, 193–204, 284
Hungary, 7, 9, 16, 26, 119–129, 154–159, 161, 164, 284, 285
Huntington, Samuel P., 6, 7, 13, 25, 27–29, 144, 146, 148, 259, 260

I
India, 7, 9, 16, 17, 48, 49, 177–182, 185–194, 196, 197, 199–204, 223, 229, 233, 235, 243, 284, 286, 288, 293
Indonesia, 7, 13–15, 46, 47, 49, 71–88, 91–96, 131
Iran, 49, 51–53, 96, 149, 265, 277, 279
Islam, 7–9, 13, 15, 27–29, 37, 40, 45–50, 53, 54, 56–76, 78, 80, 82–88, 90–93, 95, 110, 113–118, 122, 131–136, 138–144, 146, 148, 152, 153, 156–159, 162–164, 178–180, 203, 224, 226, 229, 236, 238, 244, 246, 260, 261, 272, 275, 286, 291, 292
Islamisation, 140
Islamic Defenders Front (FPI), 14, 15, 40, 46, 47, 71–88, 90, 92–94, 96
Islamism, 13, 45, 54–56, 60–62, 73, 75, 86, 94
Israel, 20, 62, 150, 151, 158, 161, 164, 257–270, 272–279, 286, 288, 293

J
Jerusalem, 69, 150, 151, 258, 266, 269–272
Jokowi, 72, 74, 76–78, 85
Judaism, 11, 20, 140, 147, 149, 157, 158, 180, 258, 259, 263, 293
Judeo-Christian, 9, 14, 16, 27, 36, 37, 112, 113, 116, 118, 119, 131, 133–140, 142–144, 146–154, 157–159, 161–164, 260, 266, 277, 279, 286, 289, 290, 293
Judeo-Christian and Humanist, 9, 113, 136, 138

Judeo-Christian values, 140, 147
Justice and Development Party (AKP), 8, 9, 14, 40, 46, 47, 58–67, 87–90, 92–95, 290, 292

K

Khamenei, Ali, 51, 52
Khan, Imran, 49, 50, 53, 54, 197, 285

L

Laclau, Ernesto, 31, 33, 34
Law and Justice Party, 116, 153, 161
Lega Nord, 116
Le Pen, Jean-Marie, 9, 114, 115, 137
Le Pen, Marine, 9, 113–115, 285
Likud, 20, 257, 259, 262–268, 276–279, 288, 293
Lwin, Kyaw, 225

M

MaBaTha (MBT), 18, 219, 220, 224, 285, 290
Macron, Emmanuel, 6, 138
Magufuli, John, 291, 292
Modi, Narendra, 9, 16, 17, 177, 180, 181, 187–192, 194, 198–200, 203, 204, 265, 285, 288
Moffitt, Benjamin, 8, 30, 33, 34
Mudde, Cas, 3, 5, 7, 10, 30–32, 34, 35, 38
Myanmar, 18, 19, 219–227, 229–232, 236, 239, 243, 244, 246, 284, 286, 287, 289

N

National Rally, 9, 113, 114, 155, 192
Netanyahu, Benjamin, 20, 257, 258, 260, 262–268, 270–278, 288, 293

North Africa, 110, 134, 139

O

Orbán, Viktor, 6, 15, 16, 26, 116, 119–130, 155–161, 164
Ottoman Empire, 8, 46, 48, 60–63, 69, 70, 90, 94, 259

P

Pakistan, 7, 13, 48, 49, 53–55, 65, 67, 96, 149, 182, 188, 190, 191, 196, 202
Pakistan Tehreek-e-Insaf (PTI), 53, 54, 194, 196–198
Party for Freedom (PVV), 9, 15, 16, 37, 113, 115, 119, 134–138, 141–143, 155, 162
Poland, 116, 124, 153, 158, 165, 287, 288, 290

R

Rajapaksa, Gotabaya, 234–236, 242
Rajapaksa, Mahinda, 19, 233
Rashtriya Swayamsevak Sangh (RSS), 16, 178, 184–190, 192, 194–196, 199–201, 203
Republican Party, 147, 148
Rizieq, Muhammad, 46, 47, 73, 76–94, 96
Russia, 2, 5, 7, 25, 26, 124, 164, 165, 290, 293
Rutte, Mark, 139

S

Salvini, Matteo, 26, 117
Savarkar, Vinayak Damodar, 183, 184
Secularism, 9, 16, 18, 37, 56, 64, 72, 81, 82, 84, 87, 110–113, 118, 126, 129, 131, 133, 138, 143,

155, 156, 160, 164, 177, 183, 203, 263, 264, 285
Shils, Edward, 30
Shiv Sena (SS), 16, 195, 203
Sinhalese Buddhist Nationalism (SBN), 19, 20, 220, 233–236, 239, 241–245, 247, 248, 285
Sri Lanka, 18, 19, 194, 219–221, 232–236, 238–244, 246, 248, 284–286, 288

T
Taguieff, Pierre-André, 3, 32, 34, 35
Tanzania, 291
Tea Party, 147, 148, 155
Transnational, 8, 11–13, 15, 21, 39, 48–50, 53, 58, 62, 75, 79, 80, 86, 88, 89, 92, 113, 124, 127, 137, 158, 159, 161, 165, 228, 244, 277, 289, 290, 293
Trump, Donald, 15, 16, 118, 137, 144, 147–156, 158–161, 164, 284, 285, 290
Tunisia, 13, 49, 55–57, 96
Turkey, 7, 8, 13, 14, 25, 40, 45, 46, 49, 58–71, 88–92, 95, 96, 124, 132, 138, 191, 284, 290, 292

U
ummah, 13–15, 45–50, 53, 54, 58, 63–66, 69–71, 75, 78, 79, 85–87, 89, 90, 92, 93
United States (US), 1, 2, 15, 25, 29, 31, 51, 112, 118, 124, 137, 144–155, 158, 164, 186, 267, 275, 276, 278

V
Violence, 9, 17–19, 28, 32, 39, 54, 62, 65, 67, 73, 74, 77, 78, 80–83, 85–87, 89–93, 140, 165, 179, 181, 188, 192–194, 197–200, 202, 204, 221, 222, 224–230, 234, 236–238, 240–242, 244–246, 248, 266, 273, 274, 278, 287–289

W
Wilders, Geert, 9, 15, 16, 113, 115, 132–135, 137–143, 155–161, 164, 285, 290
Wirathu, Ashin, 227–232

Z
Zionism, 258, 259, 261, 262, 266, 275, 293

Printed in the United States
by Baker & Taylor Publisher Services